Praise for Wilbert Rideau's

In the Place of Justice

"Incisive. . . . As emotional as any words I've read in a long time." —Dwight Garner, *The New York Times*

"Riveting. . . . Amazing. . . . The picture of prison life painted by Rideau isn't the one portrayed in many movies. . . . Now he has provided a wonderful chance to share his remarkable life." —Associated Press

"A masterpiece in the realm of autobiographies."
—*The Anniston Star*

"Fascinating and inspiring. . . . This book is a gift to all of us in so many ways." —*BookPage*

"Rideau comes across as truthful, remorseful, and straightforward. . . . *In the Place of Justice* is remarkably even-handed and generous."
—*Palm Beach Arts Paper*

"Searing, suspenseful, stomach-churning and soul-stirring. . . . A sobering indictment of the criminal justice and penal systems in Louisiana over the past half century—and testimony to the triumph of the human spirit."
—*Tulsa World*

Wilbert Rideau

In the Place of Justice

Wilbert Rideau was editor of *The Angolite*, a prison newsmagazine that during his tenure was nominated seven times for a National Magazine Award. While in prison, he was a correspondent for NPR's *Fresh Air*; coproduced and narrated a radio documentary, "Tossing Away the Keys," for NPR's *All Things Considered*; served as correspondent for "In for Life" for ABC-TV's "Day One"; and codirected the Academy Award–nominated film *The Farm: Angola, USA*. He is the recipient of a George Polk Award and an American Bar Association Silver Gavel Award, among others. He was awarded a Soros Justice Fellowship in 2007 and works as a consultant with the Federal Death Penalty Resource Counsel Project. He lives in Louisiana.

www.wilbertrideau.com

IN THE

PLACE OF JUSTICE

A Story of
Punishment and Deliverance

Wilbert Rideau

VINTAGE BOOKS
A DIVISION OF RANDOM HOUSE, INC.
NEW YORK

FIRST VINTAGE BOOKS EDITION, MAY 2011

Copyright © 2010 by Wilbert Rideau

All rights reserved.
Published in the United States by Vintage Books,
a division of Random House, Inc., New York,
and in Canada by Random House of Canada Limited, Toronto.
Originally published in hardcover in the United States by Alfred A. Knopf,
a division of Random House, Inc., New York, in 2010.

This book was supported in part by a grant from the
Soros Justice Fellowship Program of the Open Society Institute.

All photographs courtesy of the author or public domain with the following
exceptions: Larry Smith (courtesy of Larry Smith); John Whitley (courtesy of John
Whitley); supporters Sister Benedict Shannon and others, and Rev. J. L. Franklin
leading a protest (Walter Jean); Wilbert Rideau with his mother (Leslie Turk).

The Library of Congress has cataloged the Knopf edition as follows:
In the place of justice: a story of punishment and deliverance/Wilbert Rideau.—1st ed.
p.   cm.
Includes index.
1. Rideau, Wilbert. 2. Louisiana State Penitentiary—History—20th century.
3. African American prisoners—Louisiana—Biography. 4. Prisoners—Louisiana—
Biography. 5. Prisoners—Louisiana—Social conditions—20th century. 6. Criminal
justice, Administration of—Louisiana—History—20th century. 7. Corruption—
Louisiana—History—20th century. 8. African American journalists—Biography.
I. Title.
HV9475.L22L646   2010
365'.440923960730763—dc22   2009038526

Vintage ISBN: 978-0-307-27730-5

Author photograph © Linda LaBranche
Book design by Soonyoung Kwon

www.vintagebooks.com

To the late C. Paul Phelps,
my mentor and friend

Success is relative.
It is what we can make of the mess we have made of things.

—T. S. ELIOT

Contents

x   *Contents*

Author's Note

All the material in quotation marks comes from court testimony, contemporaneous notes made either by me or by others, published sources, or the best of my recollection. I have worked scrupulously to ensure that all the conversations within these pages are faithful in content, if not always to the exact words spoken.

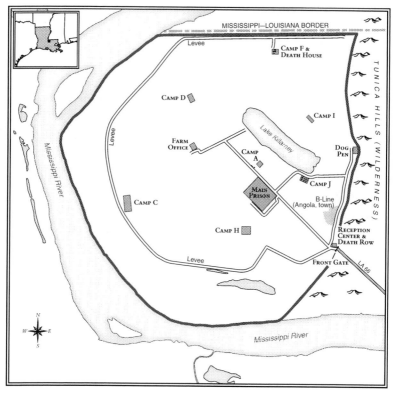

MISSISSIPPI—LOUISIANA BORDER

Levee

Camp F &
Death House

Camp D

TUNICA HILLS (WILDERNESS)

Camp I

Lake Killarney

Farm
Office

Camp
A

Dog
Pen

Levee

Camp J

Camp C

Mississippi River

Main
Prison

B-Line
(Angola, town)

Camp H

Reception
Center &
Death Row

Levee

Front Gate

LA 66

N
W E
S

Mississippi River

ANGOLA

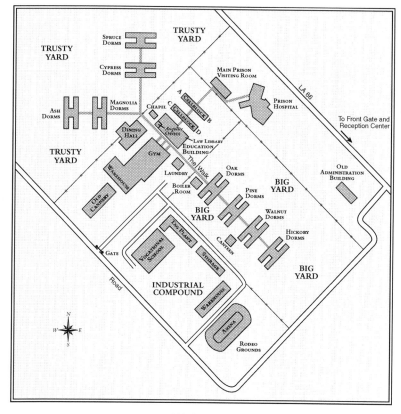

TRUSTY YARD

TRUSTY YARD

SPRUCE DORMS

CYPRESS DORMS

MAIN PRISON VISITING ROOM

PRISON HOSPITAL

LA 66

ASH DORMS

MAGNOLIA DORMS

CHAPEL

CELLBLOCK A

CELLBLOCK B

CELLBLOCK C

CELLBLOCK D

To Front Gate and Reception Center

DINING HALL

Angola Office

LAW LIBRARY

EDUCATION BUILDING

TRUSTY YARD

GYM

The Walk

OAK DORMS

OLD ADMINISTRATION BUILDING

LAUNDRY

WAREHOUSE

BOILER ROOM

PINE DORMS

BIG YARD

OLD CANNERY

BIG YARD

WALNUT DORMS

TAG PLANT

VOCATIONAL SCHOOL

STORAGE

CANTEEN

HICKORY DORMS

Gate

BIG YARD

INDUSTRIAL COMPOUND

WAREHOUSE

Road

ARENA

N
W   E
S

RODEO GROUNDS

MAIN PRISON

In the Place of Justice

Ruination

1942—1961

"Kill that nigger!" a voice barked into the winter night.

The headlights of the state troopers' car blinded me. I was hand-cuffed and in my stocking feet on the shoulder of a two-lane road, standing between the headlights of their car and the taillights of the one I had been driving before they pulled me over. Murmurs ran like the scent of prey through the small crowd of shadowy figures that rustled on the roadway beyond the lights. I wondered how they had gathered so quickly. An arm punctured the pool of light as a man lunged toward me, intercepted by the young trooper who, responding to a police radio bulletin, had captured me. I didn't need to see the faces to know that they were white.

"Give him to us," one man shouted.

"Just give us the boy, and go on your way," another said, more kindly.

A second, older trooper looked indecisive as the crowd grew more restless. I felt only fear. The younger trooper cautiously interceded. "Look, we've already called this in to headquarters. They know we have him, and they're on the way. We can't give him up. We'll never be able to explain it." The older cop fingered his holstered revolver and told the men he couldn't do what they wanted but assured them that I would be "dealt with."

It was a reprieve, but I felt certain this business could end only one way. It was 1961, and we were in Louisiana.

Within minutes more official vehicles arrived, and the road was flooded with law enforcement officers huddled in talk. Then two deputy sheriffs came over, took me roughly by the arm, and hustled me to the troopers' car. One of them, red-faced, punched me in my side and shoved me onto the floor of the rear seat. Then he kicked me hard with his cowboy boot as he climbed in. "Uh-uh—can't have that," the older trooper said. "We're taking him to the sheriff."

"He's a dead sonuvabitch anyway," the deputy said, leaning back into the seat and pinning me with his foot. The policemen drove in silence. When the car slowed and turned into a gas station on the edge of the small town of Iowa, I wondered if this was where they were going to kill me. My fear virtually disconnected me from my body.

The deputy led me gruffly to a car occupied by two large white men, who got out to talk to the men who had brought me. I was led into the car, where I sat alone in the back seat, hands cuffed behind me. When the two big men returned to the car and were settled in the front seat, they turned to introduce themselves: The driver was Henry A. "Ham" Reid, Jr., longtime sheriff of the parish we were in, Calcasieu; the other was Deputy Charles Barrios. The sheriff had questions.

My name? Wilbert Rideau. Address? 1820 Brick Street, Lake Charles. No, it's my mother's home. Age? Nineteen. I work at Halpern's Fabric Shop in the Southgate Shopping Center.

Barrios got out of the car and went into the gas station.

"Where's the gun?" Reid asked.

"Threw it away," I said.

"You have any other weapons?"

"A knife."

"Where is it?"

"Threw it away."

Barrios returned. "They're going to pick up his mother and bring her to the jail," he told the sheriff.

"My mother don't have anything to do with this," I said, alarmed.

"Well, you're gonna have to help us understand that," Reid said. "You can start by showing us where you threw the gun and knife." I directed them off the highway and onto back roads until we reached the spot. In the dark, they couldn't find the weapons in the grassy pasture. Thirty minutes and eleven miles later we were in Lake Charles, a booming oil city of sixty-three thousand.

Its four-story brick jail rose behind the parish courthouse on Ryan Street, the major downtown traffic artery. Reid drove past the courthouse and came to an abrupt halt when he saw several hundred whites gathered in front of the jail.

"We can't go through the front," Barrios said, staring at the scene before us.

"Let's try the rear," Reid said, as he put the vehicle in reverse.

People recognized the sheriff's car and ran toward us. My heart raced as Reid spun the car around and drove away from the mob.

I was living the nightmare that haunted blacks in the Deep South—death by the mob, a dreaded heirloom handed down through the generations. We had seen the photographs, heard the tales. They would beat me and stomp me, then hang me from a tree on the courthouse lawn, castrate me, douse my body with gasoline, and set it afire. The white spectators would revel in the bonfire. Afterward they would cut off my fingers and toes, ghoulish souvenirs of "white justice." They'd leave my charred remains on display as a useful reminder.

"You gonna turn me over to 'em?" I asked the sheriff.

"That's not gonna happen," he replied. He talked into his car radio, then made his way, headlights off, creeping toward the jail, stopping beside a large stand of bushes near the jail's rear parking lot. Barrios got out of the car to scout the situation.

"Sheriff, you're not gonna bring my mother into that crowd?" I asked.

"She'll be okay," he said, staring intently down the street. Then he turned to look at me. "But you have to cooperate with us. A lot of people are mad at you right now. The quicker we can get to the bottom of what happened, the quicker we can explain things and calm people down—and your momma can go back home. It all depends on you."

We sat in silence until Barrios returned. "We can go in through the back," he said, "but we have to move fast."

The sheriff gunned the motor and sped up to an inconspicuous steel door at the back of the jail. He and Barrios leaped out of the car and sandwiched me between them, each holding me under an arm. They hurried me through the door, my feet in the air. As they spirited me into an office, I heard the roar of voices even before I saw the sea of white men stirring around in the lobby of the jail. Standing in a hallway facing them were more white men, in uniforms, with guns—plenty of guns.

The office door closed, leaving me alone with a handful of men.

Barrios removed my handcuffs and seated me in a chair next to a wooden desk. He offered me water and a cigarette, which I accepted. The sheriff soon returned, pulled up a chair to face me, and asked if I was okay. I nodded.

"I need you to tell me what happened," he said in a kindly voice. "Start from the beginning."

Gladys Victorian was born January 8, 1924. It was a time of postwar prosperity in America and a time of great promise: Telephones were already in widespread use, the first regular licensed radio broadcasting had just begun, and the first sound-on-film motion picture had been shown at the Rivoli Theater in New York City. The Nineteenth Amendment had just been ratified, giving women the right to vote.

Those historic milestones, however, were far removed from Gladys's existence. More immediately affecting her world was the violent revival of the Ku Klux Klan and its campaign of terror dedicated to the subjugation of the "coloreds" and the separation of the races. Membership in the racist organization had peaked at one hundred thousand in the year of her birth, and it was sweeping to unprecedented power throughout the South and Midwest, controlling many local and state governments. The colored population lived in perpetual dread of it.

Gladys was one of fourteen children born to Victor Victorian and Anna Guillory, members of a Creole-speaking farming community of colored sharecroppers outside the small white town of Lawtell, Louisiana. Victor worked a farm with his own animals and his family, without cost to the white landowner, who received a share of the profits from the harvest of "money crops"—cotton, soybeans, and Irish and sweet potatoes.

Sharecropping was hard work, but when plummeting stock prices on Wall Street in 1929 precipitated the worst economic depression in American history, the Victorians, like many who lived on farms during the "terrible thirties," were able to escape the hardships, deprivation, hunger, and misery experienced by millions of their fellow citizens. Not only were they able to grow and raise the things they needed themselves, but they could also sell to others.

"I heard how people suffered, even saw pictures of people standing in soup lines, starving in the streets with no place to stay, cold," Gladys remembered. "But I never experienced nothing like that. We always had plenty to eat. None of us ever went hungry."

Sharecropping also allowed Victor and Anna to provide their children with an education. The kids would get up at daybreak and do their chores, including milking all the cows, before setting out for school. They'd get to class by 8:00 a.m. and get back home about 3:00 p.m., then work on the farm until sundown. That didn't leave much time for homework, but understanding teachers allowed a little spare time for students to do their homework at school. School closed in May, and the children joined their parents working full-time on the farm until September, when the new school year began.

Studying old textbooks handed down from Lawtell's white students, Gladys acquired a fifth-grade education—she and her siblings were the first generation of Victorians who were able to read and write—at the Lawtell Colored Elementary School, a clapboard building with "five or six rooms, one for each grade." The only education beyond that available to colored kids was in the town of Opelousas, seven miles away. The daily commute, at a time when most colored families traveled by horse and buggy or wagon, was daunting. So Gladys joined her parents on the farm as a full-time worker.

The freedom the Victorians enjoyed from the Depression came at a price. Bringing in the crop required the effort of the entire family. "Working the farm was hard physical labor," Gladys recalled. "We didn't have a tractor or anything like that—only mules and horses to work with—which is why all us kids wanted out and, as soon as we could, we left, one by one."

Life for girls like her was sheltered. Wherever they went, they were chaperoned. Church on Sunday was the biggest social event of the week and often the only one. There were few parties, an occasional wedding, and a school dance or function now and then. Escape meant marrying the first decent guy to come along. "Back then, love wasn't the main reason girls got married," said Gladys. Her opportunity came when she was sixteen.

Ferdinand Rideau had been living in Plaisance, a dozen miles away, when he decided to move his family to Lawtell in 1940. "Aww, he was the big man, had a brand-new black buggy that he kept polished and a big fine horse," Gladys recalled. Among the Rideau children was nineteen-year-old Thomas, whom she met at a local dance. She loved to dance, and he was good at it. Since they lived close by, Thomas soon joined the Victorian sisters on their Sunday-morning walks to the only Catholic church nearby, where blacks were allowed in the rear pews. Afterward, they would visit the general store, where Thomas would treat Gladys to a nickel's worth of candy or an ice-cream cone. "Tom was kind of hip and a neat dresser, and had a line," she said. "I liked him." He quickly asked Victor Victorian for permission to marry Gladys.

Having known each other only three months, Thomas and Gladys married in the spring of 1941 at the home of her parents. According to Thomas's older brother Lennis, Thomas wanted to marry Gladys quickly because he had gotten a girl pregnant in Jeanerette, sixty miles south toward the Gulf, and didn't want to marry that girl because she was too dark-skinned. Gladys, on the other hand, had long black hair that fell in soft ringlets and skin so pale she could have passed for white, making her more desirable to a color-conscious Creole black man.

Within several months, to earn extra money, Gladys and Thomas joined migrant workers cutting sugarcane in Jeanerette for the old black man Thomas had worked for before, and they lived there through the harvest. The old man liked Thomas and wanted them to stay to work the farm and look after him, telling the newlyweds he'd will the place to them when he died. "It was a big old run-down house and wasn't being taken care of," Gladys recalled. "When you hit the corn-husk mattress, a cloud of dust would rise from it. We had a little army foldaway cot that me and Tom slept in. Put coal oil on the wooden legs to keep the ants from crawling into the cot with us. We didn't know a soul there, and everywhere you looked was sugarcane, too much of it. We left after the crop."

They returned to live with her parents in Lawtell, where I was born in 1942. We soon moved seventy-seven miles due west to DeQuincy, where my father got a railroad job doing hard labor; then he worked at an oil refinery in Sulphur, eighteen miles south of DeQuincy, just west of Lake Charles. When he was drafted into the army in 1944, we followed him to Oakland, California. He was discharged when the war ended—he never saw action—and we returned to the Victorian home in Lawtell. By 1946, I had two brothers, Raymond and Roland.

Then came more short-term jobs for my father—one at an oil refinery in Port Arthur, Texas; then one at Memorial Hospital in Lake Charles, where my mother worked as a $2-a-day domestic for a wealthy white family. We rented briefly, and then Thomas bought a tract of land adjacent to an old cemetery for $245 and a "shotgun" house (three rooms in a straight row, front to back) for $150, which he transported to the property. "He'd add on to it whenever he got lum-

ber," Gladys recalled, ultimately expanding it to a five-room house at
1820 Brick Street. My sister, Pearlene, was born in 1947.

To all appearances, our family seemed normal enough, headed by a
hardworking husband and father. We never missed church or school;
we were well behaved, neatly dressed, cooperative, courteous, and
respectful of our elders and our betters. But there was a dark side, too.

After my father returned from that first cane harvest in Jeanerette,
he began drinking and partying with newfound and rowdy juke-joint
buddies. He first hit my mother a year after I was born because she
nagged him about going out to honky-tonks, where liquor flowed and
loose women were ever present. Womanizing outside of marriage was
characteristic of Rideau men. My mother had never witnessed violence
in her parents' home, and it chilled her. She was trapped by it, though,
a simple country girl with little education and very little income, the
mother of one child with another in her womb. She stayed with my
father, and things got worse.

As whatever romance had existed receded, my mother became little more than my father's personal slave. He was the master of the
household; the rest of us were to be ruled, to do his bidding, to be disciplined when we displeased him. He'd order my mother to kneel and
hold still for him to whip her with his belt, just as he did us kids.
"Thomas—don't. Please. Don't do this," she'd beg. When she rebelled,
he beat her with his fists, the locked doors and closed windows muf-
fling the thumps and screams. At some point, she learned that one way
to end a beating was to simply fall on the floor, lie still, and feign
unconsciousness, throwing my father into a panic for fear he might
have seriously injured or killed her, which could send him to prison.
He would carry her limp body to the car, babbling pleas to God that
she not die, and, with us in the back seat, speed to Memorial Hospital,
where he'd rush her into the emergency room. It wasn't a tactic she
used frequently, resorting to it only when the beating was more than
she could bear. When she realized that her ploy also threw me into a
panic, she explained it to me so I wouldn't be frightened. Although
neighbors would sometimes call the police, nonfatal domestic disputes
did not interest them in general, especially when they were between
colored people. The white officers would simply talk understandingly
to my father in the driveway, caution him to "keep the noise down,"
and drive away without ever setting foot in the house to see my mother
or investigate.

The fence surrounding our yard pretty much formed the boundaries of our lives, except for school. "Stay in the yard!" was a daily refrain of my childhood. Only rarely were we permitted to play with the kids next door. At the end of the school day, I had to go straight home, so I had no opportunity to form relationships with the other students. I couldn't visit their homes, so they didn't visit mine. I was lonely, driven by a desire to belong. In addition, on the first day of school in the fall, I felt the sting of how different I was from them when our teacher would make us stand in front of the class and tell what we did over the summer break. The other kids told about doing things with their families: going to the Grand Canyon or a lake, visiting relatives in California and seeing the ocean, camping. Our family didn't do things together. My father had no interest in us except as evidence of his manhood. Every summer, I was dropped off either at my maternal grandparents' farm in Lawtell or at my other grandparents' house in Opelousas. Although I liked the farm, I yearned to be somewhere else. I learned to avoid the first day of school by feigning illness or simply playing hooky, so I wouldn't have to describe where I went.

Initially, I loved school. I learned through history and geography that the world was larger than Lake Charles. I wanted to fit in with the new people I met, but my social ignorance predisposed me to blunders. Once, in the sixth grade, our teacher asked each student to get up and sing his or her favorite song. While the other students sang standard American pop songs and ballads, I stood up and wailed out John Lee Hooker's gutbucket "Boogie Chillun." It was met with snickers and laughter. I was a joke.

It never occurred to my parents to teach us what was expected of us in relation to others, and what we could realistically expect in return. They didn't talk to me about how to handle problems, deal with girls, or make friends. It never occurred to them that their children should be nurtured at home, encouraged to study, write, and be thoughtful. They saw their duties as disciplining us and providing us with the basic necessities of life—food, clothing, and shelter. They sent us to church and Sunday school, where they expected us to learn right from wrong, and to public school, where they expected we would learn everything else we needed to know about life and the world. They never involved themselves with the PTA, never inquired about what was going on at school. Once, longing to be a part of something, I acted in a school play. My parents didn't come to see it. After the performance, the other parents rushed over to their children and praised them for doing so well. I felt foolish and awkward standing there alone, and I never acted again. Nor did I go out for sports. I knew it cost money to travel to games. No one had to tell me we couldn't afford it. I became ever more isolated, more of an outsider. A puny kid, I was often picked on and pushed around by bullies. My shyness and cowardice didn't help. I grew like an untended weed, without guidance, confronting the world on my own and learning by trial and error.

My native intelligence, though, allowed me to solve some of my problems. I never had to study. I could walk into a classroom, skim the lesson or listen to the teacher or discussion, and instantly grasp the essentials. I was a straight-A student. Often I would help less intelligent kids by providing them answers for tests or letting them copy mine. They gave me their lunch money in return, but I would have helped them simply for the price of acceptance. I wanted the same things in life that everyone wants: friends, validation, to matter. But I felt I was being told on a daily basis that I didn't measure up and wasn't worth bothering with, that I shouldn't waste time dreaming about the future, that I was an outsider with my nose pressed up against the window of life, through which I saw other people living.

I took refuge in comic books. My earliest ambition was to be a spaceman like my hero, Flash Gordon. Later, I wanted to be an inventor or a scientist so I could change things, starting with my own life. I received no encouragement from my family. "You better get your head out of them clouds, boy," my parents would often say.

I was thirteen when my father's womanizing finally disrupted my world. My mother and I were driving in the family car to get ice cream when we spotted my father's motor scooter on the porch of a woman my mother suspected was one of his girlfriends. She pulled over and knocked on the door. After a while, my father came out. He lied about his reason for being there, berated my mother for following him, said he had done nothing wrong. When he got home, he whipped her.

My mother sought revenge by having a fling of her own. Returning from an out-of-town tryst, the couple had an almost fatal accident that sent my mother to the hospital with broken ribs, internal injuries, and a fractured skull. My dad hovered at her bedside, playing the betrayed but loving and forgiving husband. When she was released from the hospital and came home, that changed.

She was to get up each morning and serve him breakfast, clean his house, do the laundry, iron his clothes, and have his supper waiting when he returned from work. He expected her to be a wife to him in every way and to be a mother to us kids despite her injuries, which he declared to be her problem, not his. He refused to let me help her as she inched her broken body about the kitchen. Every night, groans of painful sex emanated from their bedroom.

We were to say nothing of my mother's ordeal upon threat of whippings. My father presented himself as a victim. He was good at manipulating appearances, mimicking responsibility, courtesy, charitableness, and friendship. He once took me along to a cousin's funeral in Beaumont, Texas, which he attended reluctantly. On the way, he told me our dead relative had been an "asshole." He instructed me to observe and learn. When we arrived, he somberly greeted everyone, then we went over to the casket and knelt. He began moving his lips as if in prayer. Then he burst into tears, crying out his cousin's name, as if overcome with grief. I stood up and stepped back, surprised, staring at my father as others rushed to console him. Between sobs, he babbled about how close he and his cousin had been, how wonderful he had been and how much he would miss him. When we finally got back to the car, he smiled, proud of himself: "Everybody there believes I cared about him. That's the way you get ahead in the world, son. You always leave people with a good impression." It was the only time he ever tried to teach me something.

As we neared home, he told me that he was leaving us, that my mother had cheated on him with another man, that he had tried to overlook it and hold the family together for us kids, but it wasn't working. He was a terrible father, grossly deficient and brutal, but I was devastated nonetheless.

His moving out surprised everyone we knew, but it was premeditated. After my mother's car accident, he had her file an insurance claim for the cost of her injuries. He handled all the negotiations, and after he won a settlement for "a lot of money," he promptly absconded with it, leaving her penniless and pregnant. We were forced to go on welfare. Then he declared the baby in her womb was not his. Ralph, my youngest brother, grew up to be the spitting image of our father.

Living on welfare brought a sharp decline in our already modest standard of living. To be sure, there were other poor kids at school, but poverty added to my shame. I focused more on the kids who didn't need to borrow lunch money from the neighbors or wheel a grocery cart full of dirty, salvaged soft drink bottles into the supermarket for a refund.

I was in the eighth grade when I burglarized a local Piggly Wiggly supermarket, not to get something I needed but for costume jewelry to give the girls in my class. I was thirteen years old, and girls had come to obsess me, especially since I didn't seem to impress them very much. I also took about $40 in change to treat the boys in school. I thought I could buy their friendship. My instant popularity faded quickly, and my act of desperation wound up isolating me even more.

The first burglary was so easy that I returned a second time, and got busted. My father came to get me at the police station. I dreaded his reaction, but he never said a word as he drove me to my mother's home. The court sent me to a nerdy white psychiatrist for counseling, and he advised me to return to school. The police had questioned some of the students and teachers, so everyone knew about the burglary: I was so ashamed that I eventually stopped going to classes. I opted to hang with the other "problem kids." We often retreated to the overgrown and neglected cemetery adjacent to the school and passed our time smoking, drinking, and shooting craps on the low-lying tombs hidden among the raised vaults and tall weeds. We'd frequent poolrooms and cafés, swapping lies about ourselves, other kids, and especially girls. It was stupid, aimless activity by stupid, aimless kids, most of whom were destined for short lives. Skinny and socially awkward, I was often the brunt of their jokes, but negative attention was better than none. Most of the kids still in school avoided me. In embracing the street toughs, I had further excluded myself from the world I yearned to be a part of.

I got a job stocking shelves and bagging groceries at Tramonte's, a family-owned Italian grocery. The store owner knew I was underage and playing hooky but was willing to overlook it in exchange for cheap labor. I was being exploited, which I didn't like, but I needed the money; besides which, I had stepped up in the world: I had a job.

One day my brother Raymond confided that he and a friend had committed a burglary. I agreed to let him tell my mother that he got the money from me, since I had a job. When they got busted, I acknowledged covering for my brother because I saw nothing wrong in what I had done. To my surprise, I was taken to the notorious State Industrial School for Colored Youths, a coed institution outside Baton Rouge, along with my brother and his friend, for an indefinite period.

Unlike other penal facilities, this one boasted a well-educated staff, ironically the result of racial segregation. Aside from the local colored schools, this institution was the only place in the area where colored educators and social workers, graduates of nearby Southern University, could find employment. But the educational level of the administration did not translate into enlightened leadership. Staff members whipped every kid in the vicinity of a fight, theft, misbehavior, or other wrongdoing, even if they were only seeking information. Shocking tales of cruelty, brutality, and even deaths occasionally appeared in newspapers after someone escaped from the facility, but staffers were seldom held accountable. Louisiana's all-white government rarely questioned the treatment of colored kids.

Some of the kids in the reform school were street thugs and gang members who carried their feuds into the facility. Most of the residents, though, were there because they were labeled as "problems" in their communities. Some had been committed by relatives who regarded them as unmanageable. These rejects, some of them innocents, did not like being imprisoned, understandably. I was one of them. I considered myself a victim of that vague, faceless, all-powerful entity coloreds knew simply as "white folks."

I simmered in my victimization until I volunteered for a part-time job sorting files and cleaning the office of the chaplain, Reverend West. It was an effort to get closer to Sexy Black, a gorgeous teenage resident I was infatuated with who had a job in the same building. Reverend West was a nice man who took the time to explain that I committed a crime when I lied to help my brother hide the fact that his money came from a burglary. I was an *accessory after the fact.* I was stunned to learn that I had done something seriously wrong. That knowledge mitigated the bitterness that had begun to build up in me.

I became a good student and a model inmate. I looked forward to seeing my mom, who visited as frequently as she could. I didn't try to escape, as others periodically did, nor did I challenge authority.

I was released after five months. Reverend West advised me to return to school, but my shame at having been in reform school was too great for that.

"You want a job?" my cousin Mason asked. He was the janitor for an exclusive women's store at one end of the Southgate Shopping Center in the white section of Lake Charles. A new shop, Halpern's Fabrics, was opening there soon. Because Mason vouched for me, Halpern's manager, Martha Irby, a pleasant, fortyish woman, hired me on the spot as janitor and general helper, what in those days was called a "porter."

The shopping center was across town from where colored folks lived, and we only went there to work or shop. I had neither a driver's license nor a car, so I commuted by city bus. The seating was segregated—blacks in the back. Most coloreds who could catch a ride after a day's work did that rather than run the risk of waiting at the bus stop, especially when it was late and getting dark, when white joyriders would often pass by to holler racial epithets and obscenities or hurl a beer can or Coke bottle from passing cars, laughter trailing behind. If you had to take the bus home, you would try to arrive at the stop almost immediately before the bus's scheduled arrival.

Since there was no place for coloreds to eat in south Lake Charles—there were plenty of whites-only cafés—we generally brought sandwiches from home or bought bread and bologna at a supermarket in the shopping center and ate in the rear of the places where we worked. We inhabited two different worlds, sharply divided by race and maintained by tradition, law, fear, and violence. Ours was always substandard and second-class, and we didn't like it very much.

I worked six days a week and earned $70 every two weeks—good pay for a colored in a non-construction job in 1959. I had never had so much money. I was able to help out my mother, purchase nice clothes for myself, and renew my efforts to buy myself some "friends."

My job introduced me to a world in which what I did mattered. I kept Halpern's Fabrics clean and served as a general helper, keeping the stock in order, running errands, and doing whatever the four white, middle-aged saleswomen needed me to do. All the women were nice to me, and I treated them with respect. Mrs. Irby, whom I really liked, was unlike any white person I had ever met, treating me with a measure of respect in turn, taking a sincere interest in me. She didn't like my having quit school and would take time to teach me about the fabrics we handled, sewing, the draperies and home decorating, how to mix paint, operate the cash register, bookkeeping, and the general operation of the business. "You never know when this might one day benefit you," she'd always say.

As things turned out, it became a benefit to the store. When the assistant manager left, she was not replaced. Instead, Mrs. Irby asked me to assume some of those duties. I leaped at the chance to demonstrate my knowledge and abilities. I helped with the books, brought deposits to the Gulf National Bank branch, tracked and ordered stock, determined discounts for damaged goods. Mrs. Irby came to rely on me, to the point that she would not go to lunch unless I was there to make sure everything went smoothly in her absence. I became her right hand. She suggested to Alvin Halpern, Jr., the store's owner, that he give me a 50 percent raise instead of hiring a new assistant manager. She was optimistic he would say yes, since it would translate into a savings for the store. Halpern said good things about my work but gave me a raise of only $2.50 a week. Mrs. Irby was embarrassed. I seethed.

I felt it was unfair, still another setback. I was fed up with a white society that marginalized me. I brooded about that, and about the fact that I had no real friends, only some people who would become chummy when they hit me up for cash. I felt my life was empty, and I despaired of things ever being different.

In fact, at that very moment the racial, social, and legal barriers separating the races in Louisiana were being challenged. On February 15, 1961, Governor Jimmy "You Are My Sunshine" Davis called the all-white Louisiana legislature into its fifth consecutive special session to wrestle with the issue of school desegregation. Ever since 1954, when the U.S. Supreme Court declared "separate but equal" school systems unconstitutional, the Louisiana government had been trying desperately to block the racial integration of its public schools. Legislators pandered to the prejudices of the white majority who wanted to keep their traditional way of life intact. The solution lawmakers hit upon bore witness to a public mood of near hysteria among whites: Rather than allow colored kids into the white schools, the legislature passed a bill to close the state's public schools and put the buildings up for sale. The governor approved it. A federal court blocked it.

I was oblivious to what was happening at the capitol, 125 miles from Lake Charles, just as I was oblivious to Harper Lee's searingly accurate portrait of Southern justice in *To Kill a Mockingbird*, her best-selling novel, which won a Pulitzer Prize in 1961. My small world revolved around the latest dance steps, my next new suit of clothes, and girls. I read neither newspapers nor books, and I didn't watch television. I didn't know who the governor of Louisiana was, much less what the legislature was doing.

For me, the most significant thing about February 15, 1961, was that it was payday. I cashed my check at the bank and, at lunchtime, caught the back of the bus to Waldmeier's Pawn Shop downtown, a couple of miles away. I made my way to the rear of the shop, where the handguns were kept. I'd been thinking off and on about getting a gun for several months. I was a puny nineteen-year-old who weighed less than 120 pounds. I'd been picked on, bullied, and harassed throughout my life, and I was tired of it. What pushed me over the edge was having been slapped and threatened in front of others at a nightclub by a guy with a knife a week earlier. As I walked back home that night, fuming, I vowed that would never happen again.

Many of my buddies had knives, but no one had a gun. I had never held, much less fired, one. I studied a .22 caliber with a price tag of $14.95. It was small enough to carry in my pocket, concealed. I had never been violent and did not want to hurt anyone. I was buying the weapon to intimidate people. I didn't expect ever to fire the gun; I felt just pulling it out would resolve any problem I faced and, as word spread, the knowledge that I carried a pistol would deter people from trying to push me around.

The pawnshop owner bagged the firearm and handed it to me. I began walking toward the front door of the store when a hunting knife in a scabbard caught my eye—a cheap, ordinary knife priced at $2. I bought it on impulse and walked out. I caught the bus back to the area where I worked and bought a box of .22 caliber cartridges at an army surplus store. Then I wandered back to work.

I got to work about nine the next morning, the weapons still in my coat pocket. I swept the floor of the shop and the sidewalk out front, cleaned the toilet, then straightened bolts of fabric and other products throughout the store. This was my future—a dead-end job. I was restless. I felt a gnawing need for things to change.

I had a week's vacation coming, starting Monday. I'd heard California was a good place for colored people, with plenty of opportunities for good jobs and a chance to be somebody. But the trip would require more money than I had.

I ate a sandwich for lunch and, not feeling well, remained in the back of the store. When Mrs. Irby returned from lunch at about two o'clock, I asked for the rest of the day off. She said that was fine as long as I made sure everything was in good order before I left. About an hour later, I walked a half block down the shopping center to a men's shop to visit with the janitor there. He asked me to help him move some things around and I did, which caused me to miss my bus. It would be an hour before the next one. I decided to wait in my cousin's car in the parking lot in the rear of the shopping center. Like most people in 1961 Lake Charles, he didn't lock it. Having been up late the night before, I fell asleep until almost 5:30. I was irritated with myself for having missed the bus again. I dreaded the prospect of having to wait at the bus stop in the dark, despite the gun in my pocket. I'd gotten it to scare people off, true, but it was difficult to scare people in a passing car.

The unseasonable warmth of the February afternoon was fading with the daylight. The smoke belching from the city's chemical plants deepened the winter evening gloom, coloring the city charcoal gray. The temperature had fallen to about 50 degrees. I zipped my jacket up halfway and meandered to Weingarten's Supermarket, where I talked to the bag boys and porters I knew and arranged for a ride home with one of them who was leaving at 7:30. It was a quarter past six, give or take.

I bought a soft drink at Weingarten's and sat on a bench outside the store, sipping it as I looked out at the overcast sky. I felt totally alone, miserable, frustrated, and desperate.

I need a new life, away from Lake Charles, I said to myself. *But that takes money.* On the heel of that thought rose a vision of the bank I had been in earlier that day. It was stuffed with money—whole drawers full of money, where the tellers made change and stuck the cash deposits people brought in. And then there was the vault, where they kept the *real* money. With that money I could buy a new life someplace else.

The idea took root quickly, and my mind raced with the possibilities. Three people worked at the bank, but on Thursday evenings only the manager, Jay Hickman, and one teller worked. Hickman was a short, overweight, mild-mannered man who often came to Halpern's to talk with Mrs. Irby. He wasn't the kind of person to put up a fight. I didn't know which of the two tellers would be on duty. One was a thirty-ish blonde who got upset when I had asked her name once when she made change for me. She had given me the strangest look, like she was scared and startled and offended all at the same time. I avoided her after that, always taking my business to the other teller, a pleasant older woman, maybe fifty. I didn't know their names, but they knew me as the boy who worked for Mrs. Irby.

I felt the gun in my pocket and knew that I could make them hand over all the money in the bank. I'd seen it done countless times in the movies. I'd get the money and tie up the two employees in the back, in that little kitchenette where they had their coffee. Better yet, I could lock them in the vault. It shouldn't take but a few minutes, after which I'd return to Weingarten's to catch my 7:30 ride home, pack some clothes, leave my family some money, and tell them I was going on vacation and not to worry about me. Then I'd catch a Greyhound bus going west. The people in the bank wouldn't be discovered until late at night or perhaps the next morning. They would tell the cops what I'd done, but it wouldn't matter because I'd be starting my life over somewhere else by then, fading into the woodwork of a black community. And I would have plenty of money, which meant I could get plastic surgery so no one would recognize me.

Driven by desperation, I convinced myself that it would work, and that it had to be done now, or never. The bank's closing time dovetailed with my ride home. When would an opportunity like this occur again? The prospect of failure, prison, even death, did not factor into the equation. I *had* to do it.

I looked at my watch: 6:30. I would wait until just before the bank's 7:00 closing time, and if there were no customers in the bank, I would go in and rob it.

I went to a department store and purchased a little bluish gray suitcase to put the money in. It was ten minutes to seven. Night had fallen. I wiped my clammy hands against my khakis as I walked out the store's back exit and stole quickly along the back of some buildings to the Gulf National Bank's rear entrance. I looked in. I didn't see any customers, but I couldn't be sure.

I checked my watch: 6:55. I had to decide. *Fuck it. What do I have to lose?* I put my right hand on the gun in my pocket and walked in the rear entrance to the bank, my pounding heart echoing in my head. I walked down a corridor, past the small kitchenette on the right. As I reached the end of the hallway, I set the suitcase down against the wall next to the vault and continued to walk into the lobby. There were no customers, but I was surprised to find both women tellers there instead of one. *This can still work, even with three of them.* I told the women I wanted to see Mr. Hickman. They pointed toward the front, near the window, where he sat at his desk. I told him there was a woman outside in back who wanted to see him, and when he walked back to see, I directed him into the coffee room. He was suddenly alarmed, nervous.

"I've come for some money. That's all I want, and no one will get hurt," I said, pulling the gun from my pocket.

"Okay, Wilbert. I'll give you all the money you want. All I ask is that you not do anything rash," Hickman said, his voice rising.

"I don't want to do anything rash. I need for you to cooperate with me," I said. "Just cooperate with me, that's all. Now tell the women up front to close the drapes and lock the door and come on back here."

Hickman stuck his head out of the coffee room and did what he was told. Looking back, it seems preposterous that I took him into a room where I surrendered my ability to see and control what was happening outside the room. It never occurred to me the women might get suspicious, simply walk out the front door and raise an alarm, in which case I would be caught. But the two women appeared shortly afterward in the doorway of the coffee room, shocked at the sight of my holding a gun on their boss. I repeated to them what I told Hickman, emphasizing that I didn't want any trouble and didn't want to hurt anyone. I just wanted money.

I waved the pistol in the general direction of the corridor and the front lobby. "Let's go get the money," I said, and followed the nervous and fearful trio out into the hallway. Before we reached the lobby, the phone rang. All of us were startled. Hickman turned his head and looked at me.

"Don't answer that," I said.

"I about have to answer it," he said. "It would be suspicious if I didn't. Most likely it's the main branch checking in with us like they always do at the end of the day."

I relented, warning him to be careful and to talk normally: "Don't try any funny stuff," I said. I stood next to him as he lifted the telephone receiver, placing my ear next to his, listening intently. The man calling asked if there was anything wrong at the branch. Hickman ignored his question, saying, "Okay, I'll be down in a few minutes." The caller asked, "Do you need a cop there?" When Hickman gave him a vague response, the caller said he was sending a car that would arrive in a few minutes. Hickman said he would call him right back and hung up.

Everything had suddenly spun out of control. The police were on the way. I didn't know what to do. I had counted on everything going right, not this.

I told Hickman to fill the suitcase, and hurry. The women stood by a table near the tellers' cages while he took stacks of bills from the cash drawers and put them in the suitcase.

"Get the big bills in there, the hundreds and whatnot. Nothing small. And hurry," I urged. "Hurry up."

I was in a state of near panic, acting on instinct. I had no time to get the money from the vault. I had to get the hell out of the bank *now*. I would have to take the three employees with me. There was no other way, not with the police on the way. We'd have to go in one of their cars. I could drop them off in the middle of nowhere and take the car. By the time they walked back to town and explained what had happened, I'd be long gone.

It felt as though everything was moving in slow motion. The police would be barging through the doors, guns drawn, anytime now.

"That's it. Shut the suitcase, and let's go," I said. *We had to get out.* I looked at the younger woman and demanded the keys to her car.

"I don't have them," she said. "I didn't drive today. My husband is picking me up."

I turned to the older woman. "Do you have yours?"

"Yes." Her car keys were in her hand.

"Where is your car parked?"

"Behind the bank," she said.

"Y'all are going to have to come with me. Let's go," I said, gesturing for them to move to the hallway that led to the rear entrance. "Come on, hurry up. Let's move it." I saw the manager was in shirtsleeves and instinctively blurted out, "Mr. Hickman, get your coat."

"I don't have one here," he replied.

"Well, you're going to be cold walking back to town."

We filed out the back door of the bank and made our way to the car, a Vauxhall, a small English four-seater roughly the size of a Volkswagen Beetle. I told the older woman to drive and the younger one to sit in the front passenger seat. I directed Hickman, with the suitcase, to the back seat behind the driver, and I sat behind the blonde. It was cramped, close quarters.

The woman drove out of the back parking lot and onto the city streets. It was about five minutes past seven. She was driving a little fast, so I cautioned her to slow down and to obey all traffic signs. I didn't want us to be stopped by the police for speeding or running a red light.

"Where are we going?" the older lady asked. "Where do you want me to drive?"

I was totally unfamiliar with the streets in this all-white section of the city. I told her to take one of the streets behind the shopping center and generally head north toward downtown, which I was a little familiar with.

The three bank employees, understandably fearful, talked constantly to me, asking that I not hurt them, that I not use the gun, that I just stop and let them out. I didn't pay much attention to what they were saying because I was trying to figure out what to do with the three of them, at which out-of-the-way place I should drop them. I was almost as afraid and desperate as they were. I knew that if other whites caught me with these three, I wouldn't survive.

We twisted and turned aimlessly through streets for fifteen minutes, passing right by the sheriff's headquarters and the heart of the downtown business district. I suddenly remembered that Opelousas Street, in north Lake Charles, petered out at the city's outskirts into the Old Spanish Trail, a country back road that went to Iowa, a small town eleven miles away. "We'll get on Opelousas Street and go east, toward Iowa," I said. "I'll let y'all out in the country. But only if y'all cooperate. Everything depends on your cooperation, remember that."

We were outside the city on Highway 171. Hickman asked if we were going to English Bayou. I said no, that I was confused. I told the driver to turn the car around. We doubled back to Opelousas Street and followed it east until it dead-ended at Ward Line Road, a narrow gravel lane. *Where was the Old Spanish Trail?* We could only go right or left. "What do you want me to do?" the driver asked. I had no idea which way to turn. No houses were visible. No house lights, no streetlights. There were no stars, no moon. It was pitch-black, the way it gets out in the country, in the woods. I thought maybe I could leave my prisoners somewhere on this road since it seemed to be in the middle of nowhere. I quickly dismissed that notion when several cars passed us after we turned left, going down the lane a mile or so through the wooded landscape. I didn't know this road or where it went, but it was obvious I couldn't leave them there, given the amount of traffic.

We came to a little bridge that crossed a bayou. There was a small clearing in the woods, next to the road, on the left-hand side. I told the driver to slow down. I was disoriented. Another car passed, and in the distance its brake lights came on. I watched the car intently through the rear window, scared it might be returning to try to help us.

Suddenly, the younger woman was bolting from the car. "Stop the car!" I yelled, grabbing at the door handle and springing out. I slipped, losing my footing. The woman ran across the road. Scrambling to break my fall, I leaned against the trunk of the car. "Stop or I'll shoot!" I yelled. Hickman, now out of the car, lunged toward me and the pistol. It went off, and he ran. I continued firing—five more shots in rapid succession—until the gun emptied. Both women fell. "Mr. Hickman!" I called, running a couple of steps after him, stopping as I realized I could not see him, then spinning around in time to see the older woman start to rise. I grabbed the knife, stabbed her, and ran to the car where I stood, shaking violently and gasping for breath. I couldn't see anything in the pitch-black night. It was deathly quiet. *Oh, God, what have I done?* I got into the car and took a deep, ragged breath. "Oh, God," I murmured, "help me—please." I took off down the gravel lane. I needed to distance myself from this horrible place, this nightmare.

Three white deputies pulled into the driveway of 1820 Brick Street. They pounded first on the front door, waking my mother, and then again at the back door. One ordered her to put on some clothes and told her she was needed at the jail. They told her that they wanted her to talk with her son but would tell her no more than that. Terrified, she dressed quickly as the cop standing in the doorway watched. They got her into the car and drove off, leaving her children behind. At the jail, they escorted her through a wild and drunken mob and left her sitting on a bench in the lobby, which was full of angry white men spilling out into the street. "I had never seen nothing that ugly in my life," she remembered. "There were about two, three hundred white mens—no women or colored folks. I was the only one there. They were drinking, cursing, and talking about how they were going to kill that nigger. They had guns. I was scared to death."

"Your momma is here. We got her in the front. You want to see her?" the sheriff asked me.

"Yes, sir. Sheriff, she's not out there with all those people, is she?" I asked.

"She'll be all right," he said. "And we gonna let you see your momma—but we need you to finish telling us what happened first. The quicker we get that done, the quicker y'all can visit."

A secretary took shorthand notes of our interview. Within an hour the police had enough of a confession, which they typed up for me to sign. Only when it was handed to me for my signature was I told that I did not have to make a statement, that I did not have to say anything at all. But I was worried about my mother being dragged into my troubles. The sheriff left to issue a statement to the media detailing the crime. I was taken upstairs, stripped of my clothing, dressed in gray jail coveralls, and locked in a cell.

I lay down on the bunk, emotionally spent and traumatized. The cops did not let me see my mother. I hoped she was all right. I wondered about the three bank employees I left out in the country. I hadn't wanted to harm them. I figured the man was okay because he ran off. I whispered a prayer that the women were somehow all right, too. Totally exhausted, I fell into a deep sleep.

The jangling of steel keys dragged my sleep-fogged mind awake. Three uniformed deputies stood before me, one in the doorway of the cell, hands on his hips: "Awright, Rideau—let's go," he said.

"Go where?" I asked, moving through the door. No response. As we walked down an empty hallway, I believed they were taking me to be killed. We went down an elevator. My legs were so weak from fear, I could barely walk. They directed me toward an extremely brightly lit area of an otherwise dark room. Sheriff Reid and the two state troopers who had captured me were waiting in the pool of light. They sat me in a chair at a long table. I wondered if it was the electric chair. The sheriff fed my fear when he sat next to me and told someone behind the light, "Tell me when you're ready." Then he offered me a cigarette, just like they did in the movies before executing someone. I snatched the lit cigarette, inhaled, and tried to see the shadowy figures in the dark behind the blinding lights. I returned the cigarette to my lips, only to find that the tension in my fingers had broken it.

The sheriff introduced the troopers flanking us on either side and then conversationally turned to me. "When you approached English Bayou off of Highway 90, on the side road there, would you mind telling me just how the car slowed up and how Mrs. McCain jumped out of the car? Would you tell me exactly how that happened, and how you shot at her?"

"One got out, and then the other two got out from the other side," I mumbled.

"Did they go in the same direction, run in the same direction?" the sheriff asked.

I nodded at him and said, "Yeah."

"And then what did you do when they ran?"

"Well, Mr. Hickman ran one way and the other two women ran another way."

"And then what did you do as they ran?"

"I shot."

"You shot? Well, uh, did you hit 'em? Did you notice?"

"I don't know. They fell, though . . ."

"How many of them fell?"

"The two women fell."

"The two women fell," repeated the sheriff. "And then, I believe that, uh, one of the women got up, and as she got up, she fell back down, and you went over to her, isn't that right?"

"Yeah."

"Well," said Reid, "tell what happened when you went back to the old woman as she was laying, as she was lying, on the road."

"I stabbed her," I mumbled.

"You stabbed her? What was it with, a hunting knife?"

"A hunting knife."

"And then you turned around after you lost them in the dark, you turned around and went back down Opelousas Street. You decided that you better not go back into town, so you reversed yourself, turned around, went back east on Opelousas Street, hit Highway 90, and proceeded on toward Iowa, Louisiana, and later on were stopped by troopers Dupin and Byon."

Reid turned first to trooper Sonny Dupin, then to trooper George Byon for a summary of how they apprehended me. "Sonny, would you mind relating the facts leading up to you spotting this car?" The sheriff slid the microphone down the table to his left for Dupin, who consulted his notes as he spoke.

The bright lights trained on the table belonged to KPLC-TV, the local Lake Charles television station, whose crew was, unbeknownst to me, capturing the event on film with a sound track.

To my surprise, and immense relief, I was returned to my cell unharmed. I sat on the bunk, shaking, until I was taken down the elevator again and led into a small barred enclosure. Frank Salter, the young district attorney who had taken office the previous month, was waiting for a photo opportunity. I recalled seeing him on the couch the previous night when the sheriff was questioning me. He pointed to *Lake Charles American Press* photographer Charles Murphy and said he should take a photo of us together. He showed me a document and explained that he was filing formal charges against me for "the murder of Julia Ferguson and . . ." That shocking information obliterated whatever else he said. The photo taken, I was returned to my cell. I lay on the thin, dirty mattress atop the steel bunk, staring unseeing at the ceiling, in shock.

In the days that followed, a parade of white men, some well dressed, some not, some cops, entered the hallway periodically to stand in front of the cell and stare at me, sometimes silently, sometimes talking to each other about me, other times cursing and telling me how many different ways they wanted to kill me. I stared back, saying nothing. What could I say?

The only non-white person I saw was my father. He stood in front of my cell, accompanied by several white men. He stared silently at me for a long time. "Dad . . . ," I said, breaking the silence.

"You sonuvabitch!" he erupted, his body shaking. "You no son of mine. I raised my children to do right. You nothing to me. You an animal, a mad dog. They say they gonna electrocute you, and I hope they do, 'cuz you a beast. If I had a gun right now, I'd shoot you myself." I was speechless. Even the white deputies seemed surprised at the venom he hurled at me. My father suddenly turned to them, his face contorted with rage: "Can I go? I can't stand the sight of him." They left.

All I had ever wanted was to fit in, to belong. Now I sat in a cell, removed from society, isolated from life. I was utterly alone, a rejection that would be complete when they executed me. Despite what I had done, I felt like a victim.

After I'd spent two weeks in isolation, the Calcasieu Parish grand jury indicted me for murder on March 1. The next day I was taken before Judge Cecil Cutrer, who arraigned me and, learning I was indigent, appointed two white attorneys, Fred H. Sievert, Jr., and James A. Leithead, to represent me. Neither had ever tried a capital case. They weren't even criminal lawyers. Plucked from different law firms, each was engaged in the practice of civil law, mostly real estate.

The first thing they said to me was, "Why did you confess on television?"

"I didn't."

"We saw you," they said. "Everybody did."

That's how I learned that my mumbled answers to Sheriff Reid under the bright lights the morning after the crime had been filmed and repeatedly broadcast throughout southwest Louisiana. The local daily newspapers had likewise saturated the community with coverage of the sensational interracial crime.

Judge Cutrer set the trial for April 10 and gave my lawyers ten days to file any motions in my case. They had less than six weeks to prepare a defense, an enormous challenge, especially since they had to fund it out of their own pockets. No money was provided for investigators, independent tests, expert witnesses. Leithead met with my mother, whom he knew because she had sometimes babysat his children.

"Gladys," he said, "if you could come up with some money to hire investigators, I think we could get to the bottom of this." He, among others, suspected that Hickman, the nephew of the city's mayor, had a hand in the robbery. I had been grilled by interrogators, especially the FBI, about that; they made the suggestion that it would go easier on me if I said Hickman was the person behind it all. I insisted he was a victim.

My mother learned she could raise some money by taking a loan against the little two-bedroom house where she lived with her four other children. She asked my father if he could come up with the rest. He told her he wasn't interested. I told her not to mortgage the house. I knew the money, contrary to Leithead's assertions, would make no difference.

Sievert and Leithead knew that a trial in Lake Charles would be a mockery. They tried to get it transferred to anywhere outside Calcasieu Parish. They presented evidence showing that seating an impartial jury would not be possible in the parish, given the nature of the crime and the amount of pretrial publicity. District Attorney Salter argued for keeping the trial in Calcasieu Parish and Judge Cutrer agreed with him.

On April 10, 1961, I went on trial for my life. Judge Cutrer warned the packed courtroom that "no laughter, no outcries, no remarks" would be tolerated. The proceeding, of course, was merely a formality. Everyone knew what the verdict would be.

On the second day of jury selection, the proceedings hit a snag when one of my attorneys noticed that the court reporter—who had recorded and transcribed all the pretrial proceedings—was not taking down the questions and answers of prospective jurors, or even the court's rulings. He made a motion that the complete trial proceedings be recorded and transcribed, but the district attorney argued that the state was not required to provide a verbatim transcript to me unless I could pay for it. The judge sided with the district attorney.

A verbatim transcript is the official record of everything that happens in the trial courtroom. Without one, a defendant cannot construct an appeal of an unfavorable verdict. We had to improvise. Every time Sievert and Leithead objected to anything during the weeklong trial, they would try to reconstruct, with agreement from the court and the prosecutor, what was said, when it was said, and, generally, what led up to the objectionable statements or testimony or ruling. Then one of my lawyers had to write down the reconstructed proceedings in longhand. It was a farce.

As the jury selection continued in the emotionally charged, crowded courtroom, my attorneys kept asking Judge Cutrer not to seat particular jurors for cause. Each time the judge refused, they were forced to use one of twelve peremptory challenges. Sievert and Leithead moved five times for a mistrial because of emotional outbursts and inflammatory or prejudicial comments made either by the prosecutor or by prospective jurors within the earshot of jurors already chosen to serve. The judge refused every request. My attorneys exhausted their peremptory challenges, and jury selection was completed on Friday morning, April 14.

Among the jurors—all white men, of course—were two special deputy sheriffs; a cousin of victim Julia Ferguson; a vice president of the largest bank in the area, who had known bank manager Jay Hickman for twenty-five years; and three persons who had seen the sheriff's televised "interview" with me.

Salter focused his presentation on making a case for premeditation and heinous, cold-blooded murder.

Sievert and Leithead tried to keep out of evidence the confession the sheriff had obtained from me the night of the crime. They argued that I confessed before anyone advised me I did not have to say anything or that I had a right to have an attorney. They objected even more strenuously to a second confession, written by FBI agent James W. Hamilton five days after the crime and based upon a session he and another agent had with me. Besides expressing a high degree of intentionality—necessary to prove premeditation and win a death penalty conviction—the FBI's version of the crime differed from my initial confession mainly in that it said I ordered the three bank employees out of the car after it had come to a stop and before I fired at them. The judge allowed the prosecutor to read both confessions to the packed courtroom.

Friday afternoon and evening were taken up with prosecution witnesses, mostly law enforcement, testifying to a pouring rain the evening of the crime, their capture of me, evidence at the scene of the crime, and the state of the bank when officers arrived after the robbery and found some $30,000 spilling from the gaping cashiers' drawers while the back door of the bank was standing wide open.

The gun used in the crime was never recovered. Salter introduced into evidence a common hunting knife a Deputy Harvey Boyd claimed to have found in a field more than a thousand feet away from the scene of the crime. Nothing tied that particular knife to the crime. The owner of the pawnshop where I bought the weapon, Robert Waldmeier, Jr., was so nervous on the stand that even the prosecutor felt obliged to remark on it. Waldmeier testified that the knife Salter asked him to identify was either the one he sold to me or one identical to it.

Sievert and Leithead asked very few questions. But on Monday they asked that a photograph be taken of the courtroom to show the incredibly crowded conditions under which the trial was occurring. The courtroom, which normally seated 300 people, was crammed with 430 spectators, by Judge Cutrer's official estimate. There were people occupying every available seat, standing against three walls, lined up in the aisles. Those who couldn't get inside the courtroom looked in from the corridors. I was the only black in sight, a fly in a bowl of milk.

My lawyers argued that the atmosphere created by the crowd was intimidating to jurors and witnesses alike. Under the weight of such community pressure, no one could be presumed to be acting or speaking freely and truthfully. Salter objected to a photograph being taken of the courtroom, saying it was irrelevant and immaterial. He brushed off the notion that there was any community pressure at work: "It is perfectly obvious that everybody in the courtroom is practicing perfect decorum."

Judge Cutrer denied the request to take a photo.

It was during the trial that I learned about the phone call that had derailed my robbery of the bank and precipitated the events that ended so tragically.

When Hickman had called from the coffee room to tell the tellers to shut the drapes and lock up, Dora McCain, the young blonde, got suspicious. She signaled to Julia Ferguson to close up, as the manager had said. Then she picked up the phone and dialed the direct extension to the bank's main office, downtown. When switchboard operator Nettie Hoffpauir answered, McCain identified herself and said, "I'm afraid there's something crooked going on. . . . Yes, I'm afraid there is."

The phone call that had panicked me had been made by Burt Kyle, a vice president from the bank's main office, phoning back after Hoffpauir told him about McCain's call.

"What's going on there, Jay?" asked Kyle.

Hickman responded as he did—"Okay, I'll be down in a few minutes"—hoping Kyle would realize his answer meant something was amiss, since Hickman never went down to the main branch after hours.

"Do you need a cop there?" Kyle asked. "I'll send a car."

"Well, maybe. I don't know. I'll call you right back," Hickman replied, hanging up the telephone.

Kyle immediately called the Calcasieu Parish sheriff's office and the Lake Charles City Police and asked them to investigate "goings-on" at the bank. A minute or two later, Murl Cormie, a radio dispatcher for the sheriff's department, sent to the bank one deputy from the station and one in a car nearby. At the same time, Mike Hogan, chief of detectives for the city police in Lake Charles, was called at home and told to go investigate a possible problem at the bank. Hogan lived about four or five minutes from Southgate Shopping Center, but he testified that because it was raining so hard, it took him maybe seven, eight minutes to get there. We were gone by then.

On the witness stand, Hickman's version of what happened on the night of the crime was essentially the same as mine—until we reached the bridge at English Bayou.

Both he and Dora McCain testified—in virtually identical language and phrasing—that I ordered them out of the car, lined them up facing me on the shoulder of the road, and, as they stood still with their hands at their sides at point-blank range, I opened fire. The bullet that struck Hickman traveled upward in his right arm, a trajectory one would find if his arm were extended outward, parallel to the ground, not at his side, when the bullet entered. Hickman, supposedly standing directly in front of me at point-blank range, suffered only a superficial flesh wound. After being shot, he ran to his left and fell into the bayou about twenty-five feet away, they said.

McCain testified that after I fired a single shot at Hickman and he ran, I ran after him. She said this after saying she had dropped face-first to the ground and pretended that she had fainted. Still, she said she was able to see Julia Ferguson about ten feet away, in the opposite direction from the bayou. McCain said that I returned from the bayou, struggled physically with Julia Ferguson, shot Ferguson twice during the struggle, then knifed her as we continued to struggle and as the older woman begged for her life. My response, she testified, was, "It'll be quick and cool."

McCain said that after I finished off Ferguson, I literally stumbled into McCain as I ran toward the car. Then, she said, I put the gun up against the back of her neck and shot her. She testified that, having just been shot at point-blank range right below her ear, she heard my footsteps on the wet grass and could detect from their direction that I had gone back toward the bayou. She said she then heard me call out to Hickman.

Hickman was no more than thirty-five feet away from the crime scene when he was in the bayou, he said, holding on to branches, treading water, and listening for every sound. Thirty-five feet is less than twice the distance of an average living room. When asked what he heard after he ran and fell into the water, Hickman said he heard two more gunshots and thought "one was for Julia and one for Dora." He also said he heard a rustling in the weeds fifteen or twenty feet away from him, which he said he thought might have been a woodland creature or me, looking for him. He testified that he heard the Vauxhall's engine start and, after a moment, heard it accelerate as the car pulled away; he heard no struggling, no begging, no talking or calling out.

McCain, however, testified that after she heard me run to the bayou and call out to Hickman, I came back to her and kicked her twice in her side, so hard that I lifted her up like a rag doll with my foot. She said that I told her, "Woman, you had better be dead because I'll run you over if you're not." McCain said that she waited a bit after I drove off and then moved toward Julia Ferguson, calling to her. Hickman heard none of that, either.

McCain testified that after I fled the scene she took off her shoes and ran barefoot down the gravel road until she found a house, and help, about half a mile away. Hickman, too, headed away from the crime scene, looking for help. He found it about three-quarters of a mile away, at the B & J Oil Well Service. He, like McCain, ended up at Memorial Hospital for treatment. Julia Ferguson reportedly died in the ambulance on the way to the hospital.

McCain's graphic details of what she said she saw and heard, if allowed to stand, closed the door on the possibility that the crime might have been manslaughter—that is, a homicide committed in the heat of passion or a state of panic rather than a premeditated murder. Her testimony was a sensational finale to the state's case, and when she finished, Salter immediately rested his case. It was Monday morning, April 17, 1961. My lawyers did not cross-examine Dora McCain. Nor had they cross-examined Jay Hickman. They made no attempt to point out even the obvious faults and inconsistencies in their testimony or even to *suggest* that it might not all be true, although I told them it wasn't. I don't think they ever believed me.

The court adjourned for lunch. When the trial resumed at 1:30, it was time for my attorneys to present my defense. In a move that probably surprised everyone, and certainly surprised me, they immediately rested without calling a single witness. The prosecution's case against me had not been challenged.

Both sides gave closing arguments. Salter told the jury the bank employees had been lined up, shot execution-style, and that I had slashed Julia Ferguson's throat. He said the crime was heinous and calculated and demanded the death penalty. Sievert and Leithead each spoke to the jury, arguing that there was no evidence I deliberately planned to harm the three bank employees when I robbed the bank and fled with them. They reminded the jury that Dora McCain testified that I told Jay Hickman he would be cold walking back to town without a coat.

Less than an hour after the jurors retired, they returned a verdict of guilty, which carried a sentence of death.

I was to be sent to the Louisiana State Penitentiary, well-known as a house of horrors. I was terrified.

2

Tribulation
1962–1970

As soon as the verdict was read, three white deputies grabbed me. They took me back to the Calcasieu Parish jail, where I was moved from total isolation on the second floor to the third floor, where the colored male prisoners were housed, and put in one of four small maximum-security cells sandwiched in the center of the building by "bullpens"—large, open rooms where sizable groups of inmates spent their days—on each side. The only other prisoner in maximum security was Ora Lee Rogers, a soft-spoken, twenty-five-year-old giant of a man sentenced to die for the rape and murder of a white woman in Evangeline Parish during an early-morning robbery in May 1959. White hostility ran high against Rogers. The Evangeline Parish coroner told newspaper reporters he didn't believe Rogers would have lived through the day at the parish jail in Ville Platte, so he was sent to Calcasieu to evade homespun justice. The day after the crime, the Baton Rouge *Morning Advocate* speculated that the attempt to hide Rogers from the public "apparently was spurred by last week's lynch-mob kidnapping from jail of Mack Charles Parker at Poplarville, Mississippi. Parker, a 23-year-old Negro, was accused of raping a white woman." The FBI found his corpse floating in the Pearl River, which divides Poplarville from Bogalusa, Louisiana.

Louisiana executions historically had taken place in the community where the crime occurred, both to satisfy the local passion for vengeance and to serve as a deterrent to potential wrongdoers. But dwindling public support for capital punishment prompted the legislature in 1956 to transfer executions to the Louisiana State Penitentiary at Angola, in the wilds of central Louisiana. Under the new protocol, a condemned prisoner remained in the local jail until the Louisiana Supreme Court reviewed the appeal of his trial. If it was found to have been constitutional, the governor was then free to schedule an execution date, and the prisoner would be transferred to Angola.

Rogers, in the cell two doors down from me, had been there two years. Our quarters were about the size of a small bathroom, each containing a bunk, face bowl, toilet, and shower. The walls of the cells were made of solid steel, except for the back wall, which was made of bars, enabling us to talk to one another across the empty cell between us. When either of us was permitted out of the cell to go to court, to see lawyers, or for some other business, we would walk over and see the other through the small hatch in the front door of our cells. We were each other's only company, segregated from the rest of the jail population and allowed only a Bible and religious material. Neither of us asked the other about the circumstances that brought us there. We accepted each other without judgment, glad for companionship.

Rogers had valuable advice for me about how to survive life in a cell, where the struggle against isolation is a battle for one's sanity. I had already slipped to the edge of madness when I first met him. Without him I would not have survived. When I'd slide off into fantasy, he'd engage me in laughter, conversation, argument, whatever it took to pull me back to reality.

He did that for nearly eight months until he lost his appeal in the Louisiana Supreme Court and was transferred to Angola in advance of his December 1, 1961, execution date. I had grown close to him. When we hustled a candy bar through a sympathetic guard or orderly, we'd split it. When we were down to our last cigarette, one of us would smoke half and toss what remained down the walkway outside the bars to the other. He was my first real friend; I finally had someone I was able to confide in and talk to about my likes and dislikes, my problems, my failings. No one had ever known as much about me as Rogers did. We were both failed human beings, social outcasts who shared the same life experiences and were now facing the same fate. When they took him to Angola, leaving me in solitude and silence, I cried—for his loss and my own.

Without a court reporter's verbatim transcript, it took Leithead and Sievert more than seven months to piece together what they felt were thirty-four constitutional violations during my trial. On November 29, 1961, they filed my appeal to the Louisiana Supreme Court, which advanced the case to the top of its docket. On January 15, 1962, the court's seven white male justices unanimously declared that I had had a fair trial.

No other institution has so fueled the imagination of the Louisiana public as the Louisiana State Penitentiary, more popularly known as "Angola," the name of the largest of several plantations merged at the turn of the century to create the institution. Its name conjures up a cacophony of horrors. It was called "the Alcatraz of the South" in 1939 by a New Orleans *Sunday Item-Tribune* reporter; its history, which has been written in the blood of those locked within its bowels, earned it infamy throughout the mid-twentieth century as the most intimidating prison in America. When deputies shackled me and put me in a car for the trip there on April 11, 1962, I feared the prison far more than my death sentence.

After I'd been on the road for half an hour, my mind fastened on the passing landscape and I calmed down. Dead stalks of the previous season's sugarcane harvest filled mile after mile of flat fields. Cows roamed free in pastures. Overhead, an occasional flock of birds took flight, whirling and turning in unison, then settling in another tree. I envied them their freedom.

Not long after we passed the state capital, Baton Rouge, the flat-lands slowly gave way to rolling hills, and we came to the quaint ante-bellum town of St. Francisville, dotted with plantations worked by slaves a hundred years earlier. We left the main highway for a narrow, winding, rutted road that snaked through twenty-two miles of some of the most rugged and forbidding terrain in the state—a wilderness of lush foliage, swamps, and deep ravines. Some of the shrubbery lining the road was deceptive: It was the tops of tall trees rooted in the bottom of an abyss far below. The dead-end road had a singular purpose—to deliver human cargo to the front gate of the Louisiana State Penitentiary.

About sixty miles northwest of Baton Rouge, the maximum-security prison sprawls on an eighteen-thousand-acre enclave surrounded on three sides by the muddy Mississippi River. The rugged Tunica Hills, replete with snake-infested woods and deep gorges, border the prison on the remaining side, completing a formidable natural barrier that makes escape extremely difficult and isolates the prison, which is accessible only by boat, plane, or this one treacherous road. The prison has twenty miles of levees, built long ago by inmates, many of whom died from the grueling labor. The levees don't always protect the prison when the Mississippi becomes swollen from melting snow and ice up north each spring.

After miles of hairpin turns and breathtaking scenery, a massive dull gray, two-story building crouching against a bluff rose out of nowhere. Its sudden appearance jolted me like a crack of lightning. The prison loomed ominously against the skies, an image of awesome power. Dread replaced shock as we grew nearer and the cast-iron front gate came into view. To the right of the gate stood a wooden guard tower that looked like an outhouse on stilts. Others were scattered nearby. My stomach clenched when I saw the colored guards. These were the infamous khaki-backs, whose rumored brutality was the stuff of legend. They were trusty prisoners armed with rifles and pistols, vested with the power to kill.

Nineteen sixty-two was an especially bad time to be entering Angola. The legislature had slashed the prison's operating budget by one-third, shutting down what few educational and vocational programs existed there and laying off 114 employees from Angola's all-white staff. The penitentiary was manned and operated by an army of khaki-backs supervised by a small contingent of actual employees, generally referred to as "free people." The Baton Rouge *State-Times* predicted that the reforms gained in the 1950s after 31 white prisoners slashed their Achilles tendons to protest conditions at Angola would be lost, and the prison would deteriorate to the point of once again becoming the nation's worst. The *Shreveport Times* saw it returning to "the medieval slave camp of the past."

Eleven men were executed at Angola from 1957 to 1961, only one of whom was white. The most recent execution had taken place in June 1961.

We drove through the front gate and parked. The deputies took me down a long walkway and into the office of the security captain for the Reception Center. I stood silently, cuffed and chained hand and foot, dreading whatever would come next.

"Well, Cap'n, we brought you another boy," one deputy said, handing over some paperwork and removing my shackles. The other deputy set down the sack of belongings I'd brought from the local jail.

"What'd he do?" the captain asked.

"Murdered a white woman."

"Okay. We'll take him off your hands."

I knew from the jail grapevine that Negroes convicted of raping or killing a white person typically got a brutal ass-whipping by Angola's white guards and their khaki-backs to "teach them their place." So when a white guard and his two trusties came to the captain's office to take me away, I was terrified. But I was spared the whipping, as I later learned, because I was going to death row. I picked up my sack, and the khaki-backs guided me down the hall, where other trusties collected vital data on me, took fingerprints, and made an official mug shot. After stripping and squatting so the khaki-backs could make sure I wasn't smuggling any contraband in my body cavities, I was given a blue-and-white pin-striped denim uniform and a new identity. I was C-18, the *C* signifying "condemned," the *18* signifying that I was the eighteenth man to be housed on Angola's death row. We headed there.

It was a makeshift affair. In 1957, when executions were moved to the prison, the expectation was that the condemned would be brought here only to die. Seven did meet their end in the electric chair that year, but three New Orleans Negroes were unexpectedly spared. Thomas Goins's execution was halted by Justice Hugo Black to allow an appeal to the U.S. Supreme Court. Alton Poret and Edgar Labat, abandoned by their attorneys, smuggled out an appeal for help that was published in the *Los Angeles Times;* a sympathetic reader hired new lawyers, who rescued them from their date with the electric chair. No one had anticipated this wrinkle in the new execution protocol. Nor had anyone anticipated that the federal courts, historically reluctant to interfere with state criminal cases, would begin staying executions frequently so they could review the fairness of state proceedings. Angola authorities were forced to create a place to house the surviving condemned, as there was no legal provision to return them to the local jails. A tier of fifteen cells on the first floor of the Reception Center building facing the bluff was designated "Death Row."

To get there, we passed through several gates and doors unlocked for us by khaki-backs. After the final door, we entered a narrow steel-

and-concrete netherworld. At the free man's instruction, the khaki-back worked a crank that opened one of the cells.

"Okay, Rideau. Go down to number nine. That's your cell," the free man said.

I picked up my possessions and passed by the cells of somber men who nodded to me as I passed. I was startled when I got to Cell 5 and saw Ora Lee Rogers sitting on his bunk looking at me. The governor had stayed his execution when his lawyers filed an appeal to the U.S. Supreme Court.

"Man, I thought you were dead," I blurted out. "They told me you were dead. You're here!"

"In living color," he said, flashing the broad smile I remembered so well.

"Rideau!" the free man yelled. "Move on down to Cell 9."

I didn't move. I wanted to talk with Ora Lee.

"Go on," Ora Lee said softly. "Go on, and we'll talk later."

I went to Cell 9 with a spring in my step, as hard as that may be to believe. My best friend, my only friend in the world, was here. I wasn't alone.

Seventeen men had escaped death since executions were moved to Angola, but only twelve were on death row. The other five, all blacks, were at the state mental hospital at Jackson, in a wing for the criminally insane. Moreese Bickham was one of them. He'd been transported to Angola for execution in 1961 for killing two white police officers. His lawyer told him the only way he could see Bickham surviving was for him to feign insanity; the state wouldn't execute an insane man. So he played crazy. Judge H. R. Reid halted the scheduled execution and ordered a lunacy hearing for Bickham, who was transferred to the state mental hospital. In 1963 he was returned to death row.

On April 11, 1962, the day I walked onto death row, there were nine colored and three white men in the cells for the condemned. The whites were all there with murder convictions.

Delbert Eyer had shot a woman in the back of the head at point-blank range during an armed robbery of a dime store. He had managed to garner considerable outside religious support because he had since "found God"; an effort was being made to get his sentence commuted based on his "rehabilitation." He was a clean-cut but standoffish young man who kept his interactions with colored prisoners to a minimum.

Brodie Byron Davis was a burly, six-foot, 220-pound ex-convict on parole from Angola when he killed an elderly man during an armed robbery. The victim was bound and beaten to death, then thrown in a river. An ex-GI, Davis was friendly and the wealthiest man on the row by virtue of a monthly disability check from the Veterans Administration.

Roy Fulghum killed four people: his wife, both of her parents, and her teenage brother. He was just a typical, everyday working stiff—until he "lost it."

Those condemned for rape were blacks: Andrew Scott, Alton Poret, Edgar Labat, and Emile Weston. Their victims had been white.

Of the other blacks there the day I arrived, Edward "Bo Diddley" Davis had been convicted of murdering a white police officer who had gone to Davis's home with other officers after Davis's wife called during a domestic dispute. Davis had previously served time in Angola for shooting his father-in-law.

Freddie Eubanks was condemned for beating and stabbing to death a seventy-year-old white woman during a burglary. He was fifteen at the time of the crime.

Thomas "Blackjack" Goins was convicted of killing a white man during an armed robbery that netted thirty-five cents.

Parnell Smith had come to Angola with a life sentence for a murder in 1956, and killed again while in prison, for which he was given the death penalty.

And, of course, there was Ora Lee.

Cell 9 was six feet wide by eight feet deep, smaller than my cell at the Calcasieu Parish jail. It contained a white ceramic face bowl, a lidless ceramic toilet, a metal table and bench affixed to the wall, and a narrow metal bunk, its hardness barely relieved by a one-inch-thick, cotton-batting mattress made at the prison factory. An electrical wire threaded its way into my cell from the hallway, connecting to a bare bulb that lightened or darkened my space as I screwed it in or out. The cinder-block walls of my cell were white on the upper half, gray on the lower. The front of the cell consisted of bars facing a ten-foot-wide hall that ran the length of the tier. On the far side of the hall there was a wall of windows that looked out onto a small grassy area directly in front of us, then the prison fence, beyond which lay the bluff. Occasionally I saw a cow or two, or an armed khaki-back walking outside the fence. Most of the prisoners would hang a sheet or blanket across the front of their cell to spend their day free from the eyes of passersby in the hall, shutting off the view outside the windows. The guards respected the crude attempts at privacy; when they needed to talk with a prisoner they would stand in front of his cell and ask the occupant to move the curtain aside.

There were few avenues of relief from the boredom and idleness of life in a tiny cage. We spent every minute of every day in our cells, except twice a week when we were permitted out one at a time for fifteen minutes to shower at the head of the tier, near the entrance. In those precious minutes, men would take a quick shower and rush down the row to talk to other prisoners. If the need to talk or conduct business was urgent, the shower was skipped. The guards didn't care how you spent your fifteen minutes.

To feed the body's need for exercise, some of us did sit-ups and push-ups or paced the small patch of floor beside the steel bunk. Full of youth and testosterone, we found masturbation a daily necessity as we passed sunless days and sleepless nights in too-hot or too-cold gray cells, waiting to die.

We were allowed visits only from our immediate family and our religious advisors. Many did not have these specific visitors and had to obtain a court order from a judge to enable others to come. A chair or wooden bench would be placed in front of our cell for visitors to sit on. There was minimal security supervision, which allowed a couple of the white guys to occasionally sneak a little sex through the bars. Unfortunately, the rest of us either had no wife or court-approved girlfriend, or the woman couldn't afford the trip. Getting to Angola was a costly endeavor for poor people, and we all came from impoverished backgrounds. The ride in 1962 was a long one over bad roads: six hours or more round-trip from New Orleans, eight from Lake Charles, ten from Shreveport. Lawyers, understandably, came only when they had to. Visitors were rare.

When my mother visited, she usually brought along one or more of my siblings. My baby sister, Mary Arlene, a toddler, would run up and down the hall, playing peekaboo with some of the guys. Visiting me on death row would become a natural part of the social context she grew up in.

We were permitted to write and receive an unlimited number of letters, but they were monitored and confiscated if authorities found them offensive. When prison officials realized in 1963 that Edgar Labat was corresponding with a white Scandinavian housewife who was trying to help him, they ended the three-year pen-pal relationship by declaring that death row prisoners could have contact only with members of their own race. The ensuing furor created an international flap and a flood of letters and petitions from tens of thousands of Scandinavians to President Lyndon Johnson and Louisiana governor John J. McKeithen requesting Labat's freedom. To avoid the charge of racism and similar problems in the future, state authorities thereafter restricted our correspondence to only those permitted to visit us—our immediate family, lawyers, and a religious advisor. While that reduced mail considerably for some, it didn't affect me. My mother, who struggled to write letters with only a fifth-grade education, was my only correspondent. Except for her occasional visits and notes, I was completely cut off from the outside world. Never had I felt so lonely; never had life seemed so futile.

We were allowed to have a small electric radio, and a small electric fan to combat the stifling summer heat in the cells. With the two-story cinder-block building at our backs and a bluff looming up in front of us blocking any possible southern breeze, death row was an inferno from May to September. During the winter, icy north winds scooped up dampness from the Mississippi River and dumped bone-chilling cold into the cells. That's when a curtain across the front of the cell proved its worth by keeping the air at bay. Our other trick for keeping warm was putting a layer of newspaper over or between the thin blankets on our steel bunks.

The radio and fan, and tobacco, were luxuries. The prison provided food, toothpaste, toothbrush, and toilet paper in restricted quantities. Everything else—deodorant, soap, hair cream, canned meat, and tuna—we had to purchase out of whatever small funds we received or could muster. My mother would send a couple of dollars regularly so that I could buy Bugler tobacco, my only indulgence. I tried to quit smoking several times to eliminate the expense, but failed. I needed the fleeting relief of a cigarette.

Death row operated independently of the rest of Angola. All files and paperwork on us were maintained in the captain's office, which was responsible for the direct management of the row. Our mail bypassed the normal process and was delivered directly to the captain's office, and our money was kept in a safe there as well. Clyde "Blackjack" Morgan was the captain when I got there, and his word was law. Morgan was a clotheshorse who favored spit-shined shoes and was also rumored to drive a Thunderbird—all on a 1962 prison salary. Like all other prison security officers, he was a white man and a staunch segregationist, but he was also basically fair, treating everyone on the row, colored and white, the same. And he'd help us if he could. He routinely informed us whenever his wife planned to go shopping in Baton Rouge, so that if any of us needed something permissible, she would buy it and be reimbursed from the money his office held for us.

Morgan was his own man. One weekend while the warden was away, a colored inmate reportedly raped or assaulted the wife of an employee somewhere on the grounds. Morgan learned that some employees planned to lynch the prisoner, who was being held in a Main Prison "Dungeon." This was an era when captains were warlords, each commanding a small clique of employees and a larger crew of armed khaki-backs who stood ready to lie, steal, fight, injure, and kill at their captain's command with no questions asked. It was a macho, arbitrary world, and captains ruled like gangsters, jealous of others' power and territorial about their turf. Morgan's authority was limited to the Reception Center, but that did not deter him. He boldly went into the Main Prison, accompanied by his own handpicked khaki-backs, snatched the offender, and immediately transported him to death row, locking him next to me in Cell 8. Angry employees stormed the Reception Center, but Morgan and his khaki-backs stopped them in the hallway, warning them that it was against the law for them to go onto death row. The employee mob dispersed unhappily. Blackjack Morgan had saved the prisoner's life.

On death row, living in such close proximity, we often got on each other's nerves. We argued, got angry, cursed and threatened each other, but since we were confined to cells there were no fights. There were, however, wars of words, of silence, and of noise, like turning a radio up to full volume to wake one's nemesis—not to mention everyone else. The biggest danger came when, on shower day, one inmate would come out of his cell and throw a glass jar or worse against someone's bars, sending shards of glass flying into other cells. Indeed, on my first night, Andrew Scott was using a tin can set over a ball of flaming toilet paper to boil his feces mixed with syrup to throw on Emile Weston, a concoction designed not only to burn but to stick to the skin. Weston, a couple of cells down from us, overheard my expression of amazement when I realized what was happening and had his blanket covering the front of his cell when Scott threw the jar of foul brew.

One condemned man tried to get another in trouble by telling

Captain Morgan the other had contraband in his cell. That was a big mistake. Morgan put both inmates in the Dungeon, then came to death row to tell us he didn't like "fucking rats, 'cause if you'll snitch on your fellow inmate, you'll snitch on me, too. But you fuckers ought not be trying to make trouble for each other. You ain't got no business playing these little fucking penitentiary games. They sent y'all gawddam asses up here to kill you—all of you. The way I see it, y'all got too much shit to deal with to be snitching on each other. Y'all all in the same mother-fucking boat. You need to be trying to paddle together."

My first lesson in life about unity occurred shortly after my arrival. The death row inmates staged a hunger strike. At each meal, we were asked if we wanted to eat, and we all refused. After the second day I was really hungry. Good smells drifted down the hall, robbing me of whatever willpower I had. When the guard announced fried chicken for lunch and asked who wanted to eat, I surrendered. After lunch, I attempted to make a joke of my weakness, but no one laughed. My calls to various guys were met with silence. Finally, I said, "C'mon, fellas, y'all not mad at me about that, huh? I was hungry, and that smell was killing me."

"We all fucking hungry, and we all smelled the same damn chicken you did," Bo Diddley said angrily, "but we didn't eat it."

"Rideau, they do this all the time," Ora Lee said kindly. "Whenever there's a hunger strike, they cook fried chicken or pork chops to tantalize you with the smell." Alton Poret yelled for him not to explain anything to me, but Rogers insisted this was all new to me, that I didn't know any better.

"I just got here," I said. "I don't know anything about how y'all do things. I don't want to be at odds with y'all, but somebody's got to teach me how things go and what to do." Several of the men began telling me about strikes, what was expected of everyone, and explained the need to act as a collective body and stick together. Afterward, I felt like a jerk and was ashamed of my selfish weakness.

Morgan eventually rose to become the head of Angola's entire security force. The captain who replaced him was a poor administrator, and we petitioned the local district court with grievances in a handwritten letter signed by most of us and sent through the mail. Then we staged a hunger strike and rebellious behavior that almost resulted in a physical confrontation with the guards. Morgan stepped in and resumed control of death row, resolving many of our grievances. He allowed us to get newspapers and magazines through the mail, and stopped guards from bringing inmates down from the second floor—where they were held in extended lockdown in isolation cells for disciplinary or security reasons—to scrub the death row hall at night, sadistically beating them before returning them to their cells.

Victor Walker was warden in 1962, but we rarely saw him except when he stood before someone's cell and read a death warrant. He would announce the date and time the governor had scheduled the inmate to be killed, then ask the inmate what he wanted done with his body. The warden performed this ritual twice in 1962, five times in 1963, and once in 1964. Executions generally took place two to three weeks after the issuance of the warrant, once as little as eleven days. They were always scheduled for a Friday, at midnight.

A hush would descend over death row when the warden departed, reflecting an unspoken understanding that Death had to be respected as it approached its prey. At some point, the executioner would come to look at the inmate and size up his physical dimensions in order to make the correct adjustments to the straps on the electric chair. Generally, the man scheduled for execution didn't sleep much. I could not fathom what he might be feeling, even though I was sitting on the tier awaiting my turn. But it was an experience that allowed some of the condemned, if they possessed any decency, to contemplate the damage they had done and feel true remorse. For some, it was a religious experience.

In my experience, the traditional last meal requested by a doomed man reflected the preferences of his friends on the row, because they would actually eat the meal; condemned men usually lost their appetites in the face of imminent death.

We discussed and debated how we would go to our deaths. Some vowed to force the guards to carry them physically to the chair, fighting and screaming all the way. "I'm gonna make them fight me, then drag me, 'cause I'm not going to cooperate with them killing me," Bo Diddley declared. Others, like me, pointed out that all we had left in life was our personal dignity and that we should not let anyone take that from us. "You don't give them the opportunity to later laugh and talk about how you squealed like a coward, afraid to die," Ora Lee said. "Make them respect you for at least being able to handle something that many of them doubt they could."

None of us died in 1962, marking only the fourth year since 1930 that no one was executed in Louisiana. All death warrants issued in 1963 and 1964 were also stayed. On a tour of the prison, newly elected governor John J. McKeithen stood before our cells and candidly told us, "If your DA doesn't push me to do it, I won't sign a death warrant and you can sit here as long as you want to, because this is not something I want to do. Do we understand each other?" We did. He advised us to get our relatives to enlist the aid of their ministers to lean on the district attorney to let our cases "just sit."

On death row, we had to build our day-to-day existence in a vacuum. The existence was senseless; we were just waiting to die. For a long time, indeed, I didn't care whether I lived or died. I had little reason to live.

Angola introduced me to the idea of reading just to kill time. The first book I read was *Fairoaks*, a historical novel by Frank Yerby that Thomas Goins recommended. "It'll give you an idea of how white folks been messing over our people as long as this country has been here," he said, handing me the paperback through the bars. "They wouldn't teach this in school." The enslavement of Africans in the American South had never received more than a passing mention in the history classes I attended. But this book brought it to life and ignited something in me. I wanted to know more—about slavery, about history, and, ultimately, about everything. From then on, I lived inside my head, in a world of books. It helped me survive the maddening monotony and boredom of the cell. Except for the unrelenting need for sexual relief and the periodic need to stretch my legs and exert myself physically, I buried myself in books. Reading obscured the dismal future I faced. Initially, I read whatever was available on the black market—smuggled books—or those owned by other death row inmates. After a prison library was created, I could be more selective, choosing what I wanted from the book cart brought in by a trusty. The more I learned, the more I sought; the more I reflected, the more I grew and matured. There were no lightning bolts, instant revelations, or overnight conversions; it was a long growth process in which I began to shed the ignorance, anger, and insecurities that had governed my previous life. I learned more from my reading on death row than I had during all my years of formal schooling, which had left me literate but uneducated. Eventually I came to see that there was so much more to life and to the world, so many options available that, as bad as things might have been, I was never as trapped in life as I had believed. I realized that my real problem had been ignorance and, as a result, I had thrown away my life.

Reading ultimately allowed me to feel empathy, to emerge from my cocoon of self-centeredness and appreciate the humanness of others—to see that they, too, have dreams, aspirations, frustrations, and pain. It enabled me finally to appreciate the enormity of what I had done, the depth of the damage I had caused others. I came to understand that the problems that overwhelmed my teenage mind could have been sorted out but instead led to a spur-of-the-moment decision that had devastating, permanent consequences. That I did not mean to kill Julia Ferguson did not change the fact that she had died because of what I did. Her family and friends lost someone they loved—in a violent manner that would pain them the rest of their days. My own family also lost someone they loved and would find it much harder to live their lives in peace.

My father fled to California and my brother Raymond joined the army, but the rest of my family, their options limited by poverty, remained behind to face the repercussions of my rash act. It was a fearful time for my mother, her existence marred by obscene phone calls and white youths drinking, firing guns, and yelling obscenities in front of her home. Welton Semien had been trying to get her to marry him for some time, to no avail, but after one terror-filled night, she accompanied him to the courthouse, where they quietly married, and he moved in, giving her and the children a little protection. The presence of his car parked in the yard helped. But he couldn't shield her from the pointing fingers, the whispers, the hostility, or the shame she bore as my mother. Yet she never complained, never reprimanded or rejected me. She stood by me unflinchingly, demonstrating a commitment, courage, and fortitude so powerful that I realized this woman loved me unconditionally, even when the world despised me and wanted to obliterate me from the face of the earth. The dreams of her girlhood had long ago been crushed by the ugly realities of her life. Like many mothers, she had transferred her aspirations to her children, especially her firstborn, and I had destroyed them just as surely as my father had done before me.

I knew there had to be moments when my mother wondered if how I turned out was somehow her fault. Once, feeling especially sad for her, I reached through the bars, put my hand over hers, and said, "You need to know that my ending up on death row—it had nothing to do with you or how you raised me."

"I had wondered," she said.

I may not have cared much about what happened to me, but I did care about my mother. As she scuffled to make the long trips to Angola and to provide for my needs out of her meager funds, I witnessed her quiet heartbreak, her suffering; and I experienced almost unrelenting guilt for having let her down, for having been responsible for her difficulties. In the wake of these feelings, though, as if one led inevitably to the other, was the blossoming awareness that the collateral damage my mother experienced paled in comparison to the loss suffered by Julia Ferguson and those whom she loved and was loved by.

Everything in me ached to make up for the devastation I'd caused, but of course I couldn't. Weighed down by guilt, remorse, and the impossible situation I found myself in, I contemplated suicide, seeing it as the least I could do, as it would not only end my mother's prolonged misery and allow her and the kids to move on with their lives, but it would also serve as atonement for the life that I had taken. Why postpone the inevitable? Why not give everyone relief, including me? Why suffer one day just for the sake of suffering the next?

"So you're ready to quit," Goins said angrily one day when I expressed these feelings. "You're lucky them white folks sent you to death row, 'cause your little ass wouldn't survive this prison. You won't fight. That means you'd be pussy, some man's old lady. You got yourself in a situation that you don't want to deal with. So you want to creep out of it like a little bitch. How is your dying supposed to benefit your victim? Or your momma? You can justify it any way you like, but it's all about you, not the people you jerked around. How can you make up for what you did if you're dead? If you wanted to do something for them, you wouldn't let their suffering be in vain. You'd fight to make some good come of it, and try to make things right. Nothing's impossible, man—until you quit. That's what cowards do. They turn tail and run. Be a man, for once in your life."

Given who I was, what I had done, and where I was—as far down in life as a person could get—that seemed impossible. I could no more change my lot than I could change the color of my skin. My prospects in life were hopeless. I had no future, and my debt could not be repaid. Yet I knew Goins was right. Suicide was a coward's way out. To be a real man, an honorable man, meant to carry on.

His words resonated in my head: "Nothing's impossible—until you quit." I had read stories of men—Malcolm X, Otto von Bismarck, Mahatma Gandhi, the nameless English convicts exiled to Australia—who rose from ashes, faced great challenges, impossible odds, and won;

scoundrels who had been as empty and worthless as I, who had gone on to re-create their lives, redeem themselves, and become respected by their fellow human beings for their good works. Maybe I, too, could be resurrected. I began to identify with these individuals and, through that newfound identity, I found hope, a burning need to live to redeem myself, to do something meaningful with my life in partial payment of the debts I owed—to Julia Ferguson and her loved ones, to my family, to society, and to God, who gave me free will to make better choices than I had.

The world could define me as "criminal," but I did not have to live its definition of me. I resolved that I would not let my crime be the final definition. I knew there was more to me than the worst thing I'd done. I knew it wouldn't be easy. I would have to survive, and that was possible only if I regarded my present circumstances as a challenge, a test. I had to prove my sincerity and determination to redefine and redeem myself, to make amends.

In the face of the Louisiana Supreme Court having affirmed my conviction and death sentence, Sievert and Leithead appealed to the U.S. Supreme Court, even though there was next to no chance my case would be one of the handful selected for review. It took them a year to prepare the petition. The crux of the appeal was the covertly filmed interview Sheriff Reid and KPLC-TV had staged and the prejudice that flowed from it. They argued that "the film so permeated the people in this area generally that it made a conviction of the Petitioner an accomplished fact, and there was no need for a mob to pound on the door of the jail demanding the prisoner."

It surprised everyone when the Supreme Court accepted my case. I did not understand at the time that, with mass civil disobedience challenging racial discrimination and the fairness of government throughout the South, the high court—which formerly had upheld many racist practices and winked at others—needed to send a symbolic message to blacks about its readiness to step in, be fair, and ensure justice. A hearing on my case, with oral arguments, was held on April 29, 1963. On June 3, the justices issued their ruling.

Justice Potter Stewart decried what he called the "kangaroo court proceedings" in my case. He wrote that the Constitution guaranteed every defendant basic rights: "Among these are the right to counsel, the right to plead not guilty, and the right to be tried in a courtroom presided over by a judge. Yet in this case the people of Calcasieu Parish saw and heard, not once but three times, a 'trial' of Rideau in a jail, presided over by a sheriff, where there was no lawyer to advise Rideau of his right to stand mute. . . . No such practice as that disclosed by this record shall send any accused to his death." My conviction was reversed and the case returned to the trial court in Lake Charles.

The Supreme Court ruled that I could not be tried within the broadcast range of KPLC-TV. That created a problem, because Louisiana law forbade moving a trial beyond an adjoining judicial district, and all of those districts were within the station's range. Judge Cutrer ruled that a judicial impasse had been reached: I was beyond the ability or authority of Louisiana courts to retry me.

Salter appealed to the Louisiana Supreme Court, arguing that my constitutional right to a fair trial must be honored. What he really asked the Louisiana Supreme Court for was permission to rewrite the law so that I could be retried in Louisiana. On June 8, 1964, the Louisiana Supreme Court was happy to oblige. Years later, the court would acknowledge it had acted contrary to law in making its ruling.

My new trial was set for December 1, 1964, in East Baton Rouge Parish, the state capital. It was a new jurisdiction, but little else changed; it was still the Old South. Moreover, because of the bitterness in Louisiana over what the ruling white power structure felt was federal interference in state sovereignty regarding the racial integration of schools and public facilities, the tongue-lashing the Supreme Court gave Calcasieu Parish when it reversed my conviction made my case even more notorious all over the state.

Frank Salter had been insistent about moving my trial to Baton Rouge. But, then, he knew something about Sargent Pitcher, the East Baton Rouge Parish district attorney who would assist in prosecuting me—something that would emerge only in the trial courtroom. My defense lawyers, who lost every battle in their attempt to have the trial moved anywhere else, probably knew it, too.

Since the civil rights movement had gotten a toehold in Louisiana, the racial climate was worse than ever. Negroes made a significant encroachment on previously all-white territory during the summer of 1964, when Louisiana State University, the state's flagship institution of higher education, enrolled its first colored undergraduates—under federal court order. As Negroes organized sit-ins, rallies, and voter-registration drives, whites banded together in violent supremacist groups and flexed their muscles, as Ralph Blumberg, who had purchased a radio station in Bogalusa in 1961, discovered when he publicly denounced the Ku Klux Klan in late 1964.

"We were called Communists, integrationists, 'nigger lovers.' We were threatened with death. Nails were put in our tires. Our car windows were smashed. Six shells from a high-powered rifle were fired into our transmitter house. Due to a kidnapping threat, I had to send my family back to St. Louis," Blumberg said in a 1966 article in the magazine *American Judaism*. The Klan boycotted and threatened his sponsors, and by early 1965 he had to sell his radio station and leave Louisiana. During this same time, the homes of numerous civil rights workers in Lake Charles were hit by midnight cross burnings, as was the home of the local NAACP president.

The Klan, which practiced violence and terror to ensure white supremacy and keep the coloreds "in their place," had its genteel counterpart in the White Citizens' Council, which employed the power of government to deprive blacks of their right to vote. Among its members and sympathizers were lawmakers, businessmen, governmental agency heads, law enforcement officials, and other movers and shakers.

The new trial judge, Elmo Lear, conceded he had serious reservations about the constitutionality of the transfer, but pointed out that it had been done on the orders of the Louisiana Supreme Court, so he had no choice but to accept my case and try it. However, he expressed the hope that, if and when this case was reversed on appeal, it would be sent to Judge John Rarick, the renowned arch-segregationist of West Feliciana Parish.

Because of the cost and time required to mount a defense 125 miles from their Lake Charles law offices, Sievert and Leithead both asked Lear to relieve them of their obligation to represent me. The judge refused, but appointed two Baton Rouge attorneys—Elven Ponder and Kenneth C. Scullin—to assist them with the case. Three weeks before the trial began, my expanded defense team moved to have the 1961 indictment thrown out on the grounds that the method used to select the grand jury pool—five white jury commissioners and the clerk of court sat around a table and handpicked potential jurors by thumbing through race-coded cards made up for that very purpose—was racially discriminatory and therefore unconstitutional under the Equal Protection Clause of the Fourteenth Amendment.

The whole criminal justice system in Calcasieu Parish, as elsewhere in Louisiana, was all white—the robed white men who sat on the bench, their white clerks, the white jury commissioners. Grand jury foremen, personally chosen by the judges, had been white men as far back as Calcasieu Parish records and living memory stretched. So were all the sheriffs who tracked down and arrested suspects, and all the coroners who sat on sanity commissions and performed autopsies for the state, and all the district attorneys and their assistants who decided which suspects would stand trial for their lives and which would be tried for lesser penalties.

Sievert and Leithead nonetheless lost their argument about racial discrimination, and on December 1, my second trial began. We had not gone far in the jury selection process when the issue of race surfaced again. Prospective juror Eddie Bates told Elven Ponder that he had been a member of the Citizens' Council for about a year. Ponder pressed him about the purposes of the organization.

"Well, we flatly don't believe in integration of the races, if that's what you mean," prosecutor Pitcher said, coming to Bates's defense. "I'd like to state for the record the purpose of the Citizens' Council, of which I am a member, is the preservation of constitutional government, and being a member of it is no more than being a member of the Presbyterian Church or any other organization." Pitcher sat on the board of directors for the Zachary, Louisiana, chapter.

Ponder jumped up and objected to Pitcher's gratuitous commentary. He moved for a mistrial on the grounds that the commentary was prejudicial and inflammatory. When the judge denied the motion, Ponder challenged the seating of Eddie Bates for cause. The judge denied that, too, and refused to let my lawyers ask Bates or any other potential jurors if they had friends and associates who belonged to the Klan. In the end, an all-white, all-male jury was chosen, as everyone knew would be the case.

The second trial was virtually a repeat of the first, but the jury was quicker, taking only fifteen minutes to conclude that I was guilty and I should die. I was returned to the East Baton Rouge Parish jail, atop the courthouse, to wait out the required appeal and review of my case by the Louisiana Supreme Court.

I had been kept in total isolation prior to the trial. After the verdict, I was instructed to pack my things because I was joining the jail's inmate population. Unlike in the Calcasieu Parish jail or Angola, prisoners here were generally kept in isolation cells for brief periods only for "mental observation" or punishment. All others were housed together indiscriminately, according to race—blacks in one part of the jail, whites in another. This marked the first time I would live among other prisoners and, like many before me, I feared entering that notorious world. The men on death row who had been in general population told me that if I entered one, especially because of my small size, I would be challenged until inmates learned I was from death row and charged with murder; that would imply I was dangerous, and therefore people would be less likely to mess with me. I began preparing myself right away. I traded some *Playboy* magazines on the black market for cash and a flat knife; I glued both inside the bottom flaps of the thick cardboard box that I would carry my personal possessions in. I was gambling that the deputies transporting me and those booking me into the jail wouldn't expect me to have contraband, since I was coming from Angola's death row, the most secure and restrictive lockup in the state. On September 29, 1964, when I entered the East Baton Rouge Parish jail, I received only a perfunctory inspection.

Heading into general population, I cloaked the knife in a damp bath towel that I held against the underside of the box as I walked beside a deputy. When I stepped inside the large, poorly lit room as a steel door slammed shut behind me, a row of metal tables was to my left, and a young, muscular, clean-cut guy sat possessively on the first table, reading a newspaper. It was the dayroom, where everyone congregated, ate, and passed time by playing cards or dominoes or talking. There were two showers against the rear wall. Large cells containing multiple bunks were on each side of the dayroom. They were sleeping quarters, where the inmates were locked in for the night. Until then, the doors remained open. More than a hundred men coexisted in quarters designed for far fewer. Many slept on the floor because there were not enough bunks.

Everyone halted his activities to see who the new person was. Their faces seemed ugly, fearsome. I was scared, but I knew that if I showed fear, they would chew me to bits. "I knew this was my lucky day!" said a young inmate sitting on the floor ten feet away, his back against bars, apparently taking part in a dice game. "There's fresh meat in the house! Lil' Man," he said, with his best tough-guy face, "there ain't enough bunks, but you can sleep in mine." There was a little laughter followed by a hush, as everyone waited for my response.

I dropped the box and towel to the floor, revealing the knife in my hand. I let a moment elapse for effect, as the youth's face turned serious, fearful. Trying to keep any trembling out of my voice, trying to sound calm and matter-of-fact, I said, "You must be tired of living." Nobody moved. I hoped he didn't call my hand. I didn't want to fight; I had no experience in fighting. I did know, though, that this moment, this encounter, would define my life both in this jail and beyond. I was going to do whatever I had to. My mouth was dry, and my hands felt clammy around the knife's masking-taped handle. The silence seemed long.

"You Wilbert Rideau?" the newspaper reader on the front table asked.

"I am," I replied, not taking my eyes off the youth in front of me.

"I'm Billy Green, and the fat mouth on the floor is Chicken," he said. "He don't mean you any harm. He just has a habit of shooting off his mouth at the wrong time." He looked at Chicken, chiding him: "Didn't I tell you about messing with people you don't know, coming through that door? Do you have any idea who you fucking with?" He lifted the newspaper, pointing to the front page. "He's from death row, getting ready to go back to death row, and he ain't got a fucking thing to lose 'cause they can't burn him but once. You're sitting there playing stupid-ass games with a dude who's gonna put your lights out. Now what is your dumb ass gonna do?"

"I'm gonna apologize, man," the youth said, rising slowly, everyone laughing at him. "I'm sorry, man. I—I made a big mistake."

I nodded, relieved. "Let me have your attention a minute," I said loudly to everyone, exploiting the moment. "I'm not sleeping on the floor. I'm willing to pay five dollars for a bunk. I'm also prepared to *take* one if I have to. So, who wants the money?" A ratty-looking guy walked up to offer me his bunk. I bought it.

The jail population was a transient one. There was no society, no commonality, no values, nothing governing behavior but the law of the jungle: strength ruled, and the only order was what it imposed. The jail was constructed in a manner that made policing of inmate activity virtually impossible; access to the bullpen was restricted to a single door, which meant jailers could not see 90 percent of it without actually entering it, which they rarely did. Jailers therefore could maintain only some degree of order through the process of accommodation, allowing the strongest clique to practice their vice with impunity in exchange for maintaining peace and managing the lockup. Billy Green, an ex-con and local street gang leader from Baton Rouge, ruled here. He coordinated the inmates' lists of orders from the commissary and turned them in to a deputy, then made sure when the items came in that they were distributed properly; he saw to it that the weak as well as the strong got their meals and that cleaning supplies were distributed and used. In short, he served as liaison for the authorities in their dealings with the inmate population.

My first major adjustment to living off death row was, understandably, to the lack of privacy—the communal toilets, showers, living quarters. Sitting on a commode in public for a bowel movement was a new and difficult experience, resulting in bouts of constipation. And there was the need to be a little paranoid: The other occupants of death row told me never to let an enemy catch me sitting on a commode with my drawers pulled down around my ankles because then I could neither run nor fight. Shortly before my trial, I had sought medical attention for an infection on my foot from Baton Rouge coroner Dr. Chester Williams, who refused, explaining that Calcasieu Parish was not paying him to provide me medical care. Expecting the same response now, to protect against becoming infected I showered every day and refused to shake hands, which earned me the reputation of being a "neat freak."

Rule of the lockup was almost always decided by violent conflict. And the inability of different personalities to get along in a lawless, idle, overcrowded environment also generated violence. The major incubator of such conflicts, however, was unmet needs, the biggest being nicotine addiction. Just about all of us smoked. Men without resources generally devised methods to take from those who had—by trade, guile, theft, or force. I was no different. The time I spent reading on death row, coupled with my eighth-grade formal education, made me the best-educated inmate in my lockup. Two-thirds of the men were barely literate; a third were unable to read or write. That provided me an opportunity. I began writing letters for them: I got a pack of cigarettes for a family letter, two packs for business, and three packs for a romantic letter, which often went to female inmates in the women's lockup adjacent to ours.

In a caged population that included a lot of young, sex-starved males at the peak of their sexuality, it was to be expected that some used gays and the weak to satisfy their sexual needs. A popular saying among the normally heterosexual youths explained their behavior: "A hard dick has no conscience." Some inmates willingly exchanged sexual favors to provide for their other needs, but violence or the threat of it was the usual method employed to force the weak into sexual slavery.

Sex was also used to express contempt. Child molesters—called "baby rapers"—were particularly reviled, but all sex offenders were regarded with scorn by both prisoners and jailers. Many viewed the jail rape of sex offenders as poetic justice, as I learned when a skinny seventeen-year-old Negro was placed in our lockup following his arrest for the rape of a fifty-two-year-old white housewife. It was like throwing meat to hungry dogs. He was locked in a cell occupied by several members of Green's clique, who took turns raping him during the night. The next night, he was placed in another cell so that other clique members could also "get their issue," after which Green announced that anyone wanting to have sex with the youngster was welcome to do so.

When the raped youth was taken to court, he complained to the white jailers, who simply shoved him back behind bars and told him, "Get your ass in there, bitch, and take care of those men. Now you know what that woman felt like." He did, but what his victim endured at his hands, as horrible as it was, paled in comparison to the nightmare of the ongoing violence and terror he was subjected to. He was beaten for "snitching" to the jailers, made a human toy in brutal games for the amusement of the men, and, of course, raped at whim, unable to resist because Green had decreed that he'd better not. When it was discovered that the youth's rectum was hanging several inches out of his backside, Green arranged for him to leave for medical treatment, after reminding him there was no percentage in snitching because the cops didn't care and the gang could get to him anywhere within the jail, on the streets, even in the penitentiary. The youngster eventually pled guilty and was sentenced to life imprisonment with the possibility of release after ten years, six months. But the sexual torment he endured changed him forever. He would, at Angola, go on to establish a pattern of violence with other inmates that would result in his spending most of his life in disciplinary cells, which doomed him to die in prison.

The men on death row had laughed and joked about prison sex, but they had not prepared me for what I found. As badly as I craved sex, I discovered that I didn't want it *that* badly. "Hey, that was my first reaction," said Big Al, an ex-con who had invited me to use the services of his sex slave. "But then, as time got hard and my dick got harder, I realized a man's gotta do what a man's gotta do. Enough time passes, you'll see it in a different light. Like they say, when you in Rome, you do as the Romans." His view was not atypical.

Having come from Angola's death row only to be reconvicted and again face the electric chair gave me stature among the other inmates. In the perverse convict culture, I was viewed almost as a martyr, since it was extremely rare for the state to seek the death penalty a second time rather than offer a plea for a life sentence. Bizarrely, it was believed that wisdom was attached to this sort of martyrdom. Inmates listened when I spoke, and my opinion was regularly sought to settle disputes. I acquired such influence that the inmates asked me to represent them in talks with jail authorities during troubled times.

Rebellious inmates would plug their commodes to protest jail conditions, flooding the courtrooms on the floors below and shutting down hearings and trials. Authorities decided I was the troublemaker, probably because the inmates often united behind me. In the wee hours one morning during a protest, I was awakened by a gloved hand over my mouth. Several deputies quietly carried me out of the lockup. Green followed us out. I realized that Green had engineered this betrayal. He later apologized, explaining that he had sold me out in exchange for leniency in his criminal case. But he had instructed all his followers in the jail to take care of me. If I needed anything, he said, I had only to send word to him.

I was taken to the Hole, an isolation cell that afforded no contact with others except when a prison guard or inmate orderly opened the metal hatch on the steel door, through which I received my food. Because of the extreme deprivation it imposed, punishment in the Hole was rarely more than a week or two, never more than thirty days. I was to become the exception.

The jail authorities had placed me in the all-white section of the jail, a move meant to isolate me and lessen my influence among the blacks. My first visitor was Sheriff Bryan Clemmons, who peered through the hatch of my cell door to tell me, "I'm the sheriff, and you're not gonna run my jail." He said I would remain in that cell as long as I was in his custody. He kept me there for more than two years. That made me special. The other inmates sympathized with me; the deputies grudgingly acknowledged my sheer endurance. After a while, many of the jailers—all of them white—came to feel I was being treated unfairly and started leaving the hatch on my door open so the white inmates could give me food or tobacco.

Some of the night deputies were Louisiana State University students. They began to let me read their textbooks while they were working. One book, *The Fabric of Society* by Ralph Ross and Ernest van den Haag, was especially compelling because it gave me a basic understanding of society and human behavior, including my own. I became so attached to the book that the deputy ultimately gave it to me. Other books that shaped my thinking and my life were Ayn Rand's *Atlas Shrugged* and *Anthem*, from which I took the message of self-reliance and the understanding that the world owed me nothing; from Machiavelli's *The Prince* I gained insight into the nature of power and politics, the forces that ruled my life; from Morris West's *Shoes of the Fisherman* I learned that pain is the price of living.

My education was advanced by the books I read, but even more by the actions of these Southern white men—"good old boys," many of them—smuggling those books in to me. It marked a turning point. From the moment I was arrested, no one from the Negro community except my family tried to help me or even visited me, not even a minister. I had been brought up in a world sharply divided by race and, for the most part, had seen white people as the oppressors. In the Hole, I saw "the enemy" trying to help me, at risk to themselves. That forced me to reexamine my racial stereotypes.

In November 1966, my attorneys appealed my conviction, specifying thirty trial errors. The Louisiana Supreme Court ruled unanimously on December 12, 1966, that all of my legal complaints lacked merit. I was returned to Angola's death row, becoming C-48. The face of death row had changed dramatically. Nine of the twelve inmates who'd been there when I'd first arrived were gone.

The governor had found Delbert Eyer, the young, white, born-again Christian, to have been rehabilitated, and commuted his death sentence to life imprisonment in July 1966, allowing him to parole out in September 1966, a free man.

Seven of the Negroes—Alton Poret, Edgar Labat, Thomas Goins, Andrew Scott, Edward "Bo Diddley" Davis, Freddie Eubanks, and Woodman Collins—had their death sentences reversed either by the U.S. Fifth Circuit Court of Appeals or by the U.S. Supreme Court because of the systematic exclusion of Negroes from the grand juries that had indicted them (the same complaint my lawyers made in my case and which the state courts had denied). Their respective prosecutors did not pursue new death sentences. They instead struck plea bargains that gave Poret, Labat, and Goins immediate release and meant freedom for Scott, Davis, and Eubanks within less than a decade. Collins remained in prison with a life sentence, leaving death row.

The death sentence of Emile Weston was thrown out by the federal court because the state had not provided him with a complete verbatim transcript of his trial so that he could appeal his conviction (another ironic echo of my experience). He was a free man.

Roy Fulghum, Brodie Davis, and Ora Lee Rogers remained. They had been joined by many newly condemned men, and death row had been enlarged to encompass three tiers of cells instead of one. The men enjoyed many more privileges, including personal TVs, hot plates, and pots and pans for cooking in the cells. The atmosphere was more relaxed and boisterous. With the state slipping into an unofficial moratorium on executions, the death sentence was not taken as seriously.

My lawyers appealed this conviction, too, to the U.S. Supreme Court. On October 9, 1967, the court declined to hear the case, and Frank Salter clamored on the front page of the Lake Charles newspaper for an execution date to be set. A gubernatorial election was less than a month away. Arch-segregationist and white supremacist congressman John Rarick was challenging the incumbent, John J. McKeithen. Since I had met McKeithen when he visited death row shortly after taking office in 1964, I wrote to him. I asked for neither reprieve nor clemency, only that I not be sacrificed to the politics of the moment.

Elven Ponder, one of my Baton Rouge attorneys, who had the offensive habit of calling Negroes "nigras," told me the governor, after reading my letter, said he was not going to sign my death warrant because he had serious legal reservations about my case. Ponder assured me that no matter what Salter said in the media, McKeithen would not execute me. William "Hawk" Daniels, the investigator for the Baton Rouge district attorney's office, had already told me, "They've done things in your case, like bringing you here, that've never been done before; things you probably can get a new trial on. I fully expect Calcasieu is going to have to try you again before it's over because there are so many issues in your case. I'm fairly certain you'll get another trial on appeal." Ponder agreed. I was heartened.

On December 8, 1967, my lawyers filed for a writ of habeas corpus in the federal district court in Baton Rouge, raising the issues of racial discrimination in the selection of my grand jury and the unprecedented change of venue to East Baton Rouge Parish. Case law on the grand jury issue was clear-cut and stretched back a hundred years. My lawyers' brief, however, landed on the desk of E. Gordon West, one of the most conservative law-and-order judges in the federal court system, a segregationist who customarily refused to see racial discrimination.

While I awaited his decision, I settled in. My first stint on death row had been submerged in reading and learning. By now I had acquired a different kind of passion. I had been defined as criminal, but I knew I wasn't an evil or monstrous person, despite my crime. I wanted the same things that everyone else wanted in life. But those things had eluded me, propelling me toward more desperate behavior that isolated me even more. I only wanted to change the way I was living. Who was criminal? I asked myself. Everyone who broke the law? Was there a criminal personality? I became intrigued by the idea of answering this question, seeing it as a way of making amends with a contribution that could help society. And I had my own personal laboratory.

I began working on an analysis of criminals. I wrote in longhand in the dead of night, when it was relatively quiet. I thought I could educate society about who turns to crime and why. That gave me a purpose and gave my mind something to fasten on.

Judge West took no action on my case for almost a year and a half. He set no date for a hearing, asked for no clarification of issues, made no ruling. I asked Ponder to do something to speed things up. He said that as long as my case was sitting there, I never had to worry about being scheduled for execution. But I didn't like being in limbo. On March 27, 1969, Ponder filed a motion with West asking to have the case transferred to another court. West denied the motion the day it was filed; he also issued an order requiring the state to show cause by May 12, 1969, why the habeas corpus should not be granted. Ponder had found a way to jump-start my case.

Less than a month later, during a hearing West called for the purpose, Ponder filed a motion to amend my habeas pleading: The U.S. Supreme Court had just made a ruling in another case, *Witherspoon v. State of Illinois*, overturning a death sentence because persons with conscientious scruples against capital punishment had been excluded from sitting on the trial jury. Ponder pointed to the verbatim transcripts of my Baton Rouge trial to show that eighteen such individuals had likewise been barred from my jury. One of Salter's assistants conceded the violations had occurred and fell under *Witherspoon*. Listening to my lawyer, the judge, and the prosecutor, I could tell that the amended habeas corpus had been filed at West's suggestion and the entire proceeding had been prearranged; they were bad actors following a script. West reversed my conviction that day in a manner that allowed him—and Salter—to sidestep the issue of racial discrimination at a time when race was a political hot button in Louisiana. By tying his ruling to the *Witherspoon* case, Judge West made the U.S. Supreme Court responsible, for the second time, for overturning my conviction. Instead of resentencing me to life imprisonment, as a number of Louisiana condemned men had been because of that case, West gave Salter the right to retry me, and a third chance to put me in the electric chair.

By this time my case had developed notoriety on the sheer strength of the state's inability to make a conviction stick. It reemerged on the front pages of the Lake Charles and Baton Rouge newspapers. I was moved back to the parish jail in Baton Rouge to await a new trial. I was well received there by the inmates, respected as a veteran sage—so much so that I was placed in my own cell to reduce my influence.

Although blacks had begun to enter some of the official corridors of power and privilege—in 1968 the capitol seated its first black state legislator since Reconstruction—the racial climate in Louisiana was as bad as ever, if not worse. As the doors to equal education and equal job opportunities were forcibly opened to blacks by a series of federal court decisions, resentment against such change festered in the hearts and minds of a large segment of white Southern society. Baton Rouge, because it housed the capitol, had become a magnet for the forces visibly, vociferously, and sometimes violently opposed to racial desegregation. As membership in the Louisiana Ku Klux Klan swelled in the mid- and late 1960s, the organization staged massive rallies in the white suburban neighborhoods south of Louisiana State University. Kleagles, Grand Dragons, and Imperial Wizards, their hooded robes glowing in the night against the blaze of forty- and fifty-foot kerosene-soaked, fire-torched crosses, revved up the passions of people resistant to the dismantling of America's caste system. The Klan members burned in effigy congressmen whose seats they had targeted, among them Jimmy Morrison, who lost the seat he had held for twenty-four years when what he intended as a negative characterization of his opponent, Indiana native John Rarick, "The Klan's Man from Indiana," backfired and swept the white supremacist to victory. The Klan met blacks head-on in the town of Satsuma, as civil rights activist A. Z. Young led a march from Bogalusa to Baton Rouge in 1967. Klansmen staged well-attended rallies—there were six hundred people at one, in 1967, just before Judge West first considered my case. Racial tension ruled in the capital city.

In 1970, at the time of my third trial, the Klan was using the kind of intimidation for which it was famous. It invaded North Baton Rouge— the black part of town—and plastered the utility poles and other upright surfaces with signs showing a rearing white-hooded horse carrying a hooded white rider, his left hand holding aloft a fiery cross. Beneath the horse's feet was the Klan's motto: FOR GOD AND COUNTRY. The poster was dominated by the horse and rider and by big, bold print in the upper left corner that read SAVE OUR LAND, and beneath the picture it read JOIN THE KLAN.

In the Baton Rouge courthouse, where my trial began on January 5, the only strand of continuity in my defense was Lake Charles civil attorney James Leithead. All of the other court-appointed attorneys had asked for and received permission to withdraw from the case. Leithead had asked to withdraw, too, on the grounds that his law partner was a special assistant attorney general, which, he argued, presented a conflict of interest; the court refused his request.

The new judge was John S. Covington, who appointed two new Baton Rouge attorneys to assist Leithead with my defense: James Wood, two years out of law school, and maritime lawyer James George. The prosecution was represented by four attorneys: Frank Salter and three prosecutors from the East Baton Rouge Parish district attorney's office. The jury for the third trial, like the other two, was composed entirely of white men. The trial, which took three days, was largely a repeat of the two earlier trials. The prosecution's case was not challenged, nor was a proper defense mounted on my behalf. The third jury returned their death verdict in a record eight minutes.

My lawyers once again began the long process of filing a mandatory appeal to the Louisiana Supreme Court, while I waited in the East

Baton Rouge Parish jail. I expected this appeal, as all my others to the state's highest court, to fall on deaf ears. Here, the reading materials I had come to rely on at Angola—a wide variety of books, magazines, and newspapers—were restricted. I filed a lawsuit demanding them, contending I had a constitutional right to educate myself. I was in court for a hearing on the issue when the judge, before the start of the formal proceedings, told attorneys representing the East Baton Rouge Parish sheriff that they had better have something to counter the merit of the suit. The parish attorneys asked for a short recess, during which I was whisked from the Baton Rouge courtroom to the airport, where a waiting airplane took me not to Angola but to Lake Charles. The East Baton Rouge Parish district attorney, with agreement from the Calcasieu Parish district attorney, but contrary to law and without telling my lawyers, had made a successful motion during the recess to have me sent back to the Calcasieu Parish jail.

To thwart any potential influence I might have among black prisoners in the Calcasieu Parish facility, Sheriff Reid shut me in a solitary-confinement cell on the jail's second floor, which housed only white inmates. I was back in enemy territory, and utterly alone.

3

Solitary

JANUARY 1972

It's late, and raining. The buildings before me have been abandoned. Life has drained from the traffic arteries below. The wet pavement of empty Lake Charles streets and parking lots doubles the glare of street lamps and neon signs, intensifying the darkness.

It's quiet. Profoundly so. Rain whispers against the open window a few feet away. The only other thing you can hear is your own heart, thumping. I've known men who could not stand this silence, but I've grown accustomed to it. I scratch a fingernail on one of the bars, to reassure myself I haven't gone deaf. I've stood here many nights staring out my second-floor window at the same scene below, week after week, month after month, year after year . . . after year. Except for the rain, it never changes.

I came from that world, was once a part of it. But it's strange to me now, like a foreign country I've only read about. I feel no love, no hate. What lies outside that window represents all of my soul's yearnings: freedom, joy, home, love, friendship, satisfaction, peace, happiness. But I feel nothing as I look. To me it is inanimate, like a picture on a wall. I'm barred from that world and old memories no longer bridge the gap. I can't relate to that world, any more than I can imagine what it would feel like to walk down one of those streets, the rain in my face. It's been too long.

I turn my attention to squashing my cigarette butt in the ashtray, then look around my cell. This is my reality. Solitude. Four walls, gray-green, drab, and foreboding. Three of steel and one of bars, held together by 358 rivets. Seven feet wide, nine feet long. About the size of an average bathroom or—and my mind leaps at this—the size of four tombs, only taller. I, the living dead, have need of a few essentials that the physically dead no longer require—commode, shower, face bowl, bunk. A sleazy old mattress, worn to thinness. On the floor in a corner, a cardboard box that contains all my worldly possessions— a writing tablet, a pen, and two changes of underwear. The mattress, the box, and I are the only things not bolted down, except the cockroaches that come and go from the drain in the floor and scurry around in the shower. This is my life, every minute of the year. I'm buried alive. But I'm the only person for whom that fact has meaning, who feels it, so it's immaterial.

My eyes return to the open window across the catwalk outside the bars. A block away, twin lights appear as a car cautiously finds its way down the rain-slicked street. A gust of wind whips at me, ice on its lash. I look at my gray, jail-issued coveralls hanging on the wall hook. I should put them on to be warmer, but I don't. After what I've been through, why should I cringe before a simple thing like cold? Strength and the spirit of contest surge through me. This is a challenge, and knowing that the cold cannot defeat me gives me pride. I remain in my T-shirt and shorts, unyielding, feeling strong and powerful. That's what I've been reduced to.

It's hard to believe that I once experienced a life in that world outside my window. Would I even be able to recognize the neighborhood I grew up in? Are kids playing hooky still shooting craps on those old tombs? Is Old Man Martello still peddling cigarettes three for a nickel to underage smokers? I wonder, but there's no one to ask. Everyone but my mother has abandoned me.

I turn from the window and walk slowly toward the heavy steel door. I'm restless again. One . . . two . . . three . . . four . . . five . . . turn. Walk back. One . . . two . . . three . . . four . . . five . . . stop. I reach for the pack of cigarettes. Light one. Puff deeply. Fan out the match, flip it out into the catwalk. I exhale the smoke, looking idly out the window, thinking of nothing, then turn lazily toward the center of my cell.

Suddenly, adrenaline is coursing through me. I freeze, like a feral cat who spots a stray dog. It's the walls! They're closer! They're moving in on me, closing up the tomb. Panic is suffocating me. *This is what they want; they want to kill me.* Somehow, I will my muscles to relax, and my mind follows. The tension dissipates. It's just my imagination. Steel walls don't move. Shit, no. I should know that better than anyone. Ridiculous. I just need something to do, that's all. But what? I look around the cell, wondering what to do. I can read, walk, shower again, or think. And I'm tired of reading, so . . .

One . . . two . . . three . . . four . . . five . . . turn. One . . . two . . . three . . . It's not right to make a man live like this, alone. But I can take it. I can whip this motherfucker. I am stronger than anything they can do to me. The more they do, the stronger they make me. I actually smile. Haven't I endured and risen above an experience that would crush most men?

One . . . two . . . three . . . four . . . five . . . turn. Yeah, I've seen men broken, destroyed by solitary. Some have come to fear every shadow. Others have committed suicide. Some men would do anything to escape this cell. Some feigned insanity so they could go to a mental institution. Even more cut themselves, over and over, until the Man, fearing a suicide on his watch, moved them out of solitary. Others stayed doped up, whenever they could get the dope. Engaging in such tricks, though, is beneath my dignity; it's unmanly. I am stronger than the punishment. The only way to beat it, to rise above it, is to regard the punishment as a challenge and see my ability to endure it while others cannot as a victory. Whenever another man falls under the pressure, it's a triumph for me. Callous, some would call me. A man falls, broken, insane, or dead, and I feel nothing except triumph. But this is no place for pity—not for the next man, nor for myself. It would break me. The hard truth about solitary is that each man must struggle and suffer alone.

One . . . two . . . three . . . four . . . five . . . turn. I wonder what time it is. It doesn't matter, except knowing the time allows me to mark the progress of the night. Breakfast shouldn't be too far off. Then lunch. Then supper. I look forward to mealtime. The food tastes awful, but I always try to eat it because I have to guard my health. Next to insanity, sickness is most to be feared in solitary, where medical help is hard to come by.

I stop at the bars, grind out my cigarette, look out the window. The rain is falling a little harder. There ought to be something I can do. Turning, I see my bunk. That's it. I drop into it, lie down. The mattress makes little difference; I'm lying on steel. I close my eyes and let my mind roam freely in search of distraction. I reject thoughts and images of past experiences as they move across the screen of my mind. Good memories are excellent distractions from this grim reality, but I possess very few of them and can't conjure one up tonight. Restless, I get back up, pace the floor for a while, then go to the steel rail that connects the two steel walls of the shower. I heft myself up, over and over, until I am in a sweat. Chin-ups have made my arms almost as strong as the steel bars that hold me. I move to the sink and push the button for some water.

As I drink, I see a black man peering at me from the polished-steel mirror over my sink. I put down my cup and carefully remove my handcrafted covering from the light fixture. The room is now flooded with light. I take a long, scrutinizing look at this fellow as he does the same to me. There's a weary slump to his shoulders. Deep furrows are etched across the brown forehead, and small wrinkles accentuate the subtle desperation in his dark eyes. Suffering is what I see in his eyes. I don't like that. If I can see it, others can also. On second thought, maybe they can't. I *care*, so I'm looking for it; but they barely even see me, much less my suffering. No, they won't see it. Satisfied, I replace the cover on the light fixture and throw the cell into twilight darkness again. It's a twilight of my own choosing, fashioned with a razor blade and cardboard—a snug-fitting cover to keep the glare of reality at bay. "Mankind cannot stand too much reality," as T. S. Eliot wrote.

I walk over to the bars, stick my arms through, lean upon them, look out the window. It's still raining. My ears suddenly pick up the distant sound of a key being fitted into a door down the catwalk. The door clangs shut. Footsteps . . . approaching. It's the Man, making his rounds. I instinctively pull my arms back into the cell. A man with his arms hanging outside the bars is vulnerable; they can easily be broken. Keys jangle loudly and another door, closer, creaks open. There are voices, movement; a door bangs shut. Men awakened down the line, outside solitary, shout curses into the night. It must be Old Asshole. The bastard. None of the others on this shift would slam doors like that. He does it deliberately, to wake me up if I am sleeping. I'm the only one back here now. Another of Old Asshole's petty tricks. I mustn't show my anger.

The trusty appears first, as usual, on the catwalk outside the bars. The trusty is the Man's first line of defense in case of danger. He's a faithful lapdog, this one, always eager to do his master's bidding. He nods at me, his eyes searching my cell, hunting for something to tell his master about. I look *through* him. Old Asshole appears at his side. He looks at me, and I look right back at him, straight into his blue eyes. I don't like him, and he knows it. He wants to be important, to feel superior, and the only way he can do it is to grind down the prisoners in his charge. He doesn't like me because I won't feed his ego.

"Still woke, huh, Rideau?"

I nod.

"How you gettin' along? Doin' all right?"

It's a meaningless greeting the world over, even among free people. But here it's stupid, too. What prisoner locked in a system designed to brutalize, crush, or destroy him has ever been "all right"?

"I'm doing just fine."

"It's pretty chilly back here. Want your window closed?"

"If you want to. It don't really matter to me."

"It's turning cold. You're gonna freeze your ass off with the window open."

"Do whatever you want. It doesn't make any difference."

He turns to his lapdog and tells him to close the window. Relief flows through my body as my muscles, taut in their struggle against the cold, begin to relax. My face remains expressionless.

Old Asshole turns back to me. "They tell me your buddy cracked this morning. Tore up his cell. Went stone crazy."

I nod.

"Guess he couldn't take that cell no more."

"Guess not."

"How long had he been in solitary? About a year, huh?"

"About."

Old Asshole shakes his head slowly like a snake charmer and tries to pin me with his gaze. "A long time. Course, that ain't nothing compared to how long you been locked down. What is it now? Ten, twelve years?"

"Something like that."

He turns his eyes away from mine, shaking his head. "I don't see how you held up this long."

I could tell him that he can't understand it because he doesn't understand what it's like to be your own man. I could tell him that he's never been a man and never will be, that he doesn't have the strength.

Take away the social props that hold him up and he'd go down like a line of dominoes. Deep down he knows it, and he expects everyone to possess the same weakness. He can't understand why I don't, and it aggravates his fears about himself and his own sense of inferiority. I could tell him all this about himself, but I say nothing.

He looks at me. "Think you'll end up like him?"

"Nope."

A smile brushes his lips. He nods his head, like he knows something I don't. I feel the urge to slap that smug look off his face.

"You think you're tough, huh, Rideau?"

"No. Just competent."

His eyes study my cell, then me. "Everybody else in this place gives, lets themselves go a little. Their cells, their appearance. I even let go sometimes, and I ain't a prisoner. But you gotta be different. Your cell always gotta be neat and clean, everything in its place. You stay shaved, hair combed—always fixed up like you waitin' to go somewhere. You don't ever bend, not even a little, do you?"

"What have you seen since you've been here?"

"Oh, I haven't seen you do it, yet. But I will."

"I wouldn't count on it if I were you."

"I *can* count on it. You're not as tough as you want people to believe. And let me tell you something," he says, tapping the bars with his keys. "No matter how tough you think you are, this steel is a whole lot tougher. You'll bend."

"Maybe. Maybe not."

He turns to leave. "We'll see."

"No. *You'll* see. I already know."

A steel door slams down the walk, and I listen to the footsteps until they fade away. Alone again. Silence engulfs me. I reach for a cigarette, feel the smoke pouring into my lungs as I inhale deeply. I smoke too much. I know I should quit. This poison only contributes to my physical deterioration, compounds the lack of exercise and poor diet. My lungs must be shit. To hell with it. Smoking is the only luxury left to me.

One . . . two . . . three . . . four . . . five . . . turn. One . . . two . . . three . . . That idiot. Old Asshole actually expects to see me break. What he doesn't know is that being broken requires my permission. I'm not about to surrender my manhood, my dignity, or my self-respect. They may have stripped me of everything else, but I will not permit myself to be reduced to a human dog. I'll die first. Of course, insanity is always possible—no, *probable.* How in hell can a man live for years like this and remain sane? It's impossi—

I halt my pacing in midstride: *I could be insane now!* I wouldn't necessarily know it. I shiver. *Suppress it, Wilbert.* I start pacing again. One . . . two . . . three . . . four . . . five . . . turn. My eyes, searching for something to latch on to, scan the walls and find the rivets. The number of rivets in here impresses me, as it has before. These walls are well held together. But, then, they'd have to be; otherwise I'd get out, wouldn't I? And they don't want that. I know the number of rivets because I've counted them before: 348 of them. Or was it 358? I frown, trying to remember. It's important to get it right. I need to know exactly the number of rivets holding me in. I decide to count them again, to be sure. I start counting, and soon I'm on my hands and knees, counting the rivets under my bunk, when a picture of what I must look like flashes through my mind. I have to smile. If Old Asshole could only see me now. He'd laugh until he shit himself, figuring for sure I'd gone crazy. And it *is* crazy. Me, down on all fours, counting the rivets in a steel tomb. It looks like insanity, but my mind is intact. Old Asshole will have to wait a little longer. When I finish counting, it's 358 rivets after all.

I crush out the cigarette, which has burned to a nub in the ashtray. I lie down, gaze up at the ceiling, walls. Aren't we always struggling against walls? I ask myself. Not always of concrete and steel, but walls nonetheless—ignorance, poverty, indifference, oppression? Yes, yes, definitely oppression. I can't remember a time when I wasn't a prisoner. But who is ever really free? "Freedom's just another word for nothing left to lose"; that's what Janis Joplin sang. I start humming "Me and Bobby McGee" until the thought of all that wasted talent, that gift, gets to me. Shooting shit in her arm. *Goddamn!* She fought her way out of this stinkhole. Port Arthur, her hometown, is right over the Texas line from Lake Charles. The girl escaped the grip of these crazy motherfuckers. She was free, whatever demons she had. A fucking shame, that was. But what the fuck do I know about freedom anyway?

Struggle is the only reality I've ever known. The world I was born into was sharply divided between black and white, good and evil, innocent and guilty. It was a world of absolutes. Whites ruled, I learned, because God demanded it. I was guilty the moment I was born. The guilty labored under the weight of poverty and misery. Locked in economic bondage, they were made servants of the innocents. The females were ravished, the males emasculated; they were insulted, humiliated, and brutalized as a matter of course. Being lynched with impunity at the pleasure of the mob was the just desert of the guilty, the wrong, the black.

I close my eyes and see a huge, ancient courtroom, built to be a temple. There is rich, dark wood that smells like lemon rind and gleaming brass everywhere. The ceiling rises several stories up into a dome, like a Byzantine church. The floors are marble, polished to a high shine. There is an altar up front where the judge sits; the choir box is off to his left, my right. To enter this temple of justice, you have to climb a mountain of marble steps to the white-columned portico that shields the front door. A huge old battle cannon squats off to the left of the steps as you approach. To the right, high atop a white pillar, a copper soldier has his left arm raised as in battle. The inscription on the topmost marble block of the base says THE SOUTH'S DEFENDERS. On the block below, 1861–1865, and beneath that, OUR HEROES. At the base of the statue, there are wreaths or flowers in a vase, with a Confederate battle flag propped alongside. I know this, even though I cannot see the statue from my seat in the courtroom. I know it because, for as long as I can remember, there have always been flowers and a Confederate battle flag there. I do not have to wonder what the city fathers meant to suggest about justice in their community when they erected a copper soldier leading the charge for the Old South on these courthouse grounds. Floodlights set in concrete ensure that every prosecutor, every lawyer, every plaintiff, every defendant, every witness, every victim, every judge, every juror, every deputy, every spectator, every reporter, every researcher, every visitor, every civil servant, every politician, and every black person who passes or enters, day or night, will see the patron saint of this temple.

Inside, a drama is taking place. A teenage boy, flanked by white lawyers, sits at a large table, a black-robed figure before him. Twelve white men, vested with the power of life and death, are seated over to the right, in the choir box. A clot of newspaper reporters sits off to the left. Behind the black boy is a sea of white faces. A carnival atmosphere prevails as characters parade to the witness stand and play their roles with unholy indifference to the significance of the drama. The performances are well received, the audience entertained.

The judge breaks for intermission and leaves the altar. The actors and members of the audience huddle in small groups, chattering gaily as if they were at a cocktail party instead of in church, completely indifferent to the shadow of death hovering nearby, awaiting the end of the play. The talk flows freely around the boy and is often about him, as though he were merely a gargoyle, an inanimate object of discussion devoid of intelligence or sensitivity.

The drama unfolding is to decide whether the boy will live or die. Curiously, the boy is relaxed and appears unconcerned, which some in the audience see as his lack of feeling. What they don't know is that the drama holds no suspense for the boy. He knows he's going to die. It doesn't matter to him. He has long since grown tired of the cruelty and meaninglessness of his existence, though his fierce pride and iron spirit will not allow him to kill himself. Someone else will have to do that. So he watches with detached interest as the drama plays out to its fateful end where absolute good will triumph over absolute evil.

"We find the defendant guilty as charged."

The jangle of keys knifes through my reverie. My eyes fly open, instantly alert. The hatch on the door of my cage swings back silently, leaving a hole in the metal the size of a shoe box. It's the Man, but a friendly one. I roll off the bunk to my feet. He stuffs several packages and some books through the hole. I grab them and quickly toss them on the bunk.

He puts his face in the hatch. He looks like mashed potatoes and redeye gravy with his bad skin and birthmark. I wonder if that's why he works here instead of in the outside world.

"They fixed some barbecue for us today. I figgered you might like some. When you finish, break the bones and flush 'em down the commode so nobody'll know."

I nod my head.

"The candy and books come from some of the prisoners down the line. They got a sex novel in the bunch. The boys swear by it—told me to tell you it's guaranteed to raise your dick all night."

Convict humor. I deadpan, "Yeah, I really need that."

He smiles. "It's supposed to be a joke. They just kiddin' you."

I nod. "I know. You want the book? My sex problem is bad enough without it."

He shakes his head. "Naw. I ain't got time to do no reading."

A quiet settles between us. The unfamiliarity of human company—other than my mother, whose face pokes through the hole every Saturday afternoon, and Sister Benedict Shannon, an activist nun who sometimes stops to see me when she visits the jail—makes me nervous and self-conscious. After so much solitude and silence, small talk comes hard to me. My mind searches for a conversation piece.

"Old Asshole came by earlier. Shooting his shit, as usual," I say.

"Yeah? Well, don't let it get to you. He ain't worth it. I don't see why they ain't got rid of that bastard a long time ago. He don't do nothing but rile everybody up and cause a whole lotta trouble."

"That's the truth."

"It's just a question of time before somebody hurts him." He moves away. "Look, I gotta go. Take it easy. I'll check you tomorrow night."

"All right."

The hatch closes; silence returns. I scan the books and stash the sex novel under my mattress. There are three food packages, and I can tell by the feel and the smell what is in each of them, but I play the old Christmas Eve guessing game anyway. Is it barbecued chicken, pork ribs, or beef ribs? Is it white bread or corn bread? Are the potatoes pan-fried or French fried? After I tease myself a bit, I open the packages and wolf down every trace of one man's human kindness. He could lose his job for bringing me this food. My eyes fall upon the candy the prisoners sent me—two little treasures that, in other circumstances, could cost a man his life in this place. A Snickers and a Butter-Nut, contraband as hell and therefore worth their weight in blood, should one man try to steal them from another. In a world defined by deprivation, things that are trivial in the outside world are magnified to a significance far beyond their street value. This Butter-Nut bar, for example, cost someone real money, which is already in short supply among the inmates. There's the cost of the candy itself, and the added value attached by every hand that facilitated its journey from the candy counter at Walgreens into the jail to the guys down the line, who sent it to me. Hell, they may even have had to grease the palm of the guard who passed it to me. Even more than the money, though, is the cost of getting caught: The guard could get demoted or fired, and an inmate could get thrown in the Dungeon for dealing in contraband.

It's strange, even to me, that men who wouldn't hesitate to rape or kill each other band together to help me, just because I've been locked down in solitary for so long. Most of them don't even know me. But my tormentors have made me a living legend in this jail: *the one they can't break.* The irony is not lost on me that it's the professed Christians who are so cruel and unmerciful, while it's the criminal misfits and social dregs who try to help me, usually without my even asking.

I flush the chicken bones and wrappings down the toilet. I turn back to the bunk, pick up the candy, and hide it for later. I light a cigarette and stand at the bars looking out into the night. The rain has stopped.

A rare sensation crawls over me—amazement at the fact that there are people out there loving and being loved or sleeping peacefully. People who experience joy, peace, and love. There are people out there who know nothing of fierce struggles for survival and sanity, struggles against aloneness, cruelty, violence, danger, rapes, rebellions, and madness. It's like knowing that Buzz Aldrin and Neil Armstrong lived in a spaceship on their way to the moon, weightless and floating on air. You can know it as a fact, but you cannot imagine the experience.

The sensation passes and an old longing surfaces—a longing to escape this harsh, ultra-masculine jungle unsoftened by love or beauty, where everyone is engaged in a perpetual battle to prove who is the toughest, the strongest, the cruelest. I long to get away from this field of pain and misery. Not to the city; that's just another jungle. I want to flee to the country, where I imagine there is no madness, no hate, no war, no animals save those that walk on four legs. Out where life is simple, peaceful, and clean. Where rippling creeks feed open meadows and green leaves dance on soft breezes to the chirpings of gaily colored birds. I long for the fragrance of honeysuckle in my nostrils, the air of innocence. And alongside the creek, clover matted from tender lovemaking. This is freedom—to work, to love, to aspire. To find my place in the world. To—

Then I think: Could I fit into that world out there? So much has changed. I was a boy when I left that world. I know nothing of the world that has taken its place. How could I adjust to that world when I couldn't even adjust to the world I knew, the world that shaped me, or misshaped me? Having lived in this jungle for so long, could I function in a civilized world?

Am I really winning my struggle to improve my mind and retain my sanity and humanness, or is my success an illusion? Am I just losing my humanity more slowly than those around me? With no guidance, and no yardstick to measure progress against, I can't tell.

I suck angrily on a cigarette. I squash it out, a fierce determination flaring in me. I *can* adjust, and I *will* adjust. If I could adjust to the cruelties of imprisonment, I can adjust to anything.

One . . . two . . . three . . . four . . . five . . . turn. One . . . two . . . three . . . four . . . five. Stop. I lean upon the bars, look about my cell.

Eat, drink, piss, shit, walk. Back and forth. Back and forth. Like a pendulum. No love, no satisfaction, no friendship, no peace—always lonely, always wanting and never having. This is not living; this is existing, like a head of cabbage on a garden row.

I look out the window and up at the heavens. It's difficult to relate to Him. He's too indifferent to pain and human misery. Most people look to Him with gratitude—for their lives, if nothing else. Gratitude eludes me. He did me no favor allowing me to be born into this world.

I suddenly feel an overwhelming sense of injustice. I want to disrupt violently the comfort of my tormentors, to impress them with my pain and misery by making them feel something of what I feel. My hands tense up, aching to hit something. I could take it out on the floor, but my knuckles are still half raw from the savage scrubbing I gave it last night. I reach for my cigarettes instead. I smoke and pace until the rebellion subsides. I return to the bars and look out the window.

The fools. Don't they realize how much of their trouble comes from making men desperate, driving them to despair and rebellion?

A heaviness settles on me, as it has before and will again—a sense of death. My chest feels tight; I feel cramped and smothered. I literally ache from despair. Long ago, a cruel world that regarded my ambition as insolence and my claim to equality as blasphemy ignited in me fires of frustration fueled by ignorance. I stand in the ominous silence of this steel tomb and contemplate the utter destruction of life that followed—my victim's, my family's, my own. I agonize for what has been lost, what could have been. From this wreckage, I *will* save something yet, though I cannot see how. I look at the books on my bunk. I know they are the keys to keeping my sanity, and they are also my salvation. If I die in here, I am not going to die an ignorant man. I am going to learn something about the world and taste something of life before I leave it, if only through books. And if I somehow survive this experience, I am going to need all the education I can milk from these books.

On the horizon the first rays of dawn appear, softening the darkened world. I am like the lone soldier trapped behind enemy lines, weary and weaponless, torn between hope and despair. I stare out the window until the flood of morning bathes the world, bringing light, hope, and life—to others. The joint awakens, and I hear the first stirrings of a new day. There are noises in the hall. It's breakfast time.

The hatch opens. "Well . . . hello there, Rideau," a voice says as I turn away from the window. The mask I wear to conceal my feelings falls into place.

"I see you're up early this morning," the Man says, slipping a tray through the hole.

I give him a smile that I don't feel. "Just looking out the window."

"It's a nice morning. Gonna be a real pretty day today." He leans against the door. He wants to talk.

I move toward the hatch and the awkward conversation I do not want. "Yeah," I tell him, "it's going to be a beautiful day."

Months passed and the raw dampness of Louisiana's winter gave way to the swelter of the Southern sun. Still there was no ruling from the Louisiana Supreme Court. The justices had not yet taken action on my appeal when in June 1972 the U.S. Supreme Court issued its *Furman v. Georgia* decision abolishing the death penalty as it then existed and voiding all death sentences in America.

In the wake of *Furman*, the Louisiana Supreme Court began ordering the state's condemned resentenced to life imprisonment and releasing them from their solitary cells on death row into the relative freedom of the prison at large, where they worked and mingled with other people. It was nearly a year before the court got around to my case. Eight of the nine justices saw no problem with anything that had ever happened in "this case [which] has been in the courts for many years." On May 7, 1973, they affirmed my murder conviction and, because of *Furman*, ordered me sentenced to life imprisonment.

The legal battle for my life was over; there was nothing left to appeal or to do, my lawyers told me. It was the last word I would hear from any of them for more than a quarter century. I was taken from the Baton Rouge courtroom where I was resentenced and ushered back to Angola.

4

The Jungle
1973–1975

Thursdays were "fresh fish" day at Angola, when new inmates joined the general inmate population. I boarded an old school bus behind the Reception Center to be transported to the Main Prison, where half of Angola's four thousand inmates lived. The other half lived in four out-camps widely scattered among fields of corn, cotton, and soybeans that stretched as far as the eye could see on the eighteen-thousand-acre prison grounds. The Reception Center housed death row, protective custody, and Closed Custody Restriction (CCR), where inmates were locked up for disciplinary reasons or because they were deemed a threat to security. Perhaps because of my slight build, the Initial Classification Board, which determined housing and job assignments, had offered me the physical safety of a cell in protective custody rather than the brutal, predatory life in Angola's general population. "It's a jungle down there," they told me, "and it can get pretty dangerous." But after twelve years of solitary confinement, I opted for the jungle.

I was dropped off behind the laundry building with my bag of personal belongings, along with the other newcomers. Then we set out on the Walk, an elevated, twelve-foot-wide concrete thoroughfare for foot traffic that ran throughout the sprawling Main Prison complex connecting cellblocks, thirty-two dormitories, the dining hall, the laundry, the education building, and various offices. Convicts lined it, leaning on the railing and studying the fresh fish. Some were merely curious; others looked for friends or enemies among the new faces; and the predators were there searching out the weak to enslave.

Slavery was commonplace at Angola, with perhaps a quarter of the population in bondage. Slaves met many needs in an all-male world shaped by deprivation. They served, of course, as sexual outlets and servants. But as capital stock, they had value and produced income. A slave also conveyed status and symbolized his owner's power. Whites, especially gangs, would enslave inmates in protection rackets, a non-sexual form of bondage in which the slave—called a "prisoner"—regularly paid money or worked for his owner in moneymaking activities. But most owners had only one slave, referred to as a "gal-boy," "whore," "old lady," or "wife." While most prisoners did not own slaves, many used the sexual services of slaves.

The enslavement process was called "turning out," the brutal rape symbolically stripping the inmate of his manhood and redefining his role as female. A prisoner targeted for turn-out had to defeat his assailant; otherwise, the rape forever branded him as property. In a violent world that respected only strength, the victimized inmate had to satisfy his master's every whim, as a displeased owner could brutalize or prostitute the slave. It was a role the victim played for the duration of his imprisonment. As property, slaves were often sold, traded, used as collateral, gambled off, or given away. They were even used as mules to transport contraband for their owners. They had no recourse. Everything in Angola reinforced the slave trade, including the security force, which benefited enormously from the oppression of one segment of the inmate population by another and the junglelike atmosphere that kept inmates paranoid and divided. These relationships were generally regarded as "marriages," and a complaining slave was more often than not returned to his old man and "counseled" by guards to be a better wife. The slave's only way out was to commit suicide, escape, or kill his master, the latter two actions drawing additional punishment.

That's what happened to James Dunn.

Dunn arrived at Angola in March 1960 at age nineteen with a three-year sentence for burglary. He was beaten and raped in the prison library by two inmates, one of whom wanted him for a wife. Since he wasn't doing much time and looked forward to making parole, he decided to make the best of it. He became a good wife, doing his old man's laundry, keeping his bunk area clean, preparing his meals, pop-ping pimples on his face, giving him massages, and taking care of his sexual needs. He paroled out but returned to Angola at age twenty-one with a five-year sentence for burglary. His former owner was still there. "[He] let me know in no uncertain terms that things hadn't changed, that I still belonged to him, and that I was still his old lady," he told me. Eligible for parole again in two years and not wanting to ruin his chance of making it, he became an obedient wife once more. All went smoothly until his master became eligible for release. If his master was released, Dunn wanted out of enslavement. He shared his feelings with his owner, who, instead of selling or giving Dunn to a friend upon his release, gave him his freedom. In an attempt to reduce his attractiveness to others, he stopped showering and cultivated a filthiness that earned him the nickname Stinky Dunn. But it wasn't enough. He fought off a number of attempts by others to claim him, finally killing Coyle Bell, a rapist. Dunn was punished with an eighteen-month stay in a cell by himself and sentenced to spend the rest of his life in prison.

While other inmates facing the prospect of going to Angola often fought and raped each other in jails to build a reputation for dangerousness that might protect them when they got to the feared prison, I was less anxious entering general population than I had been when I first stepped into the inmate bullpen in the Baton Rouge jail in 1964. Twelve years spent contemplating the prospect of being executed had brought me to terms with dying; prison had taught me not to be intimidated. I knew that I'd probably be tested and I'd probably have to fight, but I was determined to stand my ground or die on it. My eyes scanned the Walk for a familiar face, someone from whom I might be able to obtain a weapon. If I knew nothing else, I knew I would need a weapon.

In 1973 in Angola, everyone needed a weapon. Not only was the prison in the throes of major systemic change precipitated by the civil rights movement, it was also seriously overcrowded and underfunded. C. Murray Henderson, a progressive penal expert and former head of prisons in Iowa and Tennessee, was the warden. Elayn Hunt, an attorney and reformist, was the new director of corrections. "I'm hoping I'm just overreacting," she told the state's largest newspaper, the New Orleans *Times-Picayune*, "but my concerns now are food and clothing; I don't even know what rehabilitation is anymore." Shortages of basic needs guaranteed violence, as convicts sought to redistribute existing goods and resources by whatever means possible. The prison was seventy guards short that summer. Sixty-seven inmates were stabbed, and five died. The clanging of steel was a familiar sound emanating from behind dormitories as men fought like gladiators with handmade shields and swords, pieces of wood, or mail-order catalogues strapped to their chests. Even in maximum-security cellblocks, men tied their doors shut for an extra measure of safety. Survival of the fittest was the only law, and fear was the supreme ruler of all.

As I stepped onto the Walk, the first familiar face I spotted was Ora Lee's. It was hard to miss his big, muscular, six-foot-seven-inch frame as he waved his arms to get my attention. I was enormously relieved. Near him I saw several death row alumni, all friends. They were waiting for me, "just to make sure you didn't have problems with any of these old bitch-ass niggers," Daryl Evans said loudly for all to hear. The slender, gregarious youth was my best friend after Ora Lee. He and Bernard "Outlaw" Butler had been sent to death row for killing a man during a New Orleans robbery. Like all the others except me, they had gotten off death row the year before and had established themselves in general population. Outlaw had earned the distinction of being a fearless fighter. Daryl, a loud but responsible-minded individual, was a popular leader and athlete.

They assured me that I had little to fear.

"These dog-breath motherfuckers not crazy," Daryl said. "They ain't challenging nobody coming off death row, not with the kind of charge you're carrying. They know who you are, and they ain't gonna fuck with you—not unless you get to messing with galboys or dope, or you let these fools think you're weak. But you not gonna do any of that. You got what you prayed for—a second chance. You don't want to blow it by getting caught up in all the dumb shit going on around here."

"Dumb shit" hardly covered what was going on at Angola, which was in turmoil on every front. In an effort to stave off a federal court order after prisoners murdered security officer Brent Miller in 1972, corrections officials and inmate representatives negotiated changes in policies and procedures, in sessions mediated by the U.S. Department of Justice, to improve conditions at Angola. The Department of Corrections agreed to improve medical care and to allow inmates to marry their outside girlfriends and wear long hair and beards. They also implemented a host of other quality-of-life changes, many opposed by security: They agreed to remove restrictions on inmates' correspondence, magazines, and literature; to install unmonitored "collect" phones for inmates to use; and to allow full media access to the prison, its inmates, and its employees. Mail between prisoners and the media was granted confidential status, the same as legal mail—meaning the inmate could seal the envelope himself and authorities could not read its contents—which was, to my knowledge, unprecedented in any American prison. Most significantly, the disciplinary system—the foundation upon which prison security, order, and stability rests—was changed. Whereas historically inmates had been locked up and punished at the whim of authorities, with no appeal, under the new system, rules would govern lockdown, the disciplinary process, and punishment, and inmates were given meaningful appeals.

Corrections director Hunt ordered an end to the racial segregation of inmates in housing, jobs, visiting, and rehabilitative programs. She banned the word "nigger" from the everyday language of prison management and decreed that blacks had to be permitted to join the prison workforce. That was apparently too much for security warden Hayden Dees, who resigned.

Workers who lived with their families in a residential section of Angola called B-Line—so named because it was built adjacent to Camp B, now defunct—formed the backbone of the security force and power structure that for generations had ruled the prison; they regarded the changes as a repudiation of them and a diminution of their authority vis-à-vis the prisoners. As if that weren't bad enough, Warden Henderson had succeeded in getting money from the state to hire three hundred new guards to replace the army of gun-toting inmate khaki-backs, which introduced a new element into the struggle for power and control of the prison. Many of the old guard, alienated and feeling threatened by the changes, abandoned the personal responsibility they had formerly taken for prison affairs, opting to "let the prison go to hell" and just collect their paychecks. They were certain the prison situation would get so bad that the governor would ultimately oust Hunt and restore power to the old guard. The new guards, who got on-the-job training and, if lucky, guidance from responsible inmates, had no stake in the old ways of doing things and were mostly open to change. The personnel, like the inmates, formed factions vying for power. Angola was a prison at war.

Daryl, despite the assurance he gave me that I would not need a weapon, owned one himself. So I followed suit, ordering a custom-made knife from an inmate who worked in the tag plant, where they turned out license plates, street signs, and other items made of metal. My knife was the length of my forearm, and I fashioned a sheath to strap it on under my sleeve, which allowed me to appear to be unarmed, unlike many inmates who wore long coats to conceal (and thereby announce) their weapons even in the summer heat. Like others, I armed myself only when there was the prospect of danger, but followed the Angola inmates' credo: I'd rather be caught by security with a weapon than by my enemy without one.

Ora Lee, Daryl, and Outlaw accompanied me down the Walk to the Main Prison control center, where I checked in, and then to Walnut 4, a dormitory for "big stripers"—as opposed to trusties—that had not yet been racially integrated. After helping me stow my belongings in a footlocker beside my assigned bunk, Ora Lee and Daryl walked me along the fence of the Big Yard, giving me a quick education about the place, the inmates there, and what would be required of me.

Unlike the silence and solitude of death row, noisiness and bustle marked life in general population, which ran according to piercing whistles. At 5:00 a.m. a whistle woke us up; fifteen minutes later, another whistle told us to sit on the end of our bunks to be counted, although some guys just rolled over and slept through it. Inmates were counted simultaneously all over the prison—at the Main Prison, the out-camps, the hospital, administrative lockdown—and the count had to "clear" before any inmate could move. The process took about forty-five minutes when there were no problems; it could take hours if the numbers didn't add up.

After the morning count, men walked single file to the dining hall as their dormitories were called. Breakfast, like all our meals, was served cafeteria-style. We got bacon about twice a week and were limited to one ration, but we could have as much as we wanted of whatever else they were serving—grits, oatmeal, biscuits, French toast, cereal, and eggs. Men went straight from breakfast to their jobs, where they were required to check in by 7:00 on pain of being written up for a disciplinary infraction, "late to work," and given weekend duty in the field, even if they weren't ordinarily assigned to fieldwork. Fieldworkers gathered at a spot near the back gate of the Main Prison called the Sally Port at 7:00 and were marched out to the farm lines or the fields by rifle-ready guards on horseback. Fieldworkers, who labored under hot sun and in bitter cold, always hoped the count got screwed up, as it meant less time in the field for them.

The 10:30 a.m. whistle signaled everyone to get back to their dorms. About half an hour later, another whistle told us to sit on the end of our bunks to be counted again. After the count cleared, we filed to the dining hall for lunch. We had to return to our jobs by 1:00 p.m. A whistle at 3:30 marked the end of the workday. Another put us on our bunks for the four o'clock count, after which we filed out for supper. The evening was ours, and men were free to stay out in the yard exercising or just hanging around until the next whistle, half an hour before nightfall, when everyone was required to be indoors. In the dorms, men showered, read, played Ping-Pong, gambled, argued, or listened to personal radios or the television over the constant sound of loud voices and toilets flushing. With sixty men using five toilets in each dorm, the commodes stayed busy.

Some men belonged to one or more of the thirty or so inmate clubs and religious groups at Angola and would attend church services or club meetings in the evening. There they could learn public speaking, practice dramatic performances, or work on staying sober, among other things. Many attended to socialize with friends from other dorms or out-camps. Those inmates fortunate enough to have a designated space and a locker in the hobby shop would pass their evenings hand-crafting belts, purses, paintings, wooden wall art, rocking chairs, and chests, which were sold in the visiting room and at the annual inmate rodeo—a spectacle open to the paying public that featured unskilled and largely urban inmate "cowboys," desperate for money and attention, in daredevil events prohibited in regular rodeos, such as snatching a silver dollar from between a charging bull's horns—which drew thousands of outsiders to the prison. Once a week, hundreds of inmates poured out of the dorms for movie night in the dining hall.

As long as a prisoner was previously approved to be on a "call-out" outside his dorm, he could be wherever the meeting or activity was taking place, from church to the gym to the education building to the visiting room. Angola was an ant pile of nonstop movement and activity, even after dark. The 7:00 p.m. whistle marked the last major count of the day, and men were counted wherever they were without having to return to the dorm until 10:00, which was followed by lights-out half an hour later.

"Are the guards going to hassle me about my charge?" I asked Ora Lee, referring to the interracial nature of my crime.

"Play safe and stay in population, where there's protection. The guards won't do anything to you in front of witnesses," Ora Lee said.

"As for the white convicts, they may be racists, but they criminals first. Problem is, they'll do a favor for your DA, the cops, or an enemy in return for help in getting out of here. Except for those on the row with us, I wouldn't go anyplace alone with white boys, not until you get to know them better. Stay around blacks, especially the Baton Rouge dudes: You got a reputation among them from the jail."

Before falling asleep that night, I thought of the armed inmates in the dark, overcrowded dorm with me and hoped Daryl was right that guys getting off death row generally weren't being messed with. I recalled Thomas "Black Jack" Goins telling me a decade earlier: "You're lucky them white folks sent you to death row, 'cause your little ass wouldn't survive this prison." I didn't understand then, but I did now. At arrest, I was just a kid, emotionally stunted, scared of my own shadow, saddled with an inferiority complex as wide as a Parisian boulevard, and sorely lacking in life skills. I was booked into the jail at five feet, seven inches tall, 115 pounds—two and a half inches shorter and considerably lighter than now. Had I been placed in Angola in 1961 with a life sentence, the prison world would have devoured me. In supreme irony, my death sentences had been blessings, protecting me long enough for me to learn and grow, literally.

When I met the Initial Classification Board, I told them I wanted to write and asked for a job on the prison paper, *The Angolite*. It was a brash request, because the paper had always been produced by an all-white inmate staff. The officials exchanged meaningful looks, then told me there were no vacancies on the paper. Security Colonel Robert Bryan observed that the prison could use my writing ability—but in a different job. The next morning, I went to the industrial compound, adjacent to the back of the Big Yard, with Daryl and Ora Lee and reported for work at the prison cannery, where food from the farming operations was processed.

I approached the foreman. "Colonel Bryan sent me to serve as your clerk."

"My clerk?" The stringy white supervisor spit a stream of tobacco juice in the dirt and stared hostilely at me. "No, you ain't gonna be my clerk. Ain't never had a nigger clerk and ain't gonna start now. Tell you what—you go back up there to the colonel and tell him I say that if he wants you to have a clerk's job, he can make you his own clerk in the security office." He angrily returned to his office, where several white inmates had watched from the windows.

Black inmate workers had also seen what transpired. They believed

Bryan was using me to taunt the cannery supervisor, with whom he was feuding. The foreman knew that the only clerks allowed to work in the security office were gay white inmates, so relaying the foreman's message would have been merely passing along the taunt. Yet, if it was learned that I wasn't working at the cannery, I would probably get sent to the field to clear land, dig ditches, pick cotton, or harvest beans—the hardest work assignments. To avoid that prospect and to give myself time to find another job, I reported to work at the cannery every day as a manual laborer, joining the other blacks in cutting okra, making syrup, canning vegetables, sweeping floors, and performing menial tasks. I ignored the derisive laughter of the foreman and his white clerks each day when I checked in and out of the cannery, taking comfort in a rebellious determination forming within me: I refused to remain powerless in a jungle where only power mattered. I would somehow acquire some control over my life. I was determined to become a writer and to make the prison recognize me as one.

I turned for help to Sister Benedict Shannon and Clover Swann, a New York book editor who had coached me on writing through a pen-pal correspondence when I was on death row. When they learned about my present job situation, their complaints and inquiries to officials initiated a quick response.

Returning from the cannery one afternoon, I was picked up by prison security guards, who drove me to the administration building. Sweaty and dirty, I was shown into the warden's office, where Henderson, Deputy Warden Lloyd Hoyle, and the prison's business manager, Jack Donnelly, were waiting for me. Henderson, a tall, lanky man, introduced me to the others, offered me coffee, and politely inquired about my transition to the general population.

"My adjustment?" I said. "I've had no problems with the inmates. My only problems come from having to deal with a white administration that has no respect for blacks. I've been jerked around because of my color. Apparently you've heard about it, if my guess is right."

Those were dangerous words to toss at all-powerful white prison officials, but I wanted them to understand that I was not the "good nigger" they were used to dealing with. Henderson surprised me by apologizing for what had happened, telling me he didn't condone racism.

"I'm glad to hear that," I said. "Does that mean you're going to move me out of the cannery and put me on *The Angolite*?"

"We'd like to," Hoyle said, "but we can't do it right now. *The Angolite* already has a full staff. But we can do something even better, and it would allow you the time and freedom to do all the writing you want to—work on a book or something.* If you'd like, we can put you at Camp H. It's about a mile away from the Main Prison—real quiet place, the kind of environment writers like." Camp H, which held both medium-security prisoners and trusties, was popularly perceived to be a dumping ground for homosexuals, the mentally ill, and the weak.

Interpreting this as an attempt to isolate me from the Main Prison population, I declined. But I accepted Donnelly's offer of a clerical job in the Main Prison's canteen. Canteen jobs were much sought after for access to the store's inventory and the opportunity to steal. Of more value to me was the ability to retreat to the seclusion of an office with a typewriter whenever the store was closed.

I hadn't been working at the canteen long when I read in a newspaper that one of the wardens said there were no blacks on the staff of *The Angolite* because it was difficult to find black prisoners who could write. Considering my conversations with Henderson, Hoyle, and Donnelly, I was peeved. I took up an offer from the all-black Angola Lifers' Association, one of the prison's biggest inmate self-help organizations, to produce a newsletter for them. I put together an all-black staff and produced not a newsletter but a newsmagazine, twice the size of *The Angolite*. I introduced it to the membership as *The Lifer* magazine, "a publication by and for black prisoners," deliberately tapping into black resentment. Blacks made up 85 percent of the inmate population and, having been historically shut out of the all-white *Angolite*, they embraced the idea of having their own magazine and competing with it. Surreptitiously printed on the classification department's copy machine, *The Lifer* was distributed free in the prison and sent out to a network of outside supporters who sold it in churches and meetings in Baton Rouge and New Orleans. Revenue from the sales financed the next edition. The New Orleans chapter of the American Civil Liberties Union served as legal counsel and held our funds in a local bank account. We succeeded in making our point that black prisoners *could* write and produce a publication. It did not mean the prison administration had to assign blacks to *The Angolite*, but it did give the lie to its claim of a lack of black writing talent.

The competition between *The Lifer* and *The Angolite* divided the

---

* I had given my manuscript on the criminal mind, written when I was on death row, to one of my attorneys, James Wood, in 1969, to have it typed and prepared to be submitted to publishers. Nothing had come of it.

inmate population along racial lines and catapulted me to instant prominence in Angola, especially among the black prisoners, as they regarded me as being unafraid to take on the white administration. For the first time in my life I was popular. I began writing press releases for black prison organizations, and as leaders of the prison's numerous self-help organizations saw positive articles about the black clubs' activities in mainstream newspapers, they asked me to do public relations for their organizations as well.

In 1973, as I was establishing *The Lifer*, I decided to apply to the Louisiana pardon board for executive clemency. By the standards of the day, I was overdue for release from my life sentence, as Louisiana's practice, since 1926, had been to release lifers who had a record of good behavior after ten years and six months, upon the virtually automatic recommendation of the warden and pro forma approval by the governor. As Louisiana Supreme Court Justice Sanders had declared in 1971, "No *true* life sentence exists in Louisiana law." My Master Prison Record reflected a long-passed "10-6" discharge date of August 16, 1971. Other lifers, including those once condemned to death, were flowing out of the penitentiary in a steady stream.

Shortly after the U.S. Supreme Court voided all death sentences in 1972, Freeman Lavergne, a lifelong friend of my mother and one of the most powerful black leaders in Lake Charles, came to see me one day in the Calcasieu Parish jail. The first black business manager for Labor Local 207, who eventually became vice president of the local AFL-CIO chapter, Lavergne was a close ally of district attorney Frank Salter, who was part owner of a construction business that hired union labor. Lavergne was the first person from the local community, besides my mother and Sister Benedict, to visit me in the eleven years since my arrest. Because of his standing in the community, I was brought to a private office for the visit.

"I have a message for you, son, and I think you'll see it as good news," the stocky Lavergne said, leaning back in his chair. "Your case has been dragging on in the courts through three trials and for more than a decade. Frank Salter wants it to die a quiet death. He doesn't need another reversal of your conviction by the federal court. So here's the deal. You don't appeal your conviction. You take the life sentence the Supreme Court's going to give you, lie low for a couple of years, apply for a ten-six time cut, and Salter won't oppose executive clemency for you."

It sounded like business as usual. It was the way the back end of the criminal justice system worked. You got your time, kept your nose clean, and got your "gold seal"—the commutation of sentence. A first offender with a sterling prison record, I had no reason to think the gold seal wouldn't come to me as it did to everyone else. But I was relieved to know the district attorney would not oppose my release via executive clemency, the only exit for lifers.

However, rather than lie low and wait a couple of years, as Lavergne advised, I sought clemency in 1973. In January 1974, the pardon board denied my application, which was not unusual. They often turned an inmate down on his first request, to see how he would respond to adversity: Would he become angry, develop discipline problems, give up trying after suffering a setback? The hearing was a low-key assessment by the lieutenant governor, the attorney general, and the sentencing judge. It didn't make the newspapers. Salter made no attempt to appear before the board to oppose my request. I took the board's rejection in stride and figured that with one denial under my belt, I'd wait a couple of years and try again.

When the canteen replaced its inmate workers with female employees to end the chronic problem of inmate theft, Donnelly arranged for me to be assigned to the classification department, where I enjoyed the support of the officers in my varied prison endeavors and freelance writing.

The popularity of *The Lifer* outside prison made me realize there was an audience for my writing. The 1971 Attica uprising and massacre followed by the San Quentin bloodbath that claimed the lives of militant convict George Jackson and five others hung over the nation's penal system and generated serious interest in what was going on behind prison walls. Questions about justice and equality were being raised everywhere. Angola was a place everyone had heard of but few knew much about. And the more I learned, the more I felt the public needed to know.

Like almost everyone else, before I found out firsthand what prison was like, I thought it was just a purgatory where criminals were warehoused and punished before being returned to society. I was surprised to learn that it was a world unto itself, with its own peculiar culture, belief system, lifestyle, power structure, economy, and currency. It had its own heroes, like Leadbelly, who sang his way out of Angola and into international stardom; and Charlie Frazier, whose cell in the notorious

"Red Hat" disciplinary building was welded shut for seven years after he shot his way out of the prison in a bloody escape. It was a world divided into "them" and "us" by a deep abyss of ignorance, prejudice, and misunderstanding. It was a world in which the forces of good and evil struggled daily with no guarantee as to which would triumph. It was a world that placed a high premium on exercising extreme care—in word, deed, and appearance—and upon keeping one's word, whether it was to help someone or to hurt them. It was a world where inmates punished unacceptable behavior even more severely than authorities did. It was a world fraught with cruelty and danger but alive with hope, aspiration, and wide-ranging activity. There was certainly human wreckage—tortured souls and destroyed lives. But people also labored and fought to create meaningful lives in an abnormal place, and to find purpose and a measure of satisfaction in a human wasteland. Prison was more than just Hell's storehouse.

There was a huge discrepancy between popular perception and the reality of what was happening behind bars. With America wracked by civil disobedience over the Vietnam War, violent revolutionary groups, black militancy, and ghetto riots, some of the nation's inmates embraced militant antiauthoritarian rhetoric. Outside supporters of political militants publicly promoted romanticized notions of Angola prisoners united in resistance to official authority; in fact, genuine militants could not get a foothold in Angola, because gangsters, inmate leaders, slaveowners, and even run-of-the-mill criminal hustlers regarded militants as a threat to their own interests. They readily identified so-called militants to security guards in exchange for favors, often naming personal rivals or enemies as "revolutionaries." While Angola was the most violent prison in the nation, the bloodletting—with a few notable exceptions—was not due to political militancy. The violence was essentially about disrespect, vengeance, sex, turf, property, criminality, money, drugs, domestic disputes, and the inability of individuals to get along peaceably in a jungle atmosphere. Although I kept a weapon handy at all times—first, the knife; later, an iron handle of a mop wringer innocently sitting in the corner of my office—I never needed to use it. Occasionally, violence was invoked as a matter of principle, to prevent a third party from being victimized. But the reality was a far cry from the militancy that many believed kept the prison bloody. As I came to understand how Angola functioned, I continued to regard educating the public about Angola as both an opportunity and a mission.

After the third issue of *The Lifer*, prison officials shut us down, say-ing our funds were beyond their ability to audit and regulate, held as they were in a bank by the ACLU; the move only increased my support from black inmates. In the autumn of 1974, I queried Gulf South Pub-lishing Corporation, which owned and operated a chain of black news-papers in Louisiana and Mississippi, about writing a weekly column on prison life for them, and they agreed. I intended "The Jungle," which is what I called the column, to be different from the usual wail of personal pain or the bitter bar-rattling rage at the system that had historically come out of prisons. I wanted it to be reportorial and, to the extent possible, nonjudgmental. I strove to convey a wider perspective on prison issues than was usually expressed by either prisoners or officials. One of my earliest columns was an insider's analysis of the internal prison economy and the correlation between the degree of material deprivation suffered by inmates and the degree of violence within the prison, an observation I first made in the Baton Rouge jail, which was reinforced when I entered the general population in Angola. It was a piece that could not have been done by an outside journalist. It rein-forced my belief that I could make a significant contribution.

In preparing the columns, I found facts and statistics to expose racial and class inequities in the criminal justice system—from the staffing of prisons to disparities in sentences, clemencies, and execu-tions. I wrote about the problems of being black in a white-ruled prison. The administration was sometimes embarrassed by things I reported—lack of soap in a prison that produced it, little old ladies delivering cases of toilet tissue to the prison gate in response to my reported shortage of it—and why prison officials stood for it as long as they did, I don't know. It was probably because it had never been done before, so they had no policy on it, and because few Angola officials read black weeklies.

In November 1974, however, Deputy Warden Hoyle and Assistant Warden William Kerr learned I had written a column criticizing the annual prison rodeo as exploiting the inmates for the amusement of outsiders, likening it to the gladiatorial games of ancient Rome that used slaves for the entertainment of the masses. Hoyle and Kerr ordered that I be removed from general population and locked up in a solitary disciplinary cell known as the Dungeon. (Warden Henderson was out of state.) A dumbfounded Major Richard Wall, the leader of the "new guard," appeared at my office door expressing disbelief at what he had been ordered to do. I had been charged with being a threat to the security of the institution, specifically for "stirring racial animosities and instigating insurrection." The newspaper chain that carried my column immediately published a front-page demand that corrections officials explain why their "correspondent" was in disciplinary lockdown. Black politicians and civil rights groups from Baton Rouge and New Orleans also protested. Prison officials responded that I had been locked up to protect me from inmates who didn't like my criticism of the rodeo. Eight hundred Main Prison inmates then responded with a petition guaranteeing my safety, resulting in my release from the Dungeon.

I had won a stunning victory over censorship. I emerged from the Dungeon a hero, my image as a fighter reinforced by the administration's retaliation. But I was in no mood for celebration. While I was in the Dungeon, word reached me that my old friend Ora Lee had died of a heart attack. I was crushed. I also felt guilty, because Ora Lee, from whom I'd gained so much, had asked only one thing of me—that I write a column about him to help in his struggle to regain his freedom—and I hadn't done it. I had promised I would, but other things kept getting in the way. Distraught, I got an inmate to smuggle paper and pencil to me in the Dungeon, and I sat down to write the long-promised column, paying tribute to an unlikely teacher who, to the world at large, was nothing more than a criminal:

> He taught me self-reliance by being self-reliant; strength, by being strong; courage, by being courageous; and to not complain or cry about the things I couldn't change merely by embarrassing me with his own lack of tears and complaints. He was a poor man even by prison standards. He owned one pair of shoes, a change of clothes, and an old coat that was useless against the cold. Abandoned by the world, he had no source of income. He could have easily secured money if he really wanted to; he was intelligent and knew every trick to exploiting others, but he refused to utilize this knowledge because it conflicted with his religious beliefs. . . . There may have been times that he was scared, but I never knew it. And the knowledge that he was there, like the Rock of Gibraltar, somehow made the going a little easier, made me feel that there was no challenge that I couldn't stand up to, no obstacles I couldn't overcome, because he believed in me and I'd remember him saying, "A man can do anything he puts his mind to." And I

knew he was right. How many men are to be found who could lose half of their hand in a grinder as he did and not even cry out, just weep silently? And in a place full of danger, tragedies and bitterness, how many men could retain their sense of humor, greeting each new day with a smile? He permitted nothing to defeat him.*

When I was released from the Dungeon, I learned that my lockup had been followed by a security search of the office I shared with my friend Robert Jackson, which revealed photos of a female security guard and romantic letters she had sent him. It wasn't an uncommon occurrence for such a relationship to take root in the fertile soil of love-starved males competing to make the female employees feel like the most desirable of women. And when staffers rubbed shoulders with convicts day in and day out, they often came to see the inmates' humanity with fresh eyes. Still, in an us-against-them world, such relationships were viewed as traitorous by the other employees and were forbidden; a guard under the emotional sway of an inmate could aid him in an attempted escape or smuggle in contraband. Robert was locked up in a disciplinary cell, the female guard was forced to resign, and I lost my office.

Warden Henderson visited me shortly thereafter to tell me he wasn't pleased with what Hoyle and Kerr had done. He assured me that it would not happen again, and told me that I was free to write for outside publications. Exhilarated, I began trying to freelance. A couple of small alternative newspapers published me, but the mainstream media still were not interested in reports about prison life, even though Angola was seen by many as the bloodiest prison in the country.

From 1972 to 1975, 67 prisoners were stabbed to death in Angola, and more than 350 others were seriously injured from knife wounds. The violence affected one of every ten prisoners, not counting those injured in fistfights or beatings with blunt objects. Another 42 died of "natural causes" in a world where the average age was twenty-three. With no doctor or nurse on staff, medical services were provided largely by a handful of employee and inmate hospital workers whose expertise had been acquired through on-the-job training. An inmate who had worked as a mortician was the most adept at suturing.

Upset by the Louisiana legislature's refusal to address the problems

---

* Excerpted from "The Jungle," December 8, 1974, Gulf South Publishing Corporation.

at Angola, U.S. District Court Judge E. Gordon West halted the flow of inmates into Angola on June 10, 1975, placed the prison under the supervision of the court, and ordered Louisiana to make wholesale changes to end the violence and improve conditions there (*Williams v. McKeithen*). His ruling would have a significant impact on criminal justice in Louisiana because Angola was the heart of the state's adult penal system.

In the wake of West's order, *The Shreveport Journal*, one of that city's two daily newspapers, devoted its entire July 2, 1975, issue to the problems of Louisiana's criminal justice system. I was invited to be the newspaper's "inside man" with three features: first, a historical overview of Angola and the state's penal practices; second, an exposé of the problems faced by military veterans behind bars, including reporting on the nation's first self-help group to aid them, which I helped establish at Angola; third, a depiction of life in prison. The special edition won the paper the American Bar Association's highest award, the Silver Gavel, for outstanding public service.

My reporting in a newspaper that white officialdom read and respected had an impact: I was finally offered a job on *The Angolite*. But by then I enjoyed greater status and credibility as an outsider independent of the institution, so I declined the offer. Also, to leave my position as senior clerk in the classification department—whose officers approved visitors, escorted tours, and determined inmate housing and job assignments—meant a real loss of power. It was a position from which I had gradually engineered the placement of my friends and allies into key jobs. The control and influence of the Main Prison that resulted, combined with that accruing from our collective political and organizational activities among the prisoners, had quickly made me, to my own amazement, one of the most influential blacks in Angola.

One warm day in October 1975, Kelly Ward, the too-young, too-blond, freckled-faced director of classification, told me that Michael Beaubouef, his assistant director, would be taking me to Warden Henderson's office after lunch.

I had been reclassified to minimum-security custody, which allowed me to work and travel outside the fenced-in Main Prison complex without an armed escort. As a trusty, I regularly accompanied classification officers when they conducted bus tours of the penitentiary for school, church, and civic groups. The "tourists" almost always asked for printed information about the prison, but there was nothing to give them. The authorities had never bothered to compile a history of Angola or information about prison operations. Sensing opportunity, I requested the warden's permission to produce and sell a tour guide for my personal profit. I hoped that was the reason for the summons.

The drive to the administration building was short and uncomfortable. I was always ill at ease around Beaubouef. Though he had earned a college degree, as the son of a prison guard, he had been raised on B-Line in the peculiar prison culture that regarded convicts as just a step above work animals. He seemed friendly and understanding when I helped him with the monthly parole board hearings. After I was thrown in the Dungeon because of my rodeo article, however, he took me to his office for a private man-to-man talk in which he tried to persuade me to stop criticizing the rodeo and the prison. When I said I couldn't do that, he angrily told me that he no longer wanted me working with him and that he was transferring me to the field. I went to Ward and suggested that Beaubouef's threatened action would make the administration appear to be continuing a vendetta against me because of my writing. After talking with the warden, Ward assured me that nothing would happen to me. Beaubouef didn't appreciate being overruled; he refused to speak to me for months.

Henderson offered me coffee and friendly small talk. A gracious host, he treated prisoners no differently than he did others, which made him quite popular among inmate leaders. He explained that one of the immediate effects of Judge West's court order was that inmate workers in vital roles at the prison hospital were being replaced by female employees.

"There are going to be many such changes in the coming months," he said. "Classification is next. Starting the first of the year, inmate clerks will be phased out."

Female guards had always been restricted to working in the visiting room and the guard towers. "Security is not going to let women work in the middle of the Main Prison," I said. "You know that as well as I do."

"I expect there to be problems, but the male security force is going to have to accept the fact that women are going to work there—just as you have to accept it, if I'm to help you," said Henderson. "I'm interested in what happens to you, as you know. At the moment you have a job you like. Before you lose it and end up in a position that you won't like, I wanted to let you know what's about to happen, so you'll have a chance to try to get another job that you might like."

"Thanks, Warden. I appreciate that."

"You have anything in mind that you think you might like?"

I shook my head. "I'd have to take a look around."

"Well, if you don't already have something specific in mind, perhaps you could help me on something and help yourself in the process," Henderson said. "You've made quite a name for yourself as a writer and, to be frank, it's somewhat embarrassing not to have our best-known writer on the prison paper. Besides, *The Angolite* has always been white and, with eighty-five percent of the prisoners here being black, that's not right. It's never been right. But one of the ugly facts about prison is that you can't always do what you want to do or what you know is right . . ." His voice trailed off, his eyes reflective.

"You're right, Warden," Beaubouef injected, speaking for the first time. "I've always felt that it was wrong for the paper to be all white when the majority of the inmates here are black. It's not fair to the black population and it's not fair to the administration because it gives the public the wrong impression about us, making it appear that we're racist when we're not."

Beaubouef's words rang false to me. Henderson's, I believed. I had found him to be a compassionate man. I figured I was a continuing embarrassment for the administration. The New Orleans *Times-Picayune* had just published a story on October 5, 1975, "The Wordman of Angola," comparing me and my writing to Robert Stroud, the legendary Birdman of Alcatraz who taught himself ornithology by studying the birds that flew into his cell. What neither man knew was that a feature about incarcerated veterans was scheduled for publication in the April 1976 edition of *Penthouse* magazine, my first national forum. I was paid a $1,000, the most money I ever legitimately possessed in my life. I took it as heady affirmation that I could write.

"That office has got to be integrated; the black population must be represented in it, and you're the logical person to do it," Henderson said, his voice forceful.

"You want me to go to *The Angolite*," I said flatly.

Henderson nodded. "You need a job, and you'd have the best one in the prison. You'd have a typewriter, privacy, and all the time you want to do whatever writing you desire. I can't imagine a better job for you. And, as editor, you'd be your own boss."

"Bill Brown is the editor," I said.

"Not if you want the job," Henderson said.

With my job in classification ending, becoming editor of *The Ango-lite* was the best move I could make. But replacing Brown, the prison's most visible white inmate, with one of its most visible blacks, troubled me. For the past few years, blacks had been gradually taking over jobs, self-help organizations, rackets, and power previously held by whites. Black inmates outnumbered whites, but there was more unity among whites—and they were better armed, believed even to have guns. Most black leaders did not want a race war, especially when the security force was still almost all white and mostly racist, despite the hiring of seventy-five black guards during the past two years, many of whom had already quit. The total number of guards was only four hundred, divided into three shifts, to oversee two thousand inmates in the Main Prison and another two thousand spread among camps A, H, I, F, RC, death row, and the hospital.

Brown had support among white prisoners and employees. An abrupt changeover carried the potential to precipitate a larger racial conflict.

"I'll take the job, but I don't want you to move Bill Brown."

"Well, it'd be best for you," Beaubouef said. "You'd be able to pick your own staff and have a free hand to do what you want to do as editor."

"The problem with that is, while I can write, I don't know the mechanics involved in producing *The Angolite*," I said, not revealing my real concerns. "Brown will have to show me. But I don't expect him to be very cooperative once you've fired him."

"That's true," said Henderson.

"I'd prefer that you simply assign me to *The Angolite* and leave him in his present position. That'll allow me to learn the operation through working with him."

"Mike, you see to it that he's assigned," Henderson said, turning to Beaubouef. "And, Rideau, when you've learned the operation, let Mr. Beaubouef know and he'll move Brown out." He looked at us, adding, "I don't see any need for us to discuss any of this with anybody else."

I returned to the classification department, where I told Ward about my going to *The Angolite*. He was pleased.

After work, I joined several friends for the walk to our dorm, listening as they related the news of the day. There had been a bloody fight with machetes in the field that morning. In a second-story toilet in the education department—where only about a hundred students attended basic academic classes in pursuit of a GED or the one college-level course, in drafting, offered there by Louisiana State University—a new inmate had been turned out and marked as a galboy. And at the industrial compound, where inmates fabricated mattresses, license plates, traffic signs, and dentures, a cache of weapons had been discovered by guards, fueling speculation that an armed confrontation was brewing.

I now lived with sixty other men in Cypress 3 dormitory on the Trusty Yard, which encompassed a recreation yard and half of the Main Prison's thirty-two dormitories; the other half belonged to the Big Yard, where prisoners who had not attained the status of trusty lived and exercised. Each yard was a grassy rectangle that accommodated several baseball diamonds, football fields, basketball courts, volleyball courts, weight piles, and jogging areas. The Big Yard was defined by a barbed wire–topped cyclone fence; there was no fence around the Trusty Yard. The yards were the after-hours complement to full workdays in Angola's effort to reduce violence by keeping inmates busy and physically spent.

One guard stationed outside in a booth supervised our dorm and three others—a total of 240 men. Under such circumstances, control and order in a dorm rested with the largest or dominant "family" living in it. The tone and quality of life in Cypress 3 was shaped by a coalition of settled lifers and the family of black clerks, artists, and prison politicians to which I belonged. Stealing, raping, fighting, and other forms of disruptive behavior were not tolerated. It was a rule our family had reinforced just the week before by throwing out a black thief who had burglarized a white inmate's locker. Ours was the most peaceful dorm in the prison, which made it a preferred choice when security needed a safe spot to house an inmate. On occasion this forced us to exert our influence with administrators to avoid having undesirables placed among us. If all else failed, an unwanted inmate was met at the door and advised bluntly that entering Cypress 3 would prove hazardous to his health. He would relate that to security, who would find somewhere else to place him. No one ignored the warning.

Like inmates all over the prison, we were sitting at the end of our bunks waiting for security to conduct the four o'clock count so we could go to the dining hall. I told three of my closest friends about my meeting with the warden. Robert Jackson, like Daryl Evans, had been on death row with me. He'd raped a Baton Rouge college student he imagined liked him, to the point of telling her his name and how to contact him. The police did. Now serving a life sentence, he was leader of Vets Incarcerated, a self-help organization for the prison's military veterans. Robert relished politics and was delighted at the prospect of acquiring more influence and power for our "family." Daryl liked it, too, but immediately recognized, "Just 'cuz the warden says that's the way it's supposed to be, don't mean it's gonna go like that. Brown might not go for it and might do some instigating with the white boys or security. On the other hand, he don't even have to say nothing, 'cuz there's other people who're not gonna like it. And the solution is real simple: If you suddenly get locked up or knocked off, the paper stays with Brown."

"Security didn't go for us putting out *The Lifer*," said Tommy Mason, the youngest member of the family. "I can't see where they're going to be any happier about a nigger taking over *The Angolite*, the prison's official paper." After unintentionally killing a woman who refused to pay him for mowing her lawn, Tommy voluntarily turned himself in to authorities. At fifteen, he was sentenced to a life term in Angola. He became the first prisoner in the cellblocks—where men lived in cells rather than dormitories—to earn a GED, and when he was released from the cellblock in 1973, I offered him the associate editor post on *The Lifer*. He was a drafting student at Angola and president of Community Action for Corrections, a statewide prison reform organization.

I had decided to talk privately with Brown after the evening meal, to try to reach an understanding with him. If nothing else, I told my friends, I might get some insight into his thinking.

Supper was awful—unseasoned boiled spinach, tasteless boiled potatoes, and boiled wieners—so I freelanced (not everyone could afford to). Daryl and Tommy sold blood to the prison plasma company, so they could also make use of the ever-present black market. The most actively traded commodity in the thriving underground prison economy was contraband food, followed by sex, narcotics, pornography, lingerie, and weapons. While eggs, bacon, and pastries were usually available, fried chicken was the special that day.

Tommy, Robert, and I left Daryl to find a food connection for us, while we headed for the education building, walking behind a squadron of Black Muslims marching in military formation to the chant of their leader, Russell X. Wyman. They marched in pairs, in lockstep, behind the flag bearer, their backs straight and eyes fixed directly ahead of them, the Islamic flag snapping in the breeze. Even in the prison's blue denim uniforms, they were a distinctive lot—neat, clean-shaven, with black fezzes, armbands, black bow ties, and spit-shined shoes. Both whites and blacks feared the Muslims and found Islam's popularity among black convicts alarming. As their public image had been shaped by the fiery Malcolm X and much-publicized street clashes with police, many regarded all Muslims as racist, militant, and violent. I found them to be a generally reserved and peaceful group, functioning as a unit and adhering to an all-for-one principle. Some youths targeted for enslavement found instant sanctuary in joining the Muslims. Penal authorities, left to their own devices, would have crushed them. But the federal courts had recognized Islam as a religion protected by the U.S. Constitution.

Penal officials, at varying levels, maintained relations with virtually every inmate group, even criminal ones, except the Muslims. Russell wanted to change this, to improve their image. I tried explaining the Muslims in one of my early "Jungle" columns, but it had little discernible effect other than winning me their support. An opportunity had arisen the previous year while several of us were trying to broker a peace between two feuding black families, neither of whom trusted the other. I suggested to Russell that he use his group to guarantee a peace between them.

"And how are we supposed to do that?" he asked.

"Simple," I said. "Each side will understand that whoever breaks the peace will have to fight not only the other family but the Muslims as well. Not only would they be outnumbered, but who wants to fuck with you guys?" I knew word would get to the authorities that the Muslims prevented a conflict by guaranteeing a peace between the hostile sides; I figured that might cause authorities to reexamine their perception of the Muslims.

Russell liked my idea. Representatives of the combatants agreed to come to my office. Once Russell's role was explained, both leaders readily agreed to a truce. Russell immediately grasped the potential of his group to prevent bloodshed and joined us on several other similar occasions. The Muslims' image gradually improved as white administrators came to see them in a more positive light.

The education building was a two-story rectangle that housed the education department on the top floor and, on the bottom, numerous offices for security, classification, legal aid, the library, the chaplain, and a variety of inmate organizations. There were more than two dozen inmate clubs and religious organizations, and, on an alternating basis, they kept the classrooms occupied with meetings every night. Meetings attended by outside guests were held in the visiting room after hours. Inmate organizations had flourished under Henderson, who encouraged the formation and operation of self-help programs, permitting inmates to run food and photo concessions in the visiting room to fund their programs and allowing them to buy and keep property related to their organizations, such as food and food-preparation equipment, cameras, and office equipment, including typewriters. Every club had an office, vacated by prison employees when their workday was done, and its officers were permitted to work in them when not on their assigned prison jobs.

The building teemed with activity, not all of it business. The education building (like the visiting room) served as the watering hole for prisoner-politicians, their friends, inmates with offices who wanted privacy, and guys out with their "old ladies" for the night. Since only one, sometimes two guards were on hand to count and supervise the hundreds of inmates involved in an evening's activities, there was ample opportunity for prettied-up gays and galboys to meet dates and for prostitutes to turn tricks wherever opportunity presented itself—in empty rooms, restrooms, mop closets, staircases, behind counters, desks, and any other nook available. Some inmates rented or loaned their offices to facilitate brief trysts between lovers who needed to keep their affairs secret. (Owners usually had sex with their slaves in more convenient locations, like their beds in the darkened dormitory or on their respective jobs.) Control and supervision of what went on in a specific location rested with the organization hosting the activity there.

We made our way through the crowded lobby to the security window to sign in for the night, then went about our business. I headed down the hall toward the *Angolite* office, which faced a restroom and the office for the Narcotics Anonymous Club. A classification office adjoined it on one side, and the Jehovah's Witnesses' office was on the other. The *Angolite* office was also used as an office for the United States Junior Chamber—or, as it is familiarly called, the Jaycees, a nationwide group that cultivates leadership among those younger than forty—since the paper's staff controlled the Angola chapter of that organization.

The office was locked. I called to Tommy, who was walking out of the nearby classification office, to tell Kenneth Plaisance, another inmate, that I wanted to see him. I went into the blue-and-red-checkered room in the classification department that I was allowed to use as an after-hours office. It was my refuge from the jungle. A place in prison where you could be *alone* was priceless. I had just crossed my feet on my desk, lit a cigarette, and gotten comfortable when the door opened.

"Tommy said you needed to see me," Plaisance said. He was a white, balding, and bespectacled typing instructor who was allowed to leave the prison as a Jaycee speaker. "I need to see you, too." He perched on the edge of my desk and spoke with a kind of hurried breathlessness. "You're jammed with some of the guys in Spruce?" Spruce was one of the tree-named dormitories at the Main Prison, along with Cypress, Ash, and Magnolia on the Trusty Yard, and Walnut, Hickory, Oak, and Pine on the Big Yard.

I nodded.

"Good," he said, leaning forward, eager. "There's this black kid. He's not a whore or anything like that. He comes from a good family, and this is his first time in prison. One of the officers of the local Jaycees asked me to see what I could do to make sure that nobody turns the guy out or messes over him when he gets here. If you could talk to some of your friends in Spruce to kind of look out for him, it would make this guy owe me a favor, and that would help me in drawing their chapter into a project I'm working on." He handed me a piece of paper with the inmate's name and number scribbled on it.

Plaisance shunned prohibited behavior and worked hard at reinforcing his image as a model prisoner. A lifer, he was dedicated to regaining his freedom and joining the woman he loved. He had no real friends in prison, but he liked me. It was a fondness that began when I unsuccessfully pushed to get him on the staff of *The Lifer*. Plaisance was an asset, an ambitious, shrewd individual with immense knowledge of the prison and the politics governing it. He cultivated officials, community leaders, security personnel, assistants, secretaries, wives, sons, and daughters, knowing that the key to success for a prisoner—whether in job assignment, housing, earning privileges, or finding help in winning release—rested upon both knowledge and the ability to influence those who exercised power, or their intimates. My prison family had a wide network of friends and allies among both inmates and personnel, but we had not penetrated the inner sanctum of power—

the administration. Plaisance knew that the inmate power structure was shifting racially as more blacks moved into jobs and organizations with clout, and he had decided to cast his lot with us. He gradually educated me about administrative personalities and factions, the strengths and weaknesses of management, and the art of maneuvering a minefield of egos and prejudices to get things done.

"No problem," I told Plaisance, "unless he's got an enemy in his past." I paused. Now was the moment to mention what was on *my* mind. "Kenny—is Bill Brown in any kind of trouble with the administration?"

Plaisance became alert. He hated Brown. "What do you mean—in trouble?"

"Would the administration have any reason for wanting to move on him?"

Plaisance thought for a moment. "He's in trouble with the parole board. I heard that the chairman and one of the board members were in Henderson's office not too long ago, demanding he fire Bill. Henderson, according to my source, refused."

That explained Beaubouef's behavior in the warden's office. He worked with the parole board and was apparently playing hatchet man for them, knowing that placing me as editor of *The Angolite* would push Brown out.

Plaisance left and I went to the *Angolite* office, which was now open. The neat room was outfitted with black-and-white décor. Brown sat behind one desk, and Joe Archer, a friend of his, sat at a facing desk. They both looked up at me, halting their conversation. Brown was a trim, well-built blondish man in his late thirties, though his Ivy League good looks made him appear much younger. Like Plaisance, he was allowed to travel outside the prison to give speeches for the Jaycees. He was rumored to be carrying on an affair with an attractive state official. My relationship with Brown was cordial but artificial, tainted by our past as competing editors, he of *The Angolite*, me of *The Lifer*.

"What can I do for you, my man?" he asked.

"I'd like to talk. Privately," I said. "It's important, and in your best interest to hear what I've got to say." Brown asked Archer to leave, and I took his seat. I told Brown about my meeting with Henderson: "Apparently, the warden wants you out, but I don't particularly like being used as the hatchet. And, if you're suddenly ousted, people will assume you've done something wrong to warrant being fired. That'll hurt your efforts to get out of here."

Brown looked crestfallen. "It's hard to believe Henderson would do that to me," he said in a voice marked with disbelief. "It's catching me at a helluva time. If everything goes right for me, man, I could be out of here in a matter of months." He shook his head. "This will hurt. How do I explain it to people?"

"You don't have to, Bill. If we cooperate and handle this thing right, the transition can be made to look natural. I'll get assigned in here as associate editor, and we'll simply pass it off as the prison complying with the federal court orders to integrate."

"I don't have much choice, do I?" He forced a slight but false laugh.

"You can fight it—but, if you ask me, that would be stupid since it's inevitable. All our cooperating does is make sure that neither one of us gets fucked. You help ease my coming in, and I help ease your going out. You've got to trust me, much like I've trusted you in telling you this."

Brown shook his head emphatically. "I wouldn't jerk you around, not when you've laid your cards on the table. Believe me, I appreciate this, and your willingness to help with it. You can count on me—there won't be any problems."

I stepped across the hall to the office of Narcotics Anonymous. I knew that's where I'd find Silky, whose family controlled all four Spruce dormitories. He was a suave young black who rarely got excited about anything and who silently conveyed strength. We were good friends. He was dictating a letter to Shaky, his favorite slave, who doubled as his personal secretary. They greeted me warmly. Rhythm and blues from a tape player filled the room.

"Get up, baby," Silky instructed. "Let him have a seat."

Shaky rose, smiling. He wore tight, light brown shorts that barely covered the cheeks of his ass, with panty hose underneath to accentuate his shaven café-au-lait legs. A scarf was wrapped around his head, hiding his hair, and he wore lipstick. He stepped slowly in high-heeled slip-ons, his ass rolling deliberately and provocatively. He had fully embraced his prison-imposed female role. Shaky moved around to stand behind his owner, his hand on Silky's shoulder, throwing a teasing smile at me.

Silky laughed. He enjoyed Shaky's taunting games with me. "Man, when you gonna come down from wherever you living at and join the real world?" He smiled. "You ought to try it—you might like it. They got whores in here that'll make you forget women. And Shaky is the best—ain't you, baby?" He pulled Shaky around, embracing him and kissing him behind his neck.

Shaky slid out of Silky's arms, moved to me, and slipped his arm around my neck. "I can show you a lot better than him telling you," he said in a soft voice, as I closed my hand around his arm and gently pushed the effeminate boy back to Silky.

"I'm sure you could, but it's not my piece of cake. Look, I need you to take care of something for me—look out for a fish coming in." I gave him the slip of paper with the name and number on it.

Silky studied it. "A friend of yours?"

"Don't even know the dude. It's business. An organization in the streets is interested in him and asked us to look out for him."

Silky handed the note to Shaky, nodding okay to me.

I returned to my friends and told them I had talked with Brown, and that all appeared to be well. It wasn't. The following night, a breathless Plaisance rushed into my office. "You didn't tell me you're taking over *The Angolite* from Bill Brown." He relished the idea. "Bill was on the phone first thing this morning, calling people he's tight with in the warden's office, wanting to know if it's true that he's being moved out." Plaisance had been listening in on an extension. "Damn, Wilbert, why didn't you let me in on something this big?"

I told him everything, including my concerns. "You should never have tried to reason with him," Plaisance said. "He's a snake and he'll lie in a minute."

I cut the conversation short and headed for the *Angolite* office. I shoved the door open. Archer was typing at the far desk. Brown, seated at his own, looked up. "You lied to me, Bill Brown," I said. "You've been discussing what I told you with every Tom, Dick, and Harry in the administration building."

"You're fucking right! You walk in here talking shit, and I'm just supposed to take your word—without checking? I've been around this place too long for that," he said angrily, rising to his feet. "Everyone I talked to, including the warden's office, says I'm not going anywhere. I don't know what kind of play you're trying to pull off, Rideau, but it's not going to work."

"I can't account for what your people told you," I said evenly, aware that I was unarmed, alone, and outnumbered. "Henderson made it clear to me that he wanted this done low-key. I asked you to keep quiet about it, but you apparently couldn't."

"You're fucking right, buddy!" Brown repeated. "I'm not going to sit back and let you or no-fucking-body else try to fuck me around, not now, not—"

The exchange had gotten out of hand. "I'm not deaf," I said, cutting him off. "Sorry to have bothered you. I won't make that mistake again." I walked out.

I was concerned. Henderson would not appreciate my not keeping the matter confidential, and Brown might instigate violence toward me.

The day I was to have been officially transferred to *The Angolite* arrived without my being reassigned. An employee forgetting to perform a direct order from the warden was inconceivable. Brown was sure to interpret it as proof that I had been intriguing against him. For the next few tense and watchful days, I did not stray from the ranks of friends. Then I received word that I had been assigned to *The Angolite*.

Again, I went to see Bill Brown—this time accompanied by several armed friends, who waited outside the door for sounds of trouble.

"Looks like you were right all along," said Brown. Archer, at the other desk, eyed me with distrust.

"I assume this is my desk," I said, pointing toward Archer.

"It's yours, buddy," Brown said.

Archer picked up a folder and walked out of the room. I sat in the warm chair, lit a cigarette, and looked long at Brown. "Things are changing, as you now know," I said. "We can work together to make this easy for both of us, or we can make it difficult for each other. We've both got a lot to lose—you more than me because you're hoping to make parole in a few months. The fact that I came to try to talk to you before tells you that I'm willing to cooperate. But that has to be a two-way street, or none at all."

"There won't be any problems."

"Then you're the editor," I said. "I'm your associate, and that's all anyone needs to know."

Brown accommodated the transition. We developed a good rapport in the office, and he accompanied me to the dining hall, the yard, and various club meetings, introducing me to whites as his friend, allowing everyone to see the formerly competing editors working together. He taught me everything there was to know about *The Angolite* and gradually got rid of his staffers so I could pick my own. Then he lost all interest in the magazine, leaving the office pretty much to me while he attended cooking school in preparation for his parole or made Jaycee drug prevention speaking trips around the state.

In the past, *The Angolite* had been hastily thrown together and published whenever its staff got around to it, so I felt no pressure to produce a magazine as long as Brown was the editor. *The Angolite* was free to report on prison policies but not to be critical of them or to investigate the causes of violence or despair at Angola. I, on the other hand, was free from censorship, so I concentrated on proposing articles to national magazines.

Meanwhile, the violence at Angola continued to escalate. Stabbings rose from 52 in 1972 to 160 in 1974, killings from 8 to 17; 1975 was already the most violent year in modern history, and it wasn't over yet. Blood stained the Walk virtually every day. Oddly, it wasn't the violence itself that affected most prisoners, because with some exceptions—rape, extortion, strong-arming—it was targeted at a specific person for a specific reason. Most inmates did not engage in behavior that would put them at risk, so we did not feel personally threatened by it. What did affect us all, though, was the official response to violence: shakedowns, in which security searched an inmate's body, housing, or work area for weapons or other contraband, or new policies that interfered with our mobility and daily life.

The rumor spread that Henderson would leave and federal penal experts would take over the prison as they had during the 1950s in response to the national scandal following the incident when thirty-one inmates slashed their Achilles tendons. Especially disturbing was the talk that a hard-nosed warden would be coming to wrest control of the prison from the inmates and give it back to the prison employees. The Louisiana legislature, which had consistently refused to appropriate a sufficient sum to operate the prison, had just authorized more than $22 million to hire additional staff and purchase equipment to bring Angola into compliance with a federal court order to curb the violence.

There was a growing consensus among the more responsible inmate leaders that if we hoped to maintain the gains we had won, we had to curb the bloodletting. Even our contact visiting program, which allowed us to visit at small tables in a large cafeteria, was at risk; some security officials wanted to make us visit through a screen or glass. With the cooperation of about thirty club leaders, we took the message to their membership meetings, telling them of the coming crackdown and educating them on what we stood to lose in terms of the quality of our lives. Those involved in activities that fomented violence were warned that unless they immediately became model prisoners, they could expect their enemies to snitch them out.

Not long after I'd settled into my new job, Warden Henderson came to the Main Prison and met with me in the parole board room. He told me he was indeed leaving for Tennessee. He inquired about my efforts to get out of prison. He told me that he had taken notice of my self-education and development as a writer and had read my published writings. "Apart from doing well for yourself, you've worked to help make this prison a better place for the inmate population," he said.

"I've got a mission," I said. "The biggest obstacle to meaningful reform is the popular misconceptions about criminals and society's misguided efforts to cope with them. Since I've got to be here, I felt I could do a little good by clarifying a lot of that."

"You've done that, but there comes a time when you need to be a little bit selfish and concentrate on getting out of this place," he said. "You don't belong here."

Louisiana had ratified a new constitution in 1974, and with it came a new system of pardons that eliminated the review by the attorney general, lieutenant governor, and the inmate's sentencing judge. The 10-6 release mechanism had been suspended pending the creation of a new five-member pardon board of "professionals," all appointed by the governor, to review applications and recommend action. The ultimate power to grant or reject commutations of sentences lay solely with the governor, who, like the board, was bound by no criteria and rules. Henderson advised me to seek the services of Camille Gravel, executive counsel to the governor and one of the state's most influential lawyers. He also informed me that he intended to recommend my release to the pardon board and guarantee me employment and housing in Tennessee, where he was going to head that state's corrections system.

I filed an application to the board for a commutation of my sentence. In preparation for the hearing, Classification Officer Mike Schilling created an official profile of me, and my former supervisor, Kelly Ward, mailed copies of my published works to several journalism schools around the nation, requesting a professional evaluation of my writing ability. Professor William E. Porter of the University of Michigan's Department of Journalism said, "I've seen a certain amount of writing from prisons and I suspect he's the best I've ever seen." Acting dean David Littlejohn at the University of California, Berkeley, said, "Though he is evidently a man of strong convictions, he is no mere propagandist. He seems imbued by an obligation to be true to the facts—the realities—of whatever he writes about. This is a prime attribute of a real journalist." All the responses were similarly positive. I was both gratified and humbled by them, and I hoped they would show the pardon board that I had spent my years in prison wisely preparing for a successful return to society.

As we approached year's end, *The Angolite*, for all practical purposes, had been shelved. Brown was preparing for his upcoming parole hearing, and I for my pardon board hearing. The head of the NAACP in Lake Charles, Florce Floyd, had checked with Frank Salter, who assured him, as he had Freeman Lavergne before, that he would not oppose my release through executive clemency. Since I was a model prisoner, had been confined almost fifteen years—far longer than the 10-6 life sentence—and had Henderson's personal recommendation and guarantee of housing and employment in Tennessee, my application to the new pardon board was impressive. Not only did I have every reason to expect to get out, but I realized that I *needed* to get out. When the governor announced that Henderson was leaving and would be replaced by a penologist on loan from the Federal Bureau of Prisons, some guards began gloating. Life was going to be much more difficult at Angola. And who knew what the new warden would think of me?

5

Mentor

1976

I was typing a letter in the *Angolite* office on December 1, 1975, when there was a knock on the door. A neatly dressed, pleasant-faced white man in his forties walked in, stood in the middle of the room, and looked around. He asked me if I was the editor.

"Bill Brown is the editor, but he isn't in right now," I replied.

"You're Wilbert Rideau, aren't you?"

I nodded. The man began to pitch me an idea for a story. I cut him off. "You should talk to the editor about that."

"He's not here. And I'm talking to you."

"And I said you should talk to the editor," I said, turning back to my typewriter.

"What if I told you to do it?" the stranger asked, studying me.

"And you would be?" I asked, with an edge.

The man looked at me curiously. "You don't know who I am?"

I didn't.

"What if I told you I'm C. Paul Phelps?"

Holy shit! Phelps was second in command of the state's penal system. Elayn Hunt, the corrections director, had named him acting warden of Angola until a replacement could be found for Henderson. Phelps was virtually unknown to Angola inmates and personnel. This was his first day on the job.

"That changes things, doesn't it, sir?" I said. I stood up, thinking I'd probably just lost my job.

"Relax," he said, taking a seat. "I've been keeping up with you. Read all your columns in that newspaper and the articles you did for the Shreveport paper."

"Did you have anything to do with my being locked up last year for the article I wrote about the rodeo?"

"No. The first I knew of it was when I read the headlines on the front page of the paper you were writing for. No, I've followed your writings because I like the things you say. You have a pretty good grasp of what prison is all about, and you've said things that need saying. You got locked up because some people don't want you writing anything negative about Angola. But you knew that before you wrote your column, I'm sure. The fact that you wrote it anyway impresses me."

I was relieved. "Warden, as I see it," I said, "the biggest problem out there is that the general public and those with the power to change things are seriously misinformed about what prison life is all about, thanks to the bullshit they've been fed by prison administrators, convicts, reform activists, and movie producers. Too many people role-play, have something to hide, or are afraid to say anything."

"You're pretty close to the truth," Phelps said. "I was involved in the federal mediation negotiations in 1972 and '73, and as I sat there every day listening to the testimony, what I was most struck by were the misconceptions about each other that inmates and staff both had. The distrust between them was made worse by the fact that the inmate population is mainly black and the guards have always been white."

Phelps believed that the inmates' readiness to think the worst of prison authorities was largely due to administrative secrecy and the entrenched attitude that inmates do not deserve explanations. "If the administration can't do something—if you don't have dentures or underwear to give an inmate—what's wrong with telling him that? He already thinks poorly of you, so what's the worst that can happen? That he might understand you don't have it to give, and that you're not just trying to be mean to him? Hell, that would be a plus."

"Well, as warden you have the power to change things," I said. "What do you plan to do?"

"I don't know. I don't have a plan."

I stared at him. "You're taking charge of the bloodiest prison in the country, and you don't know what you're gonna do?"

"I answered your question truthfully. As you come to know me, you'll learn that I'm not going to lie to you. That doesn't mean that you'll always like what I tell you. But it's always going to be the truth. And the truth is that I honestly don't know what I'm going to do yet. I don't know enough about prisons in general and Angola in particular to formulate any plans. I need a little time to educate myself first, find out what's going on here and what the problems are. Then I'll be able to be more definite about what I'm going to do."

I could not believe my ears. This forty-three-year-old warden was unlike any I'd met before. I would come to realize that his friendly, laid-back manner belied the force of his character and an intelligence as penetrating as an X-ray. Although he was only a decade older than me, he was worldly and educated. He was a sociologist with a master's degree from Louisiana State University in social work, an air force veteran, and a career corrections bureaucrat with no actual prison experience. He had worked ten years in the probation office before being tapped to head the state's juvenile corrections system in 1967. His background in juvenile corrections, he observed wryly, would be a great help to him at Angola because he already knew many of the inmates by name; this was his way of saying that the state's juvenile corrections system was ineffective in deterring youthful offenders from becoming adult felons. Unpretentious and mild-mannered, Phelps boldly roamed Angola's violent world, chatting with inmates and employees. Warned of the danger of his forays, he said, "I'm not going to learn anything sitting on my ass in an office."

In the prison's dining hall during the noon meal one day, Phelps stepped in line, got a tray, and came over to the table where I was eating with friends. "Mind if I join you?" he asked.

My friends and I exchanged glances. We knew the whole room was watching. "Not at all," I said. "Pull up a chair."

Phelps made small talk and picked at his food while we prisoners hurried through our meal. He asked why everybody was watching us.

My friends laughed. "Chief, free people don't eat with the inmates in here—neither the warden nor the security officers," I said. "Inmates are inmates and free people are free people, and they live on different sides of the fence. What you just did, nobody does."

"I didn't know," he said. "Have I jeopardized you all in some way?"

"It's kind of late to start worrying about it. You're through eating?" I asked. He nodded. "Then let's get out of here."

Outside the kitchen, my friends headed back to their jobs as Phelps and I made our way through the throngs of prisoners on the walkway. In the *Angolite* office, Phelps fell into a chair. "I'm sorry if I've made things uncomfortable for you as a result of what I did in the dining hall," he said. "I didn't see anything wrong with it."

I stared at him. "Warden, there are certain rules of behavior, certain appearances, we're all expected to observe—both inmates and employees. It doesn't matter what you think of them. The normal rules of conduct in your world don't apply here."

"I don't know how people live in here, what's acceptable and what isn't," he said. "It's an entirely new experience for me. We've talked about a lot of things during my visits, and the more we talk and come to understand each other, the more that I see that we—you and I—basically want the same things. You tell me you don't like the corruption, the brutality, and the violence in here. I don't either, and I want to change it. But to be effective, I need to know what I'm dealing with. Why do you think I come here every day? You've been here longer than most of my employees, and you've made it your business to know this place and its problems, to understand what makes it tick. I can't change things overnight, but if you help me understand what needs to be done, I assure you I'll give it my best shot."

"If you're going to be pulling off stunts like you did in the dining hall, I don't see where you give me much choice," I said with a smile.

"You have a choice," Phelps said. "Anytime you get tired of me coming 'round to visit you, for whatever reason, all you have to do is tell me to stop, and I won't come anymore. But I don't mind telling you that I enjoy my visits to this office. It's the only place I can go in the prison where I'm not asked for personal favors."

Either Phelps was as sincere and uneducated about prison life as he appeared or he was conning me. But I liked the man. I enjoyed our discussions, which ranged beyond prison to life, state politics, and the events of the day. And, to be honest, I knew that Phelps would soon return to his full-time job as deputy director of corrections; being on good terms with him could only help.

We often talked of the need for meaningful communication between inmates and prison authorities, of the need to disseminate information about things that affected inmates. Phelps believed that the single biggest source of inmate hostility toward the administration was rooted in secrecy on how decisions were reached. He thought such secrecy sowed distrust and paranoia among both employees and con-victs. Having read my newspaper articles, he had also begun wondering how the inmate press might facilitate meaningful communication.

I heard opportunity knocking. I said *The Angolite* could certainly report on developments and put them in the proper context, but only if we were uncensored. "A censored publication has no credibility," I said.

"Okay," said Phelps.

I was surprised by his response. Censorship was the official religion of penal authorities everywhere. From the creation of the first prison in America, authorities had insisted upon reading inmates' correspon-dence; listening in on conversations; limiting what an inmate saw, heard, and read, as well as who was permitted to visit him; restricting his communications with the news media and anyone else they felt might potentially be problematic—all in the name of the "security of the institution" or "in the interests of the inmate's rehabilitation." While restricting prisoners' access to certain kinds of information is essential to the peace and security of the prison—maps showing the layout of the facility and manuals for making explosives come to mind—courts had historically blessed the blanket silencing of the nation's inmates without authorities having ever proven a genuine need for it. Penal authorities had always intimidated judges with predictions that dire consequences—disorder, riots, violence—would follow the granting of any freedoms. But in fact the opposite was quite often true: The first demand of rioting prisoners was frequently to speak to the media or someone in charge in order to have their collective voice heard. Censoring freedom of expression served mainly to shield prison officials from public scrutiny and criticism, permitting them to operate behind closed gates without accountability.

"You know," Phelps said, "after the courts legitimized the role of jailhouse lawyers, prison authorities accepted 'inmate counsels,' who now play an important part in giving inmates access to the courts. By the same token, we have all the elements of outside society here, except a free press. I think there's a role for the press to play here. The thing is to get you started."

I told him that in prison a free press faces difficulties jailhouse lawyers don't. "The truth will upset people, and people play for keeps in here, both inmates and employees. Your employees will do every-thing they can to pressure you to censor us. And, of course, we'd need access to information."

"Information is no problem. I'm the warden. If I want you to have access to information, you'll have it. Of course, you can't have confidential security information or personal information on inmates or employees, but pretty much everything else can be made available to you. If you're willing to gamble with me on this, I'll see to it that you get what you need." Phelps said I would have his backing to investigate and publish whatever I wanted, as long as I followed the same ethics and standards that professional journalists do; what I published had to be the truth, supported by evidence.

I asked if he would trust me to make responsible decisions, to give me the benefit of the doubt. I knew there would be people who trashed me to him because they didn't like something I wrote. "I've already got enemies," I said, "plus I'm black in a place run by rednecks."

"I know," Phelps said, rising from the chair to stand at my desk. He looked down at me. "You said I'll have to trust you. Tell me—can I trust you?"

His eyes engaged mine, and I knew the moment of truth had come. "Despite my crime," I said, "I'm a good person. And I'm a man of my word. That's all I've got—my word, my honor—and that's important to me. You can trust me."

"Good, then," Phelps said, as we shook hands. "Let's give it a try and see what happens." He asked me to write out new operational procedures for a reorganized *Angolite*.

Toward the end of December, Elayn Hunt was hospitalized with terminal cancer, leaving Phelps to manage both Angola and the state corrections system. He spent half a day at headquarters in the state capital, then flew his own plane to Angola, where he'd spend the remainder of the day. His executive assistant at the prison was Peggi Jo Gresham. Since he couldn't devote much attention to *The Angolite*, Gresham was made its official supervisor and given the task of resolving problems, removing obstacles to information for me, and ensuring that other prison officials did not interfere with the magazine's new mission.

Gresham, forty-two, was a chic, petite brunette with a fondness for short skirts, which earned her the moniker "Leggy Peggi" among male employees—out of earshot. She was sharp, intelligent, knowledgeable, and efficient. She had initially come to Angola in 1952 with her husband, Carl, who worked in the prison's agribusiness division. She started as a clerk-typist in the records office. When H. L. Hanchey became warden in 1964, she became his secretary. When Henderson became warden in 1968, he encouraged her to continue her education and made her his executive assistant. Her duties, power, and visibility increased dramatically under Phelps, who relied upon her to run the administration for and with him. Gresham had become a genuine success in a male-dominated world that was hostile to females. She valued power not for its status but for its usefulness to effect improvements, to make prison operations better, to serve the interest of inmates, employees, and society. She was representative of a substantial number of employees—sincere, honest, and decent—who struggled often with indifferent, corrupt, and mean-spirited counterparts over the prison's mission.

Gresham approved additional staff that I requested, assigning Tommy Mason to the magazine as a full-time staff writer; Daryl Evans as a part-time sports reporter; and Eugene Morrison, a white, as the illustrator. I had selected them based upon their character; journalism, I could teach them. (Bill Brown was still the figurehead editor.) Some black inmate leaders objected to the integrated staff. But I recognized that the publication could never be fully credible if it discriminated against any segment of the population it served, which is why all-white authority and Southern publications enjoyed no credibility with most blacks.

Under the new regime, the first conflict came when a group of prison officials objected to Gresham's instructions that they provide me copies of meat purchase orders and warehouse delivery receipts, and make themselves available for interviews. They went to Phelps, complaining that requiring prison personnel to explain their decisions and behavior to inmates was totally unacceptable. Phelps disagreed and ordered the officials to cooperate.

They were furious. Though Phelps normally ruled through persuasion, he reminded them that, given his dual positions, there would be no appealing his decision. Disobedience was grounds for dismissal.

He stopped by the *Angolite* office and let me know what had transpired. I told him that the meat situation was one of the inmates' biggest complaints because we had been getting wieners and bologna almost every day—sometimes twice a day—when the prison had purchased beef that we were never served, not to mention all the hogs inmates raised and slaughtered at Angola.

"The free people say that inmates are stealing it and smuggling it down to the dormitories, where they cook and eat it," Phelps said. "They've caught enough inmates doing it to make a legitimate argument."

"Chief, that's bullshit," I said. "They allow, if not encourage, the inmates to do that, and bust some every now and then, just enough to be able to make that very point. Inmate workers have told me how much meat they steal, and that it's impossible for them to take more because they have to smuggle it inside their shirts. Now, if you multiply the number of inmates working in the abattoir and warehouse times two smuggled steaks per man per day for a month, it doesn't add up to the five thousand pounds of meat that disappeared. I know from inmates how the meat was ripped off and who did it, and I can lay you a trail that ends with one of your assistant wardens, who got a piece of the action last week, as well as the names, dates, times of day, and locations where the free folks made their pickups."

The following week, Gresham escorted Stan Williams, director of food services for the Louisiana Department of Corrections, and Judy Sims, who headed a training program for inmate culinary workers, to the *Angolite* office for us to interview. Having Williams come from corrections headquarters to answer questions about his operation was as unique an event as Gresham and Sims being physically in our office. Women were never permitted inside the Main Prison. Prison authorities, all white males, traditionally held that a woman entering a prison compound full of sex-starved men, predominantly black, would inevitably be sexually assaulted, reflecting the historical Southern white belief that black males lusted after white women and could not control their sexual impulses. We asked difficult, even embarrassing questions about the discrepancy between warehouse delivery receipts for meat and the bologna diet we'd been fed. We found out what we wanted to know.

When the story was published in the first "new" *Angolite* in six months, it was more aggressively written than stories had been in the past, but there was no mention of the theft of meat. Phelps, who expected an exposé, came to the office wanting to know what happened.

"The people involved have all resigned or been fired or transferred," I said. "The problem has been solved, and we're eating better. The only point in running an exposé would be for the sake of scandal, which would have offended some people and generated a lot of hostility toward *The Angolite*."

I knew that my freedom to operate without censorship could be lost if I didn't handle it carefully. My adversaries were waiting to pounce. The inmate population wanted *The Angolite* to be a journalistic gun to shoot the administration with, but I wanted there to be a gradual, two-way education process.

Elayn Hunt died on February 3. I was in the warden's office the next morning to ask Phelps who would replace her.

"I'd hope it would be me," he said.

I hoped so, too. While I was there, I tried to persuade him to rescind a few orders he had issued with a view to "rehabilitating" the employees as well as the inmates. He had had all the guards' chairs removed because, he said, "I want them on their feet, walking, moving around, seeing what's going on."

"But that's not stopping them from sitting," I said. "It only forces them to sit on desks, on the walkway, on the railing—which pisses them off. These are the people you have to rely upon to achieve whatever changes you want made in this prison."

He'd expressed his intention to do away with inmate orderlies, coffee boys, shoe-shine boys. "There are prisoners here who don't do anything but wait on some officer, bring him coffee, make him comfortable, help him do his job," he said. I pointed out that both sides benefited, as those inmates enjoyed more privileges because of the relationships.

Phelps had also ordered that all inmates except night workers rise at 5:30 a.m., make their bed, and be prepared to go to breakfast by 6:00, then to work. That did not make most inmates happy, including me. My routine was to sleep through breakfast, rise around 8:00, shower, get to the *Angolite* office by 9:00, brew coffee, and read the Baton Rouge newspaper. I could begin my day late because I worked late into the night writing, my day having been spent gathering prison news from inmates or employees and listening to the problems of both. Rising at 5:30 would dramatically disrupt my schedule.

I argued to Phelps that this wasn't the time to take on the prison culture on multiple fronts. I suggested that during the search for a new corrections head, he might want to back off a little. His new policies would alienate both guards and inmates, who might join forces against him. That would lead to nothing good.

He fell silent for a moment. Then he said: "I think my orders perhaps need to be changed because they're not accomplishing what I had hoped they would."

"Good," I said. I shared with him my view that although prison authorities possess the power of law and the gun, prisoners are not powerless. They possess the power of disobedience, rebellion, disruption, sabotage, and violence. A peaceful maximum-security prison owes its success to the consent of its prisoners, a consent that comes from mutual understanding and reasonable, commonsense accommodations at almost every level of interaction. And the one thing prisoners hate most is what seems to them to be nonsensical, arbitrary rules and actions.

Phelps invited me to review and assess proposed rules and actions from the inmate perspective before their implementation. This was no small thing. In prison, it is almost impossible to get authorities to rescind a rule already enacted.

"Your guards would shit bricks if they knew you were listening to me," I said to Phelps.

"Why? They all listen to somebody, usually snitches," he replied. "Every smart manager, whether in government, the corporate world, or corrections, listens to those whose opinions he values. You've demonstrated in your writing that you understand this world better than most. That makes your perspective potentially more valuable to me than any of my top officials', because yours is one that none of us has."

I educated Phelps on the inmate economy, on how the need for everything from deodorant to appellate lawyers to dope drove initiative as well as violence. Men earned money by mending clothes, repairing watches, writing letters for illiterates, and loan-sharking. They sold plasma, food stolen from the commissary or kitchen, drugs smuggled in by visitors or employees, handcrafted weapons, and the services of their sexual slaves. Some redistributed wealth by strong-arming and stealing; others sold protection to the weak. The security force would not tolerate the drug or weapons trade but largely accommodated whatever divided rather than united the inmate population. Sexual slavery, in particular, made security's job easier: They could gain cooperation from the master, who did not want to lose his slave, and if he was a good master—one who did not pimp out or beat his slave—the "wife" would also become an informant for security, on threat of being transferred to an out-camp, where "she" had no protection from new predators. I told Phelps how inmates, in turn, sometimes exploited the administration's fear of militants to get revenge on an enemy by identifying him as a militant, which would get him thrown in the Dungeon until he could convince authorities that he was not a radical.

Just as Phelps knew little about the world that I was unveiling for him, I knew next to nothing about the world of management to which he introduced me, often taking me along to official prison business meetings, which brought a startling new element into the otherwise all-white, all-staff affairs. More than that, he gave me an education in morality, personal responsibility, goal setting, and civic duty.

I suggested to Phelps that he might enhance his bid for the director's job by taking credit for the lull in violence at the prison. There had been no stabbing deaths in the three months since he became warden.

"Do you know why there haven't been any?" he asked.

"Well, let's see," I said. "The prison is still flooded with weapons. Guys are still unhappy about the same things. Emergency medical care hasn't improved. So what's different?" I told him that a lot of inmates knew a crackdown was imminent—Judge West's order to clean up Angola had been well publicized on television and in the newspapers—and the smarter ones had been lying low as a result. The new pardon board had begun reviewing clemency applications, promising to free prisoners who demonstrated rehabilitation, so eligible inmates were on their best behavior.

"It makes sense," he said, "but I can't take credit for the drop in deaths since I've been here. I can't take credit for something I didn't do."

One afternoon I entered the lobby of the Main Prison Office (MPO), where a noisy crowd of demanding inmates had encircled Phelps. "They got another food-poisoning incident going down," Daryl explained to me.

"How much of it is real?" I asked.

"I don't know. The shit is just on the Big Yard. Trusties ate the same thing—ain't none of them sick. Dudes on the Big Yard are talking about boycotting the chow hall. They not talking strike yet—just boycott."

The year before, massive food poisoning had resulted from contaminated roast beef served in the Main Prison dining hall. The demand for toilets outstripped availability as diarrhea ran through the facility, forcing inmates to resort to buckets and necessitating the creation of makeshift medical stations. The incident triggered an inmate strike that lasted several days. The state health authorities investigated and condemned the Main Prison dining hall and kitchen: Poor drainage had caused a swamp of sewage to collect beneath the huge, elevated structure; it was infested with vermin; and flyovers by the nesting bird population put every plate at risk of droppings. The food manager was fired, and numerous prisoners filed lawsuits. Now, a year later, we were still being fed in the same dining hall, which was still condemned. It was a source of continuing discontent among the inmates.

I told Daryl that our friends and allies were to steer clear of the boycott as much as they could.

He promised to spread the word and find out what was being planned. He gestured toward Phelps. "We need to rescue your boy."

Phelps was talking earnestly to the inmates. He still hadn't learned that you can reason with inmates only when they want to listen. The men around him were more interested in confronting authority than they were in solving any problem.

Soon afterward, Phelps came to my office. "There are a lot safer situations to be in than the one I saw in the lobby," I said, pouring myself a cup of coffee.

"I'm sure there are," Phelps answered, seating himself in front of my desk. "But the Big Yard is complaining of food poisoning. The inmates talking to me in the lobby actually believe the administration poisoned them—and that's ludicrous. I tried to make them understand that it is not in our best interest for them to be ill."

"Those guys were role-playing, and the situation isn't as simple as you think," I said. "Without knowing the details of what's happening on the Big Yard, I can tell you there's a radical element down there fanning the flames, trying to assert themselves. Last year, they lost out to more rational leaders, but they came close." I explained that there were other factors at play—bitter inmate rivalries, ambitious men eager to challenge established leaders, personality clashes. I said there were racists among the employees who would like to see a race riot, to defeat integration, and those who wanted a riot as evidence of how dangerous their work was, which would be helpful when they asked the legislature for a pay hike. Those were the components of *every* disturbance.

By morning, Big Yard inmates boycotted the dining hall and asked the trusties to support them. Trusties had more to lose, having spent years acquiring minimum-security status, which carried the prospect of better jobs, outside travel, and transfer to better facilities, not to mention a better chance at parole or executive clemency. Yet, on occasion, the trusty population had shown itself capable of being every bit as rebellious and violent as inmates on the Big Yard. Political militants among the trusties were calling upon us to boycott the dining hall at noon. Two trusties from rival families got into a fight, which was soon broken up. Many of the trusties just wanted to distance themselves from any conflict.

We were all strung out in a neat single line stretching from the dormitories to the dining hall when someone up the line hollered, "Will y'all look at this crazy motherfucker!" Major H. D. Byargeon, the morning security shift supervisor, was shouting curses at the inmates in line. "That stupid sonuvabitch better not holler no crazy shit at me when I pass," someone near me said. I could not believe my eyes when I saw Byargeon was carrying a baseball bat! He was clearly trying to incite a major disturbance. Adrenaline surged through me. We were ordered to return to the Trusty Yard, where violence was festering, rather than to our job assignments elsewhere. My friend Robert went to Byargeon. "Major, I think there's some kind of misunderstanding here about—"

"Git yoah gawdam ass back in line!" the major said, pointing to the Trusty Yard.

Trusties living in Ash and Magnolia proceeded toward their dormitories. A large number of inmates I recognized as being from Spruce and Cypress dorms milled around the gate and barbershop area, indicating the action would be on that side of the yard. There were about fifty inmates, divided into two groups. The conflict hadn't begun, but it was about to.

"Say, man—them goddamn hacks in that guard shack act like ain't nothing happening!" Daryl said to me.

The guard at the gate appeared oblivious to what was taking place a short distance away. I looked up at the guard tower and saw the officer there smoking a cigarette, gazing idly at the empty sky. All my instincts told me this whole scene was wrong. Those guards knew something was about to go down in the clearing in front of them.

Daryl, who had left us briefly, returned. "Jive motherfuckers got the goddamn gates locked," he said in a low voice.

"We all locked in," said one of the inmates from our dorm. Like most men who did not belong to any clique or family, he was hunting for a safe harbor to weather the storm. Other inmates drew near us for the same reason. They knew that while my family was powerful and would fight if we had to, we were reasonable men who did not like violence. We were mostly model prisoners whom they could trust.

There were now about three hundred prisoners outside the dorms, and another hundred or so inside the dorms seeking sanctuary there. Family clashes were generally confined to those involved, but because security was interfering with the natural course of things, there was no way of gauging how wide this would spread. Big Lionel Bowers suggested we all go to our dorm, pointing out that if things got bad we could hold and defend it.

As we neared the dorm, I spotted Silky and several members of his family leaning against the railing of the Walk, idly watching the growing belligerence taking place in the clearing. "What are you up to, Silky?" I asked. "Going to referee this shit?"

"Motherfuckers want to kill each other—I say let 'em."

I leaned against the railing, staring out at the men. I could see some had weapons. "Can you stop that?" I asked Silky.

"Probably—but I thought we agreed to stay out of shit, to be low profile?"

"We did, but this needs to be stopped. Security wants it to happen, which means it's not in our best interests." I shared my suspicions with him. He studied the guard tower and the general nonchalance displayed by the security officers. He leaped off the Walk with a couple of buddies following him. Voices twittered around me as we watched the young gang leader as he half walked, half ran over to the two groups about to spill each other's blood. He stood between them, talking. The heads of the men turned, looking in the direction of the guard tower, the checkout point, the gate, and finally back at each other. They began to disassemble, slowly at first, then more quickly, anxious now to stash their weapons.

"It's still on between them—they just postponing it," Silky said on his return. "They might want to kill each other, but they'll wait and see what security has up their sleeve before they get it on again."

After twenty minutes, a whistle sounded, signaling everyone to report to their jobs.

The security shifts changed at two o'clock, and the incoming shift supervisor, Major Richard Wall, made his way to the *Angolite* office, where several of us were discussing the situation. A short, stocky man who bristled with energy, the thirty-five-year-old was a career correctional officer who commuted daily to the prison from his home across the river in Simmsport. He had been the prison training officer before being promoted and transferred to the Main Prison. Old-line security officers regarded him as a maverick, and by traditional prison standards he was. A progressive thinker, aggressive and forceful, he would buck the established way of doing things for a new way he thought was superior, kinder to the inmate population, and more practical for management. As leader of the "across-the-river crew" of mostly Cajun officers who had traditionally been discriminated against and treated as outcasts by the ruling redneck old guard, he had the kind of backing he needed to force change in the treatment of his own men or the prisoners under his control. When other security officials refused to permit concerts in the rodeo arena, Wall, at the request of the inmates, went to Warden Henderson and got the permission, accepting personal responsibility for security at the events. Wall enjoyed enormous popularity among the prisoners and a working relationship with most of their leaders.

"When you consider all that I've done for the population, will someone please tell me how the hell my shift comes on duty and gets boycotted?" he asked.

We laughed. "That's got nothing to do with you, Major," one of my friends said. "It started at breakfast on the morning shift."

"I don't have anything to do with that shift," said Wall. It was common knowledge that the mostly redneck morning crew and the mostly across-the-river afternoon shift did not get along. "I'm talking about my shift. How did we end up with this?"

"They tried to leave you with more than just a boycott," I said. We told him what had taken place. He shook his head and cursed under his breath. "Those sonuvabitches just dropped this shit in my lap and split."

"They're up to something," I said. "The question is, what?"

"My guess is that this is to discredit me and my shift," he said. "And if the trusties stage a sympathy boycott at supper, then the whole thing will have escalated under me, the shift that is supposed to have the best rapport with the inmate population." He shrugged, breathed deeply. "This is going to shoot my credibility to hell. Can you hear them laughing next time I vouch for something on behalf of the population?" He paused, then looked meaningfully at me. "Won't help your boy Phelps, either. In fact, this could all be aimed at sabotaging his chances of becoming corrections director. If this place blows up, his enemies will use it as proof that he can't handle the job. Byargeon and the morning crew hate Phelps. They don't want to see him get that job."

The employees' choice for director was rumored to be Ross Maggio, head of the agribusiness division of the corrections department. He would be bad news for the inmates, and he would reempower the guards.

"You doing anything for Phelps on this boycott business?" Wall asked.

"No," I said. "He didn't ask for help."

"Well, I'm asking: Can y'all do something about this? The Big Yard ain't gonna convince nobody they're suffering from food poisoning when the trusties ate the same food, from the same pots, and not one has complained. The health department got food samples and they're analyzing them right now, and common sense tells you they ain't gonna find nothing. Look, I got a responsibility to see that my men return home to their families in good health and without a scratch on them, but I have that same kind of obligation to all those inmates in the Main Prison who don't want trouble, who just want to do their time and tend to their own business. If you can do something about straightening up this mess before it turns ugly, I'd appreciate you doing it—as a favor to me and my men. We'll owe you one."

After he left, we all looked at each other. "He's right," Daryl said, speaking for all of us.

"Okay—we all agree it's stupid and that Wall is right," Robert, the most political of us, said. "But he wants us to cut our own throats. There are some dangerous fuckers on that yard who're gonna look at us as selling them out."

That was always the problem. Even when you had reason on your side, the fear of being perceived as a coward, of surrendering, or of selling out, often prevented inmates from doing the right thing. In a world so given to extreme machismo and the criminal ethic, the appearance of having violated the tenets of that world could cost one dearly.

"It's all in how you present it to them," I said. I recalled what Silky had done. "You just point out what happened at noon and ask, Why? In fact, we owe it to them to give them that information."

Robert rose from his chair enthusiastically. "Look, if everything goes down right, we benefit from both sides," he said. "Wall and his shift will owe us a favor, and the dudes down the Walk will appreciate our rescuing them from a bad situation, 'cause you know they're going to think that security was setting them up for a kill."

We split up and headed to different areas to spread our information. But stopping the boycott would require more than information; it would require physical leadership. I found Wall and told him we needed the dormitories to be released for supper in a precise sequence. When the whistle sounded at five o'clock, our dorm, Cypress 3, was released first. Although my guts were in a knot, I betrayed no anxiety as my family stepped onto the Walk and began marching toward the dining hall as hundreds of trusties watched us. After a pause that seemed longer than it was, the rest of our dorm fell in behind us. Our strongest allies, from Cypress 4, followed suit, and their whole dorm joined in. We were 120 men strong as we filed past Cypress 1 and Cypress 2, doubling our strength as we picked up their numbers. Silky and his family brought all four Spruce dorms into the march. There were nearly 500 men on the Walk by the time the men in Ash and Magnolia caught sight of us. As we led the way, all 1,000 trusties went to supper. With no support from our ranks, the Big Yard inmates went to breakfast the next morning. We had broken the boycott while maintaining the peace.

Phelps visited the *Angolite* office the next day, wondering how it was that everything had returned to normal.

I told him the whole story, but said I wasn't quite sure why the whole thing had gotten started.

"The inmates said it was food poisoning," said Phelps.

"There was no food poisoning. I ate the same food," I said. "This was about you. Nothing else makes sense."

"Me?"

"It might come as a surprise to you, but prisoners don't always start the disturbances. I know the morning security shift was trying to instigate something more than a boycott. We got involved because one of your better security officers asked for help."

"Tell me—had I asked, would you have interceded?"

I smiled. "You know, when we last talked, I was kind of expecting you to. But you didn't."

"No, I didn't. I don't feel that I should have to ask," he said. He told me I was as responsible for the prison as he was.

"Whoa, Chief—we live in two different worlds," I said, a bit heatedly. "Your free world is about the pursuit of happiness; this prison world, the struggle to survive." He had the luxury of being moral and civic-minded, of believing in justice and that right triumphs over wrong. Prison required me to tend to my own business and interfere in others' only at my own peril.

"What I'm saying is that you live here; you can't just criticize what's wrong and do nothing about it," he said. "Who do you expect to fix it—me, alone? The prison employees? Most of them are here only because they need a job. As soon as they find something better, they'll leave this place behind without a thought. Besides, when you leave a problem to be fixed by others, you may not like the way they do it."

"Don't throw that responsibility on me," I said. "Your society created this system and has had the power to fix it anytime it chose. Even the reformers of your world only want to sweep the streets of Hell clean."

"You can't always do what you want or be what you want. Sometimes circumstances impose obligations on you," he said. He told me change would come only through strong individuals who knew what to do, if they were not afraid to do it. In his view, I was obliged to be one of them, like it or not.

"You operate in the background, removed from the chaos of this place. Even with *The Angolite*, Bill Brown is the putative editor. I wonder how you would behave if you were forced to operate in the open."

"That's not likely to happen," I said.

"We'll see, because you're coming out from behind the scenes."

On a Friday afternoon, two white police officers from the town of LaPlace, where Bill Brown was to give a speech, arrived at the prison to pick Bill and me up. I had recently been approved as an outside speaker. The trip would be a learning experience for me. It was the first time in my fifteen-year imprisonment that I was allowed out of Angola without having to wear handcuffs and shackles. We reached the local jail after a three-hour drive. The sheriff, Lloyd Johnson, welcomed us and invited us to consider ourselves guests, not prisoners. Our cell remained open so we could go in and out as we pleased. In the employees' coffee room we chatted with a couple of female officers and answered their questions about Angola.

The next morning, accompanied by an unarmed plainclothes officer, we went to the local community center, where an all-day drug-abuse-prevention fair was being conducted for the general public by narcotics law enforcement agencies and the local Jaycees chapter. I felt a little uneasy and out of place at the virtually all-white event until I was introduced to a group of Jaycees and their wives, who immediately lavished attention on me the way whites do with lone blacks to make them feel comfortable.

I was acutely aware that I could simply excuse myself to go to the restroom and walk off into freedom at any time. In the not-too-distant past, this opportunity would have been a dream come true. I had twice planned to escape from the East Baton Rouge Parish jail; the first plan failed when my compatriots neglected to unlock my cell before running off (and promptly getting caught), and I scuttled the second plan when I saw cigarette tips glowing against the night in police cars waiting just outside the jail for us. During the twelve years Louisiana was trying to execute me, I had been desperate.

Things were different now. I was serving life in a system that had historically required only ten and a half years to satisfy that sentence. Lifers going before the new pardon board had been winning recommendations for sentence commutations. Robert Jackson, who had been on death row with me, had his life term reduced to thirty years, which made him eligible for parole. I had recently been visited by pardon board member William Carroll and the board chairman, John Hunter. Carroll patted my file, sitting on the table in front of him, and said, "I don't have any questions about you. I see no problems—none at all." Hunter agreed. I felt I was merely biding my time until I was freed.

Becoming an outside speaker was the most sought-after brass ring inmates at Angola reached for, the one that would bring contact with society and the hope of getting help or a girlfriend. Model prisoners could also become visiting-room concession workers; drivers of trucks, patrols, or ambulances; hospital workers; administration building order-lies, clerks, or B-Line workers; workers at satellite facilities, such as the minimum-security state police barracks; even servants at the governor's mansion. But being an outside speaker required a unanimous vote of all the wardens, a difficult feat. The speaking program had been created to convince the public there was a need for prison reform. Inmates were effective public relations agents because the media and the public saw them as being more credible than officials.

When the day's program ended, we returned to the local jail. "The

Jaycees' people been telling me that you boys put on a real good presentation today," Sheriff Johnson told us over coffee. "That's good. They're a large and influential organization here. I like to keep 'em happy. They asked me to get y'all for them and, to be frank, I wasn't sure I could do it. The warden told me it was voluntary, and y'all come only if y'all want to. So I sure appreciate y'all coming. Now the Jaycees owe me a favor, and that's what it's all about." He laughed. "I feel like I oughta do a little something for y'all." He paused. "You think if I call the warden and told him that we needed y'all to stay over for another meeting tomorrow, that he'd okay it? If y'all have girlfriends, call them to come meet you, and y'all just have a little holiday on me." He smiled knowingly.

I couldn't believe my ears. I did have a girlfriend, Dot, a beautiful black-haired white woman of about forty with a figure years of dancing had given her. I had met her the previous year at a Jehovah's Witnesses' gathering at Angola. She tried to interest me in the Word, and we fell in love. She was my first girlfriend. She had told her husband, a business executive, who had no objection to Dot and me exchanging passion-filled letters. But he did not know about her prison visits, granted at the discretion of prison authorities for inmates who got few or no visits, or about the speaking trips for which Phelps had just made me eligible. I knew Dot would go anywhere to be with me, although her race might sometimes present problems.

Bill Brown assured the sheriff that last-minute requests for speakers to stay over were routinely granted. When he called, Peggi Gresham said she would normally approve it, except that we had to be in Denham Springs, sixty miles away, for a Jaycees meeting the next day. I was crushed.

On the trip back from LaPlace, we passed a Klan rally, where a flaming cross burned brightly in the night. Still, the speaking trip was like heady wine. I wanted to travel as much as possible. But the administration would send speakers out only at the specific request of a school, or a social, civic, religious, or police organization, and speakers were prohibited from soliciting such requests. The more innovative inmates created all sorts of public service programs that would appeal to social-minded citizens and outside organizations, resulting in requests for speakers. The most alluring incentive securing the inmates' cooperation was, unofficially, sex. Speakers always tried to set up schedules that lasted at least several days—many were a month or longer—

preferably in smaller cities and towns, because local cops there were generally not hampered by big-city-type policies and procedures on the treatment of visiting prisoners. Most small-town officers saw no reason why inmate speakers should not be rewarded with "a little nooky" on a trip. Like so much else in Louisiana, it was unofficially okay as long as you didn't get caught and it didn't become public.

6

Crackdown

1976

Speculation about who would fill the top jobs in the penal system had become feverish. "It's gonna be a whole new ball game when Maggio takes over, Rideau," one security officer said to taunt me.

One afternoon in mid-March, I was sitting behind my desk in the *Angolite* office with my feet up when the door opened. A well-built, good-looking blond man wearing a tan leather blazer stepped into the room. His movements exuded confidence, strength, and power, like the gunfighters in the cowboy movies of my childhood. "I'm looking for Rideau," he said, walking over to the large chair and sitting down. "I'm Ross Maggio."

I didn't move. "Glad to make your acquaintance," I said. "From the way security talks, you're the new warden, even though the governor hasn't made a decision yet."

"I heard a lot about you and wanted to come by and see you. You're the one who wrote that article on the rodeo a couple years ago, eh?"

"I did. And did you give the behind-the-scenes order to have me locked up for writing it?"

Maggio smiled. "Didn't have anything to do with it," he said. "What makes you think I had something to do with it?"

I shook my head. "Just asked."

Ross Maggio, Jr., began talking about himself, his years with the corrections department, his philosophy. He was thirty-six, with a degree in agriculture. He looked and talked like he could have been a rancher, a businessman, or a hit man. There was a hint of violence about him.

The next time I saw him was on March 20, 1976, the day after the governor appointed Phelps to head the corrections system. Griffin Rivers, thirty-six, the only Louisianian in the corrections system to hold a master's degree in criminal justice, was to serve as his deputy, the first black ever to occupy that position. Maggio was named warden of Angola, the youngest ever.

I went out that morning to cover the transfer of seven hundred Angola prisoners to Dixon Correctional Institute, a new facility opened to relieve overcrowding, and found Maggio supervising the operation. Beaubouef, no friend of mine, was at his side, implying a relationship between the men that gave me pause.

That afternoon, a cheerful Phelps and Rivers visited the *Angolite* office. I had met Rivers some years before when, as a criminal justice instructor at Southern University, he brought his class on a tour of the prison. He was hip and sophisticated. He greeted me like a long-lost friend. "You know, walking through this place is sort of like walking through the old neighborhood where I grew up in New Orleans," he said. "Man, I recognize a lot of old faces I came up with, men who disappeared somewhere along the way. Now I see where they disappeared to."

When Rivers left, I said to Phelps, "I'm glad for your appointment, but your new warden bothers me."

"He shouldn't," he said, looking into my eyes. "I'm his boss, and he'll do what I tell him to do."

"Your office is in Baton Rouge," I said, implying it was far removed from what was happening at Angola.

"It may have been that way in the past, but it's going to be different as long as I'm director," Phelps said. "You're going to see me around this prison almost as much as you did when I was warden. And I'm going to be dropping in on you to see how *The Angolite* is coming along and to visit and talk with you, just like I've been doing since we first met. There are a lot of things wrong with this place, and it's going to take some drastic changes to put it in order. You've got a role to play because I want us to do with *The Angolite* what we said we'd do with it—I want it to be a meaningful source of information for the inmates and not some boarding-school newsletter. Nothing is changed in that respect. You are the editor. Peggi is your supervisor. Anytime you disagree with her on something, you can appeal her decision to Warden Maggio. And if you're not satisfied with his decision, then you appeal it to me. I'm the publisher.

"Don't get pessimistic on me before you give it a chance to work. And the same applies to Ross—don't prejudge him. He might surprise you. I've known him for a long time. We started working in corrections across the desk from each other on the same day. And Ross is who Angola needs as warden right now. This prison has been a headache for the state for longer than anyone can remember. If I do nothing else during my tenure as director, I'm determined to clean it up. We're going to regain control of this penitentiary, end the violence and bloodshed, and make it safe."

As Phelps warmed to his subject, he grew indignant. "The inmates are going to holler that we're fucking them over, but they don't have to strong-arm, rape, and kill each other. I'm not going to let that happen. Ross is the right personality for this situation. The inmates will find that he's willing to deal with them on any terms they choose. They want to cooperate—fine. They want to fight—Ross will oblige them. He has a job to do and how he does it is going to be primarily determined by the inmates themselves. But make no mistake—the job is going to be done."

While Phelps in his new job coped with the lawsuits, political pressures, and the howls of a public made even more hostile by the massive relocation of prisoners throughout the state, Maggio cracked down at Angola. Personnel were hit first; scores of entrenched employees were fired, demoted, transferred, or forced into retirement. "You can't expect to rehabilitate the prisoners until you rehabilitate the staff," Phelps explained. Among the first to go were Lloyd Hoyle and William Kerr, the two officials who had ordered me locked up in the Dungeon over the rodeo article.

When a prisoner escaped from the cellblock, Maggio unprecedentedly suspended the top cellblock supervisor. "Whenever something goes wrong, they point the finger at the bottom-line correctional officer and fire him," he said. "The way I see it, the man on the bottom will only do his job to the extent his supervisor makes him do it. When something goes wrong, it's the supervisor's ass I want, and I don't care if he was a thousand miles away from the incident when it happened. Hold the supervisor responsible for what his men do, and he's gonna make it his business to see to it that they do their job right."

Maggio also introduced surprise roadblocks along Angola's black-tops to search employees' vehicles, seeking to halt the flow of narcotics, weapons, and other contraband into the prison.

In his first meeting with inmate leaders, Maggio brushed aside questions about his plans for rehabilitating them. "Rehabilitation has a hollow sound to it when you've got people being killed as they've been killed here," he told us. "Before you can think about rehabilitation, you've got to have a degree of order and discipline. No prisoner should have to wonder whether he's going to walk out of this place alive."

Unlike typical corrections officials who resort to wholesale lock-downs—where prisoners are confined to their cells or dorms, and all inmate movement is halted throughout the prison—to combat violence, Maggio shunned actions that punished rule-abiding inmates. He ordered the immediate but selective lockup of all known and suspected gang leaders and members, drug dealers, homosexuals who created problems, and suspected strong-armers who raped weaker inmates or forced them to pay protection. When lifer Terry Lee Amphy was stabbed to death in his dormitory—the first prisoner to be killed in 1976—Maggio swiftly ordered every inmate found with anything resembling a weapon to be locked up. Sophisticated electronic devices and walk-through metal detectors were installed. Searching—"shaking down"—prisoners at every gate inside the prison was now required, and there were surprise shakedowns as well. A special detail of officers was assigned the task. Officers could no longer warn inmates with whom they had alliances, something that had become a common practice. So many men were locked up that each of the prison's two-man disciplinary cells overflowed with as many as eight men.

Those prisoners without jobs or who had been ducking work were now sent to the fields. Prisoners complained that picking cotton would not train them for jobs in society. Maggio agreed, but told me, "We've got to have something to occupy their time, burn off some of their energy. Otherwise, they'll just sit around, figuring ways to beat us or each other."

With the grip of the former inmate power structure and cliques broken by the massive transfer of prisoners out of Angola as well as the lockups, new and strict security regulations went into effect. The freedom of movement formerly enjoyed by inmates came to an abrupt end; passes were required to go through gates and to travel from one area to another. The security force grew from 450 officers to 1,200. An officer was stationed in every area of work and play, even locked inside the dormitories at night with the prisoners, armed with only a beeper that, when sounded, brought fellow officers stationed elsewhere in the prison rushing to his aid.

Prison employees replaced prisoners who had previously served as clerks in many key prison operations, positions that enabled those prisoners to profit by exploiting other inmates. Inmates complained to Phelps about the shakedowns and charged that the stringent measures imposed by Maggio were unnecessary. "None of this had to happen," Phelps replied, "but you've made it happen. You don't have to do the things that you do to each other."

Maggio continued Phelps's practice of not operating the prison from the warden's office. He ordered all top officials to create a "floating administration," moving about the prison and accessible to the inmate population. Maggio popped up everywhere, at any time, dressed in anything from a business suit to the blue denims worn by the prisoners. That kept his employees doing their jobs, which in turn kept them riding herd on the inmates—exactly what he wanted.

Maggio was a man given to action, tolerating no nonsense and accepting no excuses. One day he fired a yard supervisor on the spot. When the officer disputed the dismissal, Maggio ripped the badge from the officer's shirt and punched him in the face, knocking him to the ground in front of inmates and other employees. Except for rare instances like that, few prisoners knew that he was cracking down as hard on his employees as he was on them.

One night he busted down doors in eliminating an illicit whorehouse on B-Line, which he had ordered closed when he took office. A week later, during a ceremony attended by employees and inmate organization heads, I asked him about the incident. He grinned, relishing it.

"Chief, you shouldn't underestimate those B-Liners," I said. "Some of them are not much different from inmate gangsters down the Walk. They play for keeps, and they've put skates under wardens before you."

Maggio's ego was pricked. "They may have run other wardens, but they're not going to run this one," he said, turning dead serious. "They may kill me, but I won't run. I don't back down."

In the beginning, he and Beaubouef roamed about the prison armed, supervising and policing everything. Maggio personally led the manhunts for escapees in the rugged wooded terrain around the prison, a pistol strapped to his leg. He got lost once and radioed in. Told to stay where he was, that a search party would go out and meet him, he replied angrily: "You just tell me my goddamn location, then tell me which way those prisoners went!" Maggio was in his element; he was a man who enjoyed the macho games and was determined to succeed at them. His behavior won him respect in Angola, to the point that inmates dubbed him "a gangster," the ultimate compliment. He loved hearing that.

As Maggio settled in, my profile grew and my writing career blossomed. *Penthouse* published my feature about the plight of incarcerated veterans in its April 1976 issue. Louisiana's second-largest paper, the New Orleans *States-Item*, did a front-page series on Angola on April 14. One article, "Rideau: Piercing the Walls with Words," was a lengthy profile by reporter Jim Amoss about my self-education and rehabilitation during the fifteen years of my imprisonment; another article, "Jungle," was by me. The timing was fortunate, I thought, because in a month the state pardon board would be hearing my plea for freedom.

But two weeks after the *States-Item* articles appeared, I received my first and only disciplinary report when a guard searched my locker and found "contraband"—a bottle of Wite-Out I had taken to my dorm so I could continue working after hours on *The Angolite*. It was the only disciplinary report ever issued in Angola's history for Wite-Out, a product universally used by inmate clerks. In an environment where strong-arming, dope peddling, prostitution, and fights were the stuff of disciplinary hearings, the disciplinary court declared me guilty but gave me only a verbal reprimand. Achieving prominence while in prison, I learned, exacts a price.

Even that reprimand anguished me, because I had hoped to present a blemish-free conduct record in support of my petition for clemency. "We're interested in what's happened to a man since he landed in the penitentiary, rather than in the circumstances of the offense," pardon board chairman John D. Hunter had explained to Amoss. "If a man has a good prison record and shows a willingness to rehabilitate himself and gives us an indication he can operate in free society, we often give him a cut to a certain number of years, if the situation warrants it." As I said, I expected a favorable response from the board.

I was not permitted to appear before the pardon board to plead my own case, so others were to appear on my behalf: my mother; Sister Benedict Shannon, who was still my spiritual advisor; Lake Charles NAACP president Florce Floyd; and Louis Smith, the director of the Baton Rouge Community Advancement Center, who sponsored Vets Incarcerated, our self-help program at Angola for military veterans.

I knew I was in trouble from the moment I awoke on May 19, the day the board convened in Baton Rouge to hear my petition. The inmate who slept in the bunk next to me told me he had heard on the radio that "Frank Salter is personally appearing with your victim to oppose your release. They talked about you pretty bad, man."

It was the first time in Salter's sixteen years as a district attorney that he made the 125-mile trip from Lake Charles to Baton Rouge to oppose clemency for anyone, including a string of murderers whose sentences were commuted during that time.

He would be there because of a scandal he was involved in. A failed extortion attempt by Lake Charles AFL-CIO union boss Donald Lovett to force Arizona industrialist Robert Kerley to hire a company partly owned by Salter to construct an ammonia plant had culminated in mob violence on January 15 and the murder of construction worker Joe Hooper. Lovett was indicted for manslaughter, and his trial was set for May 10, nine days before my pardon board hearing. Salter had by then become the subject of increasing criticism as his long, corrupt relationship with Lovett was exposed by the media. His appearance at my hearing was a public relations ploy on his part to win back some public favor.

I went to my office and sat quietly behind my desk. An hour or so later, a classification officer came to the door. "Long distance," he told me in a hushed, conspiratorial tone as we moved toward his office, where I closed the door behind me to take the unapproved call. It was Louis Smith.

"Man, it's all bad news," he said. "We had everything down pat and the board had told us it was a sure thing, especially since Warden Henderson was requesting that you be released to him in Tennessee. We were all waiting for the hearing to begin when Salter showed up. Florce Floyd looked like he had seen a ghost. He walked up to Salter and said, 'Frank, you promised me that you wouldn't come.' The bastard just smiled and said, 'I changed my mind.' He came with Baton Rouge district attorney Ossie Brown, and they brought their own reporters. They set up TV cameras in the pardon board room, and you could just see the reaction on the board members' faces. They were intimidated."

I thanked Smith for his efforts and returned to my office.

Salter's appearance gave him the desperately needed dose of law-and-order publicity he was looking for. He exaggerated and even fabricated various aspects of my crime. I couldn't challenge him, because the board's policies forbade granting clemency to a prisoner who disputed the facts of his case; that was seen as a refusal to accept responsibility for his crime. In my office, I suddenly felt old and very, very tired.

I don't know how long I sat staring at the framed painting on my wall that an inmate artist, Oscar Higueras, had given me. A single warrior stood on a small hill, a bloody sword in his hand, surrounded by hordes of enemy warriors, some lying dead at his feet. His situation was hopeless, but his face and posture bespoke a determination to die fighting. I related to it. I pulled a cassette tape out of my desk drawer. I listened to Sam Cooke singing "A Change Is Gonna Come," then the gutbucket blues of Guitar Slim, wailing, "The things that I used to do / Lord, I won't do no more." It was the way I dealt with hurt, loss, depression. After sinking as far as I could emotionally, I would emerge strengthened, with an angry determination to prevail over my situation.

There was absolutely nothing I could do about the politics and politicians that sandbagged me. So I plotted escape. I planned to set up a speaking engagement for that purpose. Dot would pick me up and drive me to a house where I would remain hidden for several weeks, until the manhunt and publicity died down. I planned to go to Brazil, which had no extradition treaty with the United States. If I was successful, she would join me there, and we'd start our lives anew. I began to study Spanish, not realizing that they speak Portuguese in Brazil.

When it came time to put my plan into action, I couldn't do it. I couldn't betray C. Paul Phelps. He had been a mentor and a friend. Phelps had told me, "If I overrule my officials and I approve you to travel out of this prison"—which he had—"and you escape, my career in corrections is finished." I had given him my word.

"I believe they're wrong about you," Phelps had said. His words haunted me. He was the only official to express a belief in my basic goodness, and the first person in my life ever to really trust me, without reservation, not only to *do* the right thing but to *be* a certain way. At the last minute, I scuttled my escape plan. I was a prisoner no longer held by force but by the person I had become.

I set about trying to improve *The Angolite*. I wanted to make it a better magazine than the whites had made it, for my ego and because, with the civil rights movement providing me a frame of reference, I felt that becoming the nation's first black prison editor had given me a chance to do something good, to redeem myself, and to make my people proud of me. And, as the first editor of an *uncensored* prison publication, I had to prove that the censorship that prevailed in the nation's prisons was unnecessary and wrong.

I had an eighth-grade education and a crew of untrained high school dropouts for a staff. I knew something about journalism from writing "The Jungle," and a little less about publishing from my experience with *The Lifer*, but I had an instinct for what I felt would be right. *The Angolite* was the only publication serving the Angola prison community of some five thousand people, including prisoners and employees. It commanded no respect from either side. Under my editorship, club, religious, and sports activities were relegated to the back pages. I had shifted the magazine's focus to studying and reporting on the Angola prison community and the corrections system in the same manner as any local newspaper covered its city, with real news and features about the world we lived in and the things that affected us. I wanted the magazine to deal with the realities of prison life. I wanted to humanize stories, to give the reader the flavor of prison and its frustrations, its people, its misery and madness, and to give keepers and kept a sense of each other.

I ordered a camera so I could expand the use of pictures, showing the prison world and its people. Security objected to Maggio on the grounds that we might take photos of an officer doing something embarrassing. I argued to Maggio that officers are not supposed to be doing anything embarrassing. He approved the purchase of the camera as well as a telephoto lens. Members of the *Angolite* staff had permission to carry a camera and a tape recorder anywhere we wanted inside the prison. It was the first time in the history of Angola that inmates had such privileges, and probably the first time it happened in any prison in America. It triggered paranoia on the part of much of the personnel. To minimize problems, Peggi Gresham often paved the way for us with the top official of whatever area of the prison we planned to visit with our camera and recorder.

My predecessor had encouraged inmates and organizations to write articles about themselves and their activities, which made his job easier. I eliminated the practice and informed everyone that all articles would be staff-written to ensure accuracy and objectivity. I vowed that *The Angolite* would never again be controlled by those wanting to promote their own interests; even staffers had to agree not to write about themselves or their cases. Still, I was confronted by those who wanted me to make exceptions to the new rules, including the chaplains, who demanded that a page be set aside exclusively for use by their office.

"Every inmate publication that I know of in this country does it," Protestant chaplain Joseph Wilson argued. "I think you have a responsibility as editor, Wilbert, to do it for the spiritual good of the inmate population."

I had known Wilson since my days on death row. He was typical of Protestant chaplains at Angola—a religious bigot and spineless bureaucrat who, unable to compete for a congregation in free society, took a guaranteed state paycheck, health care, and a pension instead. It was a waste of tax dollars. More prisoners attended religious services conducted by inmate preachers than by Wilson. The Catholic chaplain was no better.

"We have a conflict of interest," I said. "Your responsibility is to save souls; mine is to produce an unbiased newsmagazine. And I can't think of any area of human thought where impartiality is more impossible than in religion. Every religionist has a different belief of what the truth is."

Wilson was indignant—especially when Phelps backed me up.

Later, when the warden's office sent me a directive to the inmate population from Phelps, I wanted to see just how far my independence went. I refused to publish it.

"Rideau, he's the director," Gresham said to me.

"I know, and he's the same man who told me that I don't have to publish anything I don't want to. The warden's office has more immediate and effective ways to get that message to the inmates."

Phelps clarified things by saying that he had merely asked the warden's office to pass his directive on to *The Angolite* for our information. Whether it was worthy of publication was left to the discretion of the editor. Phelps's personal support gave me freedom to do whatever I thought necessary to improve the publication. It was an entirely different story with the inmates.

Most of the problems during the early stage of my editorship came from blacks who, having been denied a voice in the past, harbored high expectations with me in control. Since getting off death row, I had been their writer—the prison's first black writer—as editor of *The Lifer*, as a newspaper columnist, and as a freelance writer. They had given me their unflinching support. Now they applied immense pressure for me to make *The Angolite* a black publication, just as it had been a white publication throughout its quarter-century history. This was my power base, the prison's overwhelming majority, whose support I would need in future battles to make *The Angolite* the publication I wanted it to become. To relieve the pressure, I made one concession: When Bill Brown paroled, I did not replace him, leaving the editorial staff—me and Tommy—all black until it became politically possible for me to add a white.

Blacks also expected favored treatment. While coverage of them, which had been minimal, would naturally be increased, I was determined that race would not influence anything in the magazine. Many blacks were urged by their leaders to shun me. Some did; most didn't.

When I refused the demand for a column by Narcotics Anonymous, the prison's black "outlaw" organization, they began their own campaign to pressure me. Confronted in the education building one night by their leaders, I told them *The Angolite* didn't belong to prisoners, that it was published to provide news and information *for* them. Besides which, I said, "*The Angolite* has been here for years, and the white boys had it all that time. But you never got these dudes together to try to pressure them like you're trying to pressure me." I paused; then in a whisper, I said, "Now, you were either scared of those white boys or—"

"I ain't scared of no fucking honkies, niggah!" was the response.

"Yeah, you were scared of 'em!" said Lionel Bowers, a "family" member who had accompanied me to the meeting. His voice boomed from behind me. He was a big man, and now he tapped his chest angrily. "That's right—I said that! Long as the white boys had that paper, you ain't messed with them. But the first time a brother get it, you can't wait to fuck with him. That's what's wrong now—y'all crying about white folks, but they don't have to hold us down, we'll do it for 'em." He turned and slammed his fist on the windowsill, furious. "And if anybody got an argument with that, then you better hit me in my face, because I'm through talking." Between the truth of his words and the obvious fury of a big man who was universally liked and respected, they weren't going to take up his challenge. The moment had been won, but it was a temporary peace.

The biggest problem, I gradually learned, was that no one wanted truth or objectivity. Personnel wanted only good things said about them (especially by a black editor). Prisoners wanted a one-sided publication lauding inmates and criticizing guards, and conveying to the public how badly they were being treated, a desire that increased in direct proportion to Maggio's increasing control of the prison and their behavior in it. Criticizing anyone in *The Angolite*, therefore, was potentially dangerous—the employees controlled my world, and I had to sleep among the prisoners. I would gradually have to condition everyone to the idea of being criticized in print.

I was undergoing an educational process that would influence the way I saw and thought about things. Phelps was taking me to meetings where I observed deliberations prisoners never had access to—on how to turn inmate labor to enterprises profitable for the Department of Corrections, on the problems field supervisors had in meeting their harvest quotas when the medical department issued light-duty status that kept too many injured or ill inmates out of the fields, on the processes by which the prison acquired goods and services needed for the inmate population, on how and where facilities within the prison were to be expanded, on how and why new rules and regulations were created, and, often, even on issues of prison security. Phelps invited me to participate in official administrative discussions, sometimes asking my opinion, which shocked many of his staffers. He brought me to corrections headquarters and introduced me to his staff. He introduced me to those who exercised power so I could see how they made their decisions. He frequently brought outside officials and state politicians to the *Angolite* office to chat about the prison, the corrections system, and political affairs, regularly referring officials, reporters, and individuals seeking assistance or information to me. In doing so, he was conferring credibility upon me.

Phelps was the first of a line of wardens to sit in my office and discuss prison issues. I learned that it really was lonely at the top. It's difficult for wardens to get honest advice from those around them. The warden is all-powerful within his prison world; it's a rare subordinate or inmate leader who is going to disagree with him. Subordinates tell the warden what they think he wants to hear as opposed to what he needs to know.

The warden is the one official—corrupt, honest, inept, or mean-spirited—who wants his prison to run smoothly because he is responsible for everything and is judged accordingly. Most prison problems occur in mid-level management, where the operable rule too often is to avoid offending the boss and to cover your ass.

Both Phelps and Maggio spent a lot of time in my office, talking and listening. My pre-*Angolite* writings in "The Jungle," *The Shreveport Journal*, the New Orleans *States-Item*, the Baton Rouge *Gris-Gris*, and *Penthouse* on the inmate economy, prison society, and veterans in Angola had led them, particularly Phelps, to feel that I had a grasp of the issues. They found it useful to have a prisoner like me as a sounding board, which is how I came to accept that they wanted to right the ship.

I realized that as long as I relied on reason and diplomacy, I could accomplish much. I had to be seen as totally trustworthy, and a useful resource. I also learned that the key to solving problems was never to present one without a proposed solution. My position allowed me to connect good people with each other, to promote good ideas and projects, and to find the resources to bring them to fruition.

I was becoming much more than an editor. The more I learned about management, politics, the decision-making process, the complaints, problems, and frustrations of personnel and management, the more my perspective broadened. I gained a greater understanding of what I wanted and needed to do as an editor. I saw I could help deserving individuals, be they employee or inmate.

Phelps and I developed a real friendship. We were drawn together for want of sympathetic understanding elsewhere. That was even more true of Maggio. He had used fear to whip personnel into shape, firing and hiring more employees than any warden in Angola's history, increasing the number of employees nearly threefold in his first two years. As I said, he cracked down on employees, who cracked down on the inmates, which dramatically reduced Angola's violence. But fear leads to avoidance, and there was little meaningful communication between Maggio and his employees. They had become sycophants, and he knew it. I could tell him things they wouldn't.

He would roam through the Main Prison and then drop in on me, unable to understand why inmates didn't approach him about problems so that he could correct them. Maggio would never admit it, but he wanted the prisoners, even more than the employees, to understand, respect, and appreciate what he was doing for them. They didn't, not then.

With both inmates and employees avoiding Maggio whenever possible, *The Angolite* became the unofficial middleman for solving problems. I could cut through bureaucratic red tape by talking directly to Maggio or Phelps, so many people brought their grievances to me. Maggio was capable of brutality and callousness, but as long as he felt himself in control of the physical circumstances, he was a soft touch, a benevolent dictator, a liberal even, although he would never think of himself as one. Neither prisoners nor employees understood that.

Maggio's desire to operate the best prison made him receptive to new ideas and improvements. He gave almost everything I asked for on behalf of the prisoners once I showed him that it posed no threat to his control or the security of the facility. He would always listen to reason, and I was able to rescue the inmate population from many harsh and unnecessary measures proposed by security officers and administrative officials attempting to impress the warden with their hard-line zeal. I had to keep both Maggio's and Phelps's confidence, not repeating what either told me; otherwise I'd lose their trust and my credibility, and my ability to help others.

Most of my friends were not caught up in Maggio's massive lock-ups. In fact, they benefited from the changes he implemented at Angola. As model prisoners, many were able to take advantage of the Department of Corrections' effort to relieve overcrowding. They maneuvered transfers to the minimum-security state police barracks in Baton Rouge, where there was not even a fence to keep them prisoner. Living there, they could work at the Department of Corrections headquarters as aides or chauffeurs, or at other government buildings as gardeners and maintenance men, or at the governor's mansion, where *only* lifers, murderers in particular, were accepted as servants—a long-standing practice grounded in statistics showing that murder is almost always a once-in-a-lifetime event and that murderers have the lowest recidivism rate of all prisoners, as well as the wardens' practical experience that murderers tended to be the most responsible of all inmates. Jobs in the mansion were the most sought-after in the system, because they included unchaperoned weekend passes into free society, among other privileges. And the ultimate prize for these servants was another tradition—governors would free their inmate domestic staff when they left office. Some of my closest friends, including Daryl Evans and Lionel Bowers, earned those jobs, shrinking my "family" considerably.

Maggio's dismantling of gangs and the massive transfer of inmates out of Angola radically altered the inmate power structure. He ordered inmates to elect representatives to a revived inmate grievance committee, which, with *The Angolite* and the elected leaders of formal inmate organizations (such as the Jaycees, the lifers' association, the boxing association, the Dale Carnegie club, Vets Incarcerated, and a host of other civic and religious organizations), formed the new power structure. My position as editor of *The Angolite* and an established inmate leader, together with my ability to get things done and my visible friendship with Phelps, made me the single most powerful prisoner in the new order. That didn't make everyone happy. One day, an angry security officer, Major Roland Dupree, gave me a direct order to begin working in the field after lunch. Frantic, I called the warden's office and was told by his secretary to stay in my office. As the appointed time approached, I grew increasingly concerned, because refusing to follow a direct order was punishable with time in the Hole. Just moments after Dupree came back to my office, Maggio strode up to him and declared: "You don't mess with him. If you have a problem with *The Angolite*, you bring it to me—*I am The Angolite*." The symbolic message conveyed in that act reinforced my status.

Phelps taught me that with power came obligation. It was a lesson that was brought home to me in a forceful way. Prisoners who violated the rules in satellite facilities were usually transferred back to Angola. Maggio required all inmates returning to Angola to work in the field hoeing, shoveling, chopping, and harvesting, whether the whip was on the winter wind off the Mississippi or the subtropical summer sun parched land and man alike. This included a large number of prisoners undergoing intensive therapy at the mental health unit near New Orleans, who would be sent back to Angola upon being pronounced cured. One of the patients, feeling his punishment was undeserved, began complaining. Although the counselors, security officials, and classification officers were all sympathetic, they told him there was nothing they could do because of Maggio's policy.

Distraught, the former mental patient timidly knocked on my door. "I understand about it being the rule and all, but that don't make it right," he said in a despairing voice. "I was sick, and they sent me to the hospital for treatment. I had a good job before I left, but when I come back they stuck me in the field and wouldn't give me my old job back. I ain't done nothing wrong to be in the field, unless I'm being punished for going to get treated. You think maybe the penitentiary didn't want me to go to the hospital and now they're punishing me for it?"

"I think it's probably just a mistake," I said.

"It can't be. I went to classification and security, too. They all told me that it ain't nothing they can do for me." He clasped his hands over his face, gulping for breath and choking back a sob. "Them white folks treat us bad out there in the field. They be cussin' and hollering at us, calling us all kinds of names. They just mess with us, and for nothing a lot of times. It ain't good for me. I can feel it. I need you to help me. I don't know what to do, and there ain't nobody else to help me. One of the security mens told me I oughta come talk to you and see what you can do. If you can't help me, I don't know what I'm gonna do."

I was offended by the obvious injustice. Phelps had once said to me: "Sometimes the mere fact that you're the only one who can do something makes you responsible for doing it, whether you want to or not." I checked with security and classification. They said they could do nothing because of Maggio's across-the-board policy. I sent messages to friends in various parts of the prison, asking for the names of all inmates sent to the fields upon their return from the mental health unit. I received two dozen names.

What I was going to do next was born of a gentleman's understanding with Maggio I had made months before in exchange for his cooperation on *The Angolite*.

Not long after becoming warden, he visited me one night. He was congenial, as always, but to the point.

"Mr. Phelps told me that he wants you to have the freedom to operate *The Angolite* as you see fit," he said. "That's fine and good. He's the boss. But you and I have got to reach an understanding, because while he's the boss, he's in Baton Rouge. Now, he can sit in Baton Rouge and give all the orders he wants to, but I'm the one who must put those orders into effect on a day-to-day basis, and I will be the one who sees to it that you get what you need to keep the magazine going as you want it. A warden has the power to make sure that if he doesn't want something to work right, it won't."

My father, Thomas Rideau.
No Prince Charming, he.

My mother, a virtual slave, trapped
by two kids, pregnancies, little education, no resources, and a brutal
husband. I'm on the right, my
brother Raymond on the left.

Southgate Shopping Center, Lake Charles, Louisiana, 1961. I worked at Halpern's Fabrics, two doors away from the Gulf National Bank, which I attempted to rob.

Gulf National Bank, site of the failed robbery that would send me to prison for forty-four years. When the holdup went bad, I left through the back door with three employees, one of whom would die by my hand in a moment of panic.

A deputy at the crime scene where my victim, Julia Ferguson, was mortally wounded, on the outskirts of Lake Charles in 1961. The site was not protected for the ensuing investigation. Most evidence was not preserved; other evidence was altered or fabricated. This would eventually lead to my release from prison— in 2005.

P.O. BOX 8066 4924 COLE AVE.
DALLAS, TEXAS COMP.

arles American Press

LAKE CHARLES, LA., FRIDAY, FEBRUARY 17, 1961   16 PAGES

CING THREE CHAR

CRIME STORY RECOUTED BY RIDEAU

By BILL MERTENA

A slightly-built Negro teenager sits dressed in drab, loose-fitting coveralls in a Calcasieu parish jail cell today, perhaps pondering the few minutes last night when he was rich and powerful.

He had $14,079 in a cheap suitcase in a stolen car and he was powerful enough to kill one woman by shooting and stabbing her, wound another woman and a man.

It lasted less than an hour and a half. Then Wilbert N. Rideau, 19, of 1820 Brick street, found himself branded a kidnaper, a murderer and a bank robber. His prospects now are the cold steel cell and the prison coveralls.

After he was arrested near Fenton by state troopers, Rideau was brought back to Lake Charles by Calcasieu Parish Sheriff Henry A. Reid.

On the trip back and later in the sheriff's office, he told his story. Here it is, as reported by Reid.

Wednesday Rideau, who had just turned 19 Monday, bought a .22 caliber pistol from a local pawn shop, apparently without any clear idea then of what he would do with it.

But last night he decided to rob the Gulf National Bank Southgate branch on Ryan street. At 7 p.m., the bank's Thursday night closing time he presented himself at the back door of the bank, and called the manager, Jay H. Hickman, 55, and told him "a woman" wanted to see him in the rear of the building.

Hickman recognized Rideau as ...ers were an employe of a fabric shop in ..., the job the shopping center where the Record bank is located, and complied. at neither Rideau told Hickman he "wanted ... or the some money" and showed him the ...pany had gun.

Rideau had come with a small ... suitcase, the kind women use for

CAPTURED! — Wilbert N. Rideau, left, is being taken into interrogation room by Calcasieu Parish Sheriff Henry A. Reid Jr. after Rideau was apprehended near Fenton. Reid later said Rideau had made a statement ad- mitting robbery of the Gulf National Bank's branch office at Southgate shopping center, and the shooting of three bank employes. (American Press Photo by Charles Murphy).

Sheriff Henry "Ham" Reid brings me into the Calcasieu Parish jail through the back door around 9:00 p.m. on February 16, 1961, to avoid the mob of several hundred angry whites awaiting my arrival in the front.

Personalities

Will Rogers Jr. Arrested

OCEANSIDE, Calif. (AP)—Will Rogers Jr., ex-actor, congressman and son of the late humorist, has been arrested near here on a morals count.

He was freed on $105 bail pending a court hearing after being booked Wednesday night on suspicion of lewd and disorderly conduct.

Rogers, 50, told The Associated Press "I will appear in court and plead innocent. I'm confident any fair judge will dismiss the case."

Rogers spoke to a newsman in Sacramento where he is attending to business of the State Park Commission, of which he is chairman.

Sheriff's Deputy Ralph D. Kratt said he arrested Rogers in his car on U. S. Highway 101 in nearby Leucadia. Kratt said Rogers was exposing himself indecently to other motorists.

New Appointment Made

WASHINGTON (AP)—President Kennedy has named Ramsey Clark, son of Supreme Court Justice Tom Clark, to be assistant attorney general in charge of the lands division. Job pays $20,000.

Clark, 33, is a Democrat and a Dallas lawyer.

Singer Returns to U. S.

FREETOWN, Sierra Leone (AP)—The body of Louis Armstrong's blues singer Velma Middleton will be flown to New York Saturday from Dakar. Miss Middleton was taken ill during an African tour with Armstrong's band and died in a hospital at Freetown last week. Her body was flown to Freetown Thursday.

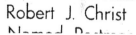

Robert J. Christ
Named Pastor

HEARING THE CHARGES — District Attorney Frank T. Salter Jr., left, last night's holdup of Gulf National Bank's Southgate branch. A woman

District Attorney Frank Salter had been in office only a few months at the time of my terrible (and sensational) interracial crime. He made his local reputation prosecuting me for it three times and opposing my release from prison for forty years, while supporting the release of numerous other convicted murderers.

The Reception Center building at the Louisiana State Prison, which housed death row, where I arrived on April 11, 1962, after being convicted of murder.

This is how I looked during my first day on Angola's death row.

Death row, where I was incarcerated from 1962 to 1973, between trials. In 2007, this facility was replaced by a new, larger death row.

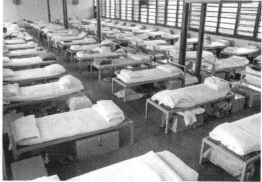

Most Angola inmates live in dormitories. *Top right:* A typical sixty-four-man dorm, and, *left,* its toilet facilities. Privacy was not part of prison life. *Left:* Inmates two abreast on the Walk, heading to the dining hall. Although the prison raised cattle and hogs, much of the meat was deemed too good for the prisoners and was sold on the open market. Cheaper food was purchased for the inmates. *Bottom:* A lone prisoner walks along the fence of the Big Yard, the recreation area for half of the Main Prison's 1,800 dormitory-housed inmates.

Relaxation takes many forms. *Top right:* A game of cards in the dorm. *Center:* Volleyball on the Yard. *Bottom left:* Basketball teams in the gym. *Bottom right:* Inmate musicians who entertain at internal prison events, such as the annual Angola Rodeo, and at church, civic, and political functions outside the prison.

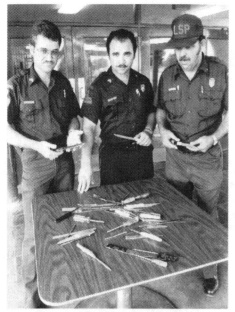

Guards survey a cache of weapons they discovered in the Main Prison. In the 1970s, everyone had weapons, most handmade. The prevailing sentiment among inmates was that they would rather be caught by security with a weapon than by a hostile prisoner without one.

James "Stinky" Dunn, seen here in 1978, was raped and sexually enslaved by another prisoner. Slaves were treated as property—rented, traded, gambled, sold. A slave won his freedom only through release from prison or the death of his master.

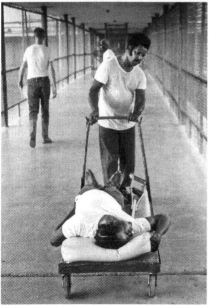

An inmate rushes another to the hospital on a buggy in the old days, before the federal court issued an order in 1975 to end the violence and improve prison conditions.

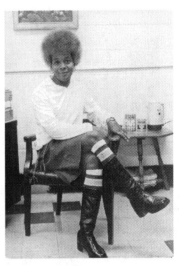

In a world without females, men sought sexual relief in masturbation and from sexual slaves, some of whom were gay but most of whom were weak inmates forced by stronger prisoners to serve as women. A slave did his master's bidding, whether that meant dancing, satisfying his sexual needs, doing laundry, prostituting, or smuggling contraband. Some embraced their prison roles as women. Most of the sexual violence in Angola was gradually ended.

Top: A seven-foot-by-nine-foot solitary-confinement cell, windowless, with a hatch in the door and a lightbulb on the ceiling, both controlled by a guard. *Left:* An isolation cell, distinguished by its front wall of bars, which lets the sights and sounds of humanity in. Either cell could be used for disciplinary reasons, protective custody, in-mates deemed a threat to security, or the mentally ill. The length of an inmate's stay in solitary confinement was at the discretion of authorities, ranging from overnight to, in some cases, more than thirty years.

All prisoners are required to work or to attend school. *Top:* Inmates study for their GEDs. *Bottom:* Paralegal students graduate.

Top: A guard marches laborers to the field. *Center:* Picking cotton by hand. *Bottom:* "Busting concrete" by hand.

Religious services conducted by inmate preachers were more popular than those led by resident chaplains, most of whom were viewed as time-serving bureaucrats. Angola has inmate-led congregations representing most Christian denominations. The Muslims, long misunderstood, became a powerful force for peace in the prison.

Ross Maggio, Jr., Angola warden, 1976–77 and 1981–84. Tough enough to tame the bloodiest prison in America in 1976, and tough enough to keep our prison newsmagazine, *The Angolite*, going when a hostile administration wanted to shut it down in 1981.

I was fortunate to be able to weave meaning and purpose into my prison life through print journalism, radio work as a documentarian and NPR correspondent, and producing television and documentary films. *Top left:* At my *Angolite* typewriter in 1977. *Top right:* At the prison radio station in 1987. *Middle:* Filming on the levee in 1994. *Bottom:* Speaking to high school students outside the prison.

"What you mean is that I could create a little problem for you with Mr. Phelps, but you can create a lot of big ones for me here," I said.

Maggio grinned. "Another thing you want to keep in mind: If a warden doesn't want a man to get out of prison, he's not gonna get out, and it doesn't matter who asks the parole and pardon boards to turn him loose." I knew that to be true.

I asked, "What kind of deal do you want to make?"

"Well, not so much a 'deal' as an understanding," Maggio said. "I'm not talking about censoring anything. Mr. Phelps doesn't want censorship. He wants you to be free to write what you want, and that's okay with me." Maggio knocked the ashes from one of the half-dozen Roi-Tan cigars he smoked daily. "But you're going to have more freedom to move and learn things than any other prisoner—and most employees—in this penitentiary, and common sense tells me that you will run across problems that I might not know exist. It's how you're going to handle that information that I'm interested in. If you're just looking for a sensational story to scandalize the prison and make me and my men look bad, then we're going to have a problem. And it's not going to be good for anyone if there's a legitimate problem that I could have solved but can't solve once it comes out. I've got to defend my men and their actions, and I'm going to do that.

"All I ask is that when you come across a legitimate problem that affects the prison, let me know about it. I'm not talking about snitching or giving me information about prisoners or other people's business. I'm never going to ask you anything like that. I'm simply talking about the kind of problems that affect the institution and my administration of it. You give me a chance to solve it first, then you can write whatever you want, stating that the warden's office either solved or didn't solve the problem. Then you're not going to have any difficulties with *The Angolite*. In fact, I want to see you and the paper do a good job because it's to my benefit."

What Maggio wanted was reasonable, and his wanting to defuse problems before they became public gave me an opportunity to approach him for solutions. Once a problem was brought to Maggio's attention, he would act on it.

So to deal with the former mental patient's problem, I called Frank Blackburn, associate warden for treatment. I explained the problem and said: "The public would never stand for this. There is something particularly offensive about sending a mentally ill person to a hospital for treatment and then punishing him for it."

"We didn't put those people in the field for punishment," Blackburn replied.

"I know—you put them out there to teach them good work habits," I said. "You can paint this thing any color you want, but there is no way you can justify sticking mental patients in the most stressful work detail in the prison."

"Warden Maggio gave the order and it's to be applied straight across the board—no exceptions. It's what he wants, and he's the warden."

"If this thing leaks to the news media," I said, "he'll get front-page coverage from New York to Bangkok. I'm sure he'd rather have you make logical exceptions."

"Well, Rideau, I don't have the authority to make an exception to Warden Maggio's orders."

I already knew that. "Then maybe you could take the policy to him and point out the need to make an exception. My guess is that when the media starts asking questions, his first question to you will be: 'Why wasn't I told about this?' "

After some more back-and-forth, Blackburn told me to send the names to him. "I'll talk to Warden Maggio," he said.

The problem was promptly resolved, and the former mental patients were reassigned to less stressful jobs.

And so I became kind of an unofficial ombudsman for the prison, solving many inmate problems through low-level prison officials who preferred to resolve the issues themselves rather than have me take them to Maggio or expose them in *The Angolite*. Indeed, many employees came to welcome my intervention. I liked being helpful, and I also liked the fact that my role as *Angolite* editor freed me from the deadening regimentation of prison routine. Unlike the lives of those who labored at difficult or mindless jobs, mine was determined rather by the events, intrigues, and problems of the day.

Instead of relieving overcrowding by releasing the old, infirm, and handicapped among its mostly black inmate population, as other states did, Louisiana, flush with oil money, instead chose in 1976 to build its way out. The state spent more than $100 million to construct and expand facilities, creating a lucrative prison-building boom for politically connected architects, contractors, and builders. Camp J, Angola's new maximum-security disciplinary cellblock, opened near the end of May 1977, just in time to take in a couple hundred of the seven or eight hundred rebellious fieldworkers staging a "work slowdown."

I rushed to the Control Center Gate, which led to the Big Yard, when I heard about the disturbance, because I wanted to photograph it. I was stopped by a guard who sent me back to the *Angolite* office. He was following the warden's instructions. Furious with Maggio, I complained to Phelps. He already knew about it.

"You probably won't appreciate this, but what Ross did was for your protection," he said. I told him I didn't need to be protected from the inmates, that Maggio did it to protect his guards from getting their picture taken doing something they didn't want anyone to see.

"A criminal will do just about anything to prevent exposure and punishment," said Phelps. "What makes you think a guard will respond any differently to your pointing that camera at him when he's beating an inmate with a baton, regardless of whether he's justified or not? Guards are like people everywhere: They don't always follow orders or obey rules or laws. Ross wasn't protecting them from you, but you from them. I can assure you those guards would have taken that camera from you, destroyed it, and probably hurt you very badly in the process. Freedom of the press is an ideal we're trying to make work in here, but our first priority is to protect life—in this instance, yours. You just confirmed that you weren't even aware of the danger you were about to walk into. Ross did the right thing."

I asked him if that meant our agreement that I wouldn't be censored was subject to the whim of the warden. He responded that there could be no free press if I was lying in a hospital bed. "In order to accomplish anything, both you and *The Angolite* have to survive," he said. "You know, Wilbert, people who have power don't always cooperate with the press. In fact, they will do almost anything to protect themselves from bad press." He told me publishing does not occur in a vacuum, and at times I would have to be creative in order to do what the power-holders didn't want me to do. He said publishers, editors, and reporters all over the world confront this same problem every day. He also pointed out that journalists didn't always have cameras. "But you still have the power of the pen," he said, "and the freedom to do what any good journalist would do—backtrack, investigate what happened, interview inmates and guards who were involved, then paint a word picture of what took place for your readers. Quit complaining—do your job."

My frustration at having been barred from covering the disturbance vanished as Phelps's lecture sank in. He had given me a broader context in which to see myself and my work. I wasn't just a prisoner who had been handed certain rights; I was a real journalist with a real job to do. Like the best journalists, I would sometimes have to be resourceful to surmount obstacles to a story. This new view of myself shaped my work in all the years to come.

7

Truth Behind Bars

1977–1981

When Tommy left to become the governor's personal valet, I decided it was time to add a white inmate to the staff of *The Angolite:* Billy Wayne Sinclair.

"You're gonna catch enough flak from blacks for putting a white boy in my place, without picking one the administration hates," Tommy said when I told him. "He's a criminal and a dopehead." Billy had recently emerged from a stint in the cellblock for possession of LSD. *Everyone* I knew advised against my bringing him on board.

I first met Billy in 1965, when he was a tall, skinny twenty-four-year-old who was shoved by angry deputies into the Hole near me behind the booking desk of the East Baton Rouge Parish jail. He had been on parole after serving a year in Angola for a sex offense, followed by a stint in the federal penitentiary at Terre Haute. He was already wanted for robberies in several states when he gunned down a popular convenience store manager in Baton Rouge. Hostile deputies perpetrated numerous little cruelties to make his stay in the Hole tough, like leaving his bright overhead light on even at night, so he couldn't sleep. To ease his misery, I passed him cigarettes and food, and once turned up my transistor radio so that he could hear a little music. For my trouble, the jailer transferred me to a solitary-confinement cell, the only black in the middle of the white section of the jail. Shortly afterward, I discovered Billy had been placed in the cell behind me. In the middle of winter, one of the jailers turned on an air conditioner that streamed cold air in on him. Freezing, his voice reduced to a whisper, Billy pleaded through a ventilation shaft for me to help him. I instigated the white inmates to rebel. Their protest brought in top officials, who rescued Billy. He would forever credit me with saving his life. As Billy was led out, the angry local sheriff vowed I would remain in my isolation cell as long as I was in his jail. He kept his word. I was there another two years, longer than any other prisoner held in isolation.

In 1966, Billy escaped. A week later, he was apprehended in Arkansas after committing another robbery. In March 1967, he was transferred to death row, where he spent much of his time loaded on drugs. At some point he began to do serious reading and ultimately filed a lawsuit against the long-term confinement of death row inmates in cells without any physical exercise. He won the suit, thereby acquiring a reputation as a jailhouse lawyer, which brought him some status among inmates.

In 1976, 63 percent of the inmates in Angola were functional illiterates. So the pool from which to draw someone for *The Angolite* who was reasonably proficient in English was small. I believed Billy had grown and improved as a result of his prison experiences, and I believed devoutly in second chances. He gave me his word that he would not use narcotics or do anything to bring disrepute upon *The Angolite*, and I knew he wasn't involved with any gangs.

When I told Maggio of my choice, he was irate: "You can forget Sinclair. He will not work on *The Angolite* as long as I'm warden." Phelps would not overrule Maggio.

The administration's hostility toward Billy stemmed from the many lawsuits he'd filed against the prison. To defuse opposition, he agreed he'd never file another suit against the warden, the institution, or any employee. The agreement entailed no real loss to the inmate population, because Billy's only success had been in the death row exercise case four years earlier. Peggi Gresham pointed out to Maggio that this was an opportunity to end Billy's legal terrorism of his employees. Maggio assigned him to *The Angolite*. To my surprise, Billy expressed relief: "That takes a big load off me, 'cause everybody wants me to file shit for them. This provides me the excuse to say no." He started work on the July/August 1977 issue.

Phelps, Gresham, Maggio, and other officials did not readily take Billy into their confidence regarding administrative processes and decision making. Gresham and I discussed the magazine's operations and management on the phone, in the lobby of the Main Prison, in her office, or wherever we met. Billy's medium-security status restricted his movement to within the Main Prison, which left me to attend conferences and meetings or to cover events elsewhere in the prison. Billy understood the officials' initial distrust of him and aimed to win them over. The Angola Jaycees, which he'd inherited when Tommy left, provided a perfect vehicle. He poured his energy into the organization and, after the Jaycees raised $1,000 for the Cystic Fibrosis Foundation, Maggio began to warm to him.

In November, Maggio revealed that he planned to leave at the end of the year to become warden of a new institution. In eighteen months, he had converted a violent Angola into one of the safest prisons in America. There had been only two killings in 1976 and one in 1977, with fewer than ten stabbings serious enough to require hospitalization. And he had done it without restricting freedom of expression for either inmates or employees. His wardenship began the most transparent and open prison administration in Louisiana history—possibly in American history—a transparency that would continue with his successor, Frank Blackburn.

As Maggio prepared to leave, the school of journalism at Southern Illinois University announced that *The Angolite*, the nation's only uncensored prison publication, had swept the American Penal Press Awards. It was cited for its "high quality and success in leading the way in new and responsible prison journalism." The awards were presented at Angola in a ceremony attended by the corrections and prison hierarchy as well as media from throughout the state. Our journalistic achievements were given widespread coverage in Louisiana, as was my editorship of *The Angolite*. I was good copy—something new and different.

I became something of a local celebrity, in demand as a speaker around the state. Shortly after the awards, the Alexandria police chief arranged for my transfer to his custody for a weeklong tour of his city's schools to talk to kids about the importance of doing the right thing in life. People wanted my autograph or a photo taken with me. They congratulated me, shook my hand, patted me on the back. Some women slipped me their phone number or address. One treated me to a tour of the city, and we made love on crushed clover on the outskirts of town, making a far-fetched prison fantasy come true.

Then came the announcement that *The Angolite* was one of five finalists in the category of specialized journalism for the 1978 National Magazine Awards. Administered by the Columbia University Graduate School of Journalism, the awards are the highest honors for the nation's magazine industry. Judges cited *The Angolite* for its "realistic reportage of what is happening behind prison walls." In the end, *Scientific American* won, but it was the first time a prisoner publication had ever been in such august company.

These were life-changing events for me. They marked the first time in my life that I had been publicly patted on the back for having done something good. It felt great. The honors increased *The Angolite*'s stature in the prison. When Warden Blackburn took over, he, like Phelps and Gresham, gave our journalism his unflinching support, and we were able to become more aggressive.

Energized, I mapped out major stories for the remainder of the year, selecting each for its potential impact or appeal to diverse segments of the prison community. The editorial mix I sought was first displayed in the July/August 1978 issue, which featured "Anatomy of a Suicide," Billy's chilling account of the life and death of his best friend, Billy Ray White, who committed suicide and slowly bled to death in the cell adjacent to Billy's while the two men talked; my profile of Peggi Gresham, the first female associate warden in a male prison in Louisiana; and an interview with New Orleans district attorney Harry Connick, the state's foremost opponent of the release of Angola prisoners. I also added a popular new section where readers could express themselves unedited. With this issue, too, I acquired illustrator Troy Bridges, which made the majority of the *Angolite* staff white.

Billy aspired to match my recognition as a professional journalist. He began to think hard about stories and to focus on writing objectively, which was difficult for him because he tended to moralize, seeing the world as black-and-white. I suggested he use his knowledge of the law to educate inmates about their rights, the workings of the justice system, and legal news and issues important to them. He took to it immediately, writing lengthy legal essays and delving into actual cases of Angola prisoners.

I concentrated on analytical features and investigative reports. In the September/October edition, I reported on old-timers lost in the bureaucracy of the system. In "Conversations with the Dead" I told of Frank "Cocky" Moore, who had been living in a tin shack and tending horses behind one of the prison's out-camps for thirty-three years—in a system that routinely released lifers after a decade of good behavior. The New Orleans *Times-Picayune* and other media picked up on my story, and Cocky was soon free.

Billy was impressed with the reaction of the outside world to the story, but I could sense his resentment, too. He was becoming more competitive. I feared that, because I didn't want there to be a winner and a loser. I asked Gresham to promote him to associate editor.

She bristled. "I am not going to promote anybody to improve their attitude," she said. She did, however, allow him to accompany me on a trip—his first—to Dixon Correctional Institute, less than an hour's drive from Angola, to do a story for our last issue of the year. Shortly afterward, we learned *The Angolite* had won top honors from the American Penal Press for best news reportage, the second consecutive year. Billy was promoted to associate editor with the publication of our March/April 1979 edition.

The Angolite's prominence grew. *Corrections Magazine* highlighted me in its March 1979 issue with a feature, "The *Angolite* Angle: A Louisiana Inmate Leads His Magazine into the Big Leagues of Journalism." The American Bar Association gave me its 1979 Silver Gavel Award for "Conversations with the Dead," for "outstanding contribution to public understanding of the American system of law and justice." It marked the first time in the ABA's hundred-year history that it had so honored a prisoner. Warden Blackburn went to Dallas to accept the award. Billy and I received a special 1979 Robert F. Kennedy Journalism Award "for bringing about a deep understanding of the lives and deaths of those imprisoned." The award was presented to Phelps and Blackburn by Senator Edward Kennedy and Ethel, widow of Robert Kennedy, during ceremonies attended by several hundred journalists at her Virginia home. Upon his return, Phelps instructed prisoner publications at other state facilities to follow our example. Supervisors and inmate staffers of the publications at both Dixon Correctional Institute and the women's prison at St. Gabriel traveled to Angola to meet us, study our operation, and discuss ways of improving their own.

My success and *The Angolite*'s were the latest signs in what I had long since begun to feel was a charmed existence. I had twice narrowly avoided being lynched following my arrest, then had been rescued from three consecutive death sentences by three unexpected landmark decisions by the U.S. Supreme Court. Thrown into the most violent prison in America, I not only survived, I thrived. "It's like something's

happening on a level that I don't understand," I told Phelps one afternoon when he stopped by my office.

"You're getting religion?" he asked, smiling.

"I don't know, but at what point do I ask, What the hell's going on?
I can't help wondering if some cosmic force or supernatural entity isn't
pushing me along a specific course in life, having saved me for some
unknown purpose I'm to serve."

"You've been blessed by an extraordinary amount of good fortune,"
Phelps said. "You want to make sense of it, and you will, eventually. But
the important thing to understand now is that you're uniquely pos-
tured to make a difference in the lives of others, to do a lot of good, and
to educate the public about the world of prison. *That* should be a personal mission with you, whether you feel a supernatural force nudging
you toward it or not. Society needs the information you are in the position to provide. This criminal justice business has a lot of experts—
we're good at studying statistics and pretending we know what we're
talking about, and while I can't speak for the other professionals, I
know we penal administrators fake it a lot. You can provide the kind of
truth that comes from firsthand experience."

I had, indeed, come to see *The Angolite* as my mission in life, my
path to redemption. It allowed me the satisfaction of helping others,
whether by educating them or solving problems. It also kept me in
touch with people outside prison, normal people, so I could mitigate
some of the effects of being institutionalized. The magazine gave me a
measure of control over my life; I could decide what stories to pursue
and set my own schedule. Every day held the promise of unpredict-
ability and discovery—giving tours, traveling, sitting in on meetings
with administrators, checking the levees that kept the Mississippi in
place, researching Angola's history, photographing the annual Angola
rodeo, and talking to scholars, media, and government officials from
Louisiana and elsewhere. Under Blackburn, *The Angolite* took flight.
Our staff began to tackle the kind of difficult subjects for which the
magazine would become famous: inequities in the system, lost and forgotten prisoners, the brutal realities of life behind bars.

We didn't do it alone. *The Angolite* gradually developed a network
of relationships with editors and journalists throughout Louisiana and
the nation upon whom I could call for information, photos, and general assistance. In return, we acted as a resource for them when they
wanted information on Angola, story ideas, or guidance on whom to

talk to—inmate or employee—about a particular issue. We became the de facto public information office for Angola and the Department of Corrections.

As we became more aggressive in covering our world, we had heated editorial conferences with Gresham and Phelps. The arguments were always over style and language. Phelps didn't want obscenities in the magazine. He wanted a publication that people could pick up off his coffee table or in a doctor's office and read without being offended. I felt we sometimes needed crude language to convey effectively the realities of prison life. "I was just thinking how my fellow penal administrators around the country would never believe what is taking place in this room," Phelps said in a flash of wry humor during one of our arguments.

But, in terms of reporting, *everything* remained fair game; officials had to cooperate and make information available. For "The Child-Savers," a story in the July/August 1979 issue, we went to Louisiana's largest reform school, the former State Industrial School for Colored Youths, where I had been sent as a teenager. My objective was to examine the prevailing view that the juvenile system was full of violent delinquents. I found what I expected: Although 68 percent of all the kids going to juvenile court in Louisiana in 1974 and 1975 were white, 68 percent of those sent to prison were black. The racial disparity held true for 1976 and 1977. Phelps, who had disagreed with my proposition of institutional racism, was surprised at the revelation. I also discovered that 85 percent of the 1,076 juveniles sent to prison in 1976–77 were there for nonviolent offenses. *Angolite* stories that exposed problems were normally followed by some type of administrative remedy, but "The Child-Savers" was not. The outside media apparently did not find these revelations of racism newsworthy; the statistics revealing lopsided juvenile justice would continue for the next quarter century.

What I felt to be my most important story, and the one that held the greatest potential to be censored, was "The Sexual Jungle." In 1979, penal administrators still universally lied about prison rape, characterizing it as an infrequent occurrence by aggressive homosexuals and sexual deviants. But, as I've said, it was an epidemic perpetrated primarily by heterosexuals, and it was an integral part of life in prison, condoned by security officers who were complicit in maintaining its existence. *Penthouse* senior editor Peter Bloch had asked me to write an article about rape and sex in prison, but he wouldn't allow me to write more than a thousand words, which, in my view, was insufficient to cover the subject. I turned down his offer of $1,000 (it wasn't easy). I decided, instead, to do an article in *The Angolite*, where I had as much space as I needed to properly deal with the subject. For the exposé, I interviewed officials, victims of sexual violence, perpetrators, and experts. To add a national perspective to the story, I turned to Ginger Roberts.

I'd met Ginger when she was a Louisiana State University law student clerking at the Department of Corrections. Phelps had asked me to look after her as she and a group of fellow students embarked upon a project to help Angola jailhouse lawyers. A New Yorker, she had done civil rights work in Mississippi before being invited to Louisiana by Elayn Hunt when she was director. We hit it off instantly, forming what would become a lifelong friendship. She became my first pro bono attorney and a staunch supporter of both my journalism and my freedom efforts. At my request, Ginger interviewed Dr. Frank Rundle in New York City for *The Angolite*. Having served as chief psychiatrist at the 2,200-man California Training Facility at Soledad and as director of psychiatry of Prison Health Services for all of the correctional institutions in New York City, Rundle provided the national overview I needed.

I opened my piece with a description of the assault I had witnessed in the East Baton Rouge Parish jail:

Leaving the bullpen, he strolled toward the cell area. Stepping into the darkened cell, he was swept into a whirlwind of violent movement that flung him hard against the wall, knocking the wind from him. A rough, callused hand encircled his throat, the fingers digging painfully into his neck, cutting off the scream rushing to his lips. "Holler, whore, and you die," a hoarse voice warned, the threat emphasized by the knife point at his throat. He nodded weakly as a rag was stuffed in his mouth. The hand left his neck. Thoughts of death moved sluggishly through his terror-stricken mind as his legs, weak with fear, threatened to give out from under him. An anguished prayer formed in his heart and his facial muscles twitched uncontrollably. He was thrown on the floor, his pants pulled off him. As a hand profanely squeezed his buttocks, he felt a flush of embarrassment and anger, more because of his basic weakness—which prevented his doing anything to stop what was happening—than because of what was actually going on. His throat grunted painful noises, an awful pleading whine that went ignored as he felt his buttocks spread roughly apart. A searing pain raced through his body as the hardness of one of his attackers tore roughly into his rectum. "Shake back, bitch!" a voice urged. "Give him a wiggle!" His rapist expressed delight as his body flinched and quivered from the burning cigarettes being applied to his side by other inmates gleefully watching. A sense of helplessness overwhelmed him and he began to cry, and even after the last penis was pulled out of his abused and bleeding body, he still cried, overwhelmed by the knowledge that it was not over, that this was only the beginning of a nightmare that would only end with violence, death, or release from prison.

Not only was the twenty-eight-page feature, illustrated with numerous photos, published in the November/December 1979 issue just as I wrote it, but Phelps and Gresham also incorporated it in Louisiana's corrections training programs as required reading for new employees. The administration's policy for dealing with sexual violence and homosexuality was revised: Once officials understood that openly gay inmates did not incite sexual violence and were often its victims, they stopped the wholesale lockup of overt homosexuals.

Later, following an American Corrections Association convention, Phelps told me that a number of corrections officials from other states could not understand why he was allowing me to do what I was doing, and they were especially displeased with "The Sexual Jungle." "We were sort of boycotted at the convention," he said, "which tells me that we must be doing something right." It was a comment that perfectly revealed Phelps's strength of character, not only to run a transparent prison but also to revel in it in the face of criticism by his peers.

My work was bringing me some much-needed positive recognition as I mounted another appeal to the pardon board. The Baton Rouge district attorney withdrew his opposition to my request for clemency. Former warden Henderson, now corrections commissioner in Tennessee, again supported my release. Phelps and Blackburn had been declaring publicly that I was rehabilitated. I had received an offer to write a book and another to make a movie about my life, offers I hoped would give me a good start when released from prison. Attorney Richard Burnes was going to make the case for my release near the end of Governor Edwin Edwards's term in office.

The hearing was held in Baton Rouge in January 1980. NAACP officers from Lake Charles and state vice president Rupert Richardson showed up to support me. Ginger got state representative Joe Delpit and Reverend T. J. Jemison, president of the National Baptist Convention, two of Louisiana's most powerful black leaders, to appear on my behalf, but only at the request of her boss, Camille Gravel, one of the state's most influential white lawyers. White Lake Charles politicians and bankers had led a letter-writing campaign against me. Frank Salter, victim Dora McCain, and staff from the Calcasieu Parish district attorney's office came to the hearing to oppose me. James Stovall, head of the Louisiana Interchurch Conference and former pastor for the McCain family, told the board that the most difficult thing he had ever done was to leave McCain's side and join those requesting my release. The board voted 3–2 against me. The crushing loss was made worse when I learned that Johnny Jackson, Sr., the only black on the board, cast the deciding vote. White reporters covering the hearing assumed the roomful of whites to be my opponents, when in fact they were predominantly supporters of mine from New Orleans and Baton Rouge.

I had been imprisoned nineteen years, longer than 99.9 percent of the inmates in Angola. I had expected to regain my freedom through the traditional 10-6 clemency process that had routinely freed lifers since 1926. Now, despite evidence in court records to the contrary, state officials alleged that no 10-6 release practice had ever existed, generating considerable frustration and anger among the lifer population, many of whom had entered into plea agreements with the expectation they would serve only ten years, six months. In 1979, the Louisiana legislature voted to repeal the very 10-6 law that officials said didn't exist. As we reported in *The Angolite*, Representative Raymond Laborde said the new law would "end the *old myth* that life in Louisiana means 10 years, six months. With this it will mean the rest of your life." That meant that the only way out of prison for lifers like me was through the new pardon board, which had just turned me down. I pulled my Guitar Slim cassette out of the drawer and closed the office door. I needed to sink down into the gutbucket blues.

· · ·

"The George Polk Award?" I asked, looking from Gresham to *New York Times* reporter Bill Stevens, who was sitting in her office.

"You don't know what you've won?" he said, then explained to me that it was one of journalism's most prestigious awards. After Stevens left, I asked Gresham to make Billy coeditor of *The Angolite*, since he had also won a Polk Award independent of my work. I told her it was the only way to ensure that he got equal media attention. She did not agree, but relented; and Billy was approved to become coeditor with publication of the May/June 1980 edition.

Following my interview with Stevens, the *Times* executive editor, Abe Rosenthal, whom I'd earlier asked for a job, phoned to congratulate me and wish me luck. He told me his paper would be keeping an eye on me. That was followed by a call from David Jones, the paper's national editor, who inquired whether any other media had shown interest in my winning the Polk Award. I told him no. "That'll change," he said. Shortly after the publication of Stevens's front-page story on me, the other national media descended. A barrage of phone calls was followed by a stream of reporters seeking interviews. One helicopter transporting an NBC team mistakenly landed in the Main Prison Trusty Yard instead of on the prison airstrip, alarming security officers. Had they landed in the Big Yard, they probably would've drawn gunfire from the tower guards.

Because neither Billy nor I could attend the awards ceremony at the Roosevelt Hotel in New York, Blackburn and Gresham stood in for us. Gresham said they were besieged by agents, reporters, and cameras wherever they went: "It was as if New York City had just gone *Angolite*-crazy!"

A month later, "The Sexual Jungle" made *The Angolite* a finalist for the 1980 National Magazine Award, though it didn't win.

Inspired by the honors our magazine received, the staff became even more aggressive. At Ethel Kennedy's suggestion, we wrote about the mentally retarded offender, who is easy prey for the rapists and strong-armers. We revealed how mail-order companies use prisons as dumping grounds for shoddy, defective products. We exposed the gross inadequacy of medical services at Angola, after which we were advised that we had better not need medical care anytime soon.

Many of our best stories originated with an official or employee. During an interview in his office, I told New Orleans district attorney Harry Connick that I couldn't imagine him being as candid with the mainstream media as he was with us. "You guys are different, Wilbert," he said. "You understand this business from the inside out; the others don't."

Now people throughout the Louisiana corrections system wanted to be in *The Angolite*. Lonely prisoners hoped exposure would get them a girlfriend or freedom. Officials and employees yearned for the professional recognition we could confer, or sought to use us as a conduit for additional resources or change. The honors and publicity we received also raised prisoners' expectations. We constantly fielded pleas to get a better prison job, improve an inmate's custody status, and address all kinds of personal problems. I once received a letter from an inmate in the mental health cellblock who believed I was responsible for "the garbage" he was being fed and demanded I change his menu "or else."

Billy and I traveled around the state unshackled and accompanied by an unarmed security officer to cover official events, to report on other facilities, to lecture at universities, and, in response to requests, to talk to at-risk kids.

We were sometimes overwhelmed by the demands on us and we knew we needed help. Tommy Mason had lost his job as the governor's valet after getting drunk and making a play for a female guest at the governor's mansion, and he had been returned to Angola. I asked him to rejoin *The Angolite*, though Billy opposed it.

I soon saw that there was a dark side to success. The ambitious and manipulative—inmates and employees alike—sought to cultivate us; the jealous and resentful, to bring us down. Some of my critics wrote letters full of lies to the pardon board (and God only knows who else) to sabotage my freedom efforts. A sympathetic official showed me some of the letters so I'd know who my enemies were and what they said and could protect myself.

More worrisome to me were the machinations of Jack Rogers, a Lake Charles attorney who, in talks with prisoners and in addressing a group of 10-6 lifers, was saying I was the biggest liability to the legal challenge they had mounted because "no judge will ever vote to let Rideau out of prison." I complained to Blackburn, Gresham, and Phelps that Rogers was creating a dangerous situation for me. They assured me they would handle it, and I never again had trouble with Rogers or with the inmates he spoke to, but I wondered, when Angola security warden Walter Pence told me there were rumors of a contract on my life coming out of Lake Charles, if it had anything to do with Rogers. The rumor mill is one of the most maddening aspects of prison life, and prisoners used it regularly to inflict anxiety—and insomnia—on a foe. My paranoia was pricked, and I sent word to all my friends and allies throughout the prison to keep me abreast of all new arrivals from southwest Louisiana and arranged to have no new inmate from that area live or work around me. I was glad I had Billy and Tommy to watch my back.

In late 1980 Elin Schoen came down to research a story on *The Angolite* for *The New York Times Magazine.* Like many outsiders, she was puzzled by my inability to get clemency in Louisiana when it was routinely given to others convicted of murder. She went to Edwin Edwards, who had left the governor's mansion some months earlier after eight years' residence. She asked Edwards, whose liberality in granting commutations was legendary, why I couldn't get one.

"Rideau was a black who had killed a white person," Edwards told Schoen. "There has never been a case where a black had killed a black where there was this kind of furor over it when the criminal came up for clemency. It's easy to raise community feelings over Rideau. But community feelings shouldn't be given that much weight."

I was stunned when I read of the nonchalance with which Edwards acknowledged the virulent racial animosity in white Lake Charles and the power that community had to enforce its will. More demoralizing still was Schoen's discovery that before my clemency hearing, Edwards "phoned a pardon board member who was known to be a Rideau supporter and requested that this person vote against Rideau." That person was, of course, Johnny Jackson, Sr. "It was just gonna be a hot potato," a source requesting anonymity told Schoen. "Edwards wasn't gonna make any friends in the Lake Charles area."

After a gloomy session listening to the blues, I took heart in the *Times Magazine* revelation that Edwards's behind-the-scenes finagling was responsible for the pardon board denial—meaning that if I had been judged on the merits, I would've gotten the recommendation. That gave me hope that I could win clemency from the new pardon board that had come in with Republican governor Dave Treen. Treen was reputed to be tough on crime and promised to be tightfisted with clemencies, but that didn't worry me, because I knew that no one could match my record and my accomplishments. Moreover, I knew a couple of members of Treen's newly appointed board to be sincere professionals, and I trusted they would be fair.

Meanwhile, Louisiana appeared to be nearing its first execution since 1961. News reporters were making the pilgrimage to Angola to do stories on the death penalty as a prelude to the scheduled April 8, 1981, execution of Colin Clark. Billy and I went to the death house at Camp F on March 17 to get photos for a single-topic edition we planned to do on capital punishment. We encountered two television crews there getting film footage of the electric chair and the death chamber. They wanted to interview us about the death penalty, and Warden Blackburn suggested we help them out.

A few days later we were interviewing Blackburn in his office when Baton Rouge WAFB-TV reporter Jodie Bell, whom we met at the death house, phoned and asked to talk to Billy. Billy took the call in a nearby office. When he returned, he said that Bell wanted to know how far it was from Angola's front gate to the death house; I wondered briefly why she hadn't just asked whoever answered the phone for that information. A couple of weeks later, Bell showed up at corrections headquarters in Baton Rouge, where we had gone to interview an official. Shortly thereafter, Billy told me he'd gotten a letter from Bell saying she had requested permission from the warden to see us again for her death penalty series.

She came alone. We saw her in a private interview room, unsupervised. We mostly chatted; occasionally she asked specific questions and jotted notes. Later she visited us again, to gather information for a story about us for *Gambit*, a New Orleans weekly.

One night soon after that, security summoned me from my office to take a phone call from the media concerning *The Angolite*. A distressed Jodie Bell told me that she had found out "everything about Billy" and angrily railed about his not having told her about his long criminal history.

"What's with you and Jodie Bell?" I asked Billy, once I had returned to my office. He told me that they had been corresponding and communicating on the phone. "She just called me, and she sounded hysterical," I said. "Call her. And tell her that she cannot call here like that again. She's putting our *Angolite* phone privileges in jeopardy."

The next morning, Billy confessed to being madly in love with

Bell, the fortyish wife of a New Orleans journalism professor and mother of three. She had recently embarked upon a career in television journalism. She did her television work in Baton Rouge during the week and visited her family in New Orleans on weekends.

Billy said he was going to continue to see Jodie in the unsupervised, closed-door privacy of the room in which we had met with her previously; that would be possible only if Jodie requested the visits as legitimate journalistic interviews. I realized that my inclusion in her last two visits had been merely to give them credence. I told him that she should leave my name out of future "interview" requests because I would not jeopardize my hard-earned credibility by participating in their ruse.

Billy's conduct put me in a bind. *The Angolite* was everything to me—both my mission and what made my life in Angola bearable and meaningful, and what I hoped would prepare me for life after my release. Billy was playing Russian roulette not only with his own life but also with mine.

What were my options? Telling Gresham about Jodie and Billy's private trysts would likely lead to Billy's dismissal from the magazine; Gresham would regard his actions as a betrayal of the trust she placed in him. Moreover, if Gresham learned that Jodie was abusing her journalistic credentials to have private romantic visits with Billy, she might severely curtail all media access to Angola and *The Angolite*, which was a benefit to the prisoners and essential to our operation. That would be good for no one.

As a man who had been deprived for far too long, I couldn't condemn Billy for wanting romance with the willing Jodie Bell. Torn as I was, I kept my mouth shut and prayed that Billy and Jodie didn't get busted.

8

Disillusion
1981—1986

The *Angolite* enjoyed remarkable freedom to investigate and criticize prison management, policies, and practices under Warden Blackburn, so it was ironic that what nearly brought us down in early 1981 was a story about a toilet and another about religion.

A maverick guard had put a lock on a communal toilet in the education building because he did not want to sit on a toilet seat used by an inmate. This was the sort of petty, arbitrary exercise of power—at once both humiliating and inconvenient to inmates—that gave daily prison life a sense of madness and superfluous cruelty. At *The Angolite*, we saw the guard's action as an opportunity for satire, which we ordinarily avoided because we felt every aspect of prison life was serious business. Billy wrote an accordingly lighthearted piece for our January/February 1981 issue called "The Locked John." The other feature in that edition was "Religion in Prison," in which I observed that the Catholic Church, the biggest and most powerful in Louisiana, had turned a cold shoulder to the imprisoned, literally abandoning ministry to them.

When the magazine was distributed throughout the prison, Billy and I were on a speaking engagement in the northeastern part of the state. Walter Pence, Angola's security warden, phoned to tell me there was growing anger among his guards, some of whom were threatening to firebomb the *Angolite* office because Billy had written "prison guards, like defensive linemen, are not known for their dazzling brilliance." Other guards complained to their state legislators that we should be shut down. Pence suggested that we consider extending our speaking trip to allow the furor to diminish. But if prison had taught us nothing else, it taught us that you can't solve a problem if you are running from it. We immediately returned to Angola, where I enlisted the help of Lieutenant Colonel Richard Wall, security chief of the Main Prison, and some other influential officers with whom I had good relations, to help mollify the angry guards.

At the same time, the bishop of the Catholic diocese of Baton Rouge, the Very Reverend John Sullivan—later discovered to have been a not-so-reverend pedophile—was offended by my article on the church and took his complaint and political clout to Governor Edwards, but Phelps stood firm.

Clinton Baudin, a vulgar, red-faced, beer-bellied officer, had meanwhile mounted a continuing vendetta against me and the magazine. On the last day of August, Louis Ortega, one of our two illustrators, overslept after working late the night before and thus missed reporting for his "extra duty" assignment that morning. Baudin cited Ortega for "aggravated work offense," a serious disciplinary infraction, and removed him to the Dungeon. Before he left, Baudin turned to Larry Stegall, our second illustrator, and said, "You're next."

Shortly afterward, Major W. J. Norwood, who had locked up Billy almost a decade before for possession of narcotics, led three officers into the *Angolite* office, where they strip-searched Billy and had him wait outside while they shook down the office. After about an hour, the officers departed. They had rummaged through photos, files, mail, confidential notes, and interviews. Worse, they had obviously listened to a cassette containing an interview with condemned prisoner Colin Clark, which we had been keeping confidential at the request of Clark's attorney.

When Phelps learned what had happened, he assured me, "I'll handle Norwood and those officers—in my own way."

A couple of weeks later, in September 1981, Phelps was fired. Republican governor Dave Treen, who'd assumed power the year before, said he ousted Phelps because of "philosophical differences." Phelps, a Democrat, had been critical of the throw-away-the-key prison-building policies that were feeding a corrections system in which more than half of its inmates were confined for nonviolent property offenses.

He was equally critical of the governor's stinginess on clemency, which he predicted would make Angola the world's largest old folks' home.

Treen replaced Phelps with John T. King, a political crony who had a background in business. Within two weeks, the new regime restricted editorial content in all prison publications. Department of Corrections headquarters shut off its flow of information to *The Angolite*, canceled equipment purchases, curtailed supply orders, and put our staff under investigation.

On October 8, King transferred Frank Blackburn out of Angola and brought Ross Maggio back as warden. Phelps and Maggio now led opposing factions of employees, and Maggio immediately got rid of Blackburn's top administrators, who were Phelps loyalists. Peggi Gresham was stripped of much of her power.

On his second night back, Maggio came to the *Angolite* office. "Been hearing all kinds of rumors about y'all," he said.

"I'm surprised at you, Warden," I said, "believing prison rumors."

He didn't smile. "Heard y'all also been running the prison."

"About as much as when you were here. People listen to us, just as you did. You know, we only have as much power as people think we have," I said.

"Well, there's some people believe you have too much, that *The Angolite* has gotten out of hand." He took a seat. "Hell, I could get elected to public office running against *The Angolite*. There's some highly placed people want y'all out of business."

"Are you putting us out of business, Warden?" Billy asked, handing him a Department of Corrections directive to all inmate organizations suspending "any type of newsletter or magazine."

"Let's put it this way," said Maggio. "I'm not gonna be the warden who shut *The Angolite* down. If they want to put y'all out of business, they are gonna have to do it themselves."

King moved quickly against us. On October 16, a Department of Corrections official wrote: "I do not feel that it is in the interest of this department or the inmates to publish derogatory information regarding public officials."

When an inmate was killed while sitting at the kitchen table in Camp H shortly after Maggio's return, neither employees nor officials would talk to us for fear of offending the new regime. Nonetheless, Maggio told us to continue to operate as we had in the past, that *he*— not corrections headquarters—would determine how we operated.

When we threatened to alert the national media about what was happening and take the King administration to court over it, Phelps sent a message advising me not to engage the new powers in a war because they were mean-spirited enough to destroy us. He assured me that whatever his faults, Maggio was his own man.

Maggio warned us that he would have "to trim [our] sails a little to pacify some people," but at least we'd stay in business. Unfortunately, that put an end to a project Phelps had approved for Louisiana Public Broadcasting, in which they were to give us cameras and train us to produce television reports. Our freedom to travel outside the prison ended, and our telephone communications with the outside world were reduced. We were unable to purchase new equipment—typewriters, cameras, tape recorders—and our yearly budget gradually dropped 40 percent even as the spending for other inmate operations increased.

Jodie Bell's visits with Billy were ended when Maggio learned of them. She then chose to quit her television job rather than give Billy up. Billy was now so stressed that he sometimes found it difficult to keep his anger under control. During one editorial conference, he was so contentious with Maggio, I was afraid the warden might lock him up. After Jodie divorced her husband, she and Billy refused to ask Maggio for permission to wed, as inmates were required to do. Instead, they married by proxy; then, as his wife, she automatically qualified to visit him.

Jodie had convinced me she was a friend, so I was surprised when one day pardon board chairman Sally McKissack came to the prison, alarmed. "Jodie has an agenda, Wilbert, and it's to get Billy out," Sally told me. "Now, there's nothing wrong with that. The problem is the manner in which she's pursuing it. In her talks with me and other board members about Billy, she deliberately misrepresents facts at your expense. To hear her tell it, Billy is the one who took over the magazine and made it into what it's become, and you're just a figurehead. You would do well to be wary of her."

Sally, whom I had known for about seven years, wanted me out of prison. Her strategy was to push a clemency application through for Billy first; she had enough votes on the board and felt certain she could get Governor Treen, despite his hard-line stance on clemency, to commute Billy's sentence. Then the board would issue a similar clemency recommendation for me, putting the governor in the position of having to commute my sentence or explain why he granted clemency to the white *Angolite* editor but not the black one. Sally was convinced that Treen would do that, particularly since he was making a genuine effort to court black voters, which Louisiana Republicans had never done before.

Billy completely surrendered himself to Jodie, who became the driving force in his life. He would echo Jodie's ideas about what we should or should not do at *The Angolite*—to the point that I had to remind him frequently that Jodie was not on the staff, nor was she knowledgeable about the world we lived in.

"The *Angolite* experiment is dead," Billy declared solemnly one day. "Jodie agrees. The concept of a free press [in prison] can't and won't work because the Department of Corrections wants us destroyed, and the only reason we're not is because of Maggio, who, while saving us, has also killed our operation."

"We're not dead," I said, urging him to keep things in perspective. *The Angolite* was still functioning at a higher level and with more resources than when Phelps initially freed the magazine from censorship in 1976. I said that no publication perpetually functioned under ideal circumstances. Important and controversial issues could still be addressed, thanks to Maggio. Billy wasn't convinced.

Louisiana's prison publications would not fare well during the King regime. Only *The Angolite* and the *Hunt Walk Talk* of Hunt Correctional Center survived. Of course, with the flow of information and physical access reduced, we couldn't do all that we wanted to. At the day-to-day level we functioned as usual, though employees erred on the side of caution by checking with Maggio before giving us an interview or solving a prison problem we brought to their attention. Billy and I redirected some of our energies into freelance writing for state and national publications, and we even produced a column, "From the Inside," for the Fortune Society of New York.

And we focused on getting out of Angola, which required patience. Because we no longer traveled outside the prison, opportunities to meet new people and advance our cause had been greatly curtailed. Jodie got a high-powered New Orleans attorney, Jack Martzell, to represent Billy before the pardon board, but we were relying primarily upon Sally's strategy.

One afternoon following Billy's clemency hearing, Tommy entered the office with a wide smile. He waved a letter and told us the pardon board had recommended that the governor commute his life term to thirty years, making him immediately eligible for parole since he had already served one-third of that term. "You have a letter from the board, too," he said to Billy, handing him the letter as he left.

Billy tore open the envelope. He looked surprised as he read, then puzzled. "I don't understand this." The pardon board had recommended a reduction in his sentence to sixty years, which, if approved by the governor, would make Billy eligible for parole in a few more years, after he had served twenty.

"This doesn't make sense," he said. "They're going backward." In 1979, a clemency recommendation urged that his sentence be reduced to forty-five years, but Governor Edwards had not approved it. "The only thing that's different is that I've won national awards since then. It's like I'm being punished for doing more. I've been locked up longer, and I've accomplished more than Tommy and all these others who're getting recommendations that will free them right away." He became distraught. "How am I going to explain this to my wife? Jodie's been preparing for my release, buying furniture and making a home for us."

I was surprised. The typical commutation recommended for someone serving a life term was for thirty or thirty-five years, maybe forty. Sally was scheduled to address an inmate organization that evening in Angola, and I suggested he ask her what happened before phoning his wife. As the day wore on, he grew angrier. He saw himself as a victim, discriminated against. There was no reasoning with him.

That evening, Sally explained to him that the board felt a recommendation for a commutation to sixty years was all the current governor would sign for him. Billy stormed away. Sally then turned to me. "Prepare yourself, Wilbert," she said. "You'll get a seventy-five-year recommendation, which will parole you out in a few more years." She saw my disappointment. "I'm sorry," she said, "but at least you'll be getting out, just not now."

A few weeks later, Billy showed me a lawsuit he had filed against the pardon board. In it, he argued that the recommended cut to sixty years was more severe than a life sentence, which traditionally had given an inmate parole consideration after ten years and six months. He also included a list of clemency recommendations for other inmates as a means of comparison. Tommy's name was among them. He told me that Jodie had "heard through a source" that the governor's office was investigating the pardon board.

"If that's true, then your putting all these guys in your lawsuit will put political heat on their recommendations. The governor won't touch them," I said.

"I can't help that," he replied harshly. "Those are the facts that show I'm being discriminated against. Besides, if I can't get out, why should they?"

"What are you doing, man?" I asked. "Sally's plan calls for me to go up next. You could be screwing things up for both of us."

"And what am I supposed to do? Keep my mouth shut and let 'em fuck over me and my wife? I can't do that, and I won't do it. I have a constitutional right to express my grievance and pursue redress. Like Jodie says, if Sally and the governor want to do something for you, they'll do it regardless of what I do."

But that's not how things worked. Sally and fellow board member Louis Jetson, a longtime black supporter, visited me soon afterward to advise me to postpone applying for clemency until some of the hard feelings among the board members had died down.

"Jodie tried to pressure the board to change their decision with threats that she and Billy might commit suicide to embarrass the board," Sally told me. "And Billy has sued the board, which makes absolutely no sense at all because he doesn't have a right to anything. Clemency is a gift of mercy." She paused.

My dream of freedom was dissolving.

"We no longer have the votes," Jetson said, shaking his head. "Those on the board who were receptive to doing something for you and Sinclair are pissed. We're hoping to salvage you, but I have to tell you, at this point, it doesn't look good."

There was no clemency hearing for me during the four years Dave Treen was governor.

I continued to work alongside Billy, though it wasn't easy. I swallowed my anger, but my friendship with him was over.

Governor Treen turned out to be so stingy in granting clemency that some of the state's newspapers charged him with abdicating his responsibilities as governor. By the end of his second year in office, he had granted only nine commutations. When he ran for reelection in 1983, he boasted of having issued only forty clemencies to prisoners as compared with the thousands granted by Edwin Edwards, who was making a bid to become governor for a third time. Treen was executing a callous political strategy, but it fueled hopelessness among the prisoner population. The situation at the prison became so incendiary that Maggio, who had never asked for the release of a prisoner, suggested to Sally that the governor commute the sentences of a couple of deserving lifers to relieve tensions at Angola. The debate over clemency took center stage at the height of the gubernatorial campaign when Edwards's brother, Nolan, was shot to death by an ex-felon whom Edwards had previously freed. Edwards nonetheless steadfastly maintained that executive clemency was an integral part of Louisiana's justice system and indicated that if elected he would again grant clemency to deserving persons.

The hope that Edwards might win staved off serious prison disturbances during the latter part of Treen's administration. Inmate organizations provided resources for the prisoner population to conduct letter-writing campaigns encouraging friends and relatives to vote for Edwards. And, for perhaps the first time in history, the entire inmate population and employee force watched the televised election results. When Edwards was declared the winner by a landslide, cheering by both the keepers and the kept erupted throughout the prison. The seething despair eating away at the Louisiana State Penitentiary was quieted overnight as hope, the balm of the prison world, was restored. Edwards reinforced it by establishing a Forgotten Man Committee to look into the increasing number of long-termers in prison.

Prisoners' expectations soared when Edwards appointed the state's first majority-black pardon board. Its chairman, Howard Marsellus, a brash, streetwise high school principal, roared up to Angola on a motorcycle, "bringing hope," he declared. "There are guys up here who deserve a second chance, and I'm gonna try to see that they get it." This had special significance to blacks, who constituted 80 percent of the state's prisoner population.

Marsellus came to personify hope to everyone—except Billy. After shaking hands with Billy during a meeting in our office, Marsellus reached for my hand and introduced himself as "the man who's gonna get *you* out of here."

"What about me?" Billy asked, smiling.

"Those white folks under Treen already took care of you. You got your issue," he said, referring to Billy's still viable recommendation for a reduced sentence of sixty years. Marsellus then told Tommy that his thirty-year recommendation was also still good. Looking back at me, he said, "It's this brother's turn. And this is the board and the governor who'll do it." He instructed me to file a clemency application. "We'll try to have you out of here for Christmas."

I fought to contain my exhilaration, and could see Tommy struggling to do the same, because we could see that Billy was ready to explode.

"I'm not accepting that shit he's talking," Billy said after Marsellus left. "He's gonna free y'all, but fuck over me because I'm white? What does he take me for?" He stormed out of the office, slamming the door.

Governor Edwards brought back C. Paul Phelps as secretary of corrections, which meant the return of freedom of expression for inmates and staff throughout the system, and the resurrection of *The Angolite* to its former status. A few months into Edwards's term, Ross Maggio retired, and Frank Blackburn returned as Angola warden. Our May/June 1984 issue reflected our restored access to information and officials: I did a major investigative report, "Dying in Prison," which revealed how terminally ill prisoners at Angola met their end—chained to a hospital bed if they were sent for treatment to one of Louisiana's charity hospitals—and, for those whose bodies went unclaimed by family or friends, a trip to a local funeral home, where the corpse was placed in a pressed-cardboard box and returned to Angola for burial in a service presided over by the prison chaplain and attended mainly by inmate gravediggers.

I resumed traveling outside the prison for speaking engagements and to pursue stories. On advice from his attorney, Billy declined trips as part of an effort to stay out of the limelight and to distance himself from me in the public mind, since I was high profile. He refused to talk to the media, leaving me to speak for *The Angolite* and about prisoner issues.

I went around the state talking to at-risk teenagers and young adults on probation about the horrors of prison life. I lectured at schools, universities, and churches, to civic and professional groups, and made numerous appearances on television to talk about prison, including a June 19, 1984, appearance on *Nightline;* unable to resist the lure of trading views with U.S. Supreme Court Chief Justice Warren Burger on national television, Billy joined me.

Once again I had access to the inner sanctum of corrections man-

agement. Phelps took me to meetings where I learned that everything about inmates in corrections was tied to dollars, that every
day an inmate wasn't working translated into money lost to Prison
Enterprises, which accounted for the constant administrative pressure on prison medical authorities to be conservative in issuing work
exemptions to inmates because it reduced the available labor pool for
agricultural and industrial operations. I also attended regulatory stan-
dardization meetings where top officials of every prison met to review
practices to achieve system-wide uniformity and end costly duplica-
tion. I learned that prison was becoming a vast business, which was a
boon to some politicians, who demanded more "law and order," which
meant more arrests, more convictions, longer jail terms, and more jobs
and contracts for goods and services they could dole out to supporters.

Where there had been only three state prisons in Louisiana when I
became editor of *The Angolite* in 1976, there were now six, with more
on the drawing board and thousands of state prisoners backlogged in
local jails around the state. Historically, jails and prisons had to be built
with voter approval, but in 1985 Governor Edwards got the legislature
to create the Louisiana Correctional Facilities Corporation, which
allowed the state to expand and build prisons without public consent.
That created a monster with an insatiable appetite for growth. The
most basic law of the prison system is that as long as there is a cell,
someone will be found to put in it. In Louisiana, the "product" would
be primarily black males, while the beneficiaries of this prison industry
were almost all white. Phelps began to despair of any meaningful
change in the way the state pursued justice. He foresaw that corrections, driven by profit and politics, would ultimately be reduced to simply warehousing people for increasingly longer periods.

If Edwards's return as governor brought hope to those in the penal
system, it did not extend to the condemned. As he was leaving office,
Dave Treen had resurrected capital punishment in Louisiana by sign-
ing off on the executions of two men. Only a couple of weeks after
Edwards moved back into the governor's mansion, his new pardon
board convened at Angola on April 1 for its first full clemency hearing:
Elmo Patrick Sonnier received a death sentence in 1977 for the kidnapping and murder, with his brother Eddie, of two St. Martin Parish
teenagers (Eddie received a life sentence).

Eddie testified at Elmo's hearing, and the brothers now claimed
Eddie actually did the killings. They weren't very convincing. Dismiss-

ing the Sonniers' claim as a ruse and rejecting an impassioned plea for
mercy from Elmo's spiritual advisor—a naive, fresh-faced Catholic nun
named Sister Helen Prejean—the board voted to let Elmo die in the
electric chair on April 5.

As the board members headed for the exit, Marsellus introduced
them to me. Lawrence Hand, the board's only white, shook my hand
politely, telling me he was impressed with *The Angolite*. Johnny Jackson, Sr., who had voted against me in the past, put his arm around my
shoulder when we were alone and whispered, "We're gonna take care
of you this time around. The last time wasn't right." A smiling Lionel
Daniels pumped my hand and told me he was from St. Landry Parish,
the family home of my parents, and winked meaningfully.

A statuesque, well-dressed, light-complexioned woman—the board's
only female—offered her hand, smiling as if she knew something that I
didn't. "I'm Margery Hicks," she said. "We've met before, but I'm sure
you've forgotten." Seeing my puzzlement, she added, "Reform school—
remember Coach Hicks? I was his wife." I remembered her husband
lining us kids up and whipping our asses with a thick strap. I nodded.
"He died four years ago," she said.

"You guys didn't do a very good job rehabilitating me back then," I
said.

"No," she said, then laughed. "But judging from what I've heard,
this place apparently did. I'm really proud of you." I felt good after
meeting her and instinctively knew she would vote to free me.

These pardon board members frequently came to Angola to interview inmate applicants and to attend administrative events and prisoner
programs, as had their predecessors. Marsellus, in particular, became a
regular at the prison, searching for "deserving" inmates to help. I also
met the board members at headquarters or outside events. Like many
in the criminal justice system, they sometimes called upon *The Angolite*
for advice or help with research, which I generally provided.

Hicks stopped by *The Angolite* whenever she came to the prison,
and I gradually got to know this strong, well-educated, brassy redhead.
She had retired from the juvenile corrections system and become a
member of the Scotlandville Area Advisory Council, a powerful black
political group in Baton Rouge. She had been given the pardon board
appointment as part of Edwards's payoff to her political group for their
support in his reelection. As time passed and our friendship grew, she
took me into her confidence and provided me with a behind-the-scenes

view into the workings of the board that would destroy all my remaining illusions about its fairness.

At an August 7, 1984, hearing, New Orleans lawyer Bill Quigley made a powerful presentation to the pardon board, arguing that his client Timothy Baldwin might well be innocent of the murder of an elderly Monroe woman. The board rejected the claim and denied Quigley's plea to have Baldwin's death sentence commuted to life imprisonment. As his September 10 execution date neared, Baldwin persisted in his claim of innocence. Then came the sensational news that Governor Edwards had flown to Angola on August 28 and met with Baldwin for an hour. The following day, Edwards flew to the women's prison to talk with Baldwin's codefendant, his ex-girlfriend Marilyn Hampton. The next day, the governor explained to the media that he had bent over backward "doing some unprecedented things to make certain in my own conscience that I was acting properly." But he was not going to stop the execution. Baldwin thanked Edwards publicly for his time and consideration. Hicks, however, was infuriated. "He shouldn't have played with Baldwin's feelings like that," she said to me. "He knew he wasn't going to do anything for the man."

I didn't understand her objection. "Edwards went the extra mile to personally find out what happened in Baldwin's case," I said. "How many governors would do that? I'm impressed."

"Everybody's impressed," she said. "That's why he did it. But Edwin Edwards is the joker who told us to deny clemency to Baldwin in the first place, just as he did with Sonnier. Now, are you still impressed?"

She told me that the governor ordered their claims denied before the hearings were even held. "He didn't care whether they were innocent or not. He doesn't want the board to send him any recommendations for clemency on death penalty cases. We were told from day one just to go through the motions, but to deny them all."

While wearing a public mask of understanding and compassion, Edwards would ruthlessly execute more men than any Louisiana governor in modern times. And I could do nothing about it because no one would go on the record.

Hicks told me that clemency proceedings were fraudulent only in death penalty cases. She assured me that although Edwards had personally sabotaged the board's decision on me in 1976 and 1980, it was extremely unlikely that he would do it again. "He got busted," she said, "and *The New York Times* told the world what he did. More importantly, he knows that he would not be governor if it weren't for us blacks. The fact that he appointed the first majority-black pardon board and chairman in history is proof of that. So you're coming out of this place. He owes us that."

The board held a hearing on my request for clemency on December 19, 1984. It was covered by *USA Today* and *The New York Times* and on the front pages of newspapers all across Louisiana. White opponents in Lake Charles cranked up their anti-Rideau machine, while the Lake Charles black community launched a letter-writing campaign on my behalf. The pardon board received nearly three thousand letters in all, which the *Times-Picayune* reported ran about 4-to-1 in favor of granting mercy.

In keeping with the board's rules, I could not attend the hearing. The board heard from both sides, and after it deliberated for fifteen minutes behind closed doors, Marsellus announced a unanimous recommendation from the four members present that the governor commute my sentence to time served. (Lawrence Hand, the only white member, was absent due to illness.)

My mother burst into tears, elated by the decision. My supporters were jubilant. Edwards had won all his elections with the solid support of the black vote—statewide, about 30 percent of the population. Given his remarks to *The New York Times Magazine* in 1980—that the feelings of the white Lake Charles community were the root of my inability to get clemency, and his comment that "community feelings shouldn't be given that much weight"—everyone assumed that I would finally receive the second chance I had worked so hard to earn and which had been given to so many others.

Two days later, Jim Amoss of the *Times-Picayune* phoned to tell me that the governor, away on a hunting trip in Texas, had rejected the recommendation of the board. Without seeing the recommendation, Edwards cited the "nature of the crime" and said that I had already been given one commutation when I was resentenced from death to life imprisonment. What he didn't acknowledge was that the forty-five or fifty unconstitutional death sentences replaced with life sentences were not grants of mercy but a legal maneuver by the state to preserve dozens of convictions that might not have stood if we had been retried. Nor did anyone note that Edwards, though he turned me down, had previously granted clemency to at least a dozen other formerly condemned murderers.

Members of the media immediately called me at the *Angolite* office. All I wanted to do was suffer my crushing defeat in private, the way other inmates did. But the reporters kept calling, and as *Angolite* editor with a phone on my desk, I felt I couldn't hide.

"Naturally, I'm floored," I told *Times-Picayune* reporter Jason DeParle. "I understand the governor's position about my having been sentenced to death before. But that's the nature of clemency—that an individual not be forever chained to misfortune, tragedy and sin. . . . I'm going to continue to be a productive individual and continue striving to earn my place among free men. I've always accepted my punishment without complaint."

Hicks was shocked at Edwards's denial, as were Marsellus and Phelps. They concluded it was a mistake to have recommended an outright discharge from prison, that it may have been too much for my white opponents to swallow. Marsellus assured me that on my next clemency application the board would instead recommend a commutation to sixty years, the same that Billy had received from the previous board. The difference was that, given my almost twenty-four years of incarceration, I would be immediately eligible for parole.

In the months following, the state executed two more inmates who had been denied clemency by the board. Then board member Lionel Daniels resigned, followed by Hicks, who was replaced by Oris Williams, a member of her political group. She assured me he would vote for me when the time came.

Meanwhile, my relationship with Billy was deteriorating. Despite his choice to remain low profile and out of the news, he felt credit due him for *The Angolite* was being buried beneath the national tide of attention that my case had garnered. He blamed me. Tension replaced the sense of calm that had long made *The Angolite* office my refuge.

April brought bad news as our supervisor, Peggi Gresham, transferred to the Louisiana Training Institute for Girls as its deputy superintendent so she could be closer to her ailing parents, for whom she had to care. Gresham and I had started on *The Angolite* a decade earlier with a shared vision. We had developed an abiding respect, trust, and fondness for each other. Like Phelps, she trusted me without reservation, as I did her. Prison power rests in personalities and in relationships. When Gresham left, she was the most powerful individual in the Angola administration. After her demotion during Maggio's second reign, she had become Warden Blackburn's right hand and confidante. In her absence, I no longer had an official I was close to in the Angola administration on whom I could count to protect my interests in conflicts.

As summer 1985 approached, Billy had lost virtually all interest in *The Angolite* and had pretty much stopped going anywhere inside or outside the prison to cover events. Since there were only three full-time writers on the staff—Billy, Tommy, and me—his withdrawal seriously affected production of the magazine, forcing me to rely more on stringers. Billy's contributions increasingly were limited to items that were essentially rewrites of published stories in the commercial media.

He became a progressively more negative force in the office. He maintained running conflicts with our new supervisor, Richard Peabody, and his assistants, whom he disliked and made no effort to work with. It made putting out a magazine even more difficult, so I asked Phelps if he could assign us a different supervisor, and assistant warden Roger Thomas was placed over us in November 1985.

One day Billy told me he was hearing rumors that pardons could be bought. "The word is that Marsellus can be gotten to," he said, "and that guys are sending their people in to him." He told me he had heard that the wife of inmate Gary Martin, a smooth-talking born-again religious con artist, had been seen on a number of occasions in the streets with Marsellus, who was said to be sleeping with her in return for getting her husband out of prison. Billy hated Marsellus, so his remarks were suspect. He suggested that I be careful about being too closely associated with Marsellus or even talking with him on the telephone, because he felt it was only a question of time before the chairman got investigated. Since we were no longer chummy, I wondered why he was telling me this.

"Billy, I don't do anything wrong," I said. "If Marsellus or any other official is doing something wrong, that's their problem, not mine. You should know me well enough by now to know that I'm *always* clean." I paused, then added, "If you know something specific that I should be aware of, tell me. If not, I don't have time for this."

I was now preparing for another pardon board hearing, which was scheduled for May 7. I had high hopes for receiving a recommendation that the governor would sign this time.

The hearing was a repeat of the previous one, attracting national media attention. Both my supporters and opponents had conducted letter-writing campaigns to the pardon board. As before, the rules barred me from attending. It was standing room only in the hearing room, which was packed with my supporters, mostly white, with the overflow outside. Margery Hicks, among others, carried picket signs advocating my release. After two hours of deliberation, the board recommended my sentence be reduced to sixty years, making me eligible not for outright discharge but for immediate parole, as our strategy dictated. The confidence of my supporters was contagious. In the privacy of my office, I planned my new life. I dreamed modestly, about walking down a street or eating in a diner, maybe going to a movie. I knew there would be enormous challenges, and I steeled myself for them. I felt that whatever life could throw at me on the outside, I was equal to it, having survived so much in Angola. I let myself drift on a tide of hope.

The media caught up with Governor Edwards the next day as he was entering the federal courthouse in New Orleans to stand trial on racketeering and conspiracy charges. He told the Baton Rouge *Morning Advocate*, "I'll take a look at [Rideau's] file when it gets to me. I'll not prejudge it."

The following day, thanks to Jim Amoss, now an editor, the conservative *Times-Picayune* did something it had never done before: It editorially called for the governor to commute the sentence of a prisoner—me. It said: "If ever a man was rehabilitated, it seems that Wilbert Rideau has been. That conclusion is not ours alone. It is shared by the professional corrections officers who have supervised him for the past 25 years."

On June 18, 1986, Edwards held a press conference where he announced that he was denying me clemency again: "If I reacted solely on my personal beliefs, I would sign the pardon," he said. "I agree with those who say he has been rehabilitated." I found it ironic that, given his previous comments to *The New York Times* that mass sentiment shouldn't overrule the ends of justice, he now justified denying me clemency because, he said, he had a responsibility to be concerned with "mass sentiment," and noted that "community feeling in the Lake Charles area" remained severely against clemency. I got the news when Warden Blackburn walked into my office and interrupted an NBC-TV news crew that was interviewing me. "Rideau, the governor just turned down the pardon board's recommendation," he said. I was devastated. The crew turned off the cameras, expressed their regrets, and left me to my disappointment.

The next day, Jane Bankston, the wife of a state senator and the director of mental health for the corrections department, came to see me. I had met her when she was working with a prerelease program several years before. She had become a good friend and, with Ginger Roberts, had coordinated my recent clemency effort. Jane had driven to Lake Charles and picked up mailbags of letters to the governor from black churches there and made sure the hearing room was filled to capacity with supporters. She asked how I was doing and requested that I accompany her to the prison hospital. There she took me into a room where there was a black inmate with whom she cheerfully began chatting. Gradually, it dawned on me that he was blind. I was intrigued. Jane introduced us. His name was Alvin Anderson. As I listened to them I became offended at a system that would keep a blind man in the biggest maximum-security prison in the nation. His blindness made him the most vulnerable person in the place. How was he to fend for himself, to survive? By the end of the visit, I was resolute, my disappointment pushed aside. "The governor may keep me in prison," I said to Anderson, "but I will make that sonuvabitch turn you loose. I promise you that."

As we left the hospital, I told Jane that I wanted all the information the department had on Anderson and other prisoners who were blind, paralyzed, or otherwise severely disabled. Then I asked her what she had come to the prison to see me about. "I wanted you to meet Alvin." She smiled. "Now I know you'll be all right." Ever the social worker, she had engineered the meeting to refocus my attention. I channeled my emotions and anger into an investigative exposé, "The Edge of Madness." The story, published in the July/August 1986 *Angolite*, was picked up by the commercial media and prompted the pardon board to initiate efforts that would ultimately free Anderson and about twenty more needlessly confined Angola inmates.

I noticed that Billy had become calmer, less negative, and much more cordial. He volunteered to do a story on Wade Correctional Institute, a prison located near the Arkansas border that was the state's only facility with a protective custody unit designated for former cops and sensitive, high-profile individuals. For someone who had shown little inclination to do any real journalism of late, this was a surprise.

During the summer, on one of my trips to Baton Rouge, Phelps expressed concern to me about Billy. Without going into details, he suggested I keep an eye on him. "Tell me," he said, "in the course of his everyday life, have you seen him behave strangely or do things that cause you to wonder about him?"

"Billy was withdrawn for a while, which we attributed to his frustration over not being able to get out, but lately he's changed. He's become more alive, more sociable, curious—always wanting to know about what's going on," I said. "Tommy believes he's up to something."

"What does he think he's up to?"

"We haven't the foggiest idea," I replied, "but if you feel he can no longer be trusted and presents a potential problem to *The Angolite*, maybe you should consider moving him into a different position."

"We'll see how things go," he said.

In August, Billy told me that Jodie heard through a source in the Baton Rouge federal district attorney's office that the FBI was now investigating pardon selling and Marsellus. He seemed quite buoyed by this fact, which I attributed to his dislike of the man. On September 4 came the news that state police had arrested Marsellus and House Speaker pro tempore Joe Delpit, one of the governor's closest political allies, on charges of public bribery and conspiracy to get convicted murderer Juan Serato out of prison for $100,000. Federal district attorney Ray Lamonica revealed he had also been conducting an investigation independent of the state police's but refused to divulge any information.

As the scandal began to dominate the news in the ensuing weeks, the governor declared that he would sign no more pardons until a grand jury investigation was over.

As the scandal grew, Billy acted increasingly odd, especially after his office was searched in a surprise security action. When I pressed him, he revealed to Tommy, me, and our illustrator, Poochie, that he and Jodie had been cooperating with an FBI sting operation on Berlin Hood, the prison's food manager, who offered to arrange a pardon for Billy for $15,000, that Marsellus was involved, and that it went all the way up the line to the governor.

We were shocked, not only because of the FBI connection but also because Billy and Hood were close, and had been for more than a decade; Hood was his mentor, protector, and advocate.

"This only has to do with Hood," Billy said, "not anyone else in this prison." He said he couldn't explain everything right then but suggested that we watch reporter Chris McDaniel's special series featuring Jodie on Channel 9 the following evening. He said that would be followed by the Baton Rouge *Morning Advocate* publishing a feature on him.

After Billy left the office, Tommy said, "Well, I'll be damned. They betrayed Hood to the FBI, then betrayed the FBI to Channel 9. This is going to raise questions about us, too."

I sat alone in the darkness of my office, deep into the night, trying to decide what—if anything—I should do. I knew that if I repeated down the Walk what Billy had told us, one of those inmates whose clemency hopes had vanished because of the scandal would take him down. I had tried hard to help Billy, yet he had caused me more problems and anguish than any other inmate during my entire prison experience.

With the morning light came clarity. Just because people labeled us criminals didn't mean we had to be criminals. I had survived everything prison had thrown at me, and I would survive this, too.

That morning Billy left Angola in the custody of federal marshals. A Channel 9 camera crew was conveniently at the front gate to film and report the story of his entering protective custody after being part of a federal investigation into pardon selling. It was headline news throughout the state.

The following afternoon, Phelps met with the *Angolite* staff.

"To answer the question foremost in your minds," he said, "Billy Wayne Sinclair is in the East Baton Rouge Parish jail, where he is being debriefed by federal and state investigators. While it's supposed to be about Hood offering him a pardon for fifteen thousand dollars, he's volunteering everything he knows about everybody to anybody who'll listen." He paused, looked at me, and continued. "He says you and Marsellus are close, that you call him at home, and he's heard you discussing the cases of inmates on the *Angolite* telephone, suggesting that your dealings with Marsellus were improper, if not criminal."

"Of course I've talked to Marsellus about inmates," I said, "just as I've talked with past pardon and parole board members who ask my opinion on trying to help inmates. I'm the editor here, and everyone calls for both information and my opinion—grant hustlers, researchers, journalists, state officials, wardens. I've been doing this for the last ten years. I've never seen it as a big deal, nor has anyone else. But in all my dealings with Marsellus he never once suggested anything improper or offered to sell a pardon, either through me or to me."

"Does anyone have any idea why Billy would want to create problems for *The Angolite*?" Phelps asked. "It's apparent that he wants to." Phelps was concerned that our staff might be seen as complicit in Billy's informant activities and his busting Hood, a popular prison employee.

"Well, we're about to learn how much respect we command and the extent of our credibility among the inmates," I said.

A less courageous man in charge would have shut us down, but Phelps used the incident as an opportunity to reinforce the administration's commitment to us. He said his concern was *The Angolite* and what Billy did. "That's something that I, as publisher, have to address," he said, "so get out your tape recorder."

He gave a lengthy statement, which I published in its entirety in the November/December 1986 issue of the magazine, following a brief report on Billy's role as an FBI undercover informant. "What Billy Wayne did certainly compromised not only the integrity of the magazine but also the safety and well-being of the rest of the staff who had nothing to do with his extracurricular activities," he said, in part.

Not long after the Sinclair affair, Phelps expanded journalism at Angola to include KLSP, the nation's only federally licensed, inmate-operated radio station.

We *Angolite* staffers met with inmate leaders, making a point of being seen with them and becoming even more accessible to the general population. Our survival required all of Angola to see that we were not part of Sinclair's sting and that we had no knowledge of it. Tensions ran rampant at the prison, with rumors of widespread investigations into individuals and operations. Inmates were on edge. Employees were wary. But our integrity remained intact.

Contrary to his expectations, Billy would serve another twenty years in prison, in protective custody. Jodie, who stuck with him, eventually went into public relations work in Houston.

9

Soldiering On
1986–1990

Which is worse: death by execution or spending the rest of your life in prison? That was a question I was asked to answer on July 1, 1986, when I went to the studios of WBRZ-TV in Baton Rouge to appear by hookup on *Nightline*. With twenty-five years served on a life sentence, I was at that time one of the longest-serving lifers in America, which qualified me as an expert on the subject. Ted Koppel was exploring it because serial killer Ted Bundy was scheduled to be executed that night—a date with death he dodged only temporarily.

A couple of weeks later I received a note from Dr. Linda LaBranche of Northwestern University, a Shakespeare scholar who had learned from my *Nightline* appearance that I "wrote for the prison newspaper" and decided—against all her instincts, she later confessed—to write to me to offer whatever I might need in the way of pens, writing tablets, or books. She sounded like a prim and proper English teacher who was patting me on the head like a good little boy. I sent a return note thanking her for her interest and asked her to write again. I enclosed articles about me from *The New York Times* and *The Christian Science Monitor* and the *Times-Picayune* editorial advocating my freedom. After reading the articles, she wrote back asking why my clemency had been denied. It made no sense to her. I wrote back, and she did, too—almost daily, telling me about her life and asking me for more information about my case. I sent her a two-inch-thick file of photocopied news clippings. In return, the following week, she sent me a thirty-page "briefing" on my case that she had prepared for the media, along with cross-indexed listings of the articles I'd sent.

I was amazed at the amount of work she'd done, even though the "briefing" was far too long to be of any value to the media. She said she was dividing the days of her summer vacation between scholarship and reading up on the criminal justice system, to which she'd never before given a thought. She found the whole thing fascinating. I wondered if she was just a crazy old lady, and if not, if she'd be willing to help me in some way that might lead to clemency. I didn't know what that might be, but the biggest problem that every prisoner faces in trying to get out of prison is a lack of help on the outside—someone to write letters, recruit other supporters, show up at pardon hearings, gather evidence, organize. When I asked her to send me a photo of herself, she sent a one-inch-square mug shot from a school ID card. *Quite possibly crazy,* I thought, trying to discern from the miniature photo what she might actually look like.

C. Paul Phelps was going to a corrections convention in Chicago in October and I asked if he would check her out for me, if she was willing to meet with him. It was a meeting that would change my life. He thought she was charming, smart, and very well informed about my case. He grilled her with questions, she grilled him, and by the end of the long dinner they shared, he urged her to come to Louisiana and talk with me in person before she agreed to put her reputation on the line to try to help me.

Linda announced she would come during the Thanksgiving break. When the day arrived, I was on edge, still a bit wary that someone might want to take out their frustrations on me because their clemency hopes were damaged by the pardon-for-sale investigation.

Linda stepped off the prison bus wearing high heels and a teal blue suit, definitely overdressed. She stood five-foot-two and weighed less than a hundred pounds, which were packed into an hourglass shape that would have been the envy of a twenty-five-year-old but that the typical black man from my era would have found too thin. Her hair was a light auburn, thanks to henna, which complemented her light complexion and highlighted big eyes that changed from bright blue to green or gray depending on the color of the sky or her clothing. She was thirty-eight years old, and although she was not beautiful in the classic sense, I could tell that she had always been a magnet for men the way pretty women are when they exude warmth. As we talked, I learned that she had left home as a teenager to find a better life than the one she was born to, that she was fiercely independent and possessed acute analytical skills that she had acquired from her life and had honed during her journey through academia. The only sign that betrayed her Ph.D. was an unrelenting desire to discuss everything from crime and punishment to politics in terms of Shakespeare's plays or dramaturgy. If it hurt her feelings that I showed no interest in what was then her life's passion, she didn't show it.

I never expected Linda to be in my life very long. She had been a rolling stone, making her way at nineteen to New York City and shifting from city to city ever since. I met her shortly after her return to the United States from Bangkok, where she'd been teaching at a university she walked into one day while backpacking around the world at age thirty-five, sleeping in youth hostels and train stations. She was clearly an adventurer, and I figured I was just the latest adventure. That was fine with me. In prison you learn to be grateful for what you can get.

"From what I gather, you have a lot of people who support you and your cause for freedom," she said to me as we sat at a concrete table, watching some inmates visiting with their families, others playing volleyball with their kids. Lush green trees formed a border around the spacious, parklike visiting grounds built into a slope of the Tunica hills. It was an oasis, a spot of beauty and peace accessible to trusties as a reward. "What you don't have—and I think you need—is a *soldier*," said Linda, "someone on the outside who will actually do for you the things that you need done. I can be that for you."

I doubted she could be the sort of foot soldier she seemed to imagine herself, since much of what might help me could be done only in Louisiana, and she lived in Chicago, far away from where any research, schmoozing, arm-twisting, or ongoing brainstorming might be done. Moreover, I could now see she didn't understand the peculiar social culture of the South and was a complete political innocent, which meant that even as smart as she clearly was, she lacked the necessary frame of reference to be an effective advisor, much less a soldier. But she was easy to talk to, fun to be with, and I figured that she might visit once or twice a year.

Several months later, Linda accepted a position on the English faculty at Loyola University in New Orleans, 140 miles from Angola.

That dramatically altered her potential to contribute to my life. Not only could she help with some of my efforts to be released from prison, she could provide companionship as well. She brought a much-needed dose of normality to my life. Twice a month I could escape the madness of prison, its pettiness, the constant need for watchfulness, the game playing and posturing of inmates and employees alike, the bickering of small minds over small matters, the daily grind of whistles and counts and forced associations. Twice a month I could sit at a picnic table, eat some barbecued chicken or pork chops, and talk to an intelligent, rational woman about anything and everything.

Linda arrived in Louisiana in the summer, a hectic time for *The Angolite*. Tommy and I were canceling speaking engagements in an effort to stay atop things. I was in the middle of an investigation into the absence of any official program in the state's penal system to deal with the threat from AIDS, then a new and little-understood disease that was generating paranoia among both guards and prisoners. But what was generating the most media interest in Angola was the resumption of executions after a two-year moratorium, with such frequency that the state briefly became the execution capital of the nation. Four inmates—Benjamin Berry, Alvin Moore, Jr., Jimmy Glass, and Jimmy Wingo—were put to death in the electric chair during a nine-day period in June, followed by three more—Willie Celestine, Willie Watson, Jr., and John Brogdon—in July.

Covering the executions strained the *Angolite*'s resources. We had to go to death row to talk to the condemned, research his legal case, talk to many of those involved, attend the all-day pardon board hearing followed by the death vigil, and then follow through with post-execution information gathering.

Determined to have a diverse staff (in part for the sake of credibility), I persuaded Ron Wikberg, an affable, blond-haired lifer and brilliant jailhouse lawyer, to join us. He had spent eighteen years in prison for the 1969 killing of a Lafayette store owner in a robbery that went bad. Like most of Angola's convicts, Ron did not participate in prison evils: drugs, homosexual rape, gambling, or gangs. He was a workaholic; he had helped run the medical clinic during the prison's bloody years, and he was now keeping warehouse inventories straight at Prison Enterprises. A decent guy with a huge heart, he was always ready to volunteer his services for activities that benefited the prison community, whether prisoner or personnel. Ron saved for years until he could pay for a paralegal correspondence course, then provided free legal services to both employees and prisoners. His most notable accomplishment was winning freedom for "Cowboy Jack" Favor, a former national rodeo champion, whose imprisonment had resulted from a criminal conspiracy. He was intelligent, perceptive, a great researcher, and a good writer, with invaluable knowledge of the prison world. Since he had reported on legal developments for *The Angolite* as a stringer after Billy stopped doing it, he knew what we needed in a staff writer.

I wanted Ron to do an insider's report from the inmates' perspective on the rash of executions and the impact it had on the world of the condemned. In the past, we had simply been able to go to death row and talk to anyone willing to talk to us. Now we were told by corrections headquarters that we were to be treated the same as commercial media, which meant we first had to obtain the permission of the attorneys, who were generally reluctant to approve our request because they feared their clients might attract media attention and thereby complicate legal efforts to avoid execution. I told Phelps that men on death row had asked to talk to us.

"The lawyers requested the restriction," he explained. "What if I, in the name of giving you an insider's view, were to allow you to view the actual execution. Would you watch it?"

I looked at him and shook my head. "Man, it messes me up every time I see those guys being led away," I said, "knowing they're gonna die, sometimes seeing the panic in their eyes."

"Why don't you turn away?"

"I can't. I've got to look at them, so they can see that I—if no one else—understand how they feel. It's never lost on me that there but for the grace of God go I."

"But if given the opportunity, would you watch the execution?"

I thought long before answering. "I don't want to watch someone die. They can dress it up in rhetoric, but they're killing a defenseless person against his will. It's a deliberate act of murder, done in as cold-blooded a fashion as is imaginable. I don't want to watch that, and I wonder about those who do."

Phelps smiled. "I haven't watched one, either—for pretty much the same reasons. Does that surprise you?"

It did. "But you're the one responsible for the human organization that kills the guy."

"Distance makes it manageable, and subordinates pretty much handle everything. We never have to worry about a shortage of curious volunteers to serve as witnesses. We get so many requests that in some cases it becomes a bit of a problem because many come from officials and politicians, and there are only a certain number we can accommodate."

Once settled into an apartment near Loyola University, Linda obtained the transcripts of my second and third trials (none existed of the first), including the voluminous appeals, and thus became the first person to read every document on file from my arrest to the present day. My revelation astonished her. "Look, I'm guilty," I explained during a visit, "and like most of these guys here, I'm not looking for excuses. I don't want to read the testimony; I heard it at trial. I'm ashamed of what I did, and I don't enjoy revisiting that."

"How much of the crime and the trials can you recall?"

"The overall crime, I remember," I said. "The actual violence—not very much. It happened so fast it was unreal, like a dream. I was so scared, and it was so dark that night that I could barely see—I have in my head murky, disconnected snapshots of what happened. But remember, I've *wanted* to forget—and that goes for the trials. I paid little attention to most of the proceedings because I felt intuitively that they were going to kill me. I knew that the trials were just a formality."

"You made it easy for the state to kill you, and so did your lawyers. They didn't challenge the evidence or even question the witnesses!" Linda said in disbelief. "They didn't even present to the jury obvious logical impossibilities or contradictions in the witnesses' testimony, or even hint that something was amiss in the state's case. What can possibly account for your lawyers' behavior?"

"Look, if they had suggested, in that 1961 Lake Charles courtroom, that the white woman might not be telling the exact truth, they could've started looking for someplace else to practice law, for one thing. Then, too, given the time and place and the mob that had gathered outside the jail the night of my arrest, and the crowd in the courtroom, I suppose they were afraid those people would just take me and lynch me if it looked like they were fighting too hard for me. Defending me couldn't have been a popular undertaking. In fact, I've wondered what the hell those two lawyers could have done to deserve the punishment of being appointed to represent me, especially since they weren't even criminal lawyers."

"But you had other lawyers and two more trials," she said.

"True, but the white folks in Lake Charles had taken what I did and refashioned it into what they wanted it to be, and once everybody involved embraced the lies, exaggerations, and fabrications of the first trial, which they conveniently made no record of, they were married to it. It became the foundation for everything that transpired afterward. It's the original prosecutor, Frank Salter, who has been keeping this thing alive long after he was forced out of office for racketeering. He's the architect of this case, the biggest of his career, and I suspect that, with my attracting media attention and scrutiny, he doesn't want it unraveling."

"Well," said Linda, "let me tell you, if I had to use your trial transcripts as a play script, it would be virtually impossible for me to re-create that crime onstage the way the prosecutors and witnesses described it. I can see that much, and I'm not a lawyer. You're guilty of robbing that bank, taking those people out into the country, and killing one, no doubt, but not the way they say you did it."

I gave her a serious look. "That's bad enough," I said.

"Have you ever heard from any of the attorneys who defended you in any of your trials?" I shook my head. "Prosecutors, judges, anyone involved in any of the trials?" I shook my head again. "Any of the media from southwest Louisiana ever try to interview you?" No again.

"Don't you think it odd that as a prisoner who has achieved a lot and received plenty of national publicity for your accomplishments, not one of your former lawyers has attempted to reach out, send you a card, congratulate you, wish you luck—nothing? I think that's telling, and I'll bet it has to do with how your case was handled. Something was rotten in the state of Louisiana, and they were all party to it, willing participants or not. To me, it sounds like what you've been hearing all these years has been the silence of the guilty." She also concluded that the justices of the Louisiana Supreme Court, with the cooperation of my lawyers, had judicially lynched me with their 1964 change-of-venue ruling, which allowed the state to retry me by setting aside the state law that forbade it. "It's the only conclusion you can draw," she said. "Your lawyers had won a judicial impasse ruling from the trial court, stating essentially that you were beyond the state's ability to retry. So why in heaven's name would they join the DA in appealing that ruling to the Louisiana Supreme Court and ask for another trial?"

"They didn't," I corrected her. "I saw the brief they filed. They asked that the DA's request be denied."

"Are you sure they filed the brief you saw? Because in its ruling the court specifically points out that you joined the DA in his request," she said, "and I can assure you there's nothing in the files to contradict that. Either the files have been laundered or your lawyers lied to you."

"No, then the court lied," I said. "I have a stamped copy from the Louisiana Supreme Court of that brief. What they did to facilitate a second trial and get me another death sentence required the court to act contrary to law. So to give it the appearance of correctness they said they were doing it at my request." I paused, trying to recall things I had not thought of in decades. "Look, what I did was bad enough, but my recollection of the trials was that there was a lot of lying and rearranging of the facts to make the crime even worse than it was." I thought back.

"Well, there's only witness testimony," Linda pointed out. "There's no other evidence to speak of because the crime scene was washed away by torrential rain that night, leaving only the knife and scabbard the deputy found, and there were no fingerprints, blood, or anything to connect it to you. I find that especially strange since there should have been blood residue inside the scabbard if nowhere else."

"That was their knife, not mine," I said. "Of that I'm certain. They said they recovered the knife but couldn't find the gun. Well, I threw them both in the same place, and it wasn't where the deputy said he found the knife. I *know* that much for sure."

"That's why no lab tests were done on the knife. It also explains why the knife disappeared after your first trial."

"Prosecutors wanted to introduce a photo of the knife at my second trial, and the judge asked if lab tests had been conducted on the knife after my arrest," I said. "They told the judge the knife had not been tested because it had rained all night, washing it clean. They lied. There was no rain."

"But, Wilbert, *everyone* testified about the rain—victims, cops, FBI, everybody," Linda said. "Everyone said it was coming down so hard that it was difficult to drive through or even to see. How can you not recall it?"

I shrugged. "I don't know." I thought for a moment, then suddenly remembered: "Look at the newspaper photos of my being brought into the jail—you'll see the clothes I'm wearing are dry; my hair is dry."

"What happened to the clothes you had on that night? If you cut

Julia Ferguson's throat, like the other teller, Dora McCain, testified, there should have been blood on your clothing."

"I don't remember cutting the woman's throat," I said. "But I do know there wasn't any blood on my clothes. Look at the picture in the newspaper. They took everything I wore, stripped me naked. Never saw my shoes and clothing again."

"Why would they all say there was torrential rain if there wasn't?"

I shrugged again. "I don't know. Look, I didn't testify, there were no witnesses for me, and my lawyers didn't challenge the prosecution, so they pretty much presented the case the way they wanted to. Especially about what happened when we got out in the country. Most of what McCain said I did out there is not true, but I can't disprove it."

"*That's* the reason for the rain," Linda said excitedly. "There was no evidence from the crime scene except for the knife that you believe was planted there. If they were going to spin this crime a different way, then they didn't want anything that might contradict what they said. The rain accounts for the absence of crime-scene evidence." She shook her head in disbelief. "But that would require everybody to lie. How did they pull that off?"

"That would've been easy," I said. "I was black, had just robbed a white bank, and killed a white woman. In 1961, every white person in the South was expected to do what was required of them. Lying and fabricating evidence to aid the prosecution would have been considered their civic duty. You know, I still marvel at the fact that they didn't simply kill me on the spot."

I explained to Linda that however interesting her discoveries and analyses were, they were irrelevant. I was trying to regain my freedom through gubernatorial clemency, and there was that pardon board policy not to entertain clemency applications when an inmate disputed the facts of the crime. Since the board had recommended my release, I had most of the battle won; all I needed now was a governor to sign off on it. Phelps had promised that he would ask Governor Edwards after the fall elections, when he had nothing to lose, to commute my sentence as a personal favor.

Linda went to the Institute of Human Relations, Loyola University's social-action arm, whose director, Ted Quant, was very interested in aiding my release efforts. The Rideau Project, the institute's first effort to aid a single individual rather than a group, was created with the blessing of Loyola's president, Father James Carter. In one of her first roles as my "soldier," Linda, along with Ted, coordinated the external effort of our Angola Special Civics Project, the first formally organized attempt by inmate leaders to get friends and relatives of the state's eighteen thousand prisoners to vote as a bloc to influence the outcome of the gubernatorial election, which experts were predicting would be very tight.

The Louisiana pardon-selling scandal gave rise to the campaign button ANYBODY BUT EDWARDS and put the governor in a runoff with reform candidate Buddy Roemer, a dark horse from Shreveport whose primary appeal may have been that few people knew who he was. He got 33 percent of the vote and Edwards 28 percent, mostly black. Edwards withdrew before the runoff.

On his way out, Edwards granted a flood of sentence commutations for prisoners, including Tommy, who was freed during the Christmas holiday. Edwards granted thousands of clemencies in all during his three terms in office, including, news reports said, more than two hundred to murderers and more than twenty to inmates formerly sentenced to death. He had said publicly that I was a model prisoner who ought to be free, but he would not free me. "I gave it my best shot," Phelps told me.

During the election campaign, Roemer had promised to appoint criminal justice professionals to the pardon board and to award clemencies based on individual merit and fairness. It may have been political rhetoric, but it was at least a ray of hope for me.

The scope of the pardon board's corruption did not come to light until Edwards was about to leave office, when his executive counsel, C. W. "Bill" Roberts, reported that there were at least 464 clemency recommendations made by the pardon board that would never reach the governor's desk for action because the governor had not asked to see them. Historically, pardon board recommendations were automatically forwarded to the governor to be granted or denied. Edwards had instructed the board to retain recommendations in their files until called for by his office. Roberts said that the only recommendations Edwards reviewed and acted upon were those brought to his attention by influential preachers, politicians, and officials.

Edwards, popularly regarded as the champion of the black, the poor, and the oppressed, dealt a crushing blow to Louisiana's long-term inmates. Prisoners who believed clemency might be likely, given historical precedents, did not pursue litigation that might have resulted in their freedom. They had no idea the deck was stacked, so they continued to cling to false hope.

When it became clear that Roemer was not going to reappoint him, Phelps retired. On March 10, 1988, I went to his retirement party at corrections headquarters. I looked around for Dorothy "Dot" Henderson, the black chairwoman of the state board of parole, and found her sitting behind her desk in a spacious office. We were chatting when a Baton Rouge attorney, Nathan Fisher, entered to see Henderson about clemency for a client. She made a phone call, told him it was done, and he left. "Hell, I didn't know you had that kind of power," I said, surprised. "So what are you gonna do for me?"

"I don't have the power it takes for you, but for almost anyone else, yes," she replied.

"If you can't get me out, at least take somebody else in my place—a gift," I said, seizing what I saw as an opportunity.

"Okay. Who do you want?"

Ron Wikberg was unearthing the identities of the state's thirty-one longest-confined prisoners (I ranked twenty-second on the list) for a story. We were certain they would die in prison anonymity unless we brought their stories to light. We had just finished interviewing fifty-three-year-old Louis "Pulpwood" Ducre, into his thirtieth year of imprisonment, and fifty-seven-year-old Jack Lathers, thirty-one years behind bars, two model prisoners who had pardon board recommendations that could free them. Their names sprang to mind, and I told Dot about them. Within a few minutes and after two phone calls, the life sentences of the two men had been commuted, and they would be freed within a day or so.

To his credit, Roemer created Louisiana's first professional, nonpolitical pardon board. Then he ignored all of the clemency recommendations they sent him. Six months after becoming governor, he granted his first commutation to a murderer, freeing Juan Serato, the key figure in the state police's sting operation that sent Howard Marsellus to prison. In explaining his decision, the governor said his criteria for clemency would include the nature of the crime, the amount of time served, prison behavior record, the inmate's rehabilitation, and prospects of support upon release. His rhetoric generated high expectations among Angola's poor and friendless long-termers whose only hope in life rested upon the system being fair. The governor then resumed ignoring all the clemency recommendations piling up in his office.

Three months later, Roemer's handpicked pardon board reviewed the recommendation of the previous board to commute my life term and forwarded it to the governor. It was done without public fanfare shortly after Thanksgiving. On December 7, 1988, Roemer plucked my recommendation from among all those awaiting his attention and denied it, despite my having served more than five times as many years in prison as Serato and having been called the most rehabilitated prisoner in America by Phelps and other Louisiana corrections officials. In announcing his decision to the media, he cited the nature of my crime and opposition from the victim and law enforcement officials in Lake Charles.

Roemer's action generated huge publicity. *The Shreveport Sun*, which served the black community in his hometown, ran two stories critical of his action. *The Shreveport Journal*, which served primarily white readers, said in an editorial that I had already served four times the national average for murderers and called Roemer's denial of clemency "a mockery of the corrections system, because Rideau has done everything the judicial system asked of him and much more."

Negative articles, features, editorials, and letters to the editor followed, which clearly annoyed the governor. In a *Times-Picayune* feature story about me in December, former district attorney Frank Salter, now Dora McCain's personal spokesman, tried to counteract the negative publicity by exaggerating the nature of my crime: "[He] lined them up military fashion and attempted to execute the three of them," he told the *Times-Picayune*. "He attempted to commit a planned mass murder."

Times-Picayune columnist James Gill wrote in January, "Of the 13 men on death row when Rideau arrived at Angola in 1962, 11 have been released and one has died. Only Rideau remains to be victimized for his achievements."

Roemer allowed the holiday season to pass without granting clemency to a single prisoner in the state, the first governor since 1892 to do so. Indeed, during his first year in office, he had compiled the most dismal clemency record of any Louisiana governor—a fact not lost upon the 3,800 long-termers at Angola who lived for a sentence reduction to rescue them from prison terms they could not outlive.

Traditionally in Louisiana, which had always pursued a criminal justice philosophy of giving a second chance to offenders, even lifers knew they would one day rejoin society, provided they survived the brutal conditions of their imprisonment. Now, Angola was fast becoming the prison where men served the longest sentences in the world. Paralleling the growing sense of despair among inmates were budget cuts, staff shortages, and growing employee dissatisfaction, all of which were adversely affecting the quality of life behind bars. Inconvenience and frustration increased in almost every aspect of everyday life for the inmates: Fewer dollars meant smaller portions of lower-quality food at mealtimes. Fewer employees meant a reduction in recreation, club activities, and church services. Because it took longer for fewer workers to process and transport visitors, visits were shorter. We highlighted the problem in "Getting Our Money's Worth," published in our first issue of 1989, reporting that Angola's employee turnover rate had jumped from 26 percent to 60 percent under Roemer, while the national prison employee turnover rate had decreased to 15 percent.

Hilton Butler was an old-line prison guard who had been "rehabilitated" by Phelps and Blackburn. As deputy warden, he had created the outdoor visiting program for disciplinary-free inmates so they would be able to play with their kids. Upon becoming warden in 1987 after Blackburn retired, he overruled his security officials' objection to congregating five thousand prisoners in the rodeo arena for a concert by the Neville Brothers. When guards were tearing down our flyers during our attempt to influence the 1987 governor's race, he ordered employees not to interfere with our political activity. He approved annual religious Prison Fellowship seminars for death row inmates, conducted in a relaxed social atmosphere outside of death row, with guests. Inmate leaders wanted him to go public about the problem of hopelessness bred by the lack of clemency. But he was hesitant to buck his superiors in a high-profile way.

Butler's security chief, Mike Gunnells, who was not hesitant to speak his mind on the subject, told *The Angolite*, "If the governor would take a close look at what's happening in the penal system, and if he'd help some of the people who deserve help, it would do a lot to improve the situation."

On March 8, Governor Roemer plucked out the board's recommendation of clemency for Ron Wikberg, a model prisoner, to deny. No reason was given.

Loren Ghiglione, president-elect of the American Society of Newspaper Editors (ASNE), flew to Louisiana on March 15 to meet with the governor and plead for my release. He left with Roemer's permission for me to fly to Washington, D.C., on April 13 to speak at the annual ASNE convention. *Angolite* supervisor Roger Thomas accompanied me. Years later, he would confess that he absolutely couldn't understand why I returned to Louisiana rather than walk off into freedom in D.C.

Although my outside travel had been approved routinely during the previous five years, I was now told that officials at corrections headquarters were concerned that I was going out too frequently. Speaking requests from Loyola, Dillard, and Xavier universities were denied.

A front-page story about me, "Free Mind Trapped in Convict Body," by Michael Kennedy in the *Los Angeles Times* in January 1989 had led Jonathan Talmadge, a producer for the ABC-TV newsmagazine *20/20*, to investigate why I was still in prison. The night following my return to Angola from Washington, *20/20* aired "Why Not Wilbert Rideau?" Correspondent Stone Phillips characterized their report as "the story of how politics, a promise, and perhaps Wilbert Rideau's very prominence have kept him behind bars." He reviewed the crime, spoke with victim Julia Ferguson's daughter, told of my three trials, and reviewed the U.S. Supreme Court's *Furman* decision, which had led to my life sentence. "He was released from death row at a time of violence in the nation's prisons," Phillips said. "Angola had a reputation as the bloodiest. Rideau was credited with helping bring peace to Angola as an articulate voice of moderation who earned the trust of inmates and of the keepers." Phillips talked to Peggi Gresham, Walter Pence, former warden C. Murray Henderson, and C. Paul Phelps. All testified that I was completely reformed. All agreed that my continued incarceration served no useful purpose.

Phillips pressed former governor Edwards about the role opposition from law enforcement and victims' friends and families played in the clemency process. He asked about Donald Wayne Owens, a murderer and armed robber Edwards had freed after only thirteen years. He asked about former death row inmate Adam Mack, the brutality of whose crime surpassed even the most sensationalized version of mine. Edwards said he couldn't remember the cases but was sure local law enforcement had not objected. Wrong, said Phillips, flashing the local district attorney's letter of objection onto the screen.

But the real bombshell that *20/20* dropped was a secret promise that Edwards had made to bank teller Dora McCain that he would never free me, no matter what. Edwards admitted to it.

Julian Murray, one of Louisiana's top criminal defense lawyers, who had represented me pro bono before the pardon board, explained to *20/20:* "No system of justice worthy of the name allows the victim or the victim's family to determine the punishment. We don't set up our system that way. . . . We set up a system of laws, not of men. We set up a clemency system, a pardon board system. And he went through all the steps. We ask for rehabilitation; we demand a certain amount of time. He's done all of those things. Then if he's going to be treated equally, he should be let out."

Stone Phillips gave the final word to Governor Roemer: "Can I ever [release him]? I don't know. Am I willing to listen? You bet! Am I willing to learn? You got it! Can he do some things to talk about the damage he did, and what he can do to restore confidence? Certainly. Got more work to do, though." Phillips ticked through a number of my public service and public education efforts, showed video of me working with New Orleans judge Miriam Waltzer and her probation-ers, and asked, incredulously, "What more *can* he do?" "His only chance to overcome what he did," Roemer said, "is what he might *pro-pose* he *could* do so that those kinds of crimes would happen *less* in the future, not more. Only *he* can address that."

I had no idea what Roemer was saying; I wasn't sure he did, either.

The Monday after the *20/20* report, Roger Thomas called to tell me that headquarters had just rescinded approval for an April 19 trip to Baton Rouge to cover a special prison ministry luncheon featuring Chuck Colson. I was given no explanation.

Roemer had appointed Bruce Lynn, a cotton farmer and banker with no experience in corrections, to replace Phelps as head of the state's penal system. Lynn called me on April 20 in response to my request. I asked if my recent trip denials represented a change in policy. "I had gotten several letters from people in Lake Charles, complaining about you going to Washington," he said, "and I just wasn't gonna let you go to that Colson thing in Baton Rouge while I'm catching flak about your other trip." He assured me that he had just approved an April 27 trip to New Orleans as part of the crime/dropout prevention program because that was "an educational kind of thing, something I can defend," he said, "but y'all going out to cover things like the Col-son event is a different matter, and you might not always be able to do things like that."

I soon learned that Lynn had denied a request for me to attend a national death penalty seminar in New Orleans in May. The following morning, a week after the *20/20* report, Ron and I went to a parole board meeting to cover a hearing for the state's longest-confined prisoner, who had spent forty-one years in Angola. We were not permitted to sit in on the hearing.

The American Society of Magazine Editors congregated at the Waldorf-Astoria in New York City on April 26 to pay tribute to the best magazines of the past year. *The Angolite* had been a finalist. Unlike in the past, no official went to represent us. It was now clear to all that *The Angolite* and its editor were out of favor.

Hopelessness is contagious. Governor Roemer's policies fed despair at Angola.

Francis "Corky" Clifton was a fifty-two-year-old lifer whose job it was to tend the prison's bloodhounds. He was a highly trusted inmate and a model prisoner, a rare trusty who lived and worked under comfortable circumstances without any supervision at all. The night after he watched the *20/20* report, he put five Moon Pies in his pocket and escaped into the Tunica wilderness. He had served twenty-seven years and had invested a lot of effort in the traditional means of earning his way out. Warden Butler, who had been working at Angola forty years, couldn't recall the last time a trusty like Corky tried to escape. After almost a week on the run, with no food or money and not wanting to steal, he surrendered. He explained that he ran off because he had given up hope of ever getting out of prison.

A rash of escapes, acts of desperation, suicides, and murders followed in the ensuing weeks. Steve "Poodle" Howard, a thirty-four-year-old trusty, took off, only to be captured several days later. Poodle, an exemplary prisoner, had served ten years of his life sentence and was active in Angola's civic and social organizations. Donald Fink, a field-worker who had served twenty-one years on a life sentence, walked out of the farm line one noon. An armed guard on horseback yelled, "Where you going?" Fink hollered back, "I'm going home," and started running. A hail of gunfire brought him down. Fink's friends told us he had come to believe he had nothing to live for. Soon afterward, an inmate was stabbed and killed, the second murder of the month.

"In all my research and prison experience, I haven't run across any other point in time where we've experienced a similar rash of desperate acts by the kind of prisoners who don't normally do these kinds of things," Roger Thomas told us.

Federal judge Frank Polozola, whose court enforced, via inspections and reports, the 1975 court order to stem the violence at Angola, expressed concern about the state of the prison; he wanted action.

Deputy Assistant Secretary of Corrections Larry Smith led a surprise shakedown of Angola on the morning of June 9 with a hundred guards borrowed from other prisons. They searched Camp C, where yet another murder had occurred the day before, but found only a two-and-a-half-inch handmade knife. A subsequent shakedown of the huge two-thousand-bed Main Prison complex produced six knives. Two hours after the outsiders withdrew, a Main Prison inmate was slashed across the face in a fight.

Ten days later, Terrance Metoyer, sentenced to eighty-seven years at Angola for armed robbery, was transported to Jefferson Parish to face more robbery charges. As he awaited his turn in court, he asked to use the restroom, where he overpowered the guard, took his gun, and fled in leg irons. Commandeering a truck, he eventually rammed into a police car. Instead of fleeing, Metoyer walked *toward* the police car, firing. He was shot three times; after surgery, he was returned to Angola.

On June 22, Judge Polozola declared a state of emergency at Angola, citing the four suicides, four murders, eleven escapes, and sixty-four stabbings there since Roemer had become governor. The judge ordered a full investigation of Angola to determine "whether the warden and others in charge of that prison are operating it in accordance with the Constitution and laws of the United States and the state of Louisiana and the consent decrees approved by the court." Polozola appointed Ross Maggio, a longtime political adversary of Warden Butler, as the court's expert to oversee the investigation. Local U.S. Attorney Ray Lamonica and the U.S. Justice Department were also ordered "to conduct such investigations—civil and criminal—which may be warranted."

Polozola did not mention hopelessness, despair, or clemency as factors in the "crisis" at Angola, but because we had kept our media friends abreast of the growing problems, they had a frame of reference for what was actually happening. We urged them not to be distracted, to stay focused on the increased number of suicides and mindless escapes, acts of desperation. "Model prisoners do not commit suicide because of drugs, mismanagement, low employee morale, corruption, or any of the things Polozola is complaining of," I told the Baton Rouge *Morning Advocate*. "They do so because of hopelessness, the same reason law-abiding citizens take their own lives. To suggest otherwise means there's some kind of political agenda."

The press interpreted my comments as criticizing the federal judge. One headline read: "Inmate Editor Declares Order 'Political.' " At a news conference, reporters alluding to my comments asked Governor Roemer if his not granting clemency might have contributed to the problem of inmate hopelessness at the prison. "I do not believe that is the problem," he said. "I think that is an excuse." He had no plans of changing his position on clemency. That night, a forty-one-year-old thief hanged himself at Angola.

We on the *Angolite* staff tried to keep the media focused on the governor's role in generating the hopelessness at the prison. We reached out to every media contact we had in Louisiana.

In a brief visit to the *Angolite* office soon after his recent appointment, Maggio stepped through the door, smiled, and said, "Don't you know to duck when a lumberjack swings an ax at a tree?"

"Roemer and Polozola are trying to lead the public to believe these guys are killing themselves because of drugs and mismanagement," I said. "They're playing politics. Somebody's got to keep things in perspective."

"Judge Polozola doesn't play politics," he said. "You have to admit there are problems here."

"There are *always* problems in this place," I said, preaching to the converted. "Are we talking about the ones Polozola wants to recognize and do something about, or the ones he wants to ignore or sweep under the rug?"

"You want to be careful," Maggio said, his tone serious. "You could end up dying in here—from old age."

"From all indications, I can expect that anyway, so I really don't have much to lose, do I?" I said. But I knew he meant well and was trying to warn me.

"There might be an opportunity to help yourself," he said.

I knew that he was offering me the chance to join forces against Butler and earn favor with the powers that be. "Chief, did I ever tell you that when you were warden in 1976," I said, "I went on a speaking trip to Baton Rouge, only to discover that some of your enemies had arranged the trip to ask me to roll over on you? I refused then, just like I have to do now. I can't do what you want me to do if I want *The Angolite* to survive."

It wasn't what he wanted to hear, but I hoped he understood.

Finally, on July 1, Roemer commuted the sentences of nine prisoners. On July 6, he acknowledged on local television that perhaps he should have been less rigid with regard to clemency. On July 10, James "Black Mattie" Robertson, whose quest for freedom after forty-one years in Angola had been front-page news, was paroled. The highly publicized event was a morale booster for the inmate population. "I thought I was going to die here," an emotional Mattie told us at the front gate, where Butler saw him off before a crowd of media. "And I sure would've if y'all hadn't helped me and made the people on the outside know what was happening with me. I appreciate the parole board and officials giving me my freedom, but y'all the ones who really got me out of Angola—*The Angolite* and the other newspaper people who was working with y'all to help me."

Ten days later, Jack Turner, sixty-eight, the inmate with the second-longest time spent at Angola, was paroled to a nursing home. He had been featured with Black Mattie and twenty-nine other inmates the year before in Ron Wikberg's article "The Long-Termers," which won honors from the American Bar Association and ultimately resulted in the release of fifteen elderly long-termers.

An angry Polozola, in a July 14 hearing in his court, expressed displeasure not only with how officials had handled the issue of Angola but also with the larger corrections problem in Louisiana. He blasted the governor and the legislature for not resolving the prison overcrowding that necessitated placing more than four thousand state prisoners in local jails. He promised to address the problem. The idea that deserving men might be released to relieve overcrowding lifted spirits throughout the prison.

Angola inmates received another powerful dose of hope from a July 23 front-page Baton Rouge *Sunday Advocate* story reporting that Roemer had rethought his clemency policy and recognized that there had to be hope and room for rehabilitation in it. In a companion story, the pardon board announced that it was undertaking a review of all seriously ill and elderly prisoners who might be candidates for nursing home or family care and was considering a similar project aimed at long-termers.

We were all smiles in the *Angolite* office. Who would have believed it? But I reminded my colleagues that you don't cross swords with a governor or federal judge and walk away buddies. It was reasonable to assume that somewhere down the line, it would cost us.

On July 24, Roemer announced a shake-up in the corrections hierarchy. Larry Smith, the only ranking black at headquarters, was put in charge of all adult prisons. By month's end, Roemer ordered the state police to conduct a criminal investigation into wrongdoing at Angola.

In August, Maggio filed a report with the federal court highly critical of management at Angola, charging the Butler administration with lax security practices that made it "relatively easy" for drugs and contraband to be smuggled into the prison. That was true, but it was true of every administration I'd known. Butler's administration was also accused of racial discrimination: only 3 of 77 security promotions at Angola above the rank of lieutenant between June 1984 and June 1989 had gone to minorities. That was also true, but racial discrimination had existed under all previous administrations as well. Maggio attributed the manpower shortage to sexual discrimination: only 3 of the 692 females who applied for a job from May 1988 to February 1989 had been hired. (The irony was that Maggio had no more wanted female guards in Angola when he was warden than did Butler.) Maggio also reported that the security deficiencies under Butler "may have been a contributing factor" in the rash of escapes, suicides, and murders.

The governor embraced Maggio's report as being "right on target" and told the media, "We expect to enact the steps brought out in that report." Butler announced his retirement the following day.

Typically, promotions in corrections were contingent upon whom you knew. Larry Smith got his the hard way. He started at Angola and worked his way up. Whenever there was a difficult task to be done, it was given to him. He earned a "troubleshooter" reputation when he was sent to assume management of the problem-plagued DeQuincy prison in 1987, making him the first black ever to run that facility. Now he was being appointed interim warden of Angola, the first black to preside over the historically white-ruled prison.

One of his first stops was the *Angolite* office for what he called a "heads-up talk" with me. "I don't think I have to tell you that you've got some officials in Baton Rouge pretty upset with you," he said. "In fact, I'm supposed to take you out of the equation. I told them I didn't think that kind of action was necessary, that I've known you as long as I've been in this business, and that I've always known you to be about the right thing, and that you could be reasoned with. And that's why we're having this talk."

"Chief, *The Angolite* is pretty much the only voice prisoners have in this state," I said. "If I don't speak for them, who will?"

"Well, you got your message across loud and clear. I'd say that you accomplished your objective. My question is: Are you done?"

I nodded. "I've done what I had to do."

"Okay, then," he said. "I have no intention of interfering with the operation of *The Angolite*. In fact, I'd appreciate you and Ron helping me. You guys know this place probably better than anyone else."

Black inmates were ecstatic about having Smith in charge, which made his job easier. For them, Smith embodied hope because he represented the impossible in their lives—a black man running Angola. If that could happen, maybe the impossible could happen for them, too. His wardenship gave rise to great expectations, from less onerous work to better treatment by the guards, from fairness in the disciplinary process to help in getting out of prison. Inmates felt Smith could ease their suffering. He met with inmate leaders and asked for their patience and cooperation; then he ordered prison-wide elections for inmate representatives who would participate in regular meetings with administrative officials and other inmate leaders to discuss and resolve issues and problems relating to prison operations and the inmate population.

Roemer authorized deficit spending to bring the prison into compliance with the law, the federal consent decree, and Maggio's report. That meant substantial improvements in security procedures, more equipment, additional staff, training programs, an employee pay hike, and a restoration of cuts that had been made in the prison's operating budgets. The court spurred the state to improve ferry service across the Mississippi River for employees who commuted and to complete improvements to the Angola Road, which had been under construction for a decade. That was an immense benefit to prison employees and visitors who had to navigate the muddy, rutted road that connected the prison to the outside world. Jobs and promotions were opened to women and blacks. The Angola prisoner population benefited from all of this: Club meetings and recreational activities were back in full swing; church services were full again; friends and family got full visits; and the stress level among inmates dropped measurably.

Smith expanded on the freedom from censorship Phelps had instituted at Angola. He gave his approval for Ron and me to collaborate with Dave Isay, a young New York radio producer, on a half-hour documentary about the state's get-tough penal practices and the hopelessness, the deaths, and the state of emergency that followed. Dave showed us how to produce, write, and record a radio program, and

then he taught me how to narrate it. The star was Moreese "Pop" Bickham, seventy-two, believed to be the state's longest-confined prisoner.
"Tossing Away the Keys" aired on National Public Radio's *All Things
Considered* and was the first such venture between convicts and a radio
producer. It won the Livingston Award for Dave, who would, in time,
get Bickham out of prison. When he returned to New York, Dave left
his broadcast-quality recorder with me in the event I might be able to
persuade the warden to allow me to do a program on death row. I was
having as full a life and as good a time as anyone who is deprived of his
freedom and a normal framework for his life could have.

I understand no more now than I did then why Governor Roemer
refused to grant me my freedom but trusted me with his political well-
being, allowing me to travel around the state without restraints or
shackles, and only an unarmed officer accompanying me when I gave
talks. I could have literally walked off at any point, which would have
done Roemer irreparable harm.

On April 3, 1990, I again flew to Washington, D.C., this time to
appear before a convention of newspaper editors to talk to them about
running a free press behind bars. I was given a warm reception by several hundred editors the next morning. I urged them to fight censorship, especially as regards prisoners. I impressed upon them that,
contrary to the claims of penal administrators everywhere, censorship
was not necessary and that a free prisoner press could benefit both
inmates and the institution. I told them *The Angolite* had proven valuable in easing tensions by dispelling rumor with truth and by helping
both keeper and kept understand one another. It wasn't always easy, I
said: "If *you* make a mistake, you get a letter to the editor. Imagine, if
you will, a guy with a bandanna around his head, an earring in his ear,
nasty scar on his face. Let's call him Bruno. If he doesn't like what I
have to say here today, Bruno is quite likely to show up at my office
door or my bedside with a clenched fist or a baseball bat. Believe me,
Bruno gives a whole new meaning to the concept of letter to the editor." They laughed.

The appearance meant a great deal to me. Three decades earlier I
had committed a terrible sin and was condemned, written off by the
world, and left to die—if not by execution, then by incarceration. But
here I was, a river of time later, after a long, hard struggle for life and a
future in the face of none. I was profoundly mindful of just how far I
was from my impossible beginnings.

Jetting through the skies on the way home, I closed my eyes and thought of Linda. The more I learned about her, the more I liked her. She was endlessly interesting. We were from totally disparate backgrounds and cultures, but we saw and thought about things similarly, to the point that I said, "Talking with you is like talking to a minature version of myself. Mind if I call you 'Junior'?"

"Why can't I be 'Senior'?" she asked.

"I don't care, but I'm older than you." She became "Junior."

In 1989 Linda became an investigator for the state board of ethics and moved to Baton Rouge. She was now less than an hour's drive from Angola, where she could conduct research and sit in on public events of interest to me. Her dedication to me was humbling.

We were optimistic about my clemency hearing, a couple of weeks away. Roemer's new pardon board was sympathetic to me. I had endeavored to "do more," as the governor had put it on *20/20* two years earlier. I had talked to at-risk schoolkids and to criminal court probationers, for which I had been awarded a certificate of appreciation by the mayor of New Orleans. I coedited a textbook, *The Wall Is Strong: Corrections in Louisiana,* for use by criminal justice students. There was the precedent-setting radio show. Columbia's Graduate School of Journalism had announced that *The Angolite* was again a finalist for the 1990 National Magazine Award, the fourth time. The most powerful element in our argument for my release, however, had been produced by Linda.

Since Governor Roemer indicated on *20/20* that he was willing to listen and willing to learn, she and Ted Quant decided that Linda would scour public records for the sort of hard data that would prove beyond a shadow of a doubt that I had been treated differently from other convicted murderers petitioning for clemency. She spent weeks in the secretary of state's office and archives recording every pardon and commutation granted to every Louisiana murderer since 1961, when I entered the system. She and Ted were shocked to see how little time many of them had served. Although ten years and six months had been the understood length of a life sentence for half a century, many murderers had been made eligible for parole after serving a third of that and were eligible to be discharged without parole after serving half of it. Linda found forty-eight executive clemencies granted to thirty-nine formerly condemned prisoners who had been freed since I entered prison in 1961. There were more than five hundred clemencies granted to murderers since 1961. None of those released had served as much time as I had.

From Ron Wikberg, who used sheriff's receipts, prison admission and discharge cards, and fingerprint cards in the prison's Identification Department to identify the arrival and departure of lifers from the penitentiary, she learned that thirty-one convicted murderers had entered the gates of Angola in 1962, the year I arrived. Six carried death sentences; the other twenty-five, life sentences. All had been freed, except me.

Since the bitter opposition to me was coming from Calcasieu Parish, Linda studied the history of murder convictions there. She discovered that up until at least 1976 (her cutoff date) Calcasieu Parish had sentenced to death every black man convicted of killing a white, the highest such rate ever documented in America. Whites who murdered whites received the death penalty 23.3 percent of the time; blacks who murdered blacks, 10.4 percent of the time. She discovered that those convicted murderers from Calcasieu who had been released from prison since 1961 had spent an average of twelve years behind bars; she also learned that no black convicted of murdering a white had ever been granted clemency and freed. At twenty-nine years and counting, I had been imprisoned longer than any offender in the recorded history of Calcasieu Parish.

When Linda first told me what she had discovered, I bristled with resentment that I had been singled out for harsher treatment than all those who did little or nothing to earn a second chance but got it anyway. Then I reminded myself that the last twenty-nine years had been a gift: I was supposed to be a dead man but had escaped execution three times. The maturity that had come with age and education was also a gift. And I had learned that optimism, the only antidote to despair, is a choice we make. I had made it long ago, and it allowed me to live a reasonably happy and meaningful life in prison. True, my life over the past twenty-nine years had almost unbearably difficult moments—years, actually—but it was also rich with significant work, friends, and love that came to me from outside the gates. It wasn't the free life that I craved, but it surely was better than the life I would have had on the streets if I had never gone to prison. Still, of course, I yearned for a normal life.

Linda's findings, based on the 101 murder convictions in Calcasieu Parish between 1889 and 1976, revealed blatant, institutionalized racism. Her exhaustive research changed the nature of the debate over me: It was now about "equal justice," not "mercy." She submitted "The Rideau Report," eighty-three pages distilling her findings, to the governor's executive counsel and the pardon board in advance of my hearing. The Institute of Human Relations of Loyola released the report to the media.

I was once again optimistic about my chances for release. But we should have taken more seriously a comment by the governor a month earlier. In March, the *Morning Advocate* reported that Roemer was not yet convinced I should be freed; he intended to meet with bank teller Dora McCain *at my request* and that of Reverend James Stovall. "I'll see if that brings any change in my attitude," said Roemer.

I had made no such request. Nor had Reverend Stovall.

As the pardon board convened on the afternoon of April 18, 1990, I heard on the radio that Roemer had met with McCain the day before and decided that he would not grant me clemency.

At two o'clock, my supporters—clustered in the hall and the lunchroom at corrections headquarters—poured into the adjoining hearing room. As usual, I was not allowed to attend. Attorney Julian Murray, who was representing me pro bono, spoke first. He said the governor was quoted as having said that he had spoken with Dora McCain, and "after speaking with Mrs. McCain, that he felt that the crime was so heinous, and it was such a terrible crime, that he was not disposed as of that given moment in time to grant any type of commutation to Wilbert. I would respectfully suggest to the governor that he got the cart before the horse, because he has appointed this board to first hear the evidence, make the recommendation, and then in due course he has to make the ultimate decision."

He continued to press his point before the board: "What [the governor] has undertaken has been an extraordinary act within the history of this state . . . we have a government of laws, not of men. And it is not appropriate that Wilbert Rideau have his future and his fate determined by the feelings of one person [Dora McCain] . . . in this society we don't allow victims to determine the punishment."

Rick Bryant, an assistant district attorney making his fourth appearance with Salter before the pardon board, suggested that my case had not been treated differently from others, emphasizing time and again that the Calcasieu Parish district attorney's office opposed the release of *all* murderers, a statement we knew to be blatantly untrue.

It was particularly ironic that on the day Salter and Bryant made the 250-mile round-trip from Lake Charles to fight to keep me in prison, the Lake Charles *American Press* ran an editorial about justice in

The annual Angola Rodeo draws thousands of tourists who pay to see convict "cowboys" in daring events. *Left:* An inmate rides a bucking bronco. *Below:* In "convict poker," the last man to remain seated at the table rather than run away wins $100. Although injuries sometimes occur, they are rarely serious.

With Ginger Roberts (later Berrigan) in 1979. She came to Angola to give legal pointers to the jailhouse lawyers. She became my first pro bono attorney, recruiting influential supporters and additional lawyers to try to win my release through clemency and the courts.

Frank Blackburn, Angola warden, 1978–81 and 1984–87. He called *The Angolite* his "conscience." Under him, the magazine won many honors for investigative journalism that exposed problems at the prison.

In the past, inmates were buried in packing crates and pressed cardboard caskets by a crew of grave diggers. After inmate leaders appealed for change, funerals became meaningful events conducted by inmates and boasting prisoner-made caskets and a horse-driven carriage.

With C. Paul Phelps, Angola warden, 1976, and Secretary of Corrections, 1976–81 and 1984–88. He taught me about friendship, civic responsibility, and moral obligation. Phelps turned *The Angolite* into the only uncensored prison publication in America because he thought it would help clean up the prison and improve inmate-employee relations—which it did.

With the decline of furloughs and the loss of other incentives to encourage good behavior, Warden Hilton Butler instituted the outdoor visiting program for trusties who remained discipline-free for one year. They could relax with their visitors in a beautiful park on the prison grounds.

Peggi Gresham, *Angolite* supervisor, 1976–85, was the best boss I ever had. The first female to become an assistant warden in the all-male prison, she commanded respect and cooperation from inmates and employees alike. Here she is with *Angolite* stringers Ashanti Witherspoon (*left*) and Woodrow Arthur.

August 7, 1984: Timothy Baldwin (*left*), with attorney Bill Quigley, declared to the pardon board that he was innocent of the murder for which he was sentenced to death. The hearing was a charade, as the governor had secretly ordered the board to deny all requests from condemned prisoners. Like many others, Baldwin was returned to death row and executed.

With Margery Hicks, member of the pardon board, in 1984. She told me about the fraudulent clemency hearings for death row prisoners and became my friend and advocate.

Billy Sinclair (*left*), *Angolite* writer, later coeditor, 1977–86, with his longtime friend and supporter, prison food manager F. Berlin Hood. In a corrupt clemency system, Hood offered to act as middleman for Sinclair to purchase the freedom he was otherwise denied. In 1986, Sinclair initiated an FBI sting against Hood, who was arrested and convicted.

Jane Bankston, the first mental health director for the Louisiana penal system, listens to Phelps and me. She recruited a staff of professionals and implemented meaningful programs for the treatment of mentally ill prisoners. She became a supporter and personal friend.

Tommy Mason (*bottom left*) arrived at Angola in 1969, at age sixteen, with a life sentence for murder. He was a model prisoner, my associate editor, and, later, Louisiana governor Edwin Edwards's personal valet. The governor freed him in 1987. A loyal friend, he returned to visit. Dr. Linda LaBranche (*center*), my unlikely knight in shining armor, saw me on TV in 1986 and spent the next two decades working to free me.

March 10, 1988: My friend "Dot" Henderson arranged freedom for two rehabilitated lifers as a farewell gift to me as her tenure as Louisiana parole board chairwoman ended.

Model prisoner and lifer James "Black Mattie" Robertson bids farewell to Warden Hilton Butler on July 10, 1989, after forty-one years at the prison. He was paroled following *The Angolite*'s profile of him as the state's longest-confined prisoner.

John Whitley, Angola warden, 1990–95, dubbed "The Man Who Tamed Hell" by *Time* magazine, was one of Angola's best wardens. With him as publisher, *The Angolite* enjoyed its heyday. He approved my becoming a correspondent for National Public Radio and my filmmaking as avenues to educate the public about the realities of prison.

Larry Smith was the only black warden of Angola, 1989–90, and the right man for the times, bringing calm to the prison during a state of emergency. He expanded the freedoms Phelps put into place and approved my entry into radio production.

Members of Angola's Vets Incarcerated honor their deceased brethren in the prison cemetery on Memorial Day. An estimated 10 percent of the nation's prisoners are military veterans.

Louisiana executioner "Sam Jones" killed twenty prisoners in this electric chair. Photographic evidence published in *The Angolite* showing the mutilation and burns inflicted upon the condemned helped facilitate the state's switch to lethal injection. "Jones" talked himself out of a job when he gave us an interview.

Ron Wikberg, my associate editor, married his sweetheart, Kay, upon his 1992 parole after serving twenty-three years for killing a man during a holdup. He was a nice guy and a brilliant jailhouse lawyer, who regarded his prison experience as "positive." Ron and Kay met when he responded to her request for information.

Prisoners meet women through friends and relatives, correspondence, and religious and civic functions at the prison. Some fall in love and marry in the prison chapel. Here, I'm attending the wedding of my associate editor Michael Glover (with a borrowed tie) and his bride, Debi.

An inmate "lawyer" interviews clients he will represent in disciplinary court. There are many self-taught jailhouse lawyers behind bars, but about fifty well-trained ones work in Angola's Legal Programs Department as "counsel substitutes" to serve the legal needs of the inmate population.

Burl Cain (*left*), Angola warden, 1995–present, and Richard Stalder, Louisiana corrections secretary, 1992–2008. They built an empire on the backs of prisoners, and Louisiana became the leading incarceration state in the country. Cain tolerated no criticism of him or his administration, and freedom from censorship became a thing of the past.

The Angolite changed constantly during my quarter-century editorship as writers were freed, quit, or died, and as successive administrations brought new supervisors and publishers. Here, with supervisor Dwayne McFatter (bottom), in January 1996: *left to right*, Lane Nelson, Michael Glover, Keith Elliott, me, Clarence Goodlow, and Douglas Dennis.

January 10, 1996: New York radio producer Dave Isay (*left*) and I await the midnight release of Moreese Bickham (*right*), star of our National Public Radio documentary "Tossing Away the Keys." He was freed by the governor after serving thirty-eight years for murder.

With Antonio James, before his March 1, 1996, execution for murder, which was the subject of my TV documentary "The Execution of Antonio James." It won me awards, which Warden Cain kept, without even telling me about them.

After four decades, freedom once again seemed within reach in 2003. Some of my defense team in New Orleans, May 31, 2003. *Left to right:* Julian Murray, Laura Fernandez, Johnnie Cochran, Linda LaBranche, and George Kendall.

Staunch supporters Sister Benedict Shannon, Johnnie Cochran, Norris Henderson, Ted Quant, and Ronald Ware appear at a June 1, 2003, Lake Charles community rally for me.

Reverend J. L. Franklin, who visited me often to monitor my welfare, led a protest at the courthouse following the rally and galvanized black community support behind me.

Free at last! With my mother, who kept the faith for forty-four years.

I married my guardian angel, Linda, in 2008, twenty-two years after she resolved to free me. Her hard work, love, and devotion allow me to wake up in heaven every morning. Here, we're at an awards dinner in the nation's capital in 2005.

Willie B, my first pet, who succumbed to oral cancer in 2006. From him I learned that unconditional love is not limited to humans and that animals are life forces with needs, feelings, fears, pain, and joys—just like the rest of us.

the Calcasieu courts. It outlined the case of a white man, former Lake Charles Dock Board member Terry Hebert, who had killed two pedestrians—a black man and woman—while he was driving drunk. A white judge, Ellis Bond, refused to take a victims' impact statement from the families and accepted Hebert's "no contest" plea. At sentencing, Judge Bond said he believed Hebert would be more careful in his drinking in the future, "considering the agony he and his family had suffered as a result of hitting and killing his two victims." Then he sentenced Hebert to two and a half years in prison, which he immediately suspended and replaced with six months in the local jail. Hebert was allowed to remain free on bond while appealing what his attorneys called an overly harsh sentence. Even the Lake Charles newspaper thought the sentence mocked justice. It was in this context that I read Bryant's front-page statement about me in the same edition of the paper: "Nothing he could do would ever be sufficient for him to be released."

The pardon board sent Roemer a unanimous recommendation to commute my sentence to fifty-five years, which would mean immediate freedom for me. Without even reviewing the board's decision or its reasoning, Roemer told an impromptu news conference that he had no plans to accept the recommendation.

As much as I tried to tell myself that this was just another glitch in a life that on balance had been pretty good, and that there would be brighter days and new ventures ahead, every rejection required more energy and faith to bounce back from. *I'll never get out of this place alive! They're going to bury me here, alone, a prisoner forever,* I thought. The image of Angola's cemetery, set on a remote patch of the prison grounds, rose in my mind: prisoners sealed up in a friendless, loveless place that no one ever visited. I pushed away the fearsome picture of my being buried there in a cardboard box. And I thought of Linda. *She's bought into this, thinking hard work and fairness would prevail. Nothing in her life prepared her for this. She must be crushed.* The telephone in my office was ringing. I somehow found a reservoir of equanimity as reporters began phoning for my response. "I appreciate the board of pardons having once again expressed their belief in my worth and potential as a human being," I said. "They have also expressed their continued belief in the American principle of equal justice, judging me the same way they judge every other person in this state who has been convicted of murder and then released."

The following day Mary Foster called from the Associated Press. "Where do you go from here, Wilbert?" she asked.

"I'll try again next year. What choice do I have? I've tried to make amends the best I could in the only ways available to me," I told her. "I've tried to do things that counted over the last twenty-nine years."

And then Francis "Corky" Clifton called. Corky and I had first met on death row, where he arrived in 1965 for killing a man during a robbery. His death sentence, like mine, was judicially amended to life imprisonment after the *Furman* ruling. Like me, Corky was a small, slight man who had entered the bloodiest prison in America. And like most of the formerly condemned, he was a model prisoner with an exemplary record of behavior. He received not a single visit from his siblings or his children, but, nevertheless, he had remade himself, teaching himself how to repair watches and to paint. Like others who thought they were serving 10-6 life sentences, he applied for clemency after a decade behind bars and was denied. A second denial followed. In 1983, he won a recommendation from the pardon board for a sentence reduction to fifty years, which was blocked by objections from law enforcement; this, in the new law-and-order climate of that time, had become routine practice for murder cases.

At the age of fifty-two, with no hope of legitimate release and after two heart attacks, feeling his time was running out, he had staged his failed "Moon Pies" escape. When he was taken back to Angola, he was placed in a small, solitary-confinement cell. Indefinite isolation was his punishment for succumbing to despair. "Having sit in this cell now for several weeks with nothing, even denied my cigarettes, I have thought a lot about suicide, and it seems to be the most humane way out of a prison I no longer care to struggle in," he said shortly after his isolation began. He had posed a difficult question to me: "Suicide, or endless torment—which would you choose?" I couldn't answer. Ron and I wrote a story about Corky. After it appeared, a woman named Betty Lung wrote to him from his hometown of Hamersville, Ohio. They corresponded, then talked on the phone. She visited him a number of times.

Now Corky was in the hospital and had sent for us. Despite the tubes delivering oxygen to his nostrils, he greeted us with a big smile. "For once in my life, something wonderful is happening," he said. "I'm getting married in five days." He handed us a photo of Betty, who had moved to Louisiana to be near him. Love had brought joy to Corky's life. "Now I've got something to live for," he said. He wanted us to know what a difference we had made in his life.

I know that among both prison authorities and the general public, the common view is that a prisoner is just waiting to find some woman to con and then leave after he is released from prison. That happens, just as it happens that scoundrels in free society take advantage of women. But in my experience, it happens far more often that a prisoner lucky enough to find a woman willing to take a chance on him, love him, and stick by him in the most challenging circumstances considers himself extraordinarily blessed and wants to keep her.

Just the day before, I had sat at a tree-shaded table on a beautiful sunny day in the spacious outdoor visiting park for trusties, watching Linda walk up the hill toward me, and I marveled at the happiness she had brought into my life. Love is a powerful, powerful force. I felt upbeat after our visit to Corky.

Two days later he was dead. Betty took his body back to Ohio, rescuing him from the Angola inmate's nightmare of being buried in the prison cemetery, a prisoner forever.

10

Hope

1990—1994

"Have you ever run across anything to indicate that an execution was botched at Angola?" asked Sarah Ottinger, a young lawyer working with New Orleans attorney Nick Trenticosta on the case of Frederick Kirkpatrick, who was scheduled to be electrocuted on September 19, 1990.

Ron and I, each with a phone to our ear, looked quizzically at one another and answered that we had not.

"In fact, prison officials have consistently expressed satisfaction at how well the executions have gone," I said, "particularly in light of news reports of bungled executions in other states."

"Like the electrocution of Jessie Tafero last May, who literally caught fire in Florida's electric chair," Ron added. "But here, neither witnesses nor news media attending Angola executions have ever reported seeing a problem."

Sarah's question was not an idle one. After an unofficial twenty-two-year moratorium on executions, Louisiana had resumed the practice with a vengeance on December 14, 1983, beginning with the electrocution of Robert Wayne Williams. By August 1990, the state had executed nineteen men. To halt Kirkpatrick's impending date with death, Ottinger and Trenticosta were mounting the first legal challenge to Louisiana's use of the electric chair, charging that it burned, tortured, and mutilated the condemned. That was confirmed by photos of Williams taken by his family at the Baton Rouge mortuary that handled his funeral arrangements.

America was marking the one-hundredth anniversary of its first execution by electric chair, an event George Westinghouse, the nineteenth-century inventor of the alternating-current technology used in that killing apparatus, had described as "a brutal affair—they could have done a better job with an ax."

I phoned Rosetta Williams, Robert's mother, and asked for copies of the photographs and permission to publish them. An *Angolite* fan and an opponent of capital punishment, she was happy to accommodate us. Because Florida law required postmortem autopsy photographs of executed inmates, Ron requested from authorities there the photos of Daniel Thomas, David Funchess, Ronald Straight, Buford White, Willie Darden, Jeffrey Daugherty, Ted Bundy, Dennis Adams, and Jesse Tafero—the last nine men to die in that state's electric chair.

Florida sent us twenty-six photos; Rosetta Williams sent thirty-three of her son. Because all incoming mail was opened and inspected for possible contraband before reaching us, the arrival of so many grisly pictures, all in color, caused a stir in the warden's office. John Whitley, who had recently replaced Larry Smith as Angola's warden (Smith had been promoted to deputy secretary of corrections), came to see us one evening and asked to see the photos. We laid them out on a long cabinet countertop, a ghoulish display. The photographs, taken soon after the men were electrocuted, vividly showed the freshly burned, mutilated flesh. I was horrified anew, and disturbed again by the shaven heads of the dead men, which seemed to strip them of their humanness. "What am I supposed to be seeing in these pictures of dead people?" the warden asked.

We pointed to the photos of Williams that showed severe burns on his head and leg where the electrodes had been placed, the areas of mutilation larger than the size of the electrodes. He had suffered first-, second-, third-, and fourth-degree burns. "When you compare how he looks with the way the inmates in Florida who were executed look," Ron said, "it's obvious the execution of Robert Wayne Williams didn't go right."

"I was a witness," the warden said, "and I didn't see anything go wrong. There were no problems."

"Chief, how do you account for these burns on him?" I asked.

"His head was covered and he had on clothes during the execution, so we couldn't see his body. When the coroner said he was dead, we were escorted out. This is my first time seeing this."

"There are no postmortem photographs of Wayne Felde, who was executed in 1988," Ron said, "but two nurses who saw him afterward have signed affidavits, describing his physical condition as being even worse than Williams's."

"Do you have photos of Dalton Prejean?" Whitley asked. He had presided over Prejean's execution on May 18, his only one.

"No, sir," Ron replied, "but you were there. Did he look anything like Robert Wayne afterward?"

"I don't know what he looked like," said Whitley. "Again, he had a hood over his head and was fully clothed. When the execution was over, I signaled the coroner, who came in to check his heartbeat and officially declare him dead."

"Chief, you didn't look at him?" I asked.

"For what?" he asked in return, a little testy. "My job was done. The witnesses left, and I left. Paramedics went in afterward and removed the body."

"Chances are your predecessors all did the same thing," I said.

Whitley, forty-six, was a year younger than me, with a fondness for Stetsons and cowboy boots. He had begun his career at the violent Angola of 1970 as a classification officer. With guts and a mind of his own, he quickly established himself as an independent power to be reckoned with, someone you wanted *with* you, never *against* you. Maggio eventually made him director of classification, and in 1978, he became deputy warden. The following year, he transferred to Hunt Correctional Center and four years later became warden of the facility. Retiring in 1989, he moved to Texas, where he served as warden of a prison operated by Wackenhut, Inc., a privately owned, for-profit enterprise to which states outsourced their excess inmate populations. He had returned to Angola earlier in the year to replace interim warden Larry Smith. Phelps assured me that Whitley would make a good *Angolite* publisher because he could be relied upon to stand his ground and not let anyone dictate to him. Phelps was right. Whitley believed in a visible and accessible administration. While he regarded himself as a criminal justice conservative, he was very much a progressive in that he did not believe in censorship or in secrecy and vowed to continue the open-door media policy at the prison. "If there's something that's wrong in the prison," he announced upon assuming the wardenship, "I want to know about it, and my staff had better correct it, because I intend to be proud of this prison and the way we operate it." Our proposed publication of the postmortem photographs of Robert Wayne Williams was his first test as publisher of *The Angolite.*

"Tell me—what are you trying to accomplish with these pictures?" he asked. "Make a case against capital punishment?"

"This is not about the issue of capital punishment," I said. I did not acknowledge that we thought publishing the sensational photos would probably result in a halt of the use of the chair. "A claim has been filed in court charging that the electric chair is defective and has been mutilating and perhaps torturing the inmates being executed. It's a legitimate story."

"The legislature just passed a law ending use of the chair," he said. "We'll switch over to lethal injection in a year."

"But the thirty-two guys currently on death row and those who will be sentenced to death during the coming year are not affected by the law," Ron said. "They have to die in that chair."

"I doubt that any newspaper in Louisiana would publish those photos," said Whitley.

"That's all the more reason we need to do it," I said. "And as publisher, you might want the distinction of having *your* magazine publish what even the professional outside press is too squeamish to print." He asked how many photos we wanted to use. I said I intended to publish only two photos of Williams to make our point—one of his head and the other of his leg, in black-and-white.

"You're saying you're not good enough writers to make your point without the pictures?" he asked.

"No writer is ever as good as a photo," said Ron. "These pictures grab your attention and make the point—without words."

I reminded the warden of his own philosophy, that if he couldn't stand having people see what he was doing, then maybe he shouldn't be doing it.

He smiled and nodded in agreement. "I just wanted you to defend your position. I think the photos will make for a great story. But you do understand there are people who are not gonna want this published," he said.

As word of the photos got around, those people did indeed arrive. Annette Viator, attorney for the Department of Corrections, came to the prison and implied I wouldn't be allowed to publish the pictures. Her boss, corrections chief Bruce Lynn, strongly suggested to me that it was not in my best interest or that of the department.

Ottinger and Trenticosta filed their lengthy legal challenge in the 22nd Judicial District Court of Louisiana, in which they included the Williams photos. There was also a report by Theodore Bernstein, a national expert on electrical engineering who had traveled to Angola and spent hours studying the chair and its equipment and found significant problems: "The buckle on the wet straps is too close to the flesh and acts as an additional conducting path to cause burns at the buckle. The buckle and leather cause arcing of the electrical current to other areas of the flesh, resulting in additional burns. The sponge utilized is too thin and therefore does not spread the current uniformly over a sufficient area, which leads to greater burns. The rough underside of the electrode and the sharp edges of the metal, as constructed, burn right into the skin because of the close spacing permitted by the thin sponge." Bernstein's conclusions were supported by another expert, Fred Leuchter, Jr., the nation's only provider of execution equipment, who stated that the Angola electrodes were "the most poorly designed . . . I have ever seen."

Bernstein told Ron and me that he was surprised to learn Louisiana's electric chair had been "put together by electricians" instead of electrical engineers. The biggest problem was the electrodes, which he said "contributed to excessive, completely unnecessary burning of the person being executed." The burns and mutilations suffered by Williams were not unique to him but were experienced by other prisoners electrocuted in Louisiana, he concluded; he predicted similar results in the future.

The court stayed the execution of Frederick Kirkpatrick. No news media in the state mentioned the photos. We decided to hold up publication of our next edition so that we could include the outcome of the pardon board's October 8 clemency hearing for Robert Sawyer, a mentally retarded inmate scheduled to die in the electric chair two days later. He was now being represented by Ottinger and Trenticosta, who had become involved in his case only the month before.

When the Louisiana Supreme Court refused to stay the execution, Trenticosta had to remain in New Orleans to file legal motions for Sawyer in the federal courts, so Ottinger had to handle a challenging presentation to the pardon board alone. After presenting evidence of

Sawyer's mental retardation, which she contended had made it difficult for him to consider the prosecutor's plea bargain offer prior to trial, Ottinger prepared to present evidence of design problems with the state's electric chair. Bernstein was to be her first witness. "I don't know where else to bring this," she told the board, "but I bring it to you because you're the conscience of the community."

The board, forewarned by Annette Viator, declared itself an improper forum. "We are not technical people. That's not our function," pardon board chairwoman Yvonne Campbell said. She disallowed Ottinger's argument and evidence of a design flaw in the chair, evidence that would have included the post-execution photos of Williams and made them part of the public record.

During a break in the session, board member Sally McKissack came over to where I was standing against the wall to say hello. Yvonne followed her. "Heard you've got copies of those photographs," Yvonne whispered.

I nodded. "They'll be in the next issue."

"The Department of Corrections isn't gonna let y'all publish that," Sally half declared, half asked.

"Whitley's the publisher. We'll see."

"You heard what we've heard, Wilbert," said Sally. "What would you do?"

"Sarah and Nick have already filed this issue in court," I said. "Having seen the pictures, I'd find a reason to dodge this execution, because if something goes wrong with it after you've refused to hear their complaint, you're going to catch flak from everywhere. But you know that."

At the end of the hearing, Campbell announced that the governor, upon the board's request, had granted Sawyer a reprieve to allow the board more time to acquire additional documents needed to make a decision.

The September/October 1990 issue of *The Angolite* featured "The Horror Show," with the postmortem Williams photographs. The magazine was being printed when we learned the closely guarded identity of the state's executioner. We asked Whitley to convey an interview request to him and stopped the presses to postpone publication of Williams's photos until after we interviewed the executioner.

"He'd have to be crazy to talk to you," Whitley said, "and once he sees those photographs in *The Angolite*, he definitely won't talk to you."

"That's why we want to interview him *before* the magazine is published," I said. I asked Whitley to let the man know that we already knew who he was, but weren't going to reveal his identity. "At least invite him to the prison; let us make our own appeal to him, and let him make his own decision." Whitley agreed to extend an invitation to the man to meet with us.

A couple of weeks later, Assistant Warden Dwayne McFatter, the new *Angolite* supervisor and Whitley's right-hand man, met Ron and me at the door of the death house at Camp F and showed us into a room, where Whitley introduced us to a bearded, dark-haired man dressed in camouflage pants, snakeskin cowboy boots, and a black T-shirt. He was a Baton Rouge electrician who had volunteered for the job of executioner and was dubbed "Sam Jones," after the governor who presided over the state's first execution by electric chair. So far, he had killed nineteen men from Angola's death row. His predecessor, Grady Jarrett, had died during the two-decade moratorium on executions, after dispatching sixty-seven men. I was intensely aware that had my death sentence stood, this man would have thrown the switch on me without batting an eyelid.

Just as many people expect me to be somehow different from them because I killed someone, I found myself expecting a man who had coolly killed nineteen people to display something in his appearance or behavior that hinted at his chilling avocation. But he appeared to be the kind of nondescript, white, working-class guy you'd find sitting at a bar, on a bus, at the supermarket—a carpenter, a locksmith, a repairman, even a cop, all of which he had been during his life.

Jones said he agreed to come and hear us out because of the reputation of *The Angolite.* Had he wanted anonymity, he would not have come to meet with us. So we appealed to his ego, telling him that we wanted to put his picture on our cover. He agreed to an interview and to being photographed. Whitley turned away in disgust as he and McFatter stepped outside the room, leaving us to our interview. We first took Jones into the execution chamber to get photos of him standing next to his instrument of death, the oaken chair that had done duty since the year before I was born. I gave him an *Angolite* to hold in his hand as I snapped his photograph.

Jones was a divorced father who didn't socialize much. He called himself "a loner" but assured us that he was just a typical citizen who lived a normal life—except for his occasional trip to Angola to push a button to kill someone. He was paid $400 each time. He insisted the money had little to do with his being an executioner. He said he did it for the victims of crime. "They don't have anyone else speaking for 'em," he said. He didn't sound convincing. He said that neither he nor his family nor anyone close to him had ever been victimized by crime. Yet it seemed clear that he liked being an executioner.

Jones said he knew nothing about executions, had never seen one performed, much less conducted one, when he executed Williams in 1983. "I didn't know what to expect," he said. We asked him about the ongoing legal challenge, the claim that the electric chair was poorly designed and caused excessive pain and mutilation to the inmate. He said there had been no problems with the chair Angola used. "I see 'em when they remove them from the chair. I haven't seen any of them burned or mutilated in the eighteen or nineteen that I've done."

"But you just admitted that you had never seen an execution before," I said, "so how would you know what the inmate was supposed to look like physically after being electrocuted?"

"I had seen people electrocuted accidentally," he said.

Ron showed him the postmortem Williams photos. "Is that the way he looked after you executed him?" Ron asked.

Jones looked through the color photographs, then shook his head. "No, I've never seen that," he said. "That's the first time I've seen that. I didn't see that on him when they had him in the chair. It may have come up later. I don't know what happens to 'em, what procedure the body goes through after they're electrocuted."

"Did any of the other inmates have burns like this on them?" Ron asked.

"No," he replied. "I don't remember seeing it on 'em. As soon as they take 'em out of the chair, they put 'em in a body bag and they're gone."

Jones admitted he had never examined the electric chair. He relied upon prison electricians—whose execution expertise was acquired, like his own, through on-the-job training—to have it in perfect working order when he arrived to perform his deed. The only test of chair readiness occurred a couple of days prior to each execution, when prison authorities put the electrodes into a tub of water to see if the electricity was flowing through them.

Jones believed the inmates he executed were human garbage, guilty and beyond redemption. Although he was highly critical of the justice system, he felt it had so many safeguards built into it that it was virtually impossible for anyone on death row to be innocent. He believed that electrocution was too quick and easy a death. "They don't feel no pain," he said, basing his statement on his own experience of having once been shocked. "It knocks them out." Yet he confessed that if he had to be executed, he would choose lethal injection over the electric chair.

"Does killing these guys bother you, just a little?" I asked.

"Nope—not at all," he replied nonchalantly. "It's never bothered me. There's nuthin' to it. It's no different to me executing somebody and goin' to the refrigerator and getting a beer out of it."

"What if it was your son?" Ron asked.

"If he did something, they sit him in the chair, he was convicted of it, I'd execute him," he said.

We left the death house convinced that Sam Jones was as remorseless a killer as any of the men he executed. And he was a free man.

"That fucker is crazier than I thought he was," said Whitley, having overheard much of the interview.

"And he's about to learn the power of the press," I said.

"No matter how this ends," said Whitley, "whether we have the needle or the chair, we won't be needing his services anymore. He talked himself out of a job."

Our September/October 1990 magazine was finally published around Thanksgiving. The photos of Williams, the medical diagnosis of his burns, and the conclusions of expert electrical engineers that Louisiana's electric chair was defective made news throughout the state. It was our hottest, fastest-selling magazine ever. Everyone wanted to see what an electrocuted person looked like, it seemed.

The corrections department, without acknowledging anything was wrong with the electric chair, announced it would ask the legislature to mandate that the present death row population be executed by lethal injection.

Our interview with the executioner was published two issues later, after which he was relieved of his duties.

A couple of weeks later I was summoned to a meeting with Governor Roemer at the governor's mansion in Baton Rouge. Whitley and McFatter accompanied me and, as usual, I wore no restraints.

Whitley said he didn't know what the governor wanted. I was concerned that it might have something to do with the post-execution photos, that the governor might want to shut down *The Angolite.* I would contest that in the most high-profile way I could, and I knew, win or lose, that would bury me in prison forever.

When I was shown into the governor's office, Whitley and McFatter waited outside with a state trooper. An attractive blonde and an old man in a suit sat on a couch to the left. Roemer stood behind a desk, a small, wiry man, dressed casually in jeans and shirt.

I recalled how he had phoned Dalton Prejean moments before his execution—causing hope for a reprieve to surge through the condemned man—only to tell Prejean he was going to let him die. I wondered now if he had been deliberately callous. He invited me to a chair in front of the desk and we both sat. He said he was honoring his promise not to make a decision on my application for clemency without meeting with me and listening to my side. "If there's anything in particular that you want to say on your own behalf, now's the time to say it," he said dispassionately.

I thanked him for meeting with me. "I don't know what to tell you that you don't already know," I said. "I've traveled throughout this state for years and could have physically taken my freedom at any point. The fact that I didn't should tell you something." I shrugged. "But perhaps you have questions for me."

"My understanding is that you took three people all the way out of the city, out into the woods, lined them up on the side of the road, and shot them execution-style." He stopped, studying me.

"No, sir," I said, shaking my head, "it didn't happen like that. I never intended to hurt anybody. If I had wanted to kill those people, I would have done it right there inside the bank, instead of running all over the place with them. In fact, they even testified that I told the bank manager to get his coat because he'd be cold walking back to town. I did not line them up and shoot them execution-style, like the DA claims. Mrs. McCain leaped out of the car and I sprang out of the other side, slipping and losing my balance. Everybody took off running and I panicked, firing impulsively as they fled."

"Why did you slash Mrs. McCain's throat?"

"I did not slash Mrs. McCain's throat."

"Don't tell me you didn't," he said, an edge to his voice. "She told me you did. She sat right there where you're at and showed me the scar on her neck."

I realized from his tone that he had granted me this audience only because of pressure from the media. This was the face-to-face version of his call to Prejean. My gut clenched.

"I don't know why she said that, Governor. In four decades, I have never heard that before. I can only tell you that it's not true."

"Wasn't there a confession?" the old man on the couch asked.

"There were two confessions," I replied. "What I'm telling you today is exactly what I told the sheriff that night at the jail. The FBI got me to sign a second one several days later that gives a different version of the crime. One of the agents wrote it himself, and had me sign it, on the promise that they would protect my mother from the lynch mob."

"You're saying the FBI statement isn't accurate?" Roemer asked.

My mind searched frantically for something he might relate to. "That statement has me eating lunch in Youngblood's Café in the shopping center next door to where I worked. It was an all-white area of town, before the civil rights movement and racial integration. It was against the law for a black person to eat in a white café. Had I tried to do so, the crime I'm in prison for would've never happened, because the whites in that place would either have killed me on the spot or the police would have locked me up." I paused, trying to gauge whether or not my words were having any impact. "There are other falsehoods in that statement."

"Why haven't you refuted any of this before now?"

"I never testified in any of the trials. My lawyers wouldn't let me. Since I had already served the required ten years, six months on a life sentence when I got off death row, I tried to get out through the clemency process, which is how all lifers get out." I told him about why I didn't challenge the facts of my case before the pardon board. "While the policy no longer exists," I said, "it's too late now for me to start refuting things. My opponents' version of the crime has been repeated in hearings and in the media for so long that it's taken on a life of its own. But that aside, what would I look like arguing that, no, I didn't cut Mrs. McCain's throat, I only shot her? What difference does that make? It certainly doesn't make me less guilty. But it would change the question from whether I merit clemency, given the amount of time I've served and my efforts to redeem myself, to a controversy over details of the crime and who's telling the truth and who's not."

Roemer switched the subject. "I guess you've seen a lot of changes at Angola during the years you've been there," he said.

"Oh, yeah—like going from night to day," I said. I started telling him about the prison and some of my experiences in it. The conversation between us relaxed, and he seemed to warm to me, asking questions about my trip to Washington and my plans if he granted me clemency. He asked about my traveling and remarked at one point, "Maybe I should make you the goodwill ambassador for the Department of Corrections." I could not tell if he was serious or joking. I remembered reading that he was a poker player and reputed to be a good one. I understood why: He was elusive and difficult to read.

Since I was doing most of the talking, in response to his questions, I lost track of time, but when he ended the meeting, he told me he was glad that we had had our talk, that it had given him a different perspective, and that he needed to reevaluate his position. He encouraged me to continue my good works and generally left me with the impression that he would do something for me. He walked me back to the door and shook my hand in a friendly fashion.

"Is he gonna do something for you?" Whitley asked as we returned to our vehicle.

"He said he was glad we met because he learned a lot that he hadn't known," I said, not wanting to divulge anything that might get back to the governor. I convinced myself that the meeting had gone surprisingly well.

In the following days, Whitley told me that the word from corrections headquarters was that the governor was going to free me. Then Department of Corrections secretary Bruce Lynn told me the same thing. Yvonne Campbell and Sally McKissack told me the pardon board had been advised that Roemer would sign their recommendation, but not until after the next year's gubernatorial campaign, because he was going to run for reelection. I was ecstatic. The wait didn't bother me a bit. The knowledge that I was going to be free made all the difference in my life. I was free to focus on making a life after prison. I *felt* free. I had hope and a future. I was on top of the world, and it was a beautiful sight.

Angola authorities dread summer. The oppressive Southern heat brings the prospect of irritated inmates who might flare up and express smoldering discontent in violence or rebellion. When a Baton Rouge judge scheduled Andrew Lee "Flash" Jones to be electrocuted on July 22, 1991, for the 1984 rape and murder of the eleven-year-old daughter of his estranged girlfriend, the pardon board recommended that Governor Roemer delay the execution until September 15, when the legislature's mandated switch to lethal injection would take effect. The governor, who was facing a tough reelection bid, refused.

Rigor mortis had not yet stiffened Jones's body when, hours later, the supervisor of the metal fabrication plant in the Main Prison industrial compound approached two inmate welders, Dan Goodson and William Stone, and instructed them to build a "restraint table" purportedly to be used on patients at the state mental hospital. He neglected, however, to remove the logo of the Colorado State Penitentiary from the photos and blueprints he provided to guide them in their work. The inmates realized they had been given the task of constructing the lethal-injection gurney that would replace Angola's electric chair. They told the supervisor they would not do anything to help the state kill an inmate. They were both locked up for disobeying a direct order.

The following morning, Tuesday, plant supervisors tried again, instructing each of the other thirty-seven inmate welders in turn—among them Eddie Sonnier, whose brother had been electrocuted in 1984—to build the gurney. But they had all decided to follow Goodson and Stone to the Dungeon. As word of what happened spread to the farm workers emerging from the dining hall and preparing to go out in the sizzling midday heat—it was over 90 degrees in the shade—there was spontaneous combustion as large numbers of them opted to join in protest, turning a collective deaf ear to the orders yelled at them to go to work.

Ron and I rushed to the scene. Ron talked to the rebelling inmates while I hurriedly photographed what was happening. It was only a matter of time before security reinforcements would rush from other parts of the prison to help deal with the uprising. We worked fast because we did not want to get caught in the middle of the potential physical clash, which could be dangerous. As we entered the Main Prison Office building, several guards stopped us and demanded my camera.

"Rideau, we got shit kicking off, and we can't have y'all running around in there with that camera," a supervisor said. "It ain't safe."

"That's our problem, not yours."

He shook his head, reaching for the camera. "Naw, y'all go on to your office. You can get your camera back when this is over."

I gave him the camera. Then I phoned the warden's secretary to report its seizure, and asked that it be returned to us.

All inmate activity in the Main Prison was being shut down, traffic frozen, and all inmates sent to their respective dormitories—except the *Angolite* staff, which was allowed to remain in our offices. Soon afterward, a small army of guards in riot gear, led by Whitley, went to the Big Yard and methodically extracted more than three hundred striking farm workers from the thousand-man population there. The strikers went peaceably to the lockdown cells, where they were crammed four and five into each one. Still, in a world that broke down under stress to us against them, tension remained, with guards and the remaining seven hundred Big Yard inmates on edge.

Later that afternoon, Whitley phoned. "I'm sure you're aware of what's been happening," he said.

"I'm told you personally led the guards down into the Big Yard."

"You'd better believe I did," he said. "There would've been a helluva lot more than three inmates injured if I hadn't." While most guards preferred to avoid conflict with prisoners, some did not. Some employees were just as radical in their viewpoint as the most radical prisoners, and the more rational always had to be on guard for them, which accounted for Whitley's decision. "If I'm going to be judged and held responsible for what my men do, then I'm going to make sure they do no more than I want them to do," he said.

"Chief, I can't believe that after executing Jones yesterday, you decided to order the inmates at the metal fab shop to build that deathbed," I said.

"Wilbert, this is so stupid that *I'm* having a hard time believing it," he said. "I've just learned that Jimmy LeBlanc and that crew in Prison Enterprises tried to pull a fast one on the inmates. They wanted the contract to build the death gurney and planned to pass it off as a hospital table, figuring the inmates wouldn't know the difference."

Then he got around to why he had called: "Our information is that the Main Prison is going to stage a general strike in the morning. I don't have to tell you that puts the inmate population and the security force on a collision course, and people are gonna get hurt."

A general strike? That quickly? My instincts told me no. "It sounds like your people are either lying to you or functioning with bad information," I said. "Think about it—the inmates were all locked in their respective dorms right after the fieldworkers struck. A general strike has to have a basic consensus among all the inmates, but they haven't had a chance to meet and discuss anything. So how could they reach an agreement to strike in the morning? I don't believe it."

"What you say makes sense. Do you think it's too late to try to resolve this before it gets out of hand?"

"It's never too late. Like always, there are those who want to see it happen and those who don't." Despite their intimidating utterances and oft-threatened violence, most prisoners shied away from trouble; they wanted to be able to pursue their prison existences with a minimum of difficulty and disruption. But I didn't tell him that. "I do know that you should let at least the lawyers and officers of all the civic and religious organizations out of their dorms. Most have a stake in the established order. They need to return to their offices and resume their normal activities after the evening meal so they can meet and communicate with each other."

"What you're suggesting runs counter to everything that's taught in corrections about how to deal with prison disturbances—and that's *not* to let inmate leaders get their heads together."

"But we both know, Warden, that all prison leaders aren't the same. Some are positive forces; others, negative. The problem will most times come from the ambitious who are trying to become leaders and the radicals," I said. "They function on emotion; they're opportunistic and will exploit any situation. If you want a solution, you have to create an opportunity for those vested inmate interests, the cooler heads, to pursue one."

Whitley was hesitant. "You're suggesting I put the welfare of a lot of people, both guards and inmates, on the line, people who could get hurt if this thing spreads and goes bad."

"Chief, you're already facing that prospect if you just wait it out and see what happens, which is what most of your colleagues would probably advise," I said. "What I'm suggesting is a small, calculated gamble that will give us a measure of the pulse of the population."

He was quiet for a while. "I *really* hate this shit," he finally said with force, exasperated. "This is one time the inmates *are* right, and they're going to end up getting fucked over because of some stupid shit that should have never happened." He paused, then said, "We need to do whatever we can do to head this off, Wilbert."

"Warden, I'm looking at getting out of here, and given my druthers, I'd *really* prefer not getting involved in something as unpredictable as a strike."

"Frankly, I don't see how you can stay out of it," Whitley said. "You know who's who, who to deal with and who not to. I don't." He was

right, and he was trying to do the right thing. I agreed to help him try
to resolve the strike, and we agreed to talk to each other only directly,
without middlemen.

He ordered the resumption of normal activities for the sixty or so
inmate lawyers and organizational officers, but the general population
remained confined to their dormitories. "You can tell the fellows that
the gurney issue is dead," he said. "It will not be built in this prison."

That evening, inmate lawyers and officers of organizations flooded
the Main Prison Office and education building to escape the stifling
heat and boredom of the dorms and gather in air-conditioned offices to
swap information and learn more about the day's events. Ron and I circulated, gathering information and conveying Whitley's message that
the gurney would not be built in Angola, and his desire to resolve the
strike.

The leaders were pleased to hear the news. Everyone sympathized
with the welders and hoped their release from lockdown could be won
by the inmate counsels representing them in disciplinary court, where
Angola prisoners challenged the disciplinary infractions they'd been
charged with. Most leaders felt that an expanded strike was unnecessary, especially because if there was one it would be almost impossible
to control the actions of the angry, the hateful, the crazy, the hopeless,
and the ambitious political opportunists on both sides, which could
result in disaster.

It had been a long time since Angola had been a violent place.
Since 1977, violent deaths at Angola had averaged about one per year,
which is probably as good as it gets in a maximum-security prison with
more than 5,000 mostly violent offenders serving sentences that pre-
clude their ever walking out, especially since the practice of paroling
lifers after ten years and six months had ended. Indeed, contrary to
popular perception, an inmate was now more likely to die of natural illness, execution, or suicide than to be killed by another prisoner. This
was also true of prison deaths nationwide—thanks to the intervention
of federal courts during the 1970s and 1980s, which forced state
authorities to curb the violence. Of the 1,729 prisoners who died in the
nation's prisons in 1990, the U.S. Justice Department's Bureau of Justice Statistics reported that only 65 had been killed by another inmate.
The major killers of prisoners in 1990 were illness (1,462) and suicide
(134). And that was among a nationwide prisoner population that now
topped a million for the first time in history.

Rule-abiding inmates—*always* the majority—would typically strike only as a last resort. A strike means disrupted lives, lost visits, and canceled activities, not to mention retaliatory administrative action. Criminal and black-marketing inmates saw strikes as interfering with their illegal pursuits. Riots, unplanned and driven by passion, are an entirely different thing. They are contagious. No one knew what morning would bring.

Norris Henderson and Gerald Bosworth were influential Big Yard residents who worked in the prison's legal assistance program. They were model prisoners concerned both about the fate of the strikers and what was happening in the prison. Norris was my close friend and ally. After ten years in the federal prison system for bank robbery, the New Orleans native had been transferred to Angola in 1985 to serve life for murder (he would win his freedom years later through litigation). He was easily the most popular of Angola's prisoners. A proficient paralegal who stayed on top of developments in criminal law, he served as librarian of the prison's law library. He was involved in sports activities, was the leader of Angola's Muslims, the president of the Jaycees, and director of the Angola Special Civics Project. He was honest and generous to a fault. Gerald was a stocky, quick-witted, real-world Cajun lawyer convicted of murder who would eventually win a new trial and acquittal. Because of his professional legal abilities, he had become a major influence among white Main Prison inmates.

Norris, Gerald, Checo Yancy of the lifers' association, Ron, and I met and concluded that the key to ending the strike lay with the thirty-nine predominantly white welders who had objected to building the deathbed as a matter of principle. They didn't know yet that their demand had been met. They had good prison jobs that they did not want to lose, so pacifying them would end their strike.

Norris and Gerald took the lead in trying to resolve the strike with the inmates. Recruiting the assistance of their colleagues in the legal aid office, they visited with the strikers in general and the welders in particular. Both groups were willing to end the strike if they were exonerated and the welders kept their jobs. I phoned Whitley at his home to convey this information.

"I won't do that," Whitley said. "Violating a rule or regulation is one thing, but they disobeyed direct orders. They have to be disciplined for what they did. They should not have been ordered to build the gurney, but this *is* prison, and I am not going to do anything that will feed the perception that it's okay for them not to obey orders."

We conveyed this message to the inmate leaders. They eventually were given a deal that would find them guilty of disobeying orders but gave them a suspended sentence and no actual punishment. We turned in for the night feeling we had accomplished something good.

The general inmate population was released from their dorms Wednesday morning and instructed to report to work at their respective jobs following breakfast. Twenty-five additional fieldworkers who hadn't heard of the settlement now refused to work and were locked up. Everyone else went to their jobs. "What the twenty-five did this morning has nothing to do with the agreement made last night between the original strikers and your administration," I told Whitley. He agreed, and his disciplinary court officers began processing the cases of the strikers, who were released from the cellblocks beginning in the afternoon and continuing late into the night.

Everyone thought the gurney affair was Whitley's fault. That bothered me. I phoned United Press International and told them, off the record, that they should question the director of Prison Enterprises, Jimmy LeBlanc. When they did, LeBlanc acknowledged responsibility and said his department's behavior had been "a mistake." I also called James Minton, local bureau chief for the Baton Rouge *Advocate*, an honest, good reporter who covered Angola. We swapped information all the time. I suggested to James that he call the warden, who liked him, and ask certain questions about the strike, in particular if he thought it was morally right to ask Eddie Sonnier (whose brother had been executed) to build the gurney. I figured Whitley would answer honestly. James called me back later that afternoon to say, "Mission accomplished. See tomorrow's paper."

On July 25, the *Advocate* carried a front-page story in which Whitley acknowledged that asking the inmates to construct the gurney was "putting them in a bad position." It also reported that the gurney would not be built in the prison. It was perhaps the first time in history that a prison warden admitted that authorities had been wrong and the inmates right, and acted to remedy the situation—a candor so unprecedented it ultimately reaped him complimentary newspaper editorials and a profile in *Time* magazine. We immediately distributed thousands of copies of Minton's article throughout the prison.

But peace would not come so easily. The skies turned dark Thursday afternoon, threatening to soak the six hundred Main Prison inmates working in the fields. The field foreman radioed his superiors for permission to begin marching the inmates back to the Main Prison.

Permission, which was granted routinely, was not given until after the rain began. Guards and inmate fieldworkers made the long march back, drenched and fuming. Whoever delayed giving permission had done it deliberately to aggravate the inmates and undermine the peace. The inmates' clothes were wet and they had nothing else to change into, since their second set of clothing had gone to the laundry earlier. The more radical inmates were urging them to strike Friday morning. Wilfred Cain, a close friend and inmate minister of the Church of God in Christ congregation, ran the prison laundry and assured me that if I could get Whitley to order the laundry opened, he would clean and dry the fieldworkers' clothes that night with a crew of volunteer workers. Whitley agreed, which calmed the smoldering dissent.

Because we on *The Angolite* had unfettered telephone access to authorities, our office had, as in former crises, become an unofficial command central for the effort to restore the peace. As several inmate leaders sat around comparing notes with us, the phone rang.

"What demonstration?" Ron asked the caller. All eyes turned to him. He listened carefully and hung up.

"That was a TV reporter. She wanted to know if the inmates here were planning any action to coincide with the demonstration tomorrow." Sister Helen Prejean had apparently announced that Pilgrimage for Life, the anti–death penalty group she headed, would demonstrate at noon in support of the striking inmates. Sister Prejean was spiritual advisor to Eddie Sonnier, one of the freed strikers Gerald overheard telling other inmates about a demonstration, which implied Sonnier and the nun were acting in concert.

"Aw, man, we've just put this thing to rest," Checo said wearily. "We don't need outside agitation. It can have the reverse effect."

Then Whitley called. His security people were hearing word of a strike being called for the next day, and he also knew of the demonstration. He asked if I knew Eddie Sonnier. "Not personally," I replied. "I know his brother was executed, which provided the strikers moral standing. Before the strike, he was just another low-key prisoner."

"He can't be that low-key," Whitley said. "As soon as I let him out of lockdown, he called the *State-Times* and made himself the spokesman for the strikers, declaring 'a big victory for human rights.' At the same time, I hear that the nun who visits him says she's going to lead a demonstration. That's no coincidence. Didn't he agree to the deal to end the strike?"

"He did, Chief," I said, "but if you're considering moving against him, I'd suggest you don't. Even if he doesn't keep his part of the bargain, it's important that the inmate population sees that you keep *your* word. Besides," I said, "what he did could have all been perfectly innocent. I mean, he's been used as part of the strike rationale, so the media naturally want to talk to him. He might just be trying to capitalize on the situation to get a little personal attention."

"Well, that's possible, I guess. What do you make of the nun?" Whitley asked.

"Sister Prejean, like most activists, means well and wants to help the inmates, but she's operating on half-baked information," I said. I told him I didn't believe she was talking to the leaders, because they would've tried to dissuade her. I thought some opportunist with his own agenda probably had gotten her ear.

"Would it do any good if you called her and explained the situation?" Whitley asked.

"Warden, I don't know how she'd interpret that," I said. "She might see me as a sellout, an administrative lackey, trying to stop citizens from demonstrating their support for prisoners who've been victimized by prison authorities. I don't need her conveying that image of me to everyone she knows." I suggested he call her.

"Wilbert," he said. "Remember? I'm the guy who's supposed to be fucking over y'all, the one y'all struck against. How much credibility do you think *I'm* going to have with her?"

Copies of a front-page story from Thursday's Baton Rouge *State-Times* about Sonnier and outside support for the strikers by a couple of groups of anti–death penalty lawyers and activists were being circulated among the inmate population by Friday afternoon. Sarah Ottinger was critical of prison officials, while Clive Stafford Smith and David Utter of the Southern Center for Human Rights threatened legal action. Prejean, the article also reported, was to lead a demonstration in support of the inmates.

This stoked the embers of the dying strike. Inmate radicals and opportunists trying to capture center stage cited the news article as evidence of public support and argued that it was *outside* pressure that had forced prison authorities to release the strikers from lockdown. They exhorted the inmates to stage a general work strike to show support for those participating in Prejean's demonstration. Our allies in the leadership argued that Prejean's demonstration would be only about supporting the inmates who refused to build the deathbed, not about the general inmate population and issues affecting them. Anti–death penalty activists cared only about stopping capital punishment.

Although the twenty-five additional striking fieldworkers had been released from lockdown, their fellow workers, Norris said, were clamoring to push for as many concessions from the authorities as they could get. "They don't really appreciate the significance of what we've accomplished because the victory didn't translate into any material benefit for them. They want to piggyback some demands." He shook his head to emphasize his sadness. "And they're *stupid* demands. They want to make the Man change their work hours, they want to be able to buy donuts X times a week, they want a different kind of peanut butter and biscuit at breakfast—*stupid* things. I had to remind one fool that he's in prison, not a luxury hotel."

Still, agitators played on emotions, resentments, us-against-them attitudes, and, by Saturday noon, the desire for a general prison-wide strike had been revived and was gathering momentum. The strike was tentatively scheduled for Monday morning. Tactical units from other prisons would arrive at Angola over the weekend in preparation for it, but would remain out of sight so as not to provoke the inmates. If the strike started, it was going to end badly.

Whitley warned me, "If someone named Norris Henderson is one of the people you're working with, you'd be wise to be very careful with him. Security has him pegged as a militant and the major instigator in this strike business." I told him that Norris had been working hard to stop the strike, at no small risk to himself, and that he now had a couple of bodyguards after a small group of black nationalists tried to put him in a dangerous predicament. "Chances are, that's who fed the false information about Norris to security."

Norris, Gerald, and allies among the inmate leadership spent the weekend cashing in their credibility, leaning on their relationships, and appealing, reasoning, and even negotiating with various individuals to back off the strike. Most inmates wanted the unrest to be over. By Sunday afternoon, the strike was called off.

There were no more disturbances during Whitley's tenure. He made it a point henceforth to cultivate a rapport and working relationship with all the inmate leaders. He would go to their offices, sit up in the middle of the night with them, discussing issues or just shooting the breeze. He wanted to solve problems and was open to new ideas, as long as they made sense. He made the inmate power structure a resource and its leaders allies in his management of the prison, enabling him to manage the prisoner population independent of his security force, which he needed only for its guard service and to operate the facility.

On September 12, 1991, Ron and I and a handful of reporters watched the prison maintenance crew remove the electric chair from the death chamber. A few hours later, we recorded the installation of the lethal-injection gurney in the middle of the chamber, which promised a less painful death for the condemned. Unlike electrocution, which required the head and portion of his lower leg shaved to accommodate electrodes, this method permitted the inmate to keep his hair and the dignity it represented. The gurney was built for $5,000 by a Baton Rouge contractor who preferred to remain anonymous.

If "Flash" Jones had been electrocuted to further Buddy Roemer's political ambitions, it was for naught. Roemer failed to make the runoff, placing third behind David Duke, a notorious white supremacist who got 32 percent of the vote, and Edwin Edwards, generally regarded as corrupt, who got 34 percent in the primary.

The runoff between Edwards and Duke was popularly dubbed "the race from hell." It was a campaign marked by the infamous bumper sticker VOTE FOR THE CROOK. IT'S IMPORTANT. The crook won the governorship with 61.2 percent of the vote. Duke won 55 percent of the white vote. That vote was a telling measure of racist sentiment in Louisiana in 1991.

Since I expected to be freed by Roemer before he left office, I wasn't concerned that Edwards, who had promised never to free me, was returning to the mansion. But as Roemer's term was running out, he commuted the sentences of forty-seven men convicted of murder, among them repeat felony offenders and some formerly sentenced to death, and denied clemency to me.

Linda, who had eagerly anticipated my release, was devastated, as was I.

In the after-hours solitude of my office and Guitar Slim's blues, I reflected deeply on my situation, and Linda's. I could not escape the conclusion that whether it was fair or unfair that I was denied clemency, I was in prison because of my own actions. Linda's only crime was compassion. We had a Sunday picnic visit scheduled; I knew it would be a dramatic one.

She had never looked more beautiful to me than when she stepped off the old cast-off school bus that delivered visitors to Butler Park. Her smile folded me into its warmth. We found a table and made out a store order for the pork chops and potatoes we would grill. Then we settled into our visit. She asked how I was holding up and wanted to figure out our next strategy.

"That's a long desert to walk through, Junior," I said. "You've blessed my life with love. You've struggled alongside me and lived for a dream. But the bubble has burst. You need to turn me loose, walk away, and go on with your life."

She gazed into the distance, fatigue and sadness in her eyes, then turned her smile on me. "Wilbert, had someone told me five years ago that so much of my life would revolve around a prison and a relentless struggle to get you out of it, I would have seriously recommended they seek professional help. But I made a promise to you back then that I would not walk away and leave you in here. Now, once you're free you can tell me to take a hike and I'll go. Until then, you've just got to put up with me trying to kick down the doors that are keeping you in. It's the only unselfish thing I've ever done, and although it's hard and sometimes painful, I'm not going to quit. I can't."

With Edwards back in office, my friends and supporters knew we would have to look elsewhere if I were ever to win my release. Hope came in the form of Gerald Bosworth, the real-world lawyer now serving time, who conceived a way to challenge the no-parole status of lifers in court. The trick lay in a basic truism about law, first told to me by Ginger Roberts-now-Berrigan: "The law is whatever a court says it is, so long as no one appeals." Many penal administrators regarded the hope generated by parole eligibility as the most effective inducement for encouraging good behavior in prisoners. We therefore wanted to test the limits of that view.

Lifer and *Angolite* staffer Gilbert Guzman won a favorable judicial ruling on the legal argument that when he was sentenced to life, his sentence did not expressly prohibit parole, as life sentences now did. He was paroled soon afterward. Then Kenneth "Biggy" Johnston, another lifer and a stringer for *The Angolite*, followed, using the same legal argument. Next, a local judge ruled in Ron Wikberg's favor on the same issue. Dorothy Henderson, who had returned to the parole board, won agreement from the family of Ron's victim, and he was quickly paroled. Three precedents for paroling lifers had been established without a single appeal from any agency. I was to be next. But instead of sending my case into the court alone, which Bosworth thought might attract opposition because of my high profile, he decided to join together all twenty-eight remaining inmates who would be eligible under this strategy. It was a grave mistake. New Orleans district attorney Harry Connick, alerted to the strategy by a parole board secretary, was adamant that one of the inmates from his city not be released. When we, as a group, won a favorable ruling in the district court, he appealed to the Louisiana Supreme Court, which reversed our victory. Another door slammed shut in my face.

The following spring, C. Paul Phelps died suddenly of a heart attack. Only weeks before, he had given *Life* magazine an interview for an eight-page feature about me, "The Most Rehabilitated Prisoner in America." He had so impressed writer George Colt with the openness and innovation he brought to prison administration that Colt wanted to follow up with a feature on Phelps.

Warden Whitley had tracked me down so he could personally tell me of the death before I heard it elsewhere. It was a knockdown blow. At sixty, Phelps was still a young man, and he was one of the fixtures in my world. Not only was he the best friend I'd ever had, he had also been the big brother and even the father figure I never really had.

The family requested I serve as one of the pallbearers at the funeral. I wanted badly to go, to help carry the man who'd had the most impact upon my life to his final resting place and to say my last good-bye. Corrections officials would not let me attend; it was felt that the many dignitaries who were expected to be there, including former governors who had denied me clemency, would find my presence discomfiting. Linda attended the event in my stead. At the funeral hour, I took a walk around the yard, remembering C. Paul, nursing my loss and my sadness. I felt his presence, as if he were walking beside me. I could hear his great words of advice: "I don't care how other people play. I play fair, and if I can't, then I won't play at all." "Sometimes life shapes roles for us not of our own making." "You have a responsibility to act for others when you're the only person in a position to do so. It's how you handle it that separates the great from the mediocre." "Always aspire to greatness." "Always take the high road; never let your enemies drag you down to their level."

God, I would miss him.

One day I was talking with Sydney Deloch, an inmate counsel substitute—one of those prisoners trained in law whose job it was to assist inmates in legal matters—when he mentioned that a prisoner had won a reversal of his conviction from the federal district court in Baton Rouge because there had never been a black grand jury foreman in the parish where he was indicted and tried in the 1980s. That triggered thoughts of my own experience in 1961, when blacks didn't have any role in the justice system, except as defendants to be tried and punished. Linda went to Lake Charles to research their records on juries and jury foremen.

Old court documents revealed without exception the method used to select grand juries in Calcasieu Parish in 1961. Five white jury commissioners sat around a table with specially confected cards that were coded *W* for white and *C* for colored. According to the undisputed testimony of clerk of court Acton Hillebrandt, himself an ex-officio commissioner who joined in the selection, the commissioners would "thumb through the cards and select whoever they saw fit" to put in the jury pool. Linda researched a dozen grand jury pools up to and including the one created for me. There was an average of one black in each pool of twenty; roughly proportionate representation would have called for between three and four. The grand juries actually impaneled were even worse: six had no blacks at all, and the other six had a single black juror.

Ed Flood, the only black man selected for the 1961 grand jury pool and grand jury that indicted me, did yard work for Hillebrandt. Linda's research showed that was typical: The token blacks selected by the white jury commissioners were janitors and laborers known to them; these simple men were in theory supposed to stand up against the wealthiest and most powerful white men in the parish to ensure fairness.

Calvin Duncan, the most brilliant legal mind in Angola, did the legal research necessary for my case, which Linda took along with her findings to Julian Murray, the lawyer who had been representing me pro bono for years. Julian filed a writ of habeas corpus for me in 1994

alleging racial discrimination in the composition of the grand jury that
had indicted me. The Calcasieu Parish district attorney did not challenge any of the facts. He argued that the white jury commissioners
didn't *intend* to discriminate during the Jim Crow era; in fact, he said,
by deliberately including a black in each jury pool, those officials had
acted quite nobly to institute an early version of affirmative action. He
also argued that I waited too long to file my claim and that I should
have known better than to believe my lawyers in 1973 when they told
me everything that could be done for me had been done, dropped my
case, and wished me well.

My petition was allotted to magistrate Christine Noland, who handled prisoners' suits for Federal Middle District Court judge John
Parker in Baton Rouge. Noland was generally considered by Angola's
jailhouse lawyers to be the most conservative jurist in the district. Still,
I was convinced my legal case was sound. So all I could do now was be
patient and wait for the ruling that would set me free.

11

Censorship

1995—2001

In prison, days inch along like snails, and years zoom past like rockets. Photos, new or old, remind you of your disappearing youth as the hours spent yearning and waiting for freedom drag by. Events make you feel your mortality and churn up your desire to "seize the day" before all your days have passed.

Such was the case when my phone rang on September 18, 1994, and my friend Ron Wikberg, after two years of freedom, told me he was dying of cancer. The doctors did not expect him to live another month. Despite that, we had a good conversation. I reminded him of the legacy he was leaving with the excellent investigative articles he wrote for *The Angolite*, some of which were collected in the anthology *Life Sentences: Rage and Survival Behind Bars*, which we coedited for Times Books, then a division of Random House, and some of which were collected in the textbook *The Wall Is Strong: Corrections in Louisiana*, which we coedited with Professor Burk Foster. Dying hadn't changed Ron's sunny nature or affected his love for his wife, Kay, and his friends or dampened his sense of humor. But he was years younger than me, and his dying hit me hard, as had Phelps's a year earlier. Ron's news came only months after Whitley told me privately that he would be leaving Angola in 1995. I felt surrounded by loss.

Whitley had been our best publisher since Phelps. There were few limits to what we could do, so long as we told the truth and held to professional standards. When corrections authorities in other states wouldn't honor our requests for information about their operations, we could rely upon Whitley or our supervisor, Dwayne McFatter, to get the data for us themselves. During Whitley's wardenship, *The Angolite* enjoyed its heyday.

Paul Slavin, an ABC-TV producer, read *Life Sentences* and wanted me to do a show for his network. With Whitley's approval, ABC brought in equipment and people to teach us how to use it. *Angolite* staffer Michael Glover was trained as my cameraman, and we followed the prison's eleven terminal inmates around for months to get their perspectives on living and dying behind bars. "In for Life," a twenty-minute report that aired March 14, 1994, on the network's *Day One* newsmagazine, was introduced as the first report ever produced by prisoners to be broadcast nationally. It won a CINE Golden Eagle, awarded for excellence in television production.

I was invited to do commentaries on prison issues as a correspondent for National Public Radio's *Fresh Air.* Whitley introduced me on the first show and said he felt the radio reports represented a good opportunity to educate the public about what prison is really like. As with the ABC project, I interviewed and recorded whoever I wanted for my reports, then shipped the tapes, unreviewed and uninspected, to Naomi Person, my producer, in Philadelphia.

The prospect of producing filmed news reports and documentaries especially appealed to me. I realized from the response to the *Day One* piece that I could have a bigger impact on educating the public and promoting prison reform through film than I ever could through print or audio. ABC-TV left their camera equipment behind for us, and I wanted to create a film production operation in Angola. The time I would have to devote to doing that, and acquiring broadcast outlets, meant I had to step down from my post at *The Angolite*, which I'd held for nearly two decades. The magazine was my baby, and it was no small thing to me to turn it loose. But I had to do so quickly, before Whitley left, because a new warden might be reluctant to allow me to relinquish my high-profile editorship for fear the act would reflect poorly on him.

Whitley allowed me to name Michael editor (he would continue to be my cameraman) provided I stayed on as editor emeritus and pursued my film projects from my desk in the *Angolite* office. "Most of the inmates and the employees respect you, and nobody's gonna challenge the magazine's operations as long as they know you're still there," said Whitley, "whereas they might try Mike."

I dove into my new job, writing to TBS, CNN, A&E, Discovery, HBO, and a host of other television companies, citing our award-winning work for ABC-TV. Aside from ABC, only CNN and TBS were interested. Thom Beer of TBS flew to Angola to meet with me and Michael, and with assistant wardens Richard Peabody and Dwayne McFatter, to hammer out working arrangements between us and his company.

Whitley had suggested we do a documentary on the prison's rodeo, but I wanted to do one first about the next execution, which, given our special access, would make it a unique report and firmly establish our new venture.

In mid-January, Whitley formally announced he would be leaving in a couple of weeks and would be replaced by Burl Cain, warden of a small satellite prison. Cain arrived at Angola just as the prison's inmate leadership of more than a hundred men threw a surprise farewell party for Whitley, who was visibly moved by the tribute. "I cannot believe that the prisoners of a maximum-security institution, with their own finances, have done a dinner to say good-bye to the warden," he told the gathering. "I've never heard of that being done before. And I can tell you, I really appreciate it." Cain, who didn't attend, ominously told a gathering of inmate leaders later that they had thrown a party for the wrong man: "If you'd been smart, you would've given a party for the new warden coming in instead of the old one going out. He can't do anything for you."

One of Cain's first acts as warden was to be the execution of Antonio James. I explained my new job to Cain and briefed him on my proposed television project, which I called "First Blood." I told him that Paul Slavin thought ABC-TV would be interested in it. Cain wanted to see a "treatment" or "script" of what I wanted to do. After reading treatments on "First Blood" and on a rodeo project, which I was going to film next in October, he enthusiastically approved both projects.

Michael and I followed Cain around with a videocam during the weeks preceding the scheduled execution as he went about familiarizing himself with the prison, selecting new uniforms for his administrative officials, learning his execution duties, moving into the warden's house, and fishing in the prison's biggest lake. Cain was a colorful personality, made-to-order for the camera. He was short, overweight, and talked like an old-time Southern Baptist preacher with a piney-woods twang. He had a certain good-old-boy charisma about him, and a knack for simplistic cornpone sayings and biblical quotes that made great sound bites. He was also a ham.

Cain assured me that we could film everything except the actual execution, which the law forbade. The state supreme court, however, halted the execution four hours before James was to die, and the project was shelved until a new execution date was scheduled.

Though Cain loved attention, he didn't fancy sharing the limelight. Shortly after he had become warden, Baton Rouge's WBRZ-TV featured the plight of Nicholas Carter, a local fourteen-year-old boy who would die without a bone-marrow transplant. I phoned reporter Margaret Lawhon, whose televised appeals had gotten a dismal response from Baton Rouge's black community, the youth's best hope for a suitable donor. I told her that Norris Henderson and I wanted to try to find a donor among Angola's five thousand predominantly black prisoners. I worked with Margaret, the medical personnel, and prison authorities while Norris recruited about fifty inmate leaders to help. Margaret got a local riverboat casino to donate $5,000 to cover the cost of bone-marrow testing of the inmates and suggested that Cain and Norris go to Baton Rouge to jointly accept the check on TV. Cain agreed, and Norris waited for him in the *Angolite* office at the appointed time, only to watch the warden accept the check on TV by himself.

Cain had a flair for endearing himself to people and making them feel like old friends. His passion in life was politics and the pursuit of power, and, I think, acceptance. To that end he became acquainted with all manner of people—rich, poor, classy, even outlaw motorcyclists.

As leader of a group of wardens of satellite facilities, he had persuaded gubernatorial candidate Edwin Edwards that they could deliver the 1991 vote of the prison employees—in exchange for the appointment of Richard Stalder, Cain's former deputy warden, as corrections chief. Intelligent, well educated, and personable, Stalder was a repressive administrator and heartless bureaucrat. Given to control and censorship, he was no fan of *The Angolite*. After Edwards won, Stalder took office in 1992, and he let us know that he was displeased that we had never published anything favorable about the American Correctional Association (ACA), whose standards he intended to employ as a way to wrest control of the state's prisons from federal judge Frank Polozola's oversight. Court supervision pretty much guaranteed that he got what he wanted from the legislature, but he had plans for the prison system and didn't want the federal courts telling him what to do.

I didn't have a high opinion of the ACA. Phelps had told me it was "about building bureaucracies, covering their asses against liability, and managing prisons with paper and pen . . . and there's no evidence that their way is better than ours." In fact, the worst massacre in modern times was in an ACA prison in New Mexico. And in another ACA facility, in Lucasville, Ohio, a riot had recently taken place.

As long as Whitley was warden, we didn't have to worry about Stalder. But Cain was his political benefactor and seemingly bullet-proof, despite having arrived at Angola with a reputation for shady dealings. The Baton Rouge *Advocate* had just written about questionable dealings involving a chicken-processing operation that used inmate labor at his previous prison. Scandals and rumors of corruption would dog Cain more than any warden in Angola's history.

Cain was about power, control, and money. His political power would enable him, as warden, to bring in unprecedented funds from the legislature, where his brother was a senator. If any reason could be found to build, repair, or replace something at Angola, money was designated for it.

Cain was like a king, a sole ruler. His favorite analogy was, "I'm like the father, and y'all are like my children." He enjoyed being a dictator and regarded himself as a benevolent one. His subordinates loathed his going into the inmate population, because if a prisoner complained or asked him about anything, he'd order it corrected instantly. Disciplinary actions were undone on the spot, as were job assignments. He wanted to be liked, and prisoners knew that.

He could also be a bully—harsh, unfair, vindictive. Subordinates who questioned his orders suffered instant demotions and transfers. Despite his spontaneous generosity to individual inmates, his idea of managing prisoners was to punish everyone for the act of one. That, he explained, was the way to "make everyone his 'brother's keeper.' "

The first significant moment that defined my relationship with Cain came one night shortly after he became warden. He took me for a ride in his Chevy Suburban out along the lonely levee that protects Angola from Mississippi River floodwaters. He wanted me to tell him who among the ranking employees were his friends and who were his enemies. I told him I wasn't a snitch. He wasn't pleased.

Matters didn't improve when I rejected his religious entreaties. A number of employees told me he wanted to bring me "to Jesus," because it would be a sensational coup for him. Once, when there was a big revival at Angola with media in attendance, Cain buttonholed me and said, "Come on, Wilbert. Come into the service with me," to which I replied, "No thanks, Warden." I knew he just wanted to exploit me, and he knew I knew.

The new editor of *The Angolite* introduced Cain to readers as "The Christian Warden," which was how he wanted to be seen. Under his tutelage, religion and moral transformation were to be the cornerstones of Angola's penal philosophy. Indeed, his wife was one of a group of visiting religionists teaching the Bible to some inmates at the start of his administration. After Cain was caught having sex with his female assistant, his wife was never again seen at the prison.

Cain, however, wouldn't let a little immorality get in the way of making Angola the focal point of an unparalleled religious crusade. He pressured inmates to participate and forced their organizations to pony up money to support it. He acquired a dubious degree from an unaccredited Bible college in Shreveport, and threw open the prison gates to churches, evangelists, and their ministries. Eager for a toehold and, dare I say, their own legitimacy as saviors of the wretched, they embraced him with evangelical fervor, singing his praises.

When Cain arrived at Angola, he assured us and the outside media that he wanted *The Angolite* to continue without censorship. "The magazine contributes so much to the prison's stability and security," he told the Baton Rouge *Advocate*. "I support what they're doing and I want them to keep doing the same job." We quickly learned that there was a wide chasm between what he said and what he did.

First, he prohibited prison employees from talking to the news media, including *The Angolite*, without prior permission. All information had to come directly from Cain or his office. The reason for this, we were told, was to ensure the accuracy of information, not to censor it. But, of course, this gradually strangled our ability to gather information independently.

All *Angolite* phone calls to people outside the prison could now be approved only by Deputy Warden Sheryl Ranatza, who was placed in charge of *The Angolite* and all media matters, the daily management of which she left to her too-young assistant, Cathy Jett. A recent criminal justice graduate, Jett was inexperienced, trusted no one, and was dedicated to covering her ass and getting favorable publicity for Cain. She could not be reasoned with. Cain's administration was concerned only with outward appearances.

The Angolite's fate was made even more precarious because of another scandal involving Cain. In October 1995, William Kissinger, a trusty who worked as an inmate lawyer, wrote a letter to federal health officials about a canned-milk and canned-tomato operation Cain was running at Angola in which inmates would scrub the rust off outdated cans and relabel them for use on the open market. When Cain found out about the letter, he had Kissinger thrown in the Dungeon, transferred from his job in the law library to fieldwork on the farm lines, and moved from his trusty dormitory to one on "the wild side" where nontrusties lived. The matter ended up in federal court, where a judge told Cain not to harass the whistleblower. The can-relabeling plant was shut down, but the whole prison got the message that Cain would not tolerate anything negative being said about Angola, even if it was true.

Michael Glover was shaken by the Kissinger incident and believed *The Angolite* would be shut down. I didn't think so, but we all recognized that we were reaching the point where we would no longer be able to do investigative exposés, the gold standard in journalism. Because of the Kissinger incident, everyone was reluctant to talk, even off the record. I felt that *The Angolite* could still serve our constituency well by doing whatever reporting we could, and analyzing things for them, while educating the outside world about life inside prison. I reminded the staff that the magazine had gone through rough times between 1981 and 1983, and we had survived by changing. We would do so again.

The end of 1995 brought more depressing news. Republican Mike Foster, who promised to end clemency for anyone convicted of a violent crime regardless of rehabilitation or the amount of time served, was elected governor. His ascension to power was a near-fatal blow to hope at Angola.

Foster reappointed Stalder, perpetuating the conversion of the corrections system into a self-serving political and money machine. Here's how it worked.

Louisiana had the nation's largest backlog of prisoners being held in local jails because of lack of space in the state penal system. Since 1992, Stalder had been partnering with sheriffs—the most powerful political figures at the local level—to house state prisoners in their jails rather than build more state prisons. The effect of this was to merge the two systems into a vast inmate-warehousing jail complex that would funnel huge amounts of state dollars to sheriffs.

Local jails were lucrative power centers for local sheriffs, who generally could not get taxpayers to fund new jails. Stalder said he would "house forty percent of the capacity" of any new local jail with state inmates. That state money would allow sheriffs to borrow the rest. "This was how, in fourteen locations, new jails have been built," Stalder told us proudly after his first four years in office, adding, "There are ninety-five local facilities in which we house state inmates."

Stalder and Cain were thus creating their own prisoner-for-profit industry. Local facilities operated at minimal expense, leaving inmates devoid of virtually all health services, legal aid from trained inmate counsel substitutes, and educational, recreational, and work opportunities available in state prisons. The state paid the jailers up to ten times the rate paid by the local parish for a prisoner. The substantial profit paid for the new jail. The more jails there were, the more jobs the sheriffs had available to fill, which increased their political manpower and their chances for reelection. New or expanded jails also meant a greater need for private contractors to provide a host of services, including telephones for inmates, and clothing, cigarettes, and snacks sold in the jail commissary. The contracts were worth big money, and the bid requirements could be tailored to effectively eliminate all bidders but one, resulting in a grateful contractor at reelection time. Once local officials became dependent upon the state-inmate funding stream, they were locked into the Cain/Stalder power network, because Stalder had the power to withdraw inmates for almost any reason and, if he did, the affected sheriff would lose the state income he now relied on as well as the political benefits that flowed from it.

As architect of this expanded system, Stalder was caretaker for the political and moneyed interests feeding off the now-fattened corrections tit. Those special interests transformed the corrections department from what had historically been the weakest state agency into a statewide political power base that would act to enlarge the penal system and keep Stalder and his patron, Cain, in control longer than anyone in the system's history. And it was an industry dedicated to physical expansion and increased political power, which meant there was no incentive to release inmates—the longer an inmate was incarcerated, the more bloated the prison population became, the more facilities were needed, and the greater the profits and political dependency of the local officials. Stalder's administration promoted incarceration by encouraging guards to increase the number of disciplinary citations, which hampered early release. The pardon and parole boards, now staffed with Foster appointees, became stingier in granting freedom, and formulated policies that reimprisoned probationers and parolees for mere technical violations. Needless to say, Louisiana quickly became the nation's number one incarceration state during Stalder's tenure.

In 1991, *The Angolite* had discovered and exposed the state legislature's quiet, hitherto-unreported passage of a rule that gave all state prisoners one year to challenge their convictions in state habeas corpus proceedings or be forever barred from doing so. The overwhelming number of inmates were unable to do so because they had no lawyers or resources. That law, along with Stalder's ascension to power, essentially extended the imprisonment of most state prisoners and pretty much buried the lifers and long-termers of Angola. Cain publicly pronounced that more than 85 percent of those imprisoned at Angola would die there.

Defending prisoners' rights had by this time come to be seen as disrespect for crime victims. The only fighters left standing in the prison reform movement were death penalty opponents, whose main aim was to substitute no-parole life sentences for capital punishment. Prison conditions, prisoners' rights or welfare, and clemency were not part of their agenda. Amid this growing desert of indifference, *The Angolite* was essentially the only voice Angola prisoners had, and it was the target of a gradual muzzling.

At this juncture, we prisoners knew we had to look out for ourselves as never before. Because I had a half-formed idea of funding a quasi-welfare program for inmates, I was elected president of the bankrupt Pardon Finance Board, the oldest of the prison's thirty-plus inmate organizations. It was renamed the Human Relations Club and changed its philosophy and direction. We acquired a franchise for the club to sell Angola Prison Rodeo souvenir T-shirts to inmates and tourists to raise revenue. I recruited the civic-minded Checo Yancy to become my vice president, assuring him that he could pursue all the good community goals that he wanted to. Since I was involved in films and radio, I needed him to steer the club in its new direction and to keep the books, sparing me the day-to-day management.

Our club teamed up with Norris Henderson's Angola Special Civics Project to maintain the prison's cemetery. We wanted to take over the handling of prison funerals. During the filming of "In for Life," dying inmates had complained that the chaplains didn't even visit them in the prison hospital, and expressed resentment at those chaplains presiding over their burial. I, along with several other leaders, asked Cain to allow us to create and handle a funeral ritual in which inmates would bury their own, with inmate preachers presiding rather than the chaplains. Cain agreed and assigned two inmate carpenters to make wooden caskets to replace the cheap pressed-cardboard coffins the prison had been buying. He assigned another crew of inmates to build an old-time funeral carriage that, when completed, was towed by big, beautiful Percheron horses. The Special Civics Project and Human Relations Club provided the manpower and footed the bill for all other funeral improvements.

We looked for ways to expand and fund our inmate-helping-inmate effort. A number of inmate organizations ran food concessions in the visiting room, selling coffee, donuts, homemade pizza, and barbecue to raise money. Some of the religious inmate organizations had been visiting men in the hospital and bringing them toiletries and books. We in turn got the clubs with food concessions to agree to give terminal patients any food they requested free of charge. The Human Relations Club offered to pay the cost of bus transportation for any terminal patient's relative to visit. Later, Cain would order Dwayne McFatter to create for inmates what turned out to be a nationally recognized award-winning hospice program.

To encourage self-education, the Human Relations Club began to reward the top inmate tutors and students in both the prison's limited academic and vocational programs by allowing them to be guests at our club's monthly socials, where they could mingle with outside guests, listen to music, eat well, and possibly win a door prize bag of food, toiletries, and other items not sold in the prison commissary.

Since most of the elderly inmates just sat around the dorms with nothing to do, the Human Relations Club created a monthly senior citizens' night, at which hundreds of the prison's elderly could congregate, be served a good meal different from their normal prison fare, play bingo for prizes, watch a movie, and socialize with their peers at our expense. It quickly became the most attended activity in the prison. We'd give them free tobacco, coffee, gloves, caps. With Cain's approval, we created an annual long-termers' day to bring together all those imprisoned more than twenty-five years for a day of good food, entertainment, and an opportunity to visit with free men and women. Our first year, singer Aaron Neville headlined the list of entertainers, and outside churches and groups volunteered their services.

The Human Relations Club quickly became the most talked-about organization in Angola, because we gave away our profits to the inmate population as quickly as we made them, a first in the prison. Prison employees who liked what we were doing volunteered their assistance, working without pay on their days off to help us stage events. As we had anticipated, other inmate organizations, not to be outdone or embarrassed, followed our lead with charitable endeavors. Checo often joked that I wanted to put a lot of programs in place in case I didn't get out of prison. There might have been some truth in that, but I took enormous satisfaction in being able to improve the lives of those around me and see the difference in their faces. Cain supported all these endeavors.

We were very pleased when, on January 10, 1996, seventy-eight-year-old Moreese "Pop" Bickham was released after thirty-eight years at Angola. We filmed it for ABC-TV's *Nightline*. The key to his freedom had been starring in "Tossing Away the Keys," the radio documentary that Ron Wikberg and I coproduced with Dave Isay in 1990. Dave had promised Pop he would get him out, and he and New York lawyer Michael Alcamo had finally pulled it off. Edwin Edwards had commuted Pop's life sentence as he was leaving office the year before. Cain hosted a small reception at the ranch house—a facility used for entertaining guests at Angola—where we all waited for midnight, when Cain personally took Pop, Angola's third-longest-confined prisoner, through the prison gate. Pop, who had been ordained a Methodist minister while in prison, knelt and kissed the ground he had longed for years to walk on.

Soon afterward, Antonio James, a "changed man" even in the opinion of the warden, lost his final court battle, and his execution was to go forward, despite evidence that he was not the shooter. His lethal injection was to be administered March 1, and Michael and I resumed filming the countdown to his death.

On February 19, Michael collapsed and died of an apparent asthma attack as he prepared for bed. I lost a valued friend and an ally in my pursuit of journalistic excellence. I mourned most, however, for his widow, Debi, a true Christian who brought love and joy into Michael's caged life and took him out of Angola at long last, though not in the way either had hoped and prayed for.

I contacted TBS Productions and CNN, asking for camera assistance to replace Michael, but their bureaucracies were too slow in responding. I appealed to Gabriel Films, a New York production company, which assured me of instant assistance to finish my film. Jonathan Stack, the head of the company, and Liz Garbus, a young filmmaker, met me at Michael's funeral in Baton Rouge, where I had been driven by a lone female security lieutenant, something so unprecedented that I spent the entire trip suspicious it was a setup.

One day during the week of the execution, we were told the surprising news that we could not film at the death house because an ABC-TV crew was filming there. They had also been on death row talking to Antonio. I asked Antonio why he was cooperating with ABC when he had committed to giving me the exclusive. He apologized and explained that Cain had brought *Prime Time Live*'s correspondent Cynthia McFadden to meet him and had asked him to cooperate with the lady. "I have to do this," James told me. "I don't have a choice." Cain was getting Antonio's son out of a juvenile prison to visit with him, and was helping his mother by providing transportation for her to visit him.

I told him that I understood. I would have done the same thing.

Cain, learning that I was angry, said that I was to continue my film, that there was no conflict, that what I would produce would be the superior film because he had made ABC promise that they had to allow me to use the footage they would tape at the death house of Antonio's walk to the execution chamber. "This way, you'll have not only what you film, but also what they do, too," he said. "This is a better deal for you."

I reminded him that I had been filming this project since the day he became warden and that he had promised me the exclusive on Antonio's last walk. He promised to make it up to me on something else. We continued filming, tweaking, and changing our project so that it didn't end up appearing to be a copy of what ABC would produce.

In June, *Prime Time Live* aired "Judgment at Midnight," a special

hour-long feature that focused on the final week's countdown to Antonio's execution. Prior to the broadcast, Cynthia McFadden appeared as
a guest on *The Charlie Rose Show* to talk about ABC's unparalleled
access to the execution. She explained that while at Angola on a totally
unrelated story about another inmate, Cain invited her to accompany
him to death row, where he introduced her to Antonio James and
suggested the story to her, guaranteeing her unprecedented camera
access to everything except the actual execution. Cain had deliberately
sabotaged my film project. McFadden, none the wiser, understandably
leaped at the opportunity.

But she also touted Cain's openness and the access accorded
ABC-TV, unaware that less than two weeks before *The Charlie Rose
Show*, Cain had punished inmate boxer Donald Vallier for his "openness" in innocent comments to the New Orleans *Times-Picayune* about
homosexuality and drugs at Angola by putting him in chains and transferring him across the state to another prison. Cain's openness and
media access were calculated and orchestrated for his own purposes.

Stack told me that Cain discouraged him from working with me.
Nonetheless, we labored on to produce the hour-long documentary,
now renamed *Final Judgment: The Execution of Antonio James*, which
was to air in August on the Discovery Channel. Stack said Cain had a
real problem with what I was doing and that it might help if I wasn't
listed as one of the producers of the film. So I reluctantly settled for the
minimal credit line "Story by Wilbert Rideau," and decided to discon-
tinue my film work until Cain became comfortable with my doing it
and I could gain more control over my work, and the credit I would
receive for it.

In the wake of Michael's death, I had reassumed control of *The
Angolite*. Cathy Jett now indicated that Cain might want to import
someone from another prison to run it. That idea stunned the entire
staff. Then *Angolite* staffer Keith Elliott died shortly after Michael, and
production of the magazine fell behind schedule. While Cain was out of
state, I phoned Sheryl Ranatza and told her that the magazine had a
contractual obligation to subscribers and that I was going to take charge
of the operation until the warden decided whom he wanted to serve as
editor. She agreed. Once I reestablished my position, I didn't think Cain
would oust me, because that would be a hugely controversial move.

It felt like death was everywhere I turned, and I wrote more about
it in the September/October 1996 issue of *The Angolite*.

While "Final Judgment" was produced, the story of another prisoner facing death went undone.

His name was Anthony Fields, but everyone called him "Beaver Duck." He came to Angola in 1971, a teenager with life terms for two New Orleans rapes. The prison was sinking into an era of barbarity that would earn it the distinction of being the bloodiest prison in the nation. It was a bad time. Beaver Duck was raped and enslaved, forced to be a wife to his rapist. Afterwards, he was used and abused by predators, traded, sold and used as collateral, escaping this role only a decade ago. Vengeful souls might regard this horrific experience as a kind of poetic justice.

Beaver Duck came to me in early February, dying of lung cancer, robbed of whatever dream for the future that had sustained him through his ordeal. He wanted to tell his story on film, to share the tragedy of his pained existence with the world. Having become a Christian, he wanted his 25 years in Angola to be of value to others, for it all not to have been a waste. His was a story I yearned to tell.

Too many things were happening, not enough time. There was the merciless countdown to the execution of Antonio James. I was committed to that story, wanting to salvage some value from his needless, yet inevitable death. Then two *Angolite* members died and the magazine fell far behind schedule.

Beaver Duck lived in my dormitory. There was no escaping him. His eyes asked when I'd bring the camcorder and begin filming. He reminded me each morning, "I'm ready when you're ready. Waiting on you." "Hang in there," I'd say. "Soon!" Though ever mindful his health was deteriorating, I was caught up in a tide of demands and activities. I was very frustrated at my inability to find the time to get back to him. Friends warned, "Time's running out." Beaver Duck became so weak he was placed on the medical ward. Still, he sent word from his hospital bed not to forget his story. I really wanted to do it, had even gotten a green light from my boss, but couldn't find the time. He remained unfinished business. I finally went to the hospital, not to film, but to tell him his request to be furloughed to die outside with his family had been denied. "That means I'm gonna die in prison, huh?" he said, his voice low and filled with despair. I watched life leave his eyes. He died a week later. He was 43.

Antonio James's story was told, but not Beaver Duck's. I failed him. His sad eyes and imploring, "I'm waiting on you," join a litany of others I could never find time to get back to. They haunt my soul during times of reflection because I understand their disappointment. Like Beaver Duck and others, I too am unfinished business. Those who promised with the best of intentions to help, and could have made a difference, couldn't make the time. They never got back.

As 1996 was drawing to a close, I was more than a little surprised to hear from Jonathan Stack. He wanted us to start working on a film I had suggested to him called "Where I Live," about life in Angola. Stack told me that Cain was okay with that. I told him that I'd seen no change in Cain's attitude, and I could do nothing until I did.

One evening soon afterward, I went to a Christmas function at the chapel, a white, high-ceilinged, octagonal building without statuary or other ornamentation save the beautiful stained-glass windows depicting symbols of the Christian, Jewish, and Muslim religions. Leaving early, I stepped onto the brightly lit Walk nearby.

"Hold up, Wilbert," said Cain, who fell in alongside me as I headed to my office. "I'll walk with you." He asked if I was going to work with Stack on another film. "Nope," I said. He flattered me about our Antonio James film and said he "knew that a little competition would make you work harder and turn out a better product." He suggested that I should work with Jonathan again. "Y'all make a good team," he said, then added meaningfully, "I like Jonathan."

A few days later, Cain phoned to tell me that Stack and Liz Garbus were at the prison to film some of the Christmas activity. They were already filming in the employee community. "But they don't know what else to film. Look," he said, "they need you to help them make this film. They don't know anything about Angola, but you know this place and how to do what they want to do. They can't do it without you, so they gonna be coming to your office to talk to you, and I'm counting on you to make this work for 'em and for us. If you have any problems or need anything, you just call."

Hardly a simple request for a personal favor, this was a nicely presented command from a dictator armed with arbitrary power. I knew I had to do what he asked.

I wondered what Stack could have done to get Cain not only to overcome his animosity toward me but to *order* me to make another film. I knew Stack had arranged speaking engagements for Cain in the northeast, even traveled with him. Now Stack had carte blanche in Angola. I had to be wary of him.

I told him and Liz, whom I liked, about various things happening in different parts of the prison that would collectively provide a slice of life in Angola. We walked over to the prison hospital with Checo and Norris to film a visit with Logan "Bones" Theriot, who was dying, and my film, now renamed *The Farm*, was under way. We filmed for months all over the prison, and despite my initial reservations, I soon warmed to the project. Filmmaking was something I enjoyed.

Two months into the project, on March 5, 1997, *Advocate* reporter James Minton phoned to ask me about an award I had won. I had no idea.

"You won the Louisiana Bar Association's top journalism award for *Final Judgment*," he said. "No one told you?"

I was stunned to learn from the front-page news story the next day that the Bar Association had requested my presence at the awards ceremony five weeks earlier. Cain had instead sent an assistant warden to the ceremony to pick up the award—actually two awards—inscribed with my name, and kept them on his desk without even telling me about them. The negative press, including an editorial critical of him in the *Advocate*, was an utter embarrassment to Cain. A week later, he struck back.

On March 12, 1997, I was ordered out of the *Angolite* office while three unidentified men in civilian clothing, carrying briefcases and black bags, went in. When I was permitted to return to the office that afternoon, I saw that our two office phones had been removed. In their place was a new phone that Cain wanted us to have, so that we could phone anyone, anywhere in the world—as long as they accepted the collect charges. (Many of our calls were to governmental agencies, libraries, and research agencies that could not accept collect calls.) The new phone, unlike our old ones, couldn't receive incoming calls and allowed us to call only outside the prison, so we could no longer have telephone contact with any official in the prison, including our own supervisor. And all our calls were now to be recorded. *The Angolite* and I were just being tolerated.

I'd spent a lifetime gaining experience and knowledge of the prison world from a unique perspective. It was my only real asset. But after two years of trying to acquire credibility as a film producer both for myself and for *The Angolite*, I had little to show for it. When *The Farm* was nominated for an Academy Award in the best feature-length documentary category, I wasn't included in the nomination. I never knew why.

Cain was doing everything he could to isolate me. He ended twenty years of my traveling outside of the prison to talk to university students, civic organizations, and probationers. My personal mail was being read. Cain was telling some of my closest allies, like Ginger Berrigan, now a federal judge, that I was no longer the upbeat, rehabilitated person they had known—that I'd given up, become depressed, let myself go. Ginger, who came to see for herself, was surprised to see me unchanged. I shuddered to think what Cain was saying to people who didn't really know me.

Cain's efforts to undermine me sometimes got me down. Now I often felt I would die in Angola, thinking all the doors were shut—state courts, federal courts, and now executive clemency.

But I would always rebound. I'd had a long life, certainly longer than anyone had expected, and that was a very precious gift, as were the opportunities and the forums given me. I had tried to make the most of them, tried to make a difference, tried to help people both in and out of prison, even helped others win the freedom that continued to elude me and that I might never know. To be sure, I regretted the suffering I had inflicted on so many innocent people with the horrible crime of my youth, the wounds that for some would never heal. Nor had my own life been easy. There had been the pain of isolation, the occasional struggle against going mad, the physical and emotional deprivations, the heartbreak of repeated denials of clemency, which forced me to dig deep within myself to find strength that I didn't even know I possessed. But I also had professional success, the blessing of remarkable supporters and friends, and the satisfaction of helping others. I felt good about myself and proud of the way I'd handled my imprisonment and, in this world of extremes, proud of the way I exercised the power I'd attained. Most of all, I had Linda, who smoothed the rough edges of my existence. I definitely was not happy; I was still a prisoner yearning for freedom, unable to make many of the decisions that controlled my life. But all in all, I had much to be thankful for.

And now hope was rekindled. In September 1997 U.S. Magistrate Christine Noland ruled that the evidence proving racial discrimination and tokenism in Calcasieu's jury selection process in 1961 was overwhelming. Citing U.S. Supreme Court decisions going back to shortly after the end of the Civil War, she recommended that my conviction be thrown out and I be given a new trial or freed.

Although Noland was not his magistrate, Judge Frank Polozola somehow came to preside over the review of her decision. He did not rush into what would normally be a formal acceptance of a magistrate's recommendation. He let it sit for a year and a half. Then, on May 5, 1999, he held a hearing on the state's objections to the magistrate's recommendations. I was brought to his Baton Rouge courtroom at Calcasieu district attorney Rick Bryant's request. The district attorney brought with him his entire top brass to fight the nearly forty-year-old case. By my side was my longtime pro bono attorney, Julian Murray. Friends and supporters of mine had come from New Orleans, Baton Rouge, Grambling, and Lafayette; three drove all night from Texas. They had come in vanloads from Lake Charles to show their support for me. Except for the seats occupied by the media, the courtroom was filled to capacity by people wearing FREE RIDEAU pins, which the judge made them remove.

As the hearing began, Judge Polozola reminded everyone that "this is not a parole or pardon board hearing. The purpose of the hearing is to determine whether or not constitutional rights were violated." The state had conceded in its pleadings that the method of selecting grand juries in Calcasieu Parish in 1961 was susceptible to racial discrimination, although they denied that the presence of Acton Hillebrandt's yardboy on my grand jury was either tokenism or discrimination. In court, however, Bryant argued that none of that mattered anyway because I had waited too long to file my habeas appeal. In earlier pleadings, he had suggested that I had deliberately sat in prison biding my time for four decades just waiting for everyone concerned with the case to die or grow so old they wouldn't be viable witnesses at a new trial. It was hard to sit still for such hallucinogenic logic.

Bryant put me on the stand and grilled me about why I hadn't filed this habeas petition in 1973 after the Louisiana Supreme Court last reviewed my conviction. I answered that I didn't know I had a basis for a claim until 1993 and explained that in 1973 my lawyers told me they had done everything for me that could be done. Bryant called James Wood, one of my 1973 lawyers, to the stand, and he confirmed what I said. The district attorney suggested that since I had educated myself as a writer, I should have also known my legal rights. Alternatively, Bryant's assistant, Wayne Frey, suggested that since I had chosen to become a writer rather than a jailhouse lawyer, I would have to live with the consequences of my choice.

Because the district attorneys could not defend against the charge of discriminatory practices, they were trying to make me the problem. In their through-the-looking-glass view, the fault wasn't what they did in 1961 but that I didn't catch them soon enough.

At the end of the daylong hearing, Judge Polozola overruled Magistrate Noland's recommendation, saying I had presented no evidence of racial discrimination in the jury or in the selection process in 1961 Calcasieu. I was immediately taken back to Angola, where Cain refused to let me talk to the media. I don't know what he told them. They reported that I either declined to be interviewed or that I would not accept their calls.

In the aftermath of Polozola's ruling, George Kendall, a nationally prominent civil rights attorney at the NAACP Legal Defense Fund, enrolled as cocounsel with Julian on an appeal of Polozola's action to the U.S. Fifth Circuit Court of Appeals. After fighting my case alone and pro bono for more than fifteen years, Julian welcomed George's help and the resources he brought to the equation. And so did I.

I watched what had been America's most transparent prison for more than two decades fade to black. The outside media was routinely denied access to me. Our original office phones were returned to us a year after they were taken following a meeting of the state senate judiciary committee at which the chairman grilled Cain about their removal. Cathy Fontenot (formerly Jett) now told me whom I could and could not speak to on the phone. Few people wanted to talk, anyway, once I informed them that all calls were monitored and recorded. Information, the lifeblood of any news operation, had pretty much dried up.

The July/August 1999 *Angolite* was the first issue to reflect that. All six of the articles I wrote were insignificant. For the next edition I managed to do a good investigative report on the unprecedented and, I thought, questionable lockup of fourteen leaders of inmate organizations. It was the last report critical of the administration to see the light of day in *The Angolite*.

Censorship was now imposed without pretense. Cathy Fontenot began giving me direct orders as to what I could and could not publish. When an employee from another prison objected to the term "guard" in one of our articles, it was banned from the magazine by administrative fiat, replaced by "correctional officer." A letter to the editor from a gay inmate grumbling about how he was treated by both inmates and employees was pulled from the January/February 1998 galleys. In 1979, you'll recall, I had published an exposé of homosexual rape and enslavement at Angola. How times had changed. Another letter to the editor, from an inmate at the women's prison, complained that certain inmates were dying from lack of medical care. Fontenot pulled that letter from the March/April 2000 galleys.

Even the mundane was now censored. For the March/April 2000 issue, I'd taken a photograph of officer Tracy Cage having her brogans shined by an elderly inmate. Fontenot called and told me I couldn't put the guard's face on the cover. I explained that I'd gotten permission from both Cage and the inmate to use the photo, but Fontenot insisted I find something else. I sent over a new cover showing just the inmate polishing the boot. My phone rang.

"Wilbert, you can't use this cover," Fontenot said.

"It doesn't show the guard's face."

"Look," she said, "I've discussed this with Warden Cain. It doesn't look right to put a picture of an inmate shining a guard's boots on the cover of *The Angolite*. It doesn't reflect well on the officers or the inmates or the institution."

"Miss Fontenot," I argued, "I don't see the problem. The photo reflects a fact of life here at Angola. The shoe-shine boy is simply doing his job—a job, I might add, that was created by Warden Cain. What's wrong with that?"

"It doesn't look right," she snapped. "Find something else for the cover."

"Is that a direct order?"

"It is," she said, hanging up.

I thought about C. Paul Phelps, who lifted censorship at Angola in 1976 because he believed that shining light on its dark spots and educating the public about its inhabitants would help stimulate reform. He and a twenty-year succession of wardens and *Angolite* supervisors had supported openness and freedom of the press because, first, they had nothing to hide, and, second, they believed that if you didn't want people seeing what you were doing, then maybe you shouldn't be doing it. I was witnessing the dismantling of everything they believed in and my own life's work, and there was nothing I could do about it.

The irony was that Cain continued to promote Angola's longtime reputation for being open to journalists. In fact, only stories that were not critical of Cain or his administration, or those that cast them in a good light, were being written or aired—stories on the rodeo, the Bible college, religious revivals, the hospice program, execution stories anchored by Cain holding the condemned man's hand and praying with him. The journalists he favored were grateful for *any* access at all to an American prison. "Half the time," I told a visiting journalist friend, "they don't even know they're being led by the nose by a warden who has co-opted them for his own agenda."

This warden surrounded himself with people notable for their blind loyalty and drove off many of the straight shooters and professionals who would second-guess him or tell him he was wrong. Mike Gunnells, Angola's most competent and knowledgeable security warden in recent times, finally left in January 1999 after being demoted and then replaced with one of Cain's cronies from a small satellite prison. Gunnells told James Minton that he feared security had been relaxed under Cain. Gunnells was no sooner off the prison farm than four inmates used two handguns smuggled in by an employee to escape on January 24, 1999.

In addition to employees who were inexperienced, corrupt, or lax, the power structure was destabilized as Cain tripled the number of assistant wardens, promoted and demoted officers, and flipped them around without regard to qualifications or experience. Opportunistic inmates used the power vacuum to make trouble for their enemies, attack guards, bribe employees to smuggle in money and weapons, and engineer escapes. On November 3, 1999, death row had been without a warden for two weeks when four men used ten hacksaw blades to escape from what was supposed to be the prison's most secure facility. It was the first such breach to occur since death row had been created in 1957. *The Angolite* was not allowed to interview either inmates or employees.

The weeks that followed brought three separate incidents of inmate attacks on guards, which were not made public by the prison. But there was no keeping the fourth incident secret.

On December 28, 1999, there was a rebellion in the education building at Camp D. One guard, the greatly disliked David Knapps, was killed. Numerous inmates, some innocent, were brutalized when employees responded. One was shot in the back of the head, a fact confirmed by the autopsy photos. When the inmate's fiancée tried to get his body, she was told he had already been cremated according to Angola's standard practice. I wondered what the hell was going on. I had never known an Angola inmate to be cremated. *The Angolite* again was refused access. The brutalized inmates were isolated. Guards were afraid to talk. Two guards who'd been held hostage during the rebellion disappeared. I sent a message to James Minton through a visitor: "Find and talk to the two hostages." He couldn't locate them. My next message to him was a prediction that Knapps's killing would never go to trial because authorities wouldn't want whatever they were hiding to come to light in a courtroom. Lawsuits by two of the inmates who were beaten were quietly settled out of court.

The outside world no longer had any way of knowing the truth of what was happening inside Angola. The policies Elayn Hunt and Phelps had put in place a quarter century before in cooperation with the Justice Department to ensure inmates had confidential telephone and mail communications with outside media, as a check against the total and arbitrary power wielded by their keepers, had been abolished. *The Angolite*'s role of ferreting out and exposing problems, or simply providing factual information, had in effect been ended. The only information coming out of Angola was what Burl Cain wanted the public to know, and there was no way for anyone to check its accuracy.

I knew, as I knew at *The Angolite*'s difficult birth twenty-three years before, that I had to tread carefully because I was no good to anyone if I didn't survive. But life without the meaning real journalism had allowed me to weave into my prison existence was tedious. There was little to look forward to. At the end of the day, I locked up the office, walked back to the dorm, and said to myself, *I've got to get out of here.* I lived from one Sunday to the next, desperate for Linda's visit. I clung to the hope that the U.S. Fifth Circuit Court of Appeals would reverse Judge Polozola's ruling denying me a new trial.

On December 22, the court did indeed reverse Polozola's ruling and threw out my forty-year-old conviction. I absorbed the miracle as I had so many miracles before and wondered what God still had in store for me. I was to remain in Angola while the state appealed the Fifth Circuit's ruling to the U.S. Supreme Court.

.   .   .

A couple of weeks later, working late, I fell asleep in my office around midnight. The faint smell of smoke awoke me. I could see smoke coming through the air conditioner on the back wall, adjacent to a small mental health office. I stepped into the hall and felt the door of that office. It was hot. Down the hall, Sergeant Francesca Tate was working the Main Prison Office alone. I ran and told her I thought there might be a fire in the office next to mine and suggested she call her supervisor and the Angola fire department. Within minutes Captain Juan Anthony and his lieutenant rushed through the MPO security gate, asking for the key to the office. Tate searched, but it wasn't where it was supposed to be. She phoned the dorm where the orderly responsible for keeping the office clean lived and instructed that he—Henry "Wali" Alfred—be sent back to the MPO. Meanwhile, I took Anthony and his colleague down to the mental health office.

They felt the door, looked at each other, and kicked it open. Flames and smoke poured out. I ran back into the *Angolite* office to grab my legal mail and notes I'd made for my lawyers. Turning from my desk, I saw smoke billowing into my office under the door. I rushed out into the hallway, which had become pitch-black with smoke. I realized I might now be trapped. The only way out was down the smoke-filled corridor. Holding my jacket to my nose, I ran blindly down the black hall until I hit the light of the Main Prison Office lobby.

"Are there any more people back in those offices?" Captain Anthony asked.

"No one but me was working down there," I said.

We all walked out of the building and stood with other inmates and officers gawking at the fire licking the night sky. It took seven fire trucks from Angola and surrounding communities to put out the blaze.

Sergeant Tate came over to me. "You saved my life," she said.

"I didn't do anything."

"If you hadn't been in your office to smell the smoke and alert me, what do you think would have happened to me, locked inside that MPO?"

We both knew the answer to that question.

The next morning Cain said firefighters thought the fire was caused by a defective electrical cord on the air conditioner.

"That's not what caused the fire that burned down your office," one of the inmate electricians who had looked at the site told me. "Something else is going on." The fire marshal who inspected the remains told me pretty much the same thing.

As the one who discovered the fire, I was called that morning to be interviewed by Ken Pastorek of WBRZ-TV, after which I was restricted to my dorm for the rest of the day. When WAFB-TV and James Minton arrived that afternoon to interview me, they were directed to Burl Cain's houseboy, Johnny Dixon, and informed that he could tell them everything about the fire because he had discovered it while doing paperwork for his religious organization in an office two doors away.

After the fire marshal and other investigators finished going through the charred offices, it was determined that Wali, the orderly, caused the fire by drying some clothing on a chair over a space heater that was left on. Two of the inmate electricians told me that could be true; they also told me this was a method of setting a delayed fire, so that the culprit is nowhere around when it begins.

I can never prove that someone set out to kill me. But I knew for certain that I had better watch my back.

12

Behind Enemy Lines

2001—2005

A black gate officer poked his head into my office and told me to call Linda immediately. I didn't stop to ask how the message made its way to me at 9:30 on a Thursday evening in July through all the forbidden levels of bureaucracy. As I walked into the office of a sympathetic captain where I was to make the call, the phone was ringing. The captain handed it to me. It was Warden Cain.

"Wilbert, I just got a court order for you to go to Calcasieu Parish. They wanted to come take you right now, tonight, but we told them we can't turn loose nobody till we can verify the court order." *Maybe I heard it wrong*, I thought. I hung on to the phone in silence.

Cain's voice picked up again: "Go on and take the rest of the night packing and telling everybody good-bye." Stunned, I raced to the dorm to call Linda. She'd seen on the five o'clock news that I'd been reindicted and had tracked down George Kendall in Washington to give him the news. I told her they were moving me in the morning. She assured me that she would arrange for either Julian or George to meet me at the Calcasieu jail in Lake Charles within a day or two. She made me promise to call her as soon as I could get to a phone in the Calcasieu jail to let her know I was okay.

My eyes scanned the office that I had made into a home for myself. Like any home, it contained mementos of people and places I treasure, evidence of my life and times. Hanging on the wall was the pen-and-ink portrait of me that Troy Bridges, our former illustrator, drew as his application for the job twenty-three years earlier. On my desk were precious photos of loved ones taken during visits, which had gotten me through long and lonely nights, along with the cassettes of various blues artists. A quarter century of notes and files sat stacked in boxes and stuffed in cabinets, along with old, unpublished manuscripts, a smattering of moldering legal documents from the first three trials, and love letters dating back to the 1970s. I couldn't even begin to sift through all this in the few hours I had.

Two *Angolite* staffers with me suggested taking only what I would need in jail to avoid giving the Calcasieu cops a chance to go through all my things.

"Look, if you win, you'll come back and pick up your stuff," said one of my colleagues. "If you lose, you'll need it all when you get back."

I took only a tiny box of essentials with me.

It was 4:00 a.m. when I showered and shaved, then woke friends to break the news to them. No one knew what to say. All the men understood the difference between local jails and Angola. They knew, as I did, that I was headed into the worst stretch of time in my entire forty years of incarceration, worse even than death row. Local jails, for the most part, are full of untamed, testosterone-charged youngsters. They're designed to be temporary holding stations for people awaiting trial or those serving short sentences. A prison like Angola is a place where inmates live for a long time, and as a result, it is a community with its own culture and with a responsible inmate power structure, social and recreational activities, sports teams, religious organizations, self-help clubs, and health care. Jails, with their transient population, have none of this: Life in a jail is idleness overlaid with chaos.

The assistant warden of the Main Prison arrived about 7:00, just as I heard again on the morning news that I'd been indicted once more. An easygoing and decent man, he assumed a confidential tone: "The people coming to get you are hateful. They've been fighting you a long time, and they won't turn the past loose. They're going to put you in chains and probably try to humiliate or hurt you in different ways. To them you're just a low-life prisoner, not a human being. You need to be prepared not to let them beat you down. You're stronger than that. I'm hoping you win this, and they don't send you back to Angola. We're keeping your bed and everything open just in case."

I had the most desirable real estate in my dorm, the second bunk from a huge fan that blew away some of the stifling heat as well as whatever germs were incubating in the dorm. I appreciated the kindness but realized, of course, that he expected me to return to Angola in no time.

At 8:00, the assistant warden and I got into a car and traveled a couple of miles across the sprawling prison complex to the Reception Center near the main gate, where I was photographed and had my fingerprints taken. Now I saw the face of doom approach—a Calcasieu deputy sheriff. He put shackles on my ankles, a chain around my waist to which he attached handcuffs, and the dreaded black iron box was affixed between the cuffs, designed to stop escape artists by holding the hands rigid and immobile, away from the cuffs so the locks can't be picked. The box tightens the chain on the handcuffs. They bit into my wrists. The deputy was all business, like a butcher tying up a rump roast. I hated the restraints, and I was scared, but I remained perfectly calm. If prison taught me nothing else, it taught me never to betray weakness.

The Calcasieu deputy loaded me into a van, and we drove away slowly. Right outside the gate, he pulled over by a car in which four armed cops were waiting. They undid the box and cuffs to frisk me and then stick me in a flak jacket.

"You expecting trouble?" I asked.

"You never know," the deputy responded grudgingly.

With me in the middle of the large van and a police car taking up the rear, we tore through the Friday-morning sunshine all the way to Lake Charles, two hundred miles away, without exchanging a single word.

About noon, we pulled up to the jail—a squat, forbidding fortress made of cinder block and brick. There are clones scattered throughout Louisiana, monuments to the runaway prison industry Burl Cain helped create.

As we wheeled into the fenced-in compound, the officer in front donned a flak jacket just before stepping out of the van into the view of cameras, both still and video, operated by other deputies. This was their own carefully controlled photo op. I was led, in shackles and flak jacket, out of the van and into the path of the cops' lenses. One backpedaled in front of me, rolling video even inside the jail. There were deputies everywhere; the sense of being engulfed by Calcasieu cops took me back forty years, except now there were some female and some black faces mixed in. *I'm fifty-nine, too old for this*, I thought.

I was put in a room and the shackles were taken off. Someone handed me a plate of food, but I was far too traumatized to eat.

A black lieutenant with a military bearing tried to explain the jail rules to me. I told him there were too many for me to digest all at once. He told me George Kendall was flying down to see me tomorrow. *Thank God, Linda reached him.*

Later, a black female deputy had me taken to her station to get background information from me.

"Why am I getting so much attention from the bigwigs?" I asked her. "I mean, I know I'm not their favorite person."

"They're scared of you."

"Why?"

" 'Cuz you're intelligent, and they know they can't treat you just any kind of way."

"Black folks, too?"

"Oh, no"—she smiled—"all them want your autograph."

The head jailer in Calcasieu, Bruce LaFargue, sent for me. About my size, he was ruddy-complexioned and friendly in a professional way. He had taken the job after retiring from Department of Corrections headquarters in Baton Rouge. One of the first things he told me was that he knew and liked Ron Wikberg. I wondered why he told me this, but I *knew* I couldn't trust him.

Placed in a solitary-confinement cell in a section of the jail called Intake, I was to be moved on Monday. *I only have to survive solitary for two days.* Next to me, separated by a cinder-block wall, was a young, dark-haired white woman whose face looked strained. She had killed her husband and three kids shortly before I arrived. Black trusties sat outside her door to guard against suicide, peeking through a small window at her every few minutes and logging their observations on a time sheet. I nodded off.

On Saturday, I woke up to grits, biscuits, and scrambled eggs that were totally tasteless. I was permitted out to shower, then returned to my cell, where I read the legal notes I'd made as I waited for George, who arrived with Linda about 1:00 p.m. George was furious because neither he nor Julian could find out what was going on. Linda pointed out to George that Calcasieu consistently refused to recognize him as my attorney, so they never notified him of anything. She showed him that he was left off the court order notification list. George scrutinized the order and saw the name of the judge who signed it: G. Michael Canaday.

"This is the judge we were informed had already been handpicked before your case had even left federal court," said George. "Judges are supposed to be selected at random, but somehow the prosecutor got him. They're playing dirty. They're rushing this case through and won't tell us a thing. We can't even get them to tell us what day they're going to arraign you."

The door to the confidential attorney interview room opened and in walked Sheriff Beth Lundy, a petite brunette with some miles on her who, in another setting, might have been attractive. She introduced herself to George and Linda and assured them that she'd do whatever she could to accommodate our legal needs.

After she left, George pushed a stack of paper toward me. "These people might try to plant a snitch on you, so be careful of what you say to anyone. Here are some agreement forms for every inmate around you to sign, saying they're not going to discuss your case with you. That should flush out a snitch."

"Do you want us to go pick up your things at Angola?" George asked. I told him no, that if I lost at trial, I'd need them when I went back. George lurched forward in the molded plastic chair. "You're never going back to that place again," he said passionately.

"You don't know what you're dealing with out here, George," I said. "This isn't just corrupt Louisiana; this is the place that throws its biggest festival every year in honor of the pirate Jean Lafitte, who smuggled contraband slaves into the territory after selling human beings was outlawed. Pay attention to your surroundings, man. You've gone backward in time to the 1950s."

"Well, trust me," George said, exuding confidence, "I've settled much more difficult cases than this one."

Linda and I exchanged a look that said, *He doesn't have a clue.*

They left, Linda for Baton Rouge and George for New York. I was returned to my cell, where I paced the floor. *I only have to get through two days of this.* Five steps, turn; five steps, turn, endlessly. The last time I was in solitary it was right here, in Calcasieu.

On Sunday I got a "recreation" reprieve from my cell from a white deputy who wore his prejudice on his face. While I walked briskly, he sat and smoked, watching me. After thirty minutes of the staggering July heat, he was ready to go in. I showered and returned to my cell, pacing and thinking. Someone told me I'd move in the morning.

The next morning, a young black female officer escorting four trusties pushing a food cart squealed, "Mr. Rideau! Oh, I've got to get your autograph before they transfer you." She slid a slip of paper at me. "I've been hearing and reading about you all my life. I admire anybody [who'd] fight that long without giving up."

That evening, I learned from a black deputy that I would appear before a judge in the morning who would appoint a lawyer to represent me if I didn't already have one. I called George at home, who said to tell the judge I was indigent but had counsel.

As night fell, I was still in solitary, pacing endlessly back and forth. I wondered why I hadn't been moved. *Are they playing a mind game with me?* Linda's words from yesterday's visit penetrated the panic rising in me: *Don't ever forget who you are. Be true to the best in yourself and they can never break you.* Fifteen minutes later my stress was under control.

At 8:00 a.m. on Tuesday I was taken to "seventy-two-hour court," a large, plain-looking room across from the attorney interview rooms. It's meant to resemble a courtroom, but nothing about it suggested the majesty of the law. Some forty pretrial detainees in orange jumpsuits and orange plastic flip-flops sat in molded plastic chairs facing the lieutenant I had met earlier, who was standing at the front explaining that they were not to talk, smoke, or sleep. About a dozen of the detainees were white. I noticed five females in the crowd; they all looked drained of spirit and tired of living. Lawyers sat off to the left, a couple of court secretaries to the right. A video camera and TV were perched behind the bench, where the judge would ordinarily be. This is the trendy video court system adopted across America. The only beneficiary is the judge, who doesn't have to leave the comfort of his office to come to this special courtroom, which was designed to spare citizens the expense and danger of transporting detainees to the courthouse downtown. The face of Chief Judge Al Gray appeared on the TV screen. As he read off the names of the detainees, they stood and answered the judge's questions about their ability to hire an attorney. One after another, they declared themselves indigent, to no one's surprise. If these people had money to pay a lawyer, they'd also have money to post bail, which is available to anyone not charged with a capital offense. So, as a rule, only poor people await their trials in jail. Judge Gray was a broken record, assigning each detainee to be represented by the public defender.

"I'm indigent, but with counsel," I announced when called.

"What does that mean?" Gray asked.

"It means I'm poor and cannot hire lawyers, but I do have attorneys at present, who've been neither hired nor court-appointed and have been fighting my case on principle."

Gray instructed deputies to bring me downtown to court at 1:30 that afternoon. A mild-mannered, light-complexioned black man in casual dress followed me into the hallway and introduced himself as Ron Ware, head of the local public defender's office.

"You Dennis Ware's son?" I asked.

"Yeah," he said, a smile breaking over a set of perfect white teeth.

I inquired about his dad, now seventy-eight. He had been a teacher of mine before I dropped out and for years was a staunch supporter, publicly taking on some of my most vocal adversaries to argue that I should be treated the same as other offenders from Calcasieu. I hoped the apple hadn't fallen far from the tree; because I was indigent, the court would automatically assign my case to the public defender, no matter what I said. I asked Ron if he could get my court appearance rescheduled so that George would have time to get back to Lake Charles (he got it switched to the next morning). He said he couldn't find any conflict of interest among his small staff that would give him the legal right to refuse my case. He expected my defense to cost a lot of money because the age of the case would require massive research into the long-defunct laws that would govern the trial as well as into the places, people, and evidence connected with the case. The cost would come out of his budget. Ninety-two percent of his budget went to defending capital cases. The rest, he lamented, was totally inadequate for the steady stream of other indigents I saw in "seventy-two-hour court."

At noon, a young female officer escorted me to my new quarters, and my relief at leaving solitary vied with apprehension about what lay before me. Mine was a unique placement: Although the jail officials were unwilling to make me a trusty, I was assigned to live in a trusty dormitory with ten detainees. In this way they avoided housing me with the general population, where they thought I could conceivably cause real problems for them; at least that's what several black deputies said to me.

My dorm was a split-level room with one wall of windows for the jailers in a glass tower to observe activity inside and three beige walls with blue trim. Intercom speakers in the ceiling provided a means of communication between the inmates and the tower jailer. Metal stairs against one wall led to the upper level, which extended halfway across the room and formed a ceiling over the bottom sleeping area. Upstairs were five double bunks, a shower, and two toilets. The floor crew, who cleaned the jail floors at night, lived there. Below there were six double bunks, one shower, and one toilet. All three toilets sat too close to the bunks on the end of the row, requiring anyone using the commode to improvise "respect" for the bunk man by stretching a bedsheet over a string in front of the toilet.

Half of the room served as a dayroom furnished with five octagonal steel tables with four round steel seats affixed to each. The seats were too small for men to sit on comfortably, raising the level of frustration in the dorm, which was obviously created by an "expert" jail designer who hadn't a clue as to what really works in day-to-day jail existence. As with the toilets, inmates improvised, using their pillows to sit on.

I was given a bottom bunk on the bottom floor, on the opposite end from the toilet and shower area, about four feet from the wall. The only person near me was an old ex-con on the bunk to my immediate right. Two night laundry workers and an orderly also slept on the bottom floor. Two ceiling fans and an industrial fan mounted on the wall above the stairs struggled to cool off the place, but it was a losing proposition. It was stifling, and all the men there wore shorts or drawers.

Unlike the harsh and barren lockup of forty years earlier, this jail had cable TV, a chest for ice and cold water, reading material, and a fledgling literacy and GED program, as well as a much more tolerant administration. Pay phones were located everywhere for inmates to make collect calls to whomever they wished at usurious rates that included kickbacks to the jail. The commissary offered small radios, cheaply made clothing, seasoning for the food, and a variety of un-healthy snacks, all at rip-off prices. Jail is a captive market where profits are guaranteed by official policy, and it has been my observation that personal friendship and political cronyism figure in who gets awarded the contracts to provide the goods and services to jails and prisons.

New detainees are stripped of everything upon entering and can have only what they purchase from the commissary. I came with pos-sessions already approved by the penitentiary, so I was told I could keep a couple of T-shirts, shorts, and a pair of socks; anything else, I would have to buy.

One thing that hadn't changed in forty years was the age of the jail population. I was the oldest in my dorm. Here, as elsewhere in the state, jail detainees were largely eighteen to twenty-eight years old, black, and poor. They were stunted emotionally, intellectually, and behaviorally, their development arrested around age fourteen or fifteen. They were basically adolescents in adult bodies—unsanitary, undisciplined, and noisy. They pretty much raised themselves, shaped by street culture, rap music videos, advertisements, needs, fears, and what little education they acquired in school before losing interest and quitting or getting expelled for behavioral problems. They regard getting arrested, shot at, or jailed as natural experiences to be taken with a shrug of the shoulders. They do not accept responsibility for what happens to them in life. They blame everyone and everything else for their frustrations, anger, and problems. Nowadays, most are crackheads and thieves. My guess is that most of these youngsters never held a job. They are not part of the American economy and exist at the fringes of its society.

They display adult comprehension and abilities in only a few things. For example, one man I met in my dorm was expert at dope pushing and the economics attached to it, but was largely ignorant of and inept at everything else. He planned on "getting some bitch pregnant" when he got out.

I asked why, and he looked at me, puzzled. "That's part of being a man. That's what you supposed to do, so your name lives on after you dead."

Love and a relationship don't enter the picture, and he had no plans to care for the child.

"That's on her," he said, then laughed. "If she don't want a baby, she shouldn't open her legs."

There is little respect among these men for females, who are viewed as prey to be conquered and used. Women are commonly referred to as "bitches" or "hoes." "Niggah" and "dawg" are the terms most frequently used for other people, and they call whites "niggah" as quickly as they do fellow blacks. Their major endeavors in the streets were hanging with the brothers, chasing sex or some form of dope, and trying to make a hustle.

When I was jailed forty years ago, a substantial percentage of the detainees were unable to read or write and many more did so only with great difficulty. Today's inmates are better schooled but more stupid. Most are dropouts who travel in marginal orbits with few perceived

options in life. They spend their time telling and retelling street experiences, talking about the personalities who populate their small
worlds, and playing cards, chess, or dominoes. They neither watch nor
read the news. Their TV fare is a diet of sports, violent action movies,
The Three Stooges, The Little Rascals, Saturday-morning kiddie car-
toons, and Discovery Channel documentaries that show violent animal
behavior. Some listen endlessly to rap music, their heads bobbing like
corks in running water, or dance by themselves in a corner. Others
engage in boisterous horseplay or argue over petty things. Their power
to reason with others is almost nonexistent, and the loud disputes that
often end in threats stem from an inability to explain their point of
view to those who don't understand. Crippled by rap slang and a deficient sense of cause and effect, they simply repeat themselves over and
over, getting louder and louder, until one of the frustrated speakers
turns to nonparticipants in search of agreement or begins to issue
threats, raising his voice to dominate and drown out the point of view
he's unable to win over.

They wear two or three pairs of underwear, each falling lower, with
the third one hanging just below the backside. They wear their pants
hanging off their asses, too. None was able to give me a reason for
doing so other than it "gangsterfies" them. Understandably, they must
constantly pull up their britches.

It was painful for me to look at these street-raised weeds, these outcasts and misfits. I knew only too well that they do not care about a
world that does not value them. This makes them walking time bombs.

My history made me a living legend in the jail. Returning to Calcasieu
after a thirty-year absence, I was at once both a heroic larger-than-life
figure and a martyr, generating admiration, sympathy, and respect
among many, especially blacks.

I settled into the dorm and stowed my meager belongings in the
footlocker bolted to the head of the bunk. Although I'd given up cigarettes a decade earlier, I brought a couple of cartons of Camels from
Angola. My immediate need was for a combination lock, which I
bought from Fred Matherne, one of the two white men in the dorm,
for two packs.

I spent the rest of the afternoon and evening listening to the
inmates' problems and their cases. I heard it all—those who claimed

they were innocent and had a witness to prove it; those whose warped sense of right and wrong convinced them they were justified in whatever they did; men who said they should have already been released but weren't because of bureaucratic foul-ups computing the "good time" credits that shorten sentences. They were all frustrated because their cases were stalled somewhere in the system and they had no one to talk to about it. Desperation tinged their voices as they unloaded their anger and grief.

Claude "Collie-Boy" LeBlanc, a stocky ex-con in on a drug charge, had been unable to get his records from the clerk of court's office.

"Did you see your lawyer?" I asked.

"Hell, I been here *six months* and I ain't seen the bitch yet, and I go to court in less than a week," another detainee, Eric Alexander, interjected.

"That's when you gonna see 'em, when you sentenced," Claude said.

"I thought the new sheriff, Beth Lundy, had a free, direct line to the public defender's office installed," I said.

"Yeah," said Eric, "but you can never get past the receptionist."

Claude continued: "I have never had a lawyer come to this jail and talk to me. Only seen a lawyer when I went to court. Look, you got a handful of public defenders and they represent everybody in the jail. Their caseload so big till everything here is plea bargains. There's no fighting here. The DA and the judges know that, at some point, you gonna come around, get tired of sitting here, and accept whatever they offer. That's the reason they set court dates so far off in the future. These people full of shit, man."

The other men said that was their experience, too. Adili Barfield, short and light-complexioned, was charged with probation violation when he was arrested for possession of marijuana and narcotics. "I've been here eight months and they haven't even arraigned me," he said. "Trial? Hell, people rarely go to arraignment to schedule a trial, and when they do, the trial date is so far off until you're ready to cop out. But I'm not copping to anything. That would put me in the joint. If I was guilty, that's one thing, but I'm not guilty, and I'm not pleading guilty."

"Do you know anyone in jail who's had a trial by jury?" I asked.

Adili thought long, then shook his head. "No, don't know anybody. The only people you see going to trial is for big charges, like murder. You barely ever see anybody else go to trial."

About 10:00 p.m. George and Linda came to prep me for the next day's hearing. They told me that the sheriff had a press conference scheduled for 10:00 a.m. to announce what the media's access to me would be. George said media from around the country had been trying to get an interview with me, either through him or Julian or directly through the jail. So far they'd all been turned down.

On Wednesday morning, I was shackled hand and foot and transported to court in a caravan of vans and escorts with two other men, each charged with triple murder.

George and Ron Ware came to my holding cell in the basement of the courthouse, where I was being held, isolated from anyone else. George handed me black trousers and a blue shirt to wear in the courtroom. Cops took the chains and flak jacket off so I could dress. One asked if I wanted to wear the body armor under or over the shirt. "I don't need it at all," I said. "I don't think anyone is going to try to do anything to me and, if they do, I have confidence that you all will stop them, in which case, perhaps one of you needs to wear this thing."

They laughed and reshackled me over the clothing. Everyone left. The cops returned shortly afterward, informing me the judge said I had to wear the orange jail uniform.

The small courtroom was just about filled, mostly with white people. I took my place between George and Ron, with two cops taking seats behind me. One leaned forward: "Take a look around the room. See if there are any hostile faces you think might try to hurt you, anyone who might be dangerous."

My eyes swept the audience, catching Linda and a few black faces, who I assumed were supporters. The white faces defied easy definition. The pockmarked district attorney was standing in the aisle talking. I leaned back to the cop. "I see one."

He stiffened into alertness. "Who?"

"Rick Bryant," I whispered.

He smiled as his body relaxed. "I think I can handle him."

Court came to order. Presiding, as predicted, was Judge Canaday, who hailed from aptly named Sulphur, a white enclave across the river in West Calcasieu, where the noxious odors emanating from chemical plants can be smelled, when the wind is right, ten miles away.

Canaday immediately rejected George's argument against disrupting an existing attorney-client relationship and then appointed the only local capital-certified attorneys he knew: Ron Ware and a New Orleans attorney who had recently lost a death penalty case in Calcasieu. Canaday announced he would compile a list of lawyers who could visit me in jail; anyone not on the list would be turned away. Ron asked the judge to allow George to stay on the case and pleaded to be taken off, saying he could not adequately defend me because he had four other capital cases and another four hundred felony cases to defend personally, in addition to his administrative duties. Canaday refused to release him but allowed George to assist in the case pro bono.

George never stood a chance of being officially appointed to defend me. He was the ultimate outsider, a Yankee from New York poking his nose where Canaday thought it didn't belong. Worse, he was a white man working for the NAACP Legal Defense Fund, still considered a betrayal among some of the locals. Julian, one of the state's preeminent criminal defense lawyers, was left completely out of the equation, even denied access to me by the judge. I wanted to ask Canaday why he was so insistent upon divesting me of my excellent lawyers and replacing them with attorneys unfamiliar with me or my case, but both Ron and George vetoed my getting into a fight with the judge.

When I was back at the jail, a couple dozen inmates and I spent an hour of recreation in a small, walled-in area with two basketball courts. Whites played at one and blacks at the other. A female officer, clearly a descendant of the long line of pale-skinned offspring that began when white Louisiana masters coupled with black slaves, sat in the shade reading want ads. I was on my fourth lap of power walking when called for a visit with George and Linda. When I arrived, they asked the officer escorting me for another room. He said there were no others. Linda had spotted former district attorney Frank Salter in the adjoining attorney room talking with an elderly man, and she refused to believe it was coincidence. We pulled our chairs close together and huddled in whispered conversation.

"You're stuck in jail until pretrial motions in the fall," said George, "but I think we'll be able to get you out on bond then; meanwhile, we'll have another hearing on getting Julian assigned to the case in about a month."

My life at the jail went on. I received several letters from female prisoners wishing me luck. I got a laundry connection, which meant I'd have bleached whites and pressed uniforms. One of my dorm mates set up a connection for salt, pepper, and sugar. Some fellow detainees made sure I saw a newspaper every day. I was grateful for even the smallest kindness.

I slept fitfully in my new environment, alert to every sound. I knew how the justice system can work under the control of ruthless individuals. Snitches can be planted. Hit men can be moved near you—men who have no history of violence but are desperate to get out from under a charge that might send them to prison for years. (At Angola, my request that no prisoners from Calcasieu live in the same dorm as me had been honored for just these reasons.)

I could afford to trust no one.

The days passed slowly. I had nothing to do—no work, no court appearances, no visits from anyone. I was still trying to digest the fact that Julian, who had represented me for fifteen years, did not have access to me. When the judge and district attorney rearranged my defense team, the local media reported nothing amiss—and no other media people came to that backwater. The sheriff did indeed hold a news conference to announce that the media would not have access to me, and it's difficult to sell an editor on the idea of a story without an interview. KPLC-TV—the same Lake Charles television station that had repeatedly aired my "interview" with Sheriff Reid in 1961—now repeatedly ran footage of me shackled or getting out of the transport van, or used the jail's ID photo of me in orange scrubs, although the televised version was darker and made me look menacing. None of this surprised me, because the Lake Charles media was little more than an arm of the prosecutor's office, at least where I was concerned. More often than not I wasn't even allowed a daily hour of recreation, despite Sheriff Lundy's public statement to the contrary.

My fellow inmates also had nothing to do until it was time to clean the floors in the afternoon, so the morning TV report of my court proceedings became a subject of conversation. All ten men in the dorm agreed that I was about to be railroaded. Eric Alexander, who after six months in jail still had not met the public defender representing him, said it most straightforwardly: "They already got their game together, dawg. They hijacked your ass from Angola where you got everything goin' for you and brought you down here where they control the game and all the players. They take your high-powered lawyers and give you some cheap-ass, overworked attorneys that guarantee you gonna lose. Then they give you this rookie-ass judge ain't been in office a year, never handled a serious case before. Them bitches railroading you, dawg. Them DAs know they ain't never dealt with heavy-hitting lawyers like you got. They ain't no match for 'em. That's the reason they takin' 'em on out and getting you some lawyers they can control. But the way I see it, they playing so dirty with you that while they think they fuckin' you, they really fuckin' themselves, 'cuz they givin' you grounds to come back on 'em and win in the future."

What Eric didn't see was that, in that scenario, I couldn't win. The appeals process would be endless. In this case, a tainted conviction would be just as good as a proper one; the district attorney knew that. What I knew was that either my lawyers would have to settle the case by getting the prosecutor to agree to let me plead to manslaughter, or we'd have to win it outright. At age fifty-nine, I couldn't lose this case. I dreaded the court proceedings, but I never lost my faith.

A month later the judge let Julian replace the other New Orleans lawyer and work with Ron Ware. George still couldn't get appointed but could work for free. In the courthouse one day, Judge Canaday took us into the back room, away from the public, and instructed my attorneys that they had fifteen days to file all the motions they intended to file in connection with the case. Ron again pleaded to be taken off the case. Canaday instead told him he was lead attorney: "You are to do the lion's share of the work on this case."

The prosecutors, who would not even speak to George or Julian, were looking smug.

I told George and Linda that we couldn't afford to trust Ron. As part of the Calcasieu justice machinery, he had hundreds of other defendants who could suffer if he pissed off the district attorney or the judge by fighting too hard for me. I even felt we had to be extremely careful about what we said around Ron, as he could hurt our case, even inadvertently.

Another Wednesday rolled around, and I rose at daybreak to get ready for Linda's weekly visit. She arrived like clockwork at 9:00.

"I've got 'em!" she said, barely able to contain her glee. "I figured out how the DA got around the random selection to have Judge Canaday assigned to this case. Look at this!" She reached into her briefcase and pulled out a sheaf of letters from the clerk of court to various judges informing them that they had been assigned to preside over a capital case. My heart was pounding.

"There's a flaw in the system. They use seven bingo balls—one for each judge—and mix them up in a hopper before selecting one at random. But the problem is, each time a judge has been selected, his ball stays out of the hopper until all the other balls are gone. The selection is only really random on the first pull, when all seven balls are in the hopper. In your case, Canaday's ball was the only one left." She lifted the cover of a manila folder to reveal a typed chart she'd constructed that graphically illustrated the cycles of cases assigned and the dwindling balls in the hopper since 1993. "There was a one hundred percent certainty that Canaday would be your judge. And, because Bryant gets copies of all of the clerk's letters assigning the judges, he knew that."

"So the sonuvabitch timed his indictment of me to get the judge he wanted?"

"Bingo! But it's worse than that." Linda shuffled her papers and brought a new one to the top. "See this? Here's a guy who was indicted on capital charges on July 19. He would have gotten the last ball in the hopper, Canaday. The next thing that happens is that Bryant turns around and indicts you on the same day, only days after telling both Julian and Judge Polozola that it would probably be about a month before they indicted you."

"That's why they yanked me out of Angola."

"But they still had some manipulating to do," Linda said, "because cases are assigned judges according to their docket number. The DA assigns the docket numbers, so he could leapfrog you in front of this other guy. Otherwise, you would have had a full bingo hopper and two out of seven chances of getting a judge Rick Bryant doesn't want handling your case."

"Oh, he's not about to let either of the black judges anywhere near this case," I said. "Junior, how did you get this information?"

"Well, you have to understand, they don't know me yet over at the clerk's office. I told one of the clerks that I was researching Calcasieu's capital allotment system and asked if there were any public records I could go through. The deputy clerk of court himself then gave me all these letters and even photocopied them for me for free. I thought I was going to have to spend a week sifting through ledgers or books of records. Can you imagine the clerk's surprise when we file all this in court and he realizes his office handed it up on a silver platter?"

"This may be what we need to oust this judge and rearrange their game plan," I said. "What does George say?"

"He's pleased."

I returned to my dorm, my spirits buoyed by Linda's discovery.

Time and time again she had come through for me. I cannot imagine where I would have been without her.

Two days earlier, I had relieved my boredom by getting involved with the plight of John Jollivette, a Creole-speaking black who slept on the bottom bunk to my right. He was forty-nine, but the guys called him "Pop" because he looked older than everyone else in the dorm, probably due to a hard and varied past. He had been a rhythm-and-blues and gospel lead guitarist when he was sent to Angola for rape. As a condition of his release, he was prohibited from working anywhere liquor was served, which effectively ended his ability to earn a living as a musician. He found work as a truck driver and as a merchant seaman. Earlier in the year, he was arrested for stealing two bottles of wine valued at $7. He was released on his own recognizance. Three months later he got into a dispute with his landlord, who called in the police. Pop was arrested for "remaining after forbidden" and "resisting an officer." Bond was set at $1,000. The next day he went to the jail's seventy-two-hour court and was appointed a public defender, who was not present. When he called the public defender's office, he couldn't get past the receptionist.

"The receptionist says the charges over the dispute with the landlord were dropped," said Pop, "and I should contact the DA or the jail to find out why I'm still being held here. When I asked the jail authorities, they said the charges weren't dropped. I don't know what's goin' on."

When he finally went to court, he learned that he was there on the old $7 wine-theft charge and was given credit for time served.

"I didn't see a public defender there," he told me. "I pled guilty. I just wanted to get it over with, so I took the deal they offered."

But he was never in jail for the theft charge; he was in for the dispute with the landlord, a charge the receptionist said was dismissed. How could he be given credit for time served on a charge that had been dropped? When Warden LaFargue came to see me that afternoon on a minor matter, I introduced him to Jollivette and explained the situation.

Looking at Jollivette, the warden said, "We don't want you here if you're not supposed to be here."

When I returned from my visit with Linda, I found Jollivette packing in preparation for his release.

Months later, I was given an office right outside my dorm, where I could listen to inmates' problems and try to facilitate solutions for those that were legitimate. Having a sense of purpose, something productive to do, was a lifeline for me, and the office provided me a quiet haven away from the constant cacophony of TV and jive in the dorm. For a while I had a computer there, until the administration tightened down on everything following an escape from the maximum-security section of the jail. I don't know if the district attorney knew about my job and office or not. I'm not even sure the sheriff knew. But the curious thing about the law enforcement and criminal justice powers in Calcasieu Parish is that once they believe they have you snared, they can be downright gracious in small ways. In my own mind, the symbol for this has always been the black-walnut ice cream deputies used to bring to Robert Lee Sauls every day in the mid-1950s as the black man awaited execution.

Saturdays always brought a visit from my seventy-seven-year-old mother. She could now visit me far more often than when I was in Angola, two hundred miles away. She would often apologize for not being able to do more to help me during the past forty years. Her sense of guilt was bitterly ironic because no one knew better than I that my actions so long ago had changed her life profoundly, causing her not only untold personal heartache but public scorn as well. Tied by poverty to Lake Charles, she was forced to remain there, mother to the most vilified defendant in the city's history, whose demonization was fueled by the vengeance reserved for black men convicted of killing a white. I told her over and over that for decades she was my only friend and visitor, that during my darkest days she was the only reason I kept going, that I became the man I am today in an attempt to make up not only for the incredible damage I caused to my victims and their loved ones, but to my own family as well. No matter what I felt, though, this was still one more thing I couldn't make right.

One Saturday in early September, my mom brought Lawrence Morrow to the jail to share the forty-five-minute visit I was allowed each week. Lawrence is a little younger than me and was publishing *Gumbeaux Magazine*, a biweekly giveaway aimed at a black audience. I first became aware of the paper when one of its writers did a nice feature on me in the mid-1990s. Morrow asked how he could help me. I told him I was being held incommunicado from mainstream media, that the district attorney would not even say hello to my attorneys much less speak to them, and that we had discovered that Judge Canaday was essentially handpicked by the district attorney. Morrow immediately commissioned a piece by Bobbie Celestine, a Lake Charles native about my age, who based his article on a face-to-face interview with the district attorney. This was the only way independent news about my case reached the local community.

I was just rinsing my coffee cup one Tuesday morning when Albert Bradley called down to me from upstairs, where he slept: "Man, there's something on the radio about a hijacked plane crashing into the World Trade Center in New York. You might wanna check the TV to see if they're showing anything."

The disaster immediately filled the screen—smoke billowing from one building, then another building, then the side of World Trade Center One crumbling and, below, people running for their lives through the streets, others looking back in stunned horror, still others sitting on curbs, shell-shocked and grieving in a landscape instantly turned ashes-to-ashes gray. My thoughts turned to all my friends in New York, and I prayed silently for their safety.

As the television kept rerunning footage of first one plane and then a second plowing into the Twin Towers, my dorm mates became increasingly excited, their fervor a mix of patriotism and glee at the prospect of our country going to war and killing people in retaliatory violence. They became so boisterous it was difficult to hear the TV. Every now and then some image would capture their attention, and a momentary silence punctuated the air before they erupted with renewed shouting and vigorous cursing. Some boasted about how they'd willingly go fight, if they could: "I'd teach them Arab terrorist motherfuckers about fucking with America." There was something bizarre about this odd blend of criminality and patriotism and their fierce allegiance to a country in which they were outlaws, lumped by politicians and society into more or less the same class as the enemy on TV.

George's wife, Tanya, saved his life on September 11 by asking him to drop their children, Hallie and Sela, off at school that morning, so he was running behind schedule. Had he been on time, he would have been getting coffee in the World Trade Center, as usual, as he passed from the train stop to the street, when the planes struck.

A week after the attack, George was one of only ten people on his flight from New York to New Orleans, a testament to the public's newfound fear of flying. A day before coming, he had finally been able to get into his office, six blocks from Ground Zero, to retrieve my case file. Going to court the next morning, I rode in a van with a young, white baby-killer chained up in the seat behind me. Hyper, almost happy, he beamed when we reached the courthouse and he saw the cameras: "Oh, we're gonna be on TV!" Of course, the media wasn't there for him, but for me.

Days turned into weeks, then into months of constant court activity that seemed to eat up the calendar of my remaining life. Judge Canaday imposed a gag order in the case and refused to recuse himself despite indisputable evidence that his appointment was subject to manipulation. He saw his selection as a "harmless error" and set a January trial date. On appeal, the Louisiana Supreme Court ordered Canaday off the case and a new judge to be selected from a full hopper of seven bingo balls. That ruling marked the first time in forty years that the Louisiana Supreme Court ruled in my favor on anything. I thought the ruling would get my case moving more quickly toward trial, but I was wrong.

Life in the Calcasieu jail became even more difficult as opportunities for recreation virtually disappeared. When we did get out of our dorms, I'd jog around the track, which ran past windows of the solitary-confinement cells; from one window, a naked white woman made a point of counting off my laps to me, while from another, an agitated white man yelled "Nigra white boy" at me. In the wee hours of a Saturday morning, eleven new men assigned to the road crew that picked up paper and trash alongside the parish roads were transferred to my dorm, filling it up. The overcrowding was awful. Clothing now hung over everything, making the place gloomier and darker. It was noisier, too. The funk of unwashed bodies was inescapable.

Several successful escapes caused authorities to curtail unnecessary movement by detainees, which didn't help the atmosphere. The authorities knew that giving inmates an outlet for their mental and physical restlessness through movies or recreation helps maintain the stability and safety of an institution. But rather than confront grandstanding politicians, who influence the media and the public, they crumbled in the face of criticism, restricting or eliminating these outlets. That, of course, made their own jobs tougher and their workplace less safe, not to mention less humane for individuals awaiting trial, who had not yet been convicted of anything.

The weather turned cold, and with flu season approaching, I asked for an immunizing injection, which I had received every year at Angola because of my history of chronic bronchitis and my age. The parish coroner, who came around once a month or so to look after the health needs of the detainees, denied my request. I was told that the only way I could get a shot was to have a private physician come into the jail to give me one. I asked Linda and George to see if they could find a doctor willing to do this—a black doctor, because I didn't feel that I could trust any white person from Lake Charles to stick a needle into my arm. The proceedings in my case and the reports on them by the local media had reignited my paranoia about local white folks. Everywhere I looked—in the jail, in politics, in local society—I saw a rift along racial lines that I hadn't seen anywhere else in decades. A black doctor volunteered to give me a flu shot and continuing care for the length of my stay.

We had no heat. The floor crew told me it worked everywhere in the jail except our dorm. We just couldn't warm up. Some men sewed caps out of the flimsy sweatshirts sold in the commissary, and I was able to buy one for some Bugler tobacco. I also scored a scanty cotton item that passes for a blanket and an extra sheet, which, when placed outside the blankets, keeps enough body heat in to warm you if you sleep in the paper-thin thermal underwear sold at the commissary under two sets of orange cotton jail scrubs, along with two pairs of socks.

After a while, a trusty who worked in the clothing office got me a jacket, but it was too late. I had picked up a bug. I got my prescribed blood-pressure medication and baby aspirin from the nurse, but she had nothing to relieve my cold. She said the best she could do was to have me fill out a medical request form and pay $5, and she'd order me Sudafed through the medical process. By the time it arrived, my cold was gone.

In December, a random selection brought Judge Wilford Carter to preside over my case. I thought once again that Divine Providence was intervening to give me a judge who, first and foremost, had the reputation of being independent of the prosecutor's office, and second, was one of the two African American judges in the district. Within days of Carter's appointment, Bryant filed a motion to recuse him on the grounds that sixteen years earlier, when he was a state representative

representing a black district in Lake Charles, Carter had appeared
before the 1986 pardon board at his constituents' request to say that
since other convicted murderers were routinely being freed on the
grounds of rehabilitation, fairness dictated I should be freed as well,
especially since my rehabilitation was universally acknowledged. The
parade of thirty-five other witnesses appearing on my behalf amply
proved his point. He told a Lake Charles television station: "We ought
to have the same standard for everybody. We don't do that in Louisiana. . . . We have one man who has been in prison longer than anybody else for the same crime under the same circumstances."

In his motion, Bryant accused Carter of working with Julian Murray in 1986 "to lobby for defendant's release on the same charge for
which he will stand trial," and demanded, "What is to stop them from
working together toward that goal today, when they are in ultimate
positions to accomplish that goal—trial judge and defense attorney?"

At a February 2002 hearing on the recusal, Carter addressed
head-on the attack on his integrity—an assault that would have been
unthinkable on any white Calcasieu Parish judge. He and Julian declared they had never met before that day and had never previously
been in contact about me or anything else. Carter turned to chief
felony prosecutor Wayne Frey, who was handling the recusal motion
for the absent Rick Bryant:

"Do you not think my oath of office would prevent me from col-
laborating with Mr. Murray? And if not that, that the laws of this state,
which would make it a crime for me to communicate with Mr. Murray
to get Mr. Rideau off, would? I would have to commit a crime; would
you say that?"

Frey responded, "I would think that you would, yes, sir."

Carter pressed forward: "What facts do you have to support such a
statement, other than the fact that I appeared at the pardon board
meeting sixteen years ago?"

Frey said he had no other facts.

Judge Carter refused to recuse himself, saying the state had presented no evidence to suggest that he was not and could not be impartial in his duties as judge and that absent such a showing, he had not
only the right but the responsibility under law to stay on the case.
Bryant appealed the ruling to the Third Circuit. The mainstream
white media in Lake Charles slanted their coverage against Carter,
referring to him as my advocate. The black community was up in arms

at the raw attack on Carter's integrity, but there was little that they could do. Lawrence Morrow ran editorials in *Gumbeaux* defending the judge. A white two-member majority of the Third Circuit panel, citing no law for their action, threw Carter off the case. We appealed to the state supreme court and waited some more.

Reverend J. L. Franklin, the thirty-six-year-old pastor of the Bethel Metropolitan Baptist Fellowship Church in Lake Charles, helped to fill the months of inactivity in my case. He had visited me one day and asked if I'd like him to pray with me, even though he was certain I had many other religious and spiritual advisors who came. I told him that the only other religious person who had come was a priest who'd been sent by his superior, at my mother's request. The priest told me that jail authorities gave the clergy a hassle when they came, so they didn't come regularly as a general practice.

Franklin and I hit it off immediately. He was a throwback to the ministers of the civil rights days, who took leadership on social and civic matters as part of their duty to their parishioners. He was deeply concerned about the poor quality of education in the black schools in Lake Charles and the indifference to it by the predominantly white school board. I urged him to run for a seat on the board in the upcoming elections. He knew nothing about politics, so I ran his campaign. We conferred during our weekly visits.

Franklin ran on the theme that a good education is the best crime prevention and announced his candidacy in front of the jail. He pointed out that Louisiana spent only $5,200 a year to educate a child, claiming a lack of money, but could find $52,446 a year to incarcerate that child in one of its hellish juvenile prisons should he steal a $500 television. He told me that a white judge had pulled him aside and told him not to mix the issues of public education and juvenile justice. "I disagreed," Franklin told me.

Franklin unseated the entrenched incumbent and immediately began working to improve education in the underperforming schools of the parish, which happened to be predominantly black. He became vocal about other local social issues, most often those concerning racial division or racial inequities. He visited me two or three times a week to consult, and he came to call me "The Professor." We became fast friends.

The state supreme court refused to consider our appeal regarding Carter, so it was back to a random allotment, now accomplished by computer. It selected Judge Patricia Minaldi. My team learned about that from media reports.

A transplant from Boston, Minaldi was reputed to be highly intelligent. She now lived in the overwhelmingly white, conservative enclave of Sulphur, Louisiana, and had ascended to the bench on a strident law-and-order platform. Because she had worked as one of Bryant's prosecutors for a decade while my case was active, the law required her to step aside as judge. Julian sent her a letter requesting she do that without our having to file a motion to recuse her. (It was also rumored that she'd had an affair with Bryant, which some people thought still may have been ongoing.) After more than a month of silence, she denied the request and invited us to do whatever we felt we had to do.

George and Linda had broadened their contacts in the law enforcement and legal communities of Lake Charles and New Orleans in order to learn more about the rumored affair between Minaldi and Bryant. Linda also pored through the Lake Charles *American Press* archives for every mention of Minaldi since her arrival in Calcasieu Parish.

By August 2002 she had learned that Judge Minaldi was given an award by Crimefighters, a victims' rights organization, whose Lake Charles chapter had come into existence with the express purpose of circulating a petition to stop me from ever leaving prison. At that time, the president of the chapter was Beth Lundy, now sheriff, who was then an employee of Bryant.

"Because race is such an integral part of this case," Linda said, "Minaldi's acceptance of an award from Crimefighters is further grounds for us to call for her removal."

Linda had identified several members of Crimefighters' board of directors who had ties to David Duke and white supremacist organizations and activities.

"We'll put it in our recusal motion," said Linda, "and send the motion to the media and then hope they show up for the hearing. After all, Minaldi is rumored to be on a short list for a federal judgeship, which makes her of more than local interest. George decided it would be good to put Sheriff Lundy on the stand, since she's the one who set up the Lake Charles chapter and gave Minaldi the award."

"You know," I said, "Lundy is going to claim she didn't know about Crimefighters' affiliation with white supremacists. And so is Minaldi."

Linda laughed. "You think?" she asked mockingly. "How politically incompetent do you have to be to crawl in bed with someone without checking them out? Can you even imagine how Julian could shred them on the stand if they made such a claim?"

"I see where you're coming from," I said. "Once we get either one in the witness box, it's a no-win situation for them. If they knowingly embraced Crimefighters, they've married themselves to racists; if they say they didn't know about the supremacists, they define themselves for their political adversaries as reckless and incompetent." We just needed the media to cover it.

We filed a motion to recuse Minaldi, claiming she should step aside because of her employment in the district attorney's office while my case was active, because of the "close, personal relationship" between her and Bryant—which was, we said, an open secret in the Calcasieu Parish legal community—and because of the award she received from Crimefighters, given that the trial would require the presiding judge to rule on issues concerning race.

On September 9, 2002, Minaldi held a brief hearing. An assistant district attorney asked the judge to hold my lawyers in contempt, claiming the language in our motion was "abusive and insulting and discourteous" to both Minaldi and Bryant, and vowed to seek sanctions with the Bar Association against them (he never did). Minaldi gave the state thirty days to file a response to our motion. She claimed that "there are things that are in this motion that are untrue and inaccurate," but she also said, "because they might establish grounds for recusal . . . I will refer it out to another judge, and that judge will make all the decisions regarding the conduct of [the defense attorneys]."

After the hearing, an incensed Rick Bryant went on the local FOX-TV affiliate and vehemently denied having had an affair with Minaldi—denying more than we had actually alleged—and insisted he would file an affidavit to that effect. An affidavit he eventually filed addressed only Minaldi's employment in his office and made no denial of an affair or even a "close personal relationship" with her.

That same afternoon, deputy clerk of court Jeanne Pugh, who had worked Minaldi's hearing, randomly allotted a judge to hear the recusal motion. The computer selected Al Gray, the only African American judge in the district besides Wilford Carter.

Chief Judge Fred Godwin, with no standing in my case, called Pugh to find out which judge would preside over the recusal hearing. That is when, apparently, the idea of a black judge hearing any kind of motion in my case caused more than a little concern in some quarters. Godwin talked with Bryant and then Minaldi. Then he instructed Pugh to undo the allotment of Gray, telling her that Minaldi intended to refer the case to another judge only *after* the district attorney filed his response to our motion. Neither the chief judge nor anyone else ever explained why, even if that were true, a random allotment that was to take effect thirty days hence had to be rescinded and later redone. Finally, the chief judge called Ron Ware and told him about his various conversations.

The next day Godwin, with clearer eyes, told Pugh he was retracting his previous instructions to her. He said it was the clerk of court's responsibility to make a determination concerning the allotment based on Judge Minaldi's statements during the hearing. Pugh's boss then withdrew the allotment "on his own authority."

This Keystone Kops routine would have been funny if the rest of my life were not at stake.

Months passed and still there was no resolution from the Third Circuit Court of Appeals as to whether Gray would be reinstated to hear the motion to recuse Minaldi. Over our objection, Judge Kent Savoie, a former prosecutor from Sulphur, was brought into the case. He set a hearing on our motions for February 13, 2003—my sixty-first birthday.

George came down from New York, as he did nearly every month, for a brainstorming session before the hearing. He had taken about a dozen "John Doe" affidavits, mainly from persons in the legal community who had heard about the affair between Minaldi and Bryant, in some cases from one of the principals. After Minaldi was nominated for a federal judgeship in January 2003, some informants began reaching out to the defense team. They wanted the protection of anonymous affidavits because they were afraid to anger either a sitting judge or the district attorney, two of the most powerful people in the parish. But if push came to shove, our John Does were willing to take the witness stand under a subpoena. We also put Bryant's wife on our subpoena list.

"I've talked to Julian and to Linda," George said, looking across the table at Linda, "and we all agree that we need to bring Johnnie in now."

I had met Johnnie Cochran in 1999 after *The Farm* was nominated for an Academy Award. He came to my *Angolite* office to interview me for two hour-long segments on his television show. After the interviews, he gave me the pin off his lapel, which said EXPECT A MIRACLE, and told me that if I won a new trial, he'd be there for me.

"I thought we were going to save him for trial," I said.

"The problem is," said George, "if we get stuck with Minaldi, she's too smart ever to let Johnnie come in as counsel. She'll keep him out."

"How can she do that?" I asked.

"He's coming in as counsel *pro hoc vice*, like me, which only means that he's not a member of the Louisiana bar but the court recognizes his credentials from other states and allows him into the case kind of like a guest. No judge has to permit someone with out-of-state credentials to practice in their courtroom. And Minaldi will realize immediately that Johnnie Cochran will rearrange the dynamics of media coverage of the case, meaning scrutiny of what is going on down here by outsiders rather than sanitation of their hijinks by the hometown cheerleaders at the *American Press* and KPLC-TV," said George, referring to Lake Charles's two main media outlets. "We're going to sneak Johnnie into Lake Charles for the hearing on the thirteenth."

George motioned across the table toward Vanita Gupta, a young NAACP Legal Defense Fund attorney he had brought into the case, and Laura Fernandez, who began working on my case in 2001 as an intern at LDF and now worked on the case in the pro bono section of her new employer, Holland and Knight. "Johnnie'll fly straight into the airport in Lake Charles, where Vanita and Laura will pick him up and bring him to the hotel. They'll use their room key to bring him through the back door, bypassing the front desk. The next morning, we'll all meet at Ron's office and walk over to the court."

"You can't let Ron know about this ahead of time," I said. "We can't trust him not to tell someone he trusts, who will tell someone they trust, and before you know it, the secret's out. Our strength here is the element of surprise, and we have to do whatever we can to keep this quiet."

"That's understood. In fact, what we'll do is have Ron meet us that morning at the hotel to prep for the hearing at one-thirty. That should prevent anyone in his office from finding out about Johnnie and getting on the phone. As you know, we've been contacted by a relative of one of Ron's employees who told us that Bryant has Ron's employee spying for inside information on your case."

"Did you ever tell Ron about that?"

"No. We don't tell him anything, anyway, except on a need-to-know basis."

"George," I said. "Do you seriously think we can sneak Johnnie Cochran into this one-horse town without everybody and his in-laws knowing about it?"

"Well, my friend," said my ever-optimistic attorney, laughing, "we're going to try."

They succeeded. When Johnnie entered the small courtroom on the thirteenth, smiles broke out on our side of the aisle, and jaws slackened or fell agape on the prosecutor's side. As word spread that Johnnie was in the courtroom, it quickly filled to standing room only.

Johnnie took his seat next to me at the defense table. "I told you I'd be here for you," he said, smiling. "I'm your birthday present!"

We had subpoenaed both Judge Minaldi and Bryant as witnesses. Minaldi had reached 125 miles to Baton Rouge to hire one of the top criminal defense attorneys in the state, Jim Boren, to represent her. Cochran called Bryant to the stand to ask him about the affidavit he'd submitted. Looking wan and uncharacteristically anxious, Bryant asked the judge if he could have a cup of water from the pitcher on the bench, which he proceeded to spill all over himself and the witness stand. A collective gasp and several giggles escaped from spectators as deputies went scurrying for towels to sop up the mess. Johnnie whipped his handkerchief from his pocket and offered it to an unaccepting Bryant, then turned his back on the district attorney and walked to the defense table, a barely perceptible smile on his face. I remained impassive, but it wasn't easy.

Once Bryant and the furnishings were dried off, Johnnie began his direct examination of the district attorney, who had sworn in his affidavit that Minaldi did not begin her employment in his office until September 3, 1986. The date was important, because we claimed in our motion that she began in February, *before* the date of my clemency hearing in May of that year. Our implied argument was that Minaldi's presence in the office—her brain was clearly superior to anyone else's there—was a factor in how Bryant proceeded.

I was blessed to have an army of help, not only some of the best lawyers in the country, but also young New York lawyers and law students who were working for free on my case. And, of course, Linda, who had encyclopedic knowledge of my case, was working for the defense full-time. We were in the fortunate position—rare for an indigent defendant like me—of having ample manpower to check out the prosecutor's statements. We had been told by a former prosecutor that Minaldi began work in February, and it was Linda who took Laura Fernandez to the courthouse and pulled a document signed by Assistant District Attorney Minaldi in *March* 1986. Confronted with this document, Bryant blamed his payroll accountant for providing him with incorrect information. Bryant had also claimed in his affidavit that he and Minaldi had never discussed my case, but Laura had tracked down a court transcript where Bryant and Minaldi were cocounsel and argued about a change of venue based on what had happened in my case. Finally, Bryant had claimed that my case wasn't active in his office after I filed my petition for habeas corpus in 1994, during the time Minaldi was there. Johnnie presented him with the docket sheet from the federal court showing all the status conferences in which the district attorney's office took part, the motions they filed and responded to, and case records they submitted during Minaldi's tenure with his office.

When Johnnie entered the docket sheet into evidence, Judge Savoie remarked, "The only purpose of this is to show that you quibble with what Mr. Bryant calls a nonissue?" to which Johnnie retorted, "I wouldn't call it quibbling, Your Honor."

In the end, Judge Savoie said he would require the district attorney to furnish us with certain information to answer the claims in our recusal motion. When it came time to consider whether Minaldi would have to do likewise, Jim Boren sent a note to the judge, who then said court would recess for ten minutes so he could read a motion Boren had filed that morning. In fact, the judge now met in the corridor behind the courtroom with my attorneys, Bryant and his team, and Boren. Boren said he was sure our evidence about Minaldi's service in the district attorney's office was sound. If the judge was recused on that basis alone, none of the other more sensational issues would have to be aired in court. Bryant was adamantly against this. Julian, who embodies old Southern gentlemanliness, was outraged that Bryant would allow his wife to be grilled in open court when he was being given a face-saving way out. Back in the courtroom, Savoie severed the grounds for recusing Minaldi and said the issue would be addressed at a hearing on February 28, which it was. After nearly eight months of combat, Minaldi was recused.

Of course, it didn't end there. When Minaldi ascended to the federal bench in April 2003, Bryant appealed Savoie's decision, arguing that only Minaldi, the individual, was recused. The division in which she served was not recused, and the judge who would replace her after a special election should inherit the case. This meant that another white judge from Sulphur would preside over my trial.

As the two-year anniversary of my return to Calcasieu approached, depression began to overtake me. My mother and Linda visited me, as did Sister Benedict Shannon, who had been my steadfast friend and supporter for thirty years—she came from Houston every other month with another friend, Geri Doucet. Reverend Franklin was a godsend. But I was increasingly fearful now that I was going to be railroaded by a system controlled by people who made up rules to suit them as they went along. I felt abandoned by the state and national media for not covering my hearings and for simply repeating what the local newspaper sent over the wire. After I talked to the *Los Angeles Times*, whose reporter exposed the vein of racism that cut from the present all the way back to 1961 in my case, the sheriff shut the lid on me completely, telling me and my attorneys that if I spoke to any more media, I risked losing all of my phone privileges, including the privilege of calling my defense team. I found this ironic, because the warden himself suggested that I put the *Times* reporter on my visiting list and because the article insinuated that I was some kind of con artist. I wanted to sue the sheriff, but my defense team convinced me that would just be one more distraction.

I realized about this time that if I were reconvicted, I would be sent to Wade Correctional Center, a small prison in the northern part of the state where high-profile prisoners are sent to live in solitary cells, for their own safety. Life there is very hard, with little in the way of clubs, activities, and the kind of opportunities to learn and grow that are part of the Angola world. This was a crushing weight on me. I came to think of suicide as an option if I wound up there. It was only when I thought of Linda and everything she had sacrificed to stand by me—her career, her pension, her savings—that I fell to my knees at the side of my bunk one afternoon and pleaded with God to show me the way out, for her sake. I was about as demoralized as I'd ever been. I'd lie in bed for hours, listless and rumpled. I went a week without shaving, wandering aimlessly from my bunk to a stool at one of the steel tables, then back again. I was physically, emotionally, and mentally adrift.

One day my dorm mate Albert Bradley said to me: "Say, man, what the fuck's wrong with you, anyway?"

"Bradley," I said, "these motherfuckers got a cake baked for me out here."

"So you just gonna lie down and die for them? Look at yourself, man. Did you lose your razor? Where are the creases in your clothes? You look like shit."

"Well, I feel like shit. Besides, I've got no visitors coming today. No one's gonna see me like this."

"What the fuck you talking about, man? *I* see you. More important, all these motherfucking inmates and jailers around here see you. Dawg, you can't go around here looking just any kind of way. You're Wilbert Rideau. You represent us all. Get your shit together."

His words snapped me out of my funk. I cleaned up and dug into my pile of legal notes and began looking for something that we could use against the district attorney. I began at the beginning. I scrutinized the indictment and Canaday's court order to return me to Calcasieu from Angola.

"This order is illegal," I told Linda on her next visit. "Look: It says that the federal court ordered me returned to Calcasieu Parish. The federal court never made such an order. What it said was that the state either had to retry me or release me. This case should have been returned to East Baton Rouge Parish, where I was tried after a change of venue in 1964. The law in 1964 was that a case could not be moved away from the changed venue *under any pretense whatsoever.* The law's been changed, but that is not supposed to apply in this case. These suckers have literally stolen this case and brought it back here illegally."

George and Julian agreed. But we were caught up in a judicial catch-22. We would have to litigate the legality of the actions of Calcasieu officials *in Calcasieu Parish*, meaning we would have to get the guilty parties to judge themselves guilty! It was at times like this that the judicial process dumbfounded me.

On May 31, 2003, Julian, George, and Johnnie held a press conference in New Orleans to announce that Ron Ware was filing a motion in Calcasieu to return the case to Baton Rouge, where the Louisiana Supreme Court had sent it because of state misconduct after the 1961 kangaroo court proceeding in Lake Charles. The motion accused Bryant of hijacking the case to Calcasieu for political purposes.

The next day, Johnnie and Julian joined Ron in Lake Charles for a prayer rally to support me, organized by Reverend Franklin and sponsored by a coalition of local black churches. The event, held at the Evergreen Baptist Church, drew more than eight hundred people to listen to a Catholic nun, a Catholic priest, a Muslim imam, numerous

Baptist pastors, a civil rights advocate, and Johnnie, who told the audience: "Many white people do not understand African Americans' distrust of the justice system, especially about all-white juries. What do you think would happen if the shoe were on the other foot? What would white folks think if white defendants, their sons, their fathers, their brothers were tried by all-black juries and black prosecutors, given the issue of race relations in America? Would they have confidence that a fair and just proceeding would take place? Of course they wouldn't."

After the rally, Johnnie joined a protest march to the old courthouse led by Franklin, who said the statue of a Confederate soldier on the lawn out front, with its pedestal inscribed THE SOUTH'S DEFENDERS, was a visible and constant reminder of white oppression to every defendant, lawyer, and visitor in the court. "It's time for this statue to come down," he said, "and time for Johnny Reb to stop standing guard over the halls of justice. All Americans deserve to be treated equally in the justice system. We've not seen equal justice here or anything remotely resembling equal justice." Franklin decried the harsher treatment given to blacks accused of crimes against whites and noted that black-on-black crimes received relaxed punishment. He pointed to a current case in which four black defendants were indicted for the murder of four black adults and an unborn baby, noting that although there was an eyewitness to the crime, Bryant had cut manslaughter deals with all the defendants, meaning none would serve even half as long as I had already served.

The prayer rally buoyed my spirits even though I wasn't able to attend. It was touching to know that so many people wished me well, and I was humbled that Johnnie and Julian took time out of their demanding schedules to participate. (George was representing an indigent in another state that day.) Ron's presence was an act of courage—and not his first on my case—as the rally and march were negatively received by much of the white community, judging from commentary in the newspapers.

The state supreme court appointed an ad hoc judge to hear our motion. Charlie Quienalty, a retired district judge from Calcasieu who had earned a reputation among defense attorneys as a hanging judge, surprised everyone when he decided after a September 5, 2003, hearing that my case did indeed belong in Baton Rouge. He also forced the clerk of court to turn over copies of all public records in their files from

1961 onward when he learned that the district attorney had given us only those snippets of the 1970 trial transcript that he intended to use at trial. We were ecstatic. We needed to escape the toxic atmosphere of Lake Charles if we were to see justice served.

Bryant appealed Quienalty's ruling and an all-white panel of the Third Circuit obligingly reversed it. The state supreme court refused to consider our appeal. So we were stuck in Calcasieu. In the election to replace Minaldi, her husband, a vice president and corporate attorney for Jack Lawton, Inc., which owned the biggest bank in the parish, ran against David Ritchie, a young Republican city councilman from Sulphur who had a private practice and also worked in Ron Ware's office as a public defender. On November 15, 2003, Ritchie won the race and inherited my case.

Ritchie arrived with some baggage. Two years earlier he had told Linda and George that when he was a law clerk, a very emotional Dora McCain came to see him when I was up for clemency and argued passionately against it. As a result, Ritchie had made it clear to others, including Ron, that he didn't think I should ever go free.

Linda and I felt Ritchie should recuse himself. George had a different take. "Look, the difference between Ritchie and the other judges in the pot—and let's be honest, we're looking at a white judge because it's not going to go any other way out here—is that Ritchie admitted his bias up front. All these other guys are too clever and too experienced to put their prejudice on the record. They'll just screw us without ever leaving a trace. And remember, until a few days ago, Ron Ware was Ritchie's boss and they had a good relationship. For that reason, if no other, maybe our new judge will want to make at least a show of fairness." We stuck with Ritchie.

Although Calcasieu's indigent defender system was financially strapped and other trials had to be put on hold, Ritchie found a funding source so the forty-three-year-old charge against me could go to trial. Things did not start well for us. Bryant made a motion, which Ritchie granted, that no mention of my rehabilitation could be made at trial; it was judged irrelevant to the question of whether I should go back to prison. Likewise, we were not allowed to bring in statistical data showing that I had already served nearly twice as long as any other man from Calcasieu serving time on a murder conviction; nor that some local boys convicted of murder since my 1961 conviction served as little as four years. We were to be confined to the crime itself. Character witnesses on my behalf would be allowed to testify only to my reputation for truthfulness.

In return, we filed a battery of motions. We argued that because of state misconduct in three previous trials, a sort of three-strikes-and-you're-out rule should apply. We moved to have Bryant recused on the grounds of prosecutorial vindictiveness, given his impassioned opinions and bitter statements, many factually untrue, about me to media over the past twenty-five years. We moved to dismiss the case on the grounds that after more than four decades, it was impossible to have anything resembling a fair trial since many of the state's witnesses were deceased and, although the prosecutor would be able to use their previous testimony by reading it for the jury from old transcripts, we could not cross-examine those witnesses, who had never been effectively cross-examined before because I had never had an adequate defense. Moreover, we argued, there was a mountain of evidence the state had not preserved that was no longer recoverable because the 1961 crime scene was now an interstate on-ramp, and none of the other pertinent sites—the bank, the fabric shop, the pawnshop, the sheriff's office, and the 1961 jail—still existed. In short, there was no longer any way to investigate adequately the facts of the crime. A new trial would be little more than reading the old transcripts into the record for a new jury, which, of course, was exactly what the district attorney wanted.

It would take more than six months for our motions, each denied by Judge Ritchie, to make their way through the rubber-stamp process of appeal in the Third Circuit and for the state supreme court to either deny them or refuse to hear them.

While there was little to do on my case except wait, Reverend Franklin provided me another opportunity to make a difference for the citizens of Calcasieu Parish. Early in 2004, he told me he was frustrated about the substandard education the students in his district were getting and the fact that the superintendent of schools was ignoring the problem. He handed me a sheaf of papers that included statistical breakdowns on the parish's school performances. The black schools performed abysmally compared to the white schools.

"Get rid of the superintendent," I told him.

"How? He's been an icon out here for a decade, a local hero who writes Cajun cookbooks on the side," he said. "They'll never fire him."

"They will if you bring enough heat on him," I said. "Get your Coalition of Pastors for Action involved. These statistics are a scandal.

The kids in the black schools are even outperformed by kids in all of the surrounding parishes, where the schools have less money and fewer resources. Educate your preachers."

Sixty pastors joined Franklin in the campaign to oust Superintendent Jude Theriot. They kept the issue on the front pages of the newspaper, circulated petitions, and would not be ignored. In June, the school board voted that Theriot would have to leave within a year.

After I helped with that campaign, I occupied myself with some other local politics. I advised the black community in the race for the congressional seat of southwestern Louisiana held by Democrat Chris John, who was making a run for retiring John Breaux's spot in the Senate. But during that contest, on July 1, 2004, we had a hearing that concerned a portion of some interviews with Billy and me that Jodie Bell Sinclair had conducted in 1981 and shared with Bryant to help prosecute me. Although the tape contained nothing that had not already appeared in print, the district attorney apparently thought that my taped admission that I killed Julia Ferguson was a smoking gun. During a break in the hearing, Assistant District Attorney Wayne Frey managed to get a copy of Jodie's tape to a reporter for local TV station KPLC, in blatant violation of the gag order that had been imposed in the case. In shades of 1961, KPLC-TV assisted the district attorney in further poisoning the potential jury pool against me not only by repeatedly airing out-of-context sound bites from the tape, but by posting them in streaming video on its website. Judge Ritchie learned of the leak only when he saw the footage on TV.

The result of this collaborative undermining of the justice system was the same as it was in 1961—a change of venue. Bryant was willing to go along with it only if he and Judge Ritchie were to retain control of the case and merely import a jury from elsewhere. We argued that an impartial jury, alone, would not ensure the fair trial demanded by law. The state had demonstrated its malfeasance over and over again. Like so many of our pleas for simple fairness, this one also fell on deaf ears. Judge Ritchie would not send my case elsewhere, and no higher Louisiana court would make him do it.

As it became clear that none of our motions to fend off a fourth trial would succeed, we began preparing in earnest for the courtroom battle. I pored over the old trial transcripts and identified for Linda where the defense team needed to focus—on "facts" that, although untrue, had been accepted as gospel for more than forty years.

Linda moved to Lake Charles for a week, typing into her laptop during our visits not only the fabrications, exaggerations, or outright lies I found in the old trial transcripts, but also everything I remembered about growing up in Lake Charles in the 1940s and 1950s. We covered my home life, school life, work life, events leading up to the crime, and everything that happened in its wake, both immediately and during the three previous trials. Linda was a thorough inquisitor, forcing me to remember more than I ever would have believed I could. Every night she returned to my mother's house, where she was staying, typed up a report, and sent it along with our day's work to Julian and George. These materials, together with the scant remaining physical evidence in the case, which George and Linda scrutinized, became the basis for our defense. George sought out the top experts in the country to evaluate the autopsy reports and photos, the handling of the crime scene and evidence, even the language used in various 1961 police reports and witness statements, which, surrealistically, we acquired from a reporter who got them from Bryant, who wouldn't disclose them to us. Linda was struck by the uncanny similarity not only in the diction and phraseology of the statements given to police first by Hickman and then McCain, ten days later, but also by the identical linear progression of the statements. The two statements, she felt, were similar far beyond what coincidence could account for. She saw that as evidence that Frank Salter had orchestrated the testimony of witnesses just as he had orchestrated the secretly filmed and televised "interview" between Sheriff Reid and me that led the Supreme Court to declare my 1961 trial "kangaroo court proceedings." Julian, who was to question me on the witness stand, began studying the earlier trial transcripts and my life and times as Linda and I set them down in the interview room.

When we were all together in Lake Charles, George and Julian were concerned that we didn't have a silver stake to drive through the prosecution's story. They felt it would be a very delicate matter to confront Dora McCain about her statements; the jury might well interpret our questions as an attack on an old woman who'd been victimized. Getting at the truth was not going to be easy.

"We'll have to hope they give us gifts at trial," George said. "Their fatal flaw—what has always caused them to lose their convictions—is that they go overboard in their rhetoric, their claims, their attitude. None of that matters when they're pitching to a hometown jury, but outsiders may not like it. We've seen that happen before. We have to hope that in this trial Bryant and his team will stay true to their tendencies to overreach, and that we can exploit them."

Shortly before trial, we learned that Dora McCain would not be appearing in the courtroom. She'd had open heart surgery a couple of years before, and a doctor said she was too frail for the stress of a trial. Her "testimony" would be that old transcript. One of our few opportunities to attack the prosecution's story had suddenly disappeared.

As things continued to go against us, I wondered, in the solitude of jail, why I had previously been rescued from the forces in Calcasieu that had tried so hard, so many times, to kill me. I had long since come to believe that I had been saved too many times to chalk it up to chance. Who would have thought that a bankruptcy and real estate lawyer would have hit upon an issue of interest to the U.S. Supreme Court in 1961 and that my case—over all others presenting the issue of pretrial publicity—would have been selected for review? And who would have thought after my second trial, as I waited on death row, that the Supreme Court would make a ruling in an Illinois case that would give me a new trial? And who would have guessed that after my third trial the U.S. Supreme Court would have, seemingly out of the blue, abolished the death penalty as it was then applied? And how could a man who had served forty years on a murder conviction get a federal court to set aside that conviction because the system used to select the grand jury that returned the indictment in 1961 was unconstitutional? All of this, together, led me to believe that a higher power than man was at work in my life. Now, lying on my bunk, I wondered: What if I had been saved only to portray prison life from the inside and never to go free? Everything in me cried out that there *had* to be more than that for me, that Providence had not saved me for a purpose that would forever chain me to guard towers and locked gates.

And yet, the judge and the prosecutor were making it almost impossible for us to mount a defense, moving us closer to yet another judicial lynching. I thought of everything I'd given up at Angola for what was my last shot at freedom. I was at the top of the pecking order in Angola's inmate society. I had the best job in the prison, where I could weave meaning into my existence. I sat on the boards of several inmate clubs, which expanded my ability to make a difference in the quality of prisoners' lives. I was the president of the Human Relations Club, which enabled me to bring resources to bear to help elderly prisoners and hospice patients. I was one of a handful of inmate leaders who worked together for the good of the whole institution, inmates and staff alike, rather than for their own personal ends. We worked to keep peace and order in the prison, though this was sometimes misunderstood by inmates who saw Angola only through the narrow lens of their personal pain. And I had perks. I worked in an air-conditioned office rather than in the field. Even though my traveling was cut out and media access to me increasingly restricted and monitored after Burl Cain's arrival in 1995, and even though *The Angolite* was increasingly censored, what I left behind at Angola was a relative paradise compared to what I could look forward to if we lost this trial. I had to believe Providence had something better in store for me; still, the specter of a cell at Wade haunted my waking thoughts and gave me night sweats whenever things took a turn for the worse.

Judge Ritchie asked both sides to submit a list of possible places from which to draw a jury. Bryant's list included the whitest judicial districts in the state, beginning with Jefferson Parish, which had gained infamy even in Louisiana as the district that sent David Duke to the state legislature. Small, rural, heavily white judicial districts completed his list. Our list included all the metropolitan areas of Louisiana. Judge Ritchie refused even to consider New Orleans, where nearly 60 percent of the voters, and potential jurors, were black. Nor would he send the case back to Baton Rouge, where it belonged. Lafayette, he said, was too close to Lake Charles; Shreveport was out, doubtless because Johnnie Cochran was its most famous native son.

In the end, Ritchie ruled that we would select a jury from Monroe, in the conservative Bible Belt reaches of the state. Carla Sigler, the prosecution team's newest assistant district attorney, hailed from there. For us, it looked like the worst of the state's metropolitan districts. One of our chief barometers for trying to gauge the jury pool was the race for governor between Edwin Edwards and David Duke in 1991. The Monroe area went solidly for Duke.

Just days before the trial was to begin, George and Julian came to the jail for a conference and gave me the dark news I'd long feared: Johnnie Cochran was too ill to participate in the trial. He'd been battling a brain tumor with experimental treatments when conventional medicine had failed him, and although he had rallied a few months earlier and even went back to work briefly, he'd gotten much worse. He was not even going to be able to travel from California to sit at our defense table. I returned to my dorm and lay on my bunk, staring into empty space, remembering the lapel pin Johnnie had given me years before that said EXPECT A MIRACLE. I remembered his deep faith and prayed for a miracle to heal him, and another to help me since he couldn't.

13

Deliverance

2005

Deputies roused me out of my bunk one Sunday morning, trussed me up with cuffs and shackles, and stuffed me in the back of a sheriff's car for the four-hour trip to Monroe, where we were to pick a jury. I felt I was heading into still another jail autocracy where I was friendless and vulnerable to being set up or sucked into violence. There was always the chance that some inmate would cooperate with Bryant in exchange for a deal, planting dope on me or making up some damaging story. I also had to be on the lookout for something the deputies might do to hurt me or set me up.

My fears were unfounded. Almost all of the jail staff knew who I was, and every one of them treated me courteously. I was held in a solitary cell—the largest cell I'd ever seen—where at the end of each day in court I could think calmly about the day's events and jot down ideas for my lawyers. Even though I sometimes returned from court after supper was served, I was always given a tray of hot food to eat, unlike the bologna sandwiches I'd gotten after a day in court in Lake Charles. I was also given medical attention. The jail would not release me for court each morning until the jail's nurses drained and bandaged an inflamed blackhead on my back. I was then able to sit attentively in court for the long days of jury selection.

On the day I arrived, there was a front-page Associated Press story about me in the Monroe *News-Star*, which the newspaper followed up with a story of its own on Monday. The two articles had an impact on the potential jurors, many of whom were dismissed for cause, either because they were convinced of my guilt or because they thought I had served enough time and weren't willing to send me back to prison whether I was guilty or not. Bryant amazed me by instructing the potential jurors that the burden was on him to prove every element of the crime with which I'd been charged and asking them, should they have *any* doubt at all about my guilt or if he failed to prove *every element* of the case, whether they could release me. He did this with an air of graciousness that I'd never seen in him, as though he wanted the jury to bend over backward to be fair to me. On the heels of that thought came the realization that he was acting so graciously because he was absolutely confident that he would be sending me back to prison for the rest of my life.

After five days, we ended up with a jury of two black women, one mixed-race woman, one black man, seven white women, and one elderly white man named Percy Ritchie—no relation to the judge—who became the foreman. Six of the whites were registered Republicans. The jurors were bused to Lake Charles on Sunday, January 9, to begin the trial the next morning. Our defense team worked out of Ron Ware's office during the day and a bloc of rooms at the local Holiday Inn at night. With Julian, George, and Ron were Vanita Gupta, now a lawyer at the Legal Defense Fund; Parisa Tafti and Chris Hsu, young lawyers George had brought on board from his new employer, Holland and Knight; and, assisting the lawyers, a battalion of New York University law students whose boundless energy and eagerness gave buoyancy to the whole team. Linda was the only non-lawyer on the team, the fact expert and a contributing strategist. Laura Fernandez, now clerking for a federal judge, came to offer moral support.

It was not lost on Judge Ritchie that the media seats in the courtroom were filled by journalists from New York, Chicago, Washington, Boston, Houston, Atlanta, New Orleans, and elsewhere. Even the local media realized that the eyes of the nation were on the trial. That made an enormous difference in the judge's rulings.

Usually quick to cave in to the prosecutors, Ritchie stood firm in ruling that we had a right to use photocopies of what were clearly authentic transcripts of court hearings from 1961, even though Bryant claimed they had "disappeared" from the clerk's office and insinuated that perhaps they had never existed or that we had somehow made them vanish. Linda found their disappearance highly suspect, since the last time she, Chris Hsu, and an investigator went to look at the files— *in the presence of a deputy clerk*—they had to be retrieved from the locked evidence room, to which only insiders, including Bryant, had access. In granting our request to use the transcripts, the judge noted that he had denied every one of our pretrial motions and I did, after all, have a right to present a defense.

In preliminary matters, George and Julian objected to Dora McCain's not appearing, because we would not be able to cross-examine one of the state's few living witnesses, but said we would waive our objection if the prosecution would agree to let us introduce into evidence comments McCain made in 1999 to a British tabloid. Wayne Frey fairly jumped out of his seat in enthusiastic agreement, as though he couldn't believe our stupidity. Since we intended to use her own statements to undermine her credibility, my lawyers were perplexed by Frey's exuberance. I wondered nervously what guerrilla assault our opposition had planned.

Mike Perlstein of the *Times-Picayune* and Laura Sullivan of National Public Radio both noted in their reporting that the courtroom was divided along racial lines (the Lake Charles press didn't), with white people sitting behind the prosecution and mostly black spectators sitting on the defense team's side of the aisle. In opening arguments, Bryant painted me as a calculating, cold-blooded murderer who ruthlessly turned on three people I knew by name, people who were my personal friends. It was the same sensational portrait Frank Salter had painted in my three previous trials. Bryant told the jury that before I entered the bank I had decided to kill the employees because they could identify me. He said I took them to a deserted spot ten miles outside town where I "lined them up and shot them." He said I kicked Mrs. McCain like a rag doll as she feigned death and physically fought with Mrs. Ferguson, yanking her to her feet, before shooting her twice. He would prove to them, he vowed, that "Julia Ferguson, who was already shot, begged—begged—for her life," saying, "Think about my poor old daddy," before I stabbed her and slashed her throat. Turning dramatically to point at me, he said, "That man committed the murder of Julia Ferguson."

George made the opening statement for our side. He told the jury that they would not have to decide whether I killed Mrs. Ferguson, because I did. The question they would have to answer was whether it was the cold-blooded murder described by Bryant, or manslaughter, defined under Louisiana law as the exact same crime as murder but committed in the heat of passion.

George told the four blacks and eight whites who would decide whether I would live free or die in prison that the ill-conceived and spur-of-the-moment bank robbery spun out of control almost before it began when a phone call came that startled everyone and I realized I wouldn't be able to just walk out of the bank as I had planned because police were on the way. He told them I put the employees in a car with the intention of dropping them off out in the country, where it would take them an hour or two to walk back to town, and that I panicked when the bank employees jumped from the car, began to flee, and wouldn't stop when I told them to stop or I'd shoot.

"As scared as he was," George said, "he shot, . . . these were the acts of an impulsive, confused teenager. He was so confused he started to head right back into town." He told jurors that in order to understand what happened that night, and what subsequently led to evidence and testimony that was not true, they had to understand the racial atmosphere of Louisiana in 1961, an atmosphere in which the community response to an interracial crime was a white mob that waited at the jail for the black defendant. "We are not suggesting in any way that what Wilbert Rideau did that night could be excused by the racial inequities of that time." But, he told them, in order to understand how authorities investigated and prosecuted the crime, including holding me in isolation with no attorney for two weeks, "it's going to be important for you to consider the mores and customs of the time."

Then Bryant began calling witnesses, most of whom were dead. Judge Ritchie may well have set a precedent in the American justice system by allowing Bryant to use testimony from previous trials for thirteen of his twenty-five witnesses. It was, essentially, a trial by transcript. Surreally, Ritchie informed the jury that Lake Charles radio personality Gary Shannon "will be playing the part of Mr. Hickman," sounding, as Adam Liptak of *The New York Times* put it, "as though announcing an understudy." The female parts were played by a local out-of-work actress.

We, of course, couldn't cross-examine the transcripts. Moreover, the jury had no way of assessing the credibility of the characters played by stand-ins. These witnesses spoke through the filter of professional voices, and without body language, shifting of the eyes, or clearing of the throat; their testimony betrayed no hesitation, no uncomfortable pauses, no nervousness, timidity, confidence, fear, anger, or arrogance—none of the usual cues we use to judge the truthfulness of what a person is saying.

To support the stories of the deceased witnesses, Bryant called to the stand Robert Waldmeier, Jr., then eighty, who owned the downtown pawnshop where I had bought my weapons. He said he couldn't remember for sure when he heard about the crime or how he heard about it, and he couldn't recall whether he contacted the sheriff or the deputies contacted him. He told Bryant he was pretty certain, though, that he didn't speak to any deputy on the night of the crime. When asked if he would have given deputies a duplicate of the cheap, common scout's knife he'd sold to me, he sidestepped by saying they would have had to buy it. When confronted with his prior testimony, in which he said he had talked with a deputy, he recanted and said, okay, maybe that was true. He described the knife blade as sharp on one side and dull on the other. He also admitted that deputies were in and out of his shop on a daily basis, that he was fishing buddies with deputy Harvey Boyd, who normally worked across the river in West Calcasieu but just happened to be the one to find the knife early the next morning, and that he and Boyd had been prepped together by Bryant before trial.

The knife was important because it disappeared from the locked evidence vault right after the 1961 trial. Only an old black-and-white photo of the weapon remained, which foreclosed any testing or examination of it. At my 1964 trial the Baton Rouge judge asked the district attorney if any fingerprints or blood residue had been found to connect the knife to me. The district attorney said there was none but explained that it had rained hard all night in Lake Charles before they found it the next morning.

After Waldmeier's testimony, during the lunch break, Linda said, "I'll go to my grave believing that Harvey Boyd got one of those knives from Waldmeier and planted it the next morning, especially since it was found three football fields away from the crime scene in a spot where you couldn't have thrown it from the car. No, that knife was planted so the court could lynch you in 1961."

Someone working for Bryant tracked down Sheriff Ham Reid's secretary from 1961, Anna Dahl, who had never before testified. On the stand, she said she helped count the recovered money and swore that there were no large crowds outside the jail when she and a deputy went from the jail to the courthouse to lock it up. Dahl was an excellent witness for Bryant, elderly and soft-spoken with no apparent grudge.

Meanwhile, Judge Ritchie was nodding off to sleep.

FBI agent James Wright testified that he and his partner, James Hamilton, interviewed me in a small room for four hours or more five days after the crime, after which Hamilton, now deceased, wrote out a confession in longhand for me to sign. Wright testified that the confession was accurate as to the facts, including my referring to McCain and Ferguson as "Dora" and "Julia." (Interestingly, I was said to have called Hickman "Mister.") Under cross-examination, Wright insisted that even in the segregated Jim Crow South of 1961, I might have addressed the women by their first names, since I knew them. As to the contention in the "confession" that I ate lunch at Youngblood's Café, he told Julian that since the café was located near the shopping center where I worked, I likely could have eaten in the otherwise all-white café if the workers there knew me. Wright denied Julian's suggestion that these details and others in Hamilton's handiwork were embellishments inserted deliberately to inflame an all-white, all-male jury, which was the standard jury makeup in Lake Charles in 1961.

Bryant introduced another new witness, Larry Lacouture, who worked for B. J. Oil Services in 1961. He said Hickman was wet from the heavy rain when he made his way to the shop for help, thus corroborating the testimony of a roster of dead witnesses who said it was a mean and tempestuous night. Murl Cormie, the sheriff's radio dispatcher, whose office was in the jail, said he saw no "non-police personnel" at the jail that night. He was backed up by another new witness, Bonnie Smith, an employee of the Gulf National Bank, who said that she was called to the sheriff's office to help count the recovered money and testified that when she arrived sometime between 9:00 and 9:30 there was no mob at the jail. She also testified that she stepped out of her car into five inches of water in the street, it was raining so hard.

Bryant's biggest surprise witness was John Holston, the ambulance driver who picked up Mrs. Ferguson from the crime scene. We had tracked him down ourselves because we wanted to ask him about what kind of equipment he had in his ambulance in 1961, and what kind of training, if any, he may have had in emergency medical services. We knew from deputies' testimony in the old transcripts that Ferguson was alive when she was picked up, and the old testimony also revealed that

Holston had stopped the ambulance shortly after picking her up when he met one of the deputies returning to the scene. We wanted to know how long Holston delayed getting Mrs. Ferguson to the hospital, what route he took, and whether he was sounding his siren. Holston refused to speak to our investigator; he said only that he was already a witness for the prosecution and that we wouldn't like what he had to say. Holston surprised us by testifying that no one else was at the crime scene with him, since testimony from earlier trials showed that both a sheriff's deputy and a local farmer helped him load Mrs. Ferguson into the ambulance and left the scene in his vehicle. We were shocked when Holston said that although his ambulance was equipped with oxygen, he didn't use it. "She didn't need oxygen," he said. "She was dead." We were shocked even more when, with great emotion, he said that Ferguson's throat was so badly slashed he had to cradle her head in his arms to prevent it from falling off when he loaded her onto a stretcher. His contribution to the prosecution—besides adding to the chorus that it was "pouring down rain like I'd never seen before"—was to take what in previous trials had been a slashed throat and ratchet it up into a near decapitation.

Upon hearing Holston's testimony, I understood Wayne Frey's delight at our wanting to use Dora McCain's 1999 comments to a British tabloid, where she described the crime with embellishments we had never heard in four decades. "He slashed [the knife] across [Ferguson's] throat until her head was nearly severed," McCain told *The Mail.*

Jodie Sinclair was the last on Bryant's list of live witnesses. He played part of that unaired 1981 interview. Though Billy and I were both told we would be discussing the death penalty on tape, Jodie began asking me questions about my crime. I had been advised, as I've said, never to publicly dispute the facts of my crime as they were established at trial, even if they were not accurate; clemency is about rehabilitation and asking for mercy, and you don't want to fight about what happened. I had followed that advice in responding to Jodie.

Bryant seemed to value the tape not for my admission that I had killed Ferguson, but for my retrospective analysis that bridged Jodie's question about my crime to the purported subject of the interview— the death penalty—"the fact that I hated white people added an extra dimension to the whole affair. I mean, you're not that concerned about the humanity of people you hate, which is why it is so easy for [society] to execute people." Although the comment was an attempt to explain the kind of anger and oppression I felt as a teenager growing up in the Jim Crow South, where my humanity was unrecognized and abused on a daily basis, Bryant tried to make it appear as though I had been a black militant just looking for an opportunity to kill white people.

On cross-examination, George got Jodie to admit that she disliked me and had worked for years to poison my reputation with the media, both in Louisiana—where she'd lambasted me on radio and in an interview with the Lake Charles newspaper as "the nation's best con artist"— and nationally. She and Billy had been trying to smear my reputation for nearly two decades, demeaning me to, among others, *Life*, *20/20*, *The Dallas Morning News*, and the Associated Press.

George questioned Jodie's journalistic ethics, eliciting from her an admission that she had repeatedly used her status as a TV reporter to enter Angola for personal visits with Billy. She was reluctant to admit that using her professional credentials to gain access to a private room in a maximum-security prison to carry on a secret love affair with a prisoner was unethical. She finally conceded not that she did anything wrong, but that "some people might call it a lapse of judgment, which I assume is the purpose of your line of questioning."

Bryant rested his case and court recessed.

The night before, Julian and George had told me that I was going to be the lead witness for the defense. "Are you crazy?" I asked. "Bryant is going to have a field day with me if I go first. Why don't we put on some of our other witnesses first so that the jury will know when I come along that I'm telling the truth? You throw me out there first and I'm like red meat for a pit bull."

"That's exactly what we want," said Julian, smiling. "That's our strategy."

"Look," said George, "Bryant has no idea who most of our fact witnesses are because we aren't bringing them under subpoena. We put you on the stand first, and he's going to think—just as he's been thinking all along—that you're basically all we've got. Since they've boxed us in by not letting us bring up rehabilitation, they'll think we're just trying to throw ourselves on the mercy of the jury based on your personality."

"So Bryant *will* go after you like a pit bull," Julian interjected. "He's going to try to make you mad, get you off-kilter, confuse you. He'll argue with you, and the judge will let him. All you have to do, no matter what Bryant does, is stay calm and tell the truth. Don't let him rattle you."

"But I still don't see why I have to go first," I said.

George smiled at me. "We've got a good case and, I think, a better than even chance of getting a hung jury. But that doesn't get us where we want to go, which is home. We need some drama to go with our facts, and since we can't get it by cross-examining dead or incapacitated witnesses, we need Bryant to supply it. He'll go so far overboard with you that it'll boomerang on him. It's a trap he was born to walk into."

I looked at George and Julian. I didn't think they were nearly as confident as they wanted me to believe. But they had gotten me this far. "You know you're asking me to jump off a skyscraper here, huh?"

Julian leaned back in his chair and smiled broadly. "Don't worry, I'll catch you. That's what I'm here for."

After the recess, I took the witness stand. I was wearing a light shirt under a dark green sweater and gray slacks that Linda had bought for me at a thrift store in Baton Rouge. My trial wardrobe had been a matter of great discussion among my defense team. Both George and Julian flatly ruled out a suit as inappropriate and artificial. "You will not be comfortable in a suit," George said, and Julian added, "Plus, you never want to outdress the jurors." The clothes were good-looking and clean, and I was comfortable in them, which was important.

Once news circulated that I was taking the witness stand to speak publicly in court for the first time about the forty-four-year-old crime, every seat in the courtroom was taken and spectators lined the walls. The judge declared that no one else would be allowed to enter unless someone left.

Julian began by asking me about my life growing up in Lake Charles in the 1940s and 1950s. I talked about the racial divide back then, and how it was drilled into me early in life to "learn my place" in a world in which I was conditioned to feel like a second-class citizen. I talked about my parents' divorce, about dropping out of school, our poverty, and collecting discarded Coke bottles on the white side of Broad Street to get money so my mother could buy us food. I recalled my resentment over being paid less than the white employees at Tramonte's grocery, one of my first direct experiences of a common complaint in my world—that whites took advantage of blacks just because they had the power to do it.

I recounted for Julian my experiences working with Mrs. Irby at the fabric shop in Southgate Shopping Center, how she tried to help me, how I felt cheated by the owner when I received only half the small raise I expected. I talked about white harassment at the bus stop coming and going from work and being barred from the whites-only restaurants there.

Julian interrupted me to ask if I maintained that any of this, or anything else that might have happened to me, justified what took place on February 16, 1961.

"No," I said. "Nothing justifies that."

I explained that at five feet, seven inches and 115 pounds soaking wet, I was a magnet for bullies not only at the bus stop in white Lake Charles but also in the black pool halls and nightclubs where I spent a lot of my time and most of my disposable income, and how this led me to think about buying a gun to protect myself, something that would make anyone wanting to mess with me back off. I recounted that incident at a black nightclub where I was slapped and threatened, and how I was determined I wouldn't be humiliated again.

Julian stopped me again to ask if I realized that most people would conclude that since I bought the gun and a knife the day before the crime, I bought them because I planned to rob the bank. I said I did realize that, and that I would have bought the gun earlier except I had to wait until payday, February 15. The knife, I said, I bought on impulse as I was setting out to leave the pawnshop and saw it in a display case. Even the pawnshop owner had testified to that. I said I fired the gun that night to see what it sounded like and took it with me to the nightclub. I intended to carry it regularly.

I explained that on the day of the crime, after leaving work early, I had fallen asleep in my cousin's car for several hours and, dreading the prospect of waiting for the bus in the dark, I had lined up a ride home at 7:30 with one of the porters from the supermarket. I recounted how, while waiting for my ride, all the problems of my life crowded into my mind, and I began to feel sorry for myself, trapped in what seemed to me to be a dead-end life. I said I was thinking then that if I could just go somewhere else I could start my life fresh in a place where I could be somebody, a place where I could matter. But that required money, and I didn't have any. That's when I thought about the bank, I said, and decided I would rob it.

My account of what happened inside the bank was essentially the same as the prosecution's. Julian brought out the half-baked nature of my undertaking with pointed questions: "Help me to understand this. When you walked up to the front of the bank, Mr. Hickman and the two women were right there where you could watch their every move and control them. Why didn't you exert control right then and there, tell them you had a gun, make them close the drapes and do as you say?"

I said I didn't know; it was my first time trying to rob anyone.

Julian asked me what my reaction was to the phone call and the caller who said that they were either sending a car out or one was already on the way.

I told him it was panic. To me, that call meant that someone knew the bank was being robbed and the police were on the way. In a moment, everything had spun out of control. I didn't know *what* to do, I said.

Julian stopped me. "You heard the DA say you took them out to the country to kill them. Why should we believe you didn't?"

"If I had intended to kill those people, eliminate witnesses, I would have done it right there in the bank. It never entered my mind that I was going to hurt anybody."

Julian asked me to recount the crime as I remembered it.

I explained that after we wound our way around Lake Charles for a quarter hour, I got lost on a gravel road looking for the Old Spanish Trail. Disoriented and lost, I'd told Mrs. Ferguson to slow down so I could think, get my bearings. I was looking through the rear window when suddenly Mrs. McCain bolted from the car. I lost my footing as I sprang out of the car behind her. As I regained my footing, leaning on the side of the trunk, yelling for her to stop or I would shoot, Mrs. Ferguson jumped out and followed McCain. Everything was going to hell. Mr. Hickman had come out of the car and tried to either hit my hand or grab the gun. The gun went off, unintentionally or not—I didn't know which. Everything happened very fast, I said, like a blur. Hickman ran, and I started firing until the gun wouldn't shoot anymore. Both women fell. Mrs. Ferguson got up. I ran to her and stabbed her. I was acting on panic and impulse. Then I ran to the car, turned it around, and headed back to Opelousas Street. All I wanted to do was to get away from there.

Now Julian resumed his questioning. He wanted to know how much time transpired from the moment Mrs. McCain jumped out of the car to the time I got back into the car.

I told him that my recollection of the crime, from the time the shooting started until I was back in the car, was like a series of disjointed snapshots rather than a streaming video, discrete moments frozen in my mind within a larger blur that seemed to me to last perhaps twenty seconds.

Julian asked me to tell about my capture, and I recalled for him the mob that quickly formed at the site of my arrest as well as the trip back to the jail in Lake Charles and the mob there, both inside and out. I talked about the confession I gave that night in the face of an overriding fear for my mother's safety once I had been told she had been brought to the jail. We went over the events of the next several days—the sheriff's "interview" that KPLC-TV secretly filmed and broadcast, the FBI statement five days later, and my belief that I was going to be executed every time they took me out of my cell.

Julian had me on the stand all afternoon, and I was exhausted by the time court adjourned for the day and I was taken back to jail. Meanwhile, Bryant bragged to reporters that he was eager to get at me on cross-examination.

"I'm looking forward to it because he's lying," he said. "But he's had forty-three years to practice. He should be pretty good at it by now."

When court resumed the next morning, Bryant opened his cross-examination with heavy sarcasm: "I've been listening to your story and I almost feel I should apologize to you. Obviously, you've been wronged all these years."

It was clear he wanted me to blame society or someone else for my actions. I had never done that, and I wasn't going to start now.

Bryant pointed to the differences in my version of the crime and the 1970 trial testimony of the eyewitnesses, particularly their account of being lined up on the side of the road and shot, and my account that I shot at them in panic as they ran.

"Either Dora McCain and Jay Hickman are lying, or you are. Which is it?" he demanded.

"I don't want to call anybody a liar," I said. I suggested it was fair to say our versions were different.

Bryant came back at me again and again, trying to force me to call the state's witnesses liars. He became increasingly frustrated the more I refused to do so. He cited my remark on the 1981 taped interview in which I said I hated white people in 1961. I'd already explained this remark under Julian's direct examination as the kind of free-floating anger a person feels toward a group or entity that oppresses him—the way some people hate the IRS, for example. In 1961 Louisiana, this kind of "hatred" was a common feeling among blacks.

Bryant whirled dramatically from me to face the jury: "Actually, you were one of the earliest perpetrators of a hate crime, were you not?"

It was a clumsy attempt to turn the underlying racial climate of the Jim Crow South on its head. I wanted to point out that the lynch mobs, the Night Riders, the Ku Klux Klan, and other groups that organized after the Civil War specifically to terrorize and kill blacks who didn't "know their place" were the earliest perpetrators of hate crimes in America, or at least right behind the thugs and thieves who raped and murdered their way through the Native American population. But the witness stand was not the place to correct Bryant's view of history, so I simply repeated my earlier statement: "It wasn't hate, it was anger."

The district attorney wanted to debate me about whether my crime was murder or manslaughter, grilling me about what I thought the difference was between the two. I didn't know what his point was, but I was amazed that the judge permitted him to keep badgering me on this point. I wanted to say that, as district attorney, he ought to know that these crimes were defined by statute and that what I thought was immaterial. But I didn't want to sound argumentative, so I said, "Murder is premeditated, something thought out."

As I continued to refuse to argue with him, Bryant began to flush. Referring to both the ambulance driver's testimony and Mrs. McCain's remarks to the British tabloid, he flung one of the autopsy photos at me and demanded I "explain how her head was nearly decapitated."

At that moment I was grateful that Linda had brought the autopsy photos into the jail and made me look at them as we were preparing for trial. I didn't want to see them, but she insisted. The sight of what I had done, the life I had taken, unnerved me and made me want to retch. I turned away, but she was not to be deterred. She had had all the photos in the evidence vault rephotographed so she could blow them up digitally and scrutinize them. She wanted to point out certain things to me, certain things in them. I told her I couldn't bear to look at them.

"You can look at them here, or you can let Rick Bryant shove them in your face in front of the jury," she said. I took her advice. Now, as Bryant shoved them in my face, I was able to keep my composure and respond to him about the throat slashing, which had become part of the myth surrounding my crime, thanks to a succession of Calcasieu Parish prosecutors and the local media.

When I said to him, "Mr. Bryant, you and I both know that didn't happen," I thought the vein standing out in his neck would burst. "Her head was not nearly decapitated. I've seen the photos. That's another exaggeration."

He asked me why I had gone after Mrs. Ferguson when I saw her trying to rise.

"It all happened so fast. I was scared," I told him. "You're asking me to rationalize what I did as a nineteen-year-old. There was no rhyme or reason for what I did. It was uncalled-for. But I was scared to death."

He wanted to prove I was lying when I said I did not call the two female bank tellers by their first names and, in fact, did not even know their names in 1961, contrary to the "confession" written up by the FBI agent. He went over my duties at the fabric shop, including the fact that for a couple of months before the crime I took the shop's daily deposit to the bank. Then he produced another of the evidence photos, which showed a placard on top of the ledge in front of the tellers' stations, and asked how I could fail to know their names, since each teller's name was clearly displayed on one of these nameplates. I said truthfully that I did not recall ever seeing their names, but my answer didn't sound convincing even to me. What would the jury think?

Bryant accused me of never having expressed remorse for my actions. What this had to do with the question of my guilt, I don't know. In criminal justice circles, taking responsibility for your actions and expressing remorse are considered primary evidence of rehabilitation. Although I had publicly expressed remorse in a number of media interviews, we didn't have them at hand because of the judge's order prohibiting any mention of rehabilitation and confining us to the facts of the crime.

I said that I had written a letter of apology to the victims a quarter century earlier. At my mention of this, the relatives of all three in the audience gasped audibly and shook their heads. I explained that because I didn't think they would want to open their mailboxes one day and find a letter from me, I gave the letter to Ginger Berrigan, who was my lawyer at the time. It was my understanding that she sent it to the original district attorney, Frank Salter—who, though out of office, had continued to represent the victims of this case in his private practice— for him to pass along to them. She also gave a copy to Reverend James Stovall, who was Mrs. McCain's minister at the time of the crime and who tried to mediate with her on my behalf.

"I guess Frank Salter never gave it to them, because they say I never expressed any remorse," I said.

Bryant sarcastically noted that those who could corroborate my story—Frank Salter and Reverend Stovall—were conveniently dead.

I realized that, as with the nameplates, it was again my word against Bryant's. I felt my heart beat faster. No one needed to tell me who had more credibility, a convict or a district attorney. I shut my eyes for an instant. *Your call, God.*

I opened my eyes and through the windows at the back of the courtroom, I saw Ginger Berrigan—now Chief Federal Judge Berrigan of the Eastern District of New Orleans—in the foyer, waving at me. Here was Johnnie Cochran's miracle. She was the one person in the world who could corroborate my testimony. Afraid she would leave the courthouse before I could let Julian and George know she was there, I tried jerking my head slightly and shifting my eyes toward the windows in the hope of alerting my legal team to her presence, but I was afraid to do too much for fear the jury would think I was acting weirdly.

I shouldn't have worried. Ginger and a colleague were in Lake Charles to talk to the female federal judge there (ironically, Patricia Minaldi) about gender issues in the judiciary, and she decided to drop in on my trial.

After Bryant was done with me, there was a short recess. Then Julian put Judge Berrigan on the stand and she confirmed my decades-old letter of apology to the victims. Bryant slumped down in his seat, his swagger gone. He declined the opportunity for cross-examination.

In quick succession, George called former Angola warden John Whitley, former assistant warden Dwayne McFatter, and corrections officer Sherman Bell as witnesses. After long bench conferences in which my lawyers were again warned not to mention rehabilitation, each testified that he had known me for decades and that I had a reputation for truthfulness at the prison. Since it was my truthfulness while testifying that was at stake, we could call "character witnesses" only to establish that single point.

Eventually, retired Louisiana Fourth Circuit Court of Appeals Judge Miriam Waltzer took the stand and testified that she'd known me since 1982 and that I had a reputation for truthfulness among her colleagues on the bench as well as educators, church people, law students, sociologists, law professors, and lawyers. "All the prestigious people in New Orleans know Wilbert to be an honest person," she said. Asked if she knew me in a setting outside of prison, she replied that she came to know me through a program she was involved with to help young first offenders change their lives. Bryant declined to cross-examine her.

I wondered what the jurors thought of all the bench conferences that were taking place. We'd call a witness, Bryant would ask for a bench conference, and the lawyers from both sides would cluster around the judge for as long as half an hour, arguing, after which a witness testified for perhaps three or five minutes. I thought that if I were a member of the jury, it would be clear to me that the prosecutor was trying to keep information from me.

Having established for the jury that I was a truthful and honest person, our next task was to begin showing how the state's case against me had been ratcheted up beginning forty years ago and continuing to the present. We began with the most gruesome element of the case, the mythical near decapitation.

George called Dr. Werner Spitz to the stand. One of the foremost forensic pathologists in the country, he served on the House Committee on Assassinations investigating the deaths of John F. Kennedy and Martin Luther King, Jr., and had testified against O. J. Simpson in his murder trial. He testified, first, that the coroner in 1961, Harry Snatic, failed to do his job in several important ways: He didn't visit the crime scene or examine the body there to form an independent opinion, which could differ from that of the police; he didn't examine the victim's clothing, which could carry trace evidence such as gunpowder and show weapons' entrance and exit points; most important, he didn't do a complete external exam of the surface of the body before beginning the autopsy, which he conducted with a cigarette dangling from the corner of his mouth. He didn't take photos of the body or of the wounds. He stuck his finger in the wounds, which altered the evidence. He never explored the path of the bullet and never photographed the bullet he retrieved. He made an assumption that there were two bullets but never looked for the second one. Dr. Spitz concluded from his own examination that there was only one bullet and that Dr. Snatic mistook the bullet's exit point for a second entry point.

Using the coroner's autopsy report and his testimony from 1970 as well as two photos of the victim taken by a sheriff's deputy—one in the emergency room and one while the autopsy was in progress—Dr. Spitz said he believed the wound to Mrs. Ferguson's neck was a tracheotomy performed in the emergency room. He noted that the incision was only one inch long and ran parallel to the elastic fibers in the neck, typical of incisions made by surgeons. The wound, he said, was superficial, made by an object with two sharp sides, such as a scalpel, rather than a knife, which has one blunt side and one sharp side. Moreover, he said that if the neck wound were a stab wound, there would have been blood in both the stomach and the lungs, neither of which was reported by the coroner in his autopsy report. Dr. Spitz pointed to the photo of Mrs. Ferguson in the emergency room and noted that one side of her mouth was open and rounded, which indicated to him that a breathing tube had been inserted in an effort to save her.

Bryant began his cross-examination by suggesting that today's technology wasn't available to the coroner in 1961, but Dr. Spitz said the basic procedures for conducting an autopsy were in place by the mid-1950s: Examine the whole body first, examine the clothing, photograph everything as evidence, don't stick your finger in the wounds. While today's methods and labs are more refined, he said, even the 1961 standards were adequate to preserve an objective record. Bryant asked how long it would have taken Mrs. Ferguson to die from the wound in her chest. Dr. Spitz said it would have taken at least twenty minutes.

When Bryant realized that Dr. Spitz had used numerous blowups of the autopsy photos that we had reshot and digitized, he stopped the proceedings and ordered his staff to obtain a huge screen so he could show the photos more graphically to the jury to shock and repulse them.

Bryant was making our case for us. The jurors were completely enthralled by what Dr. Spitz was telling them, and I saw at least two mouths drop open in stunned disbelief when they saw that the "decapitation" was a one-inch incision.

Dr. Spitz was on the stand most of the morning. We had just enough time before the lunch break to start making our argument about the role race and race relations in the Jim Crow South played in the way my case was handled.

George called Weldon Rougeau to the stand. A few months earlier he'd been on the front page of the Lake Charles newspaper as a home-grown boy who'd made good. He was now a settled pillar of the Washington, D.C., community, where he practiced in a huge law firm. He looked for all the world like a banker: tall, erect, distinguished, dignified. He testified that the Lake Charles he knew in the 1960s was rigidly segregated: "We were not allowed to talk about the schools

being all black, and the teachers were prohibited from discussing desegregation in the classroom." He played in a rock-and-roll band at
both white clubs and black, and told how at the white clubs he had to
come in through the back door and couldn't mingle with the patrons.
In high school, he worked at a car wash in south Lake Charles and testified that he never would have referred to white customers by their
first name. When George asked him why, he replied, "We were taught
to respect our elders, black or white, and to say 'Yes, ma'am,' and 'No,
sir.' " He noted that while he could shop in Woolworth's, he could not
have eaten at the lunch counter there because of his color. He had no
white friends and was called "boy" or sometimes "nigger" by whites.
Like so many African Americans of that era, he was deeply bitter as a
youngster about a world in which blacks were raised "not expecting to
be respected but were expected to respect whites." He testified that it
was this bitterness that drove him to become active in civil rights.

Weldon was an effective counter to the white FBI agent who
claimed that back then a black teenager might call white grown-ups by
their first names. I thought we were doing okay. Linda ate lunch with
me and said the defense team felt good about how the morning went.

After lunch, Ron put my mother on the stand, where she "offered a
narrative that harkened back to the Old South," according to one
reporter. Her soft voice barely audible, she told how three white
deputies came to our house the night of the crime and woke her by
pounding on both the front and back doors. Hustled into the night, she
was forced to leave her other three children, one only three months
old, asleep and unattended. When they reached the jail, she said,
deputies led her into the building through a mob of about two hundred
white men, some of whom were saying things like "Hang that nigger"
and "Shoot him." She said the deputies put her on a wooden bench in a
corridor where a large number of men both in uniform and in street
clothes were drinking, cursing, pushing each other, and saying they
were "gonna get that nigger." Although she asked to see me, she was
left sitting on the bench, afraid, with no explanation of why she was
there or where I was. It was nearly 3:00 a.m. before deputies took her
back to our house. She found out what happened the next day from a
neighbor. She testified that in the days that followed, whites in cars
would come and sit in front of our house next to the cemetery and
sometimes make loud and rude remarks. She told how a white man
came to our house and asked my terrified younger brother through the

screen door whether he didn't agree that something should be done about me. She testified about phone calls she received, one from a woman who said: "If he doesn't get electrocuted, he'll get the rope."

Ron introduced a photo published by the local press in 1961 showing her sitting on the bench at the jail the night of the crime. Nonetheless, Bryant succeeded in confusing the frail eighty-one-year-old by repeatedly asking her what she wore that night and if the clothing in the photo matched her description.

"You love your son, and you'd do anything to help him, wouldn't you?" he asked, more accusation than question. In trying to discredit her testimony about the mob, Bryant disrespected her, badgered her, and confused her. I had always protected my mother from public attention, so this hit me hard.

Ron called Jackie Lewis to the stand. She had been fourteen in 1961, when her mother worked five to midnight as a maid in the Pioneer Building across the street from the courthouse. Jackie said her father became upset after he heard the bulletins on TV about the robbery and Mrs. Ferguson's death, and about my identity. He got his gun and told Jackie and her sister to stay in the back of the house, away from the windows. After her father received a call from her mom, she said, he "had a look on his face I never saw before." He put the girls in his truck and went down Broad Street, the main thoroughfare leading downtown and the street that severed black from white in Lake Charles. A block away from the courthouse and jail, they saw a mob of at least a hundred white men, Jackie said, walking around and shouting.

Her father stopped the car some distance off, pointed to the mob, and told the children: "Look and never forget." Jackie said that the scene she saw that night was etched in her mind forever, and those who doubted her testimony "don't understand how fear lasts in a child's heart or how a group of angry white people looks to a black child."

Jackie testified that later that night and in the coming days, her father and some of his friends armed themselves and took turns standing watch over their neighborhood, which was flooded with cars of whites running through it. That night, she said, was a "major event" in her life and in Lake Charles.

Strong and eloquent on the stand, Jackie reinforced what my mother and I said about the mob. Confirming my testimony, she said that in 1961 blacks never caught a bus in south Lake Charles after dark and confirmed Weldon Rougeau's earlier testimony that blacks were never allowed to call whites by their first names but were required to show respect to white adults by addressing or referring to them as "Miss" or "Mr." She added that the reverse wasn't true, and it pained her to see even small white children call her mother "Hazel" rather than the respectful "Miss Hazel."

We now called Harvey Boyd to the stand. He was the deputy sheriff who supposedly found the knife used in the crime. In a pretrial hearing, both he and Bryant were taken aback when my lawyers grilled him about his recent remarks to the *Los Angeles Times* in which he said of 1961 Lake Charles: "It was a good little town back then. Ever'body did their job. The prosecutors, the law enforcement. You didn't have to worry about lynching because they lynched 'em for you."

Boyd on the stand denied making that statement. Like so many of the state's witnesses before him, he swore it was raining "cats and dogs" when he got to the jail between 8:30 and 9:00 on the night of the crime. He swore there was no mob outside the jail, either at the time of his arrival or until he left at about midnight. He said there was no mob inside the jail either, that at most there were half a dozen or so deputies who had come inside the jail to dry off and get coffee, like he did. He said deputies didn't search the crime scene until the next morning because it was raining so hard, and no one, to his knowledge, preserved the crime scene or guarded it overnight.

Julian now began to dismantle Boyd's testimony. First, he introduced into evidence a certified copy of the February 16, 1961, National Weather Service report for Lake Charles, broken down by the hour. It showed no precipitation until after 9:00 p.m. and no significant rain until after midnight.

Next, he entered into evidence a transcript from a change-of-venue hearing held in 1961 and read into the record the testimony of Sheriff "Ham" Reid, who said there was a crowd of about three hundred people outside the jail when he brought me in.

He then read into the record the 1961 testimony of Mike Hogan, chief of detectives for the Lake Charles city police, who said the inside of the jail, including the lobby and corridors, was jammed with people. Julian read the words of Gerald Campbell, a civilian who came to the jail that night when he heard about the arrest; he put the number of men inside the jail lobby between fifty and one hundred. Chief Deputy Sheriff Sam Mazilly estimated there were still sixty-five or seventy-five men outside the jail at midnight.

As Julian continued his direct examination, Boyd said that, to his knowledge, neither he nor any of the other deputies walked across the street to the pawnshop owned by his friend Robert Waldmeir to see what kind of knife or gun they should search for.

I wondered if anyone on the jury could possibly believe that.

We called to the witness box Louisiana writer Anne Butler, whose 1989 book written with her husband, former warden C. Murray Henderson, *Angola: A Century of Rage and Reform*, included a chapter on me and contained the verbatim transcript of a long interview I gave her. It offered a more detailed explanation of the anger, resentment, and frustration I felt as a teenager toward white people than the brief comment on Jodie Sinclair's tape. As soon as Julian asked her whether I'd ever discussed my feelings about race with her, Bryant called for a bench conference, after which Anne was asked to leave the stand without testifying further.

Court adjourned after what felt like a very long day. Once I was back at the jail, alone, questions haunted me. Did it raise red flags with the jury that so many of the character witnesses for me were prevented from saying much? I prayed that having a federal judge, a state appellate judge, two wardens, and a corrections officer vouching for my truthfulness would mean something to those all-important ten women and two men who held my fate in their hands. Did the jury, eight of whom were white, understand what we were trying to explain about the racial climate in 1961 and how it affected the prosecutor's handling of my case? Four of the jurors had not even been born in 1961. They had no frame of reference for the Jim Crow South. Would they get it? Could the jury ignore the irrefutable proof that there was indeed a mob at the jail that night, despite the parade of witnesses Bryant introduced who said otherwise? Could they ignore all of our proof that contradicted Bryant's case?

I woke up at 3:00 a.m. and felt my anxiety level rise with the sun. Logic told me that we had already shown the prosecutor's case to be full of exaggerations and outright lies. We should get a hung jury, at least, and if it hung evenly or in my favor, perhaps Bryant wouldn't want to press for another trial but would finally settle for a manslaughter conviction. But so much of what had transpired in this case had nothing to do with logic.

I've always been his ticket to national attention and to votes from the whites who put him in office, I thought to myself. *He'll never give up this case.*

Take a breath, Wilbert. Calm down.

*Yes. Okay. Whatever comes at the end of this, I will handle it as I've han-
dled every adversity for the past quarter century. I'll summon the strength
that allowed me to transcend the worst days in prison. I'll survive. If the jury
sends me back to prison for the rest of my life, I will find a way to carve out
some meaning for the remainder of my days because I just can't believe that
Divine Providence has saved me so many times without some purpose. No, I'll
be fine. But Linda? What would happen to her? She'd stick by me for the rest
of my life, or hers. That was her promise, years ago—that she would never
leave me while I was still in prison. That was when she thought it would take
six months or a year to get me out. Nearly twenty years have passed. I can't let
her throw away the rest of her life visiting me twice a month in prison, forever. Her life is as much on the line as my own.*

Our last day in court was Martin Luther King, Jr.'s birthday, January 15. We needed to further chip away at the credibility of the statement the FBI agent wrote out in longhand five days after the crime for
me to sign, which Bryant had always called my "handwritten confession." George called to the stand Ronald Butters, a cultural linguistics
expert from Duke University, who testified that the FBI statement did
not originate from the same source, meaning me, as the one I gave the
night of the crime. The sheriff's confession, he said, used language in a
way that would be expected from a young person without a high school
education, speaking colloquially under stress. Its structure was chaotic
in the way that spoken narratives usually are. The word choice in the
FBI document, by contrast, was more educated and methodical, almost
characteristic of an essay. He said that the most significant difference
between the two documents was the emotional connotation given to
the events in the FBI document. In conclusion, he said that my confession to the sheriff was likely my confession and the FBI statement was
the work of someone else.

Julian called our final witness, Paul Carroll, who had retired after
thirty-one years with the Chicago police and had authored or coau-
thored numerous articles in the field of criminal investigations, most
significantly for us, "Crime Scene Investigation: A Guide for Law
Enforcement," published by the U.S. Department of Justice. Bryant
tried to disqualify him on the grounds that he couldn't contribute
much because of the age of the case. Judge Ritchie certified him.

Carroll thoroughly discredited the sheriff's investigation of the
crime scene and his handling of the case in 1961. As for the two "con-

fessions," he said that generally the one closest in time to the crime itself will be the more accurate. He added that when law enforcement has one confession, taking a second is dangerous because it opens the door for discrepancy and doubt about which one is correct. He said the old 1961 filmed "interview" with Sheriff Reid and me wasn't a statement but a "press conference," a public relations piece, and I should not have been a part of it.

Carroll came down hard on local law enforcement for not protecting the crime scene. He said if bad weather was expected, the scene should have been covered with a tarp, or it should have been photographed. He concluded that because the crime scene was not preserved and an arrest had already been made, law enforcement had its mind on something other than collecting evidence.

He noted that they did not keep my clothing or examine it for gunpowder, mud, or blood, which would have been an invaluable source of evidence, nor did they examine or keep the clothing of any of the victims. They did not take photos of anyone's wounds. The victim's shoe should not have been moved from where it was found and placed next to the body by a deputy before the crime scene was measured, documented, and photographed. Evidence, he said, should be preserved until the completion of a defendant's sentence or until he dies.

On cross-examination, Bryant suggested that the technology and methods used in a big city like Chicago might have been more sophisticated than what was known in a small town like Lake Charles in 1961. Carroll said that the basic techniques used in investigating crimes, preserving evidence, and interrogating suspects were the same everywhere. In response to one of Bryant's questions, Carroll said that the FBI had jurisdiction only in the bank robbery, not the homicide, so there was no reason for them to question me about Julia Ferguson's death five days after the crime. He said he'd never seen a case in which the FBI took a statement in a bank robbery case after a confession had already been obtained by police. He said this, too, would be bad procedure.

And with that, we rested our case.

Bryant's closing argument held no surprises. The same old story, four decades old: I planned the robbery, took the hostages because they could identify me, lined them up, and killed them execution-style. He told the jury that this was a hate crime, that I killed Ferguson because I hated white people.

He said I picked a very convenient time to tell my story since so many witnesses were now dead. Sarcasm rolled off his tongue when he said, "I thought the most interesting part of his story was, 'I didn't murder her, I killed her,' " which he called "a distinction without a distinction."

Frustration leaching into his voice, Bryant told the jury, "Race permeated this trial." Though acknowledging that the social and racial injustices of the early 1960s were reprehensible, he scoffed at the idea that they played any role in the way this interracial crime had been handled. "The only decision you must make in this case," he argued, "is whether Wilbert Rideau murdered Julia Ferguson."

It was Julian's turn, and now he was fully in his element, like a veteran warhorse coming alive at the smell of gunpowder. Looking every bit the Southern gentleman he is, with his stately bearing and full silver mane, he commanded the rapt attention of every person in the room the moment he rose from the defense table.

Provocation sufficient to deprive a person of his cool reflection was the defining factor in manslaughter under Louisiana law, he told the jurors, and the provocation did not have to be instigated by the victim. He reminded them of the phone call that threw me into a panic and prompted me to take the bank employees out of the bank. He reminded them that if I had wanted to kill the employees, I could have killed them right there and simply walked away. He reminded them that I told Jay Hickman to take his coat because it would be cold walking back to town. He reminded them that I was lost and confused— according to the victims' own testimony—while meandering through white Lake Charles trying to figure out where to drop off the bank employees, and that I myself was terrified, riding around with a car full of whites in a place where I could never explain being after dark in 1961. He reminded them that I panicked when Dora McCain bolted from the car and began running, and that it was in this panic—this loss of cool reflection—that I fired at the employees and killed Ferguson.

He explained that we were not using the racial climate of the Jim Crow South to mitigate in any way the crime I committed. Nothing, he said, justified the crime. Race, however, did affect the way both law enforcement and the district attorney handled the case, including holding me in isolation with no access to an attorney and coercing statements from me. The times being what they were, Julian said, the prosecutor could count on having an all-white, all-male jury hear the case against a black teen accused of murdering a white woman. The crime was distorted, witnesses lied, and evidence was inflated to inflame that jury.

"They were never satisfied. They wanted to ratchet this up, ratchet this up," Julian said as he swept an open arm toward me. "They were making it as bad for this man as they could."

Julian approached the jury and looked each person in the face. "This case," he said, "is about a one-inch cut, a tracheotomy," not a decapitation. "For forty-four years," he said, people had been led to believe "that Wilbert Rideau slashed Mrs. Ferguson's throat from ear to ear." He reminded them that they had seen the autopsy photos themselves.

He turned to look at Rick Bryant and reminded the jury that a prosecutor's job is to get to the truth, not to convict. "Why did he bring in the ambulance driver to convince us of what really didn't happen?" Why had the prosecutor insinuated that the mob Jackie Lewis saw outside the jail wasn't real but merely a story that cropped up in the black community? Why indeed, when the truth, in the sheriff's own testimony, was right there in the old record?

Why, he asked the jury, had all of the state's witnesses testified for four decades that it rained, and rained, and rained "cats and dogs" the night of the crime, when the National Weather Service showed otherwise? Because the rain was needed to explain why evidence was destroyed and the crime scene was not preserved, he said.

Again referring to the Jim Crow South, Julian said, "You have to understand that time, and then it comes together. You think they would hesitate to exaggerate the facts of the case to get the result they wanted?"

And that nameplate in the photo, the one Bryant said proved I knew the ladies in the bank by their names? Julian pulled a jeweler's round magnifying glass from his pocket. "Our public defender, Ron Ware, blew this photo up last night on his computer," Julian said. Then he bent dramatically over the table in front of the jury box to eyeball the photo. "You want to know what this sign really says?" He turned to the twelve men and women and lowered his voice almost to a whisper. "It says, 'Pay Electric Bills Here.' "

He faced the jury squarely to admit that my killing Ferguson was "a terrible act, a criminal act, one for which he deserves great punishment, but not one for which he deserves to be locked up for the rest of his life." Waving his arm toward me, he said, "He did a terrible thing, but it wasn't murder."

Julian paused and in a quiet voice made his final plea: "It's time to put this case to rest. Not just for Wilbert Rideau but for the whole community. It's been going on too long. He's been punished. Bring back a verdict of manslaughter."

Bryant's rebuttal was short, his arrogance gone. He told the jury that even if they believed my version of events rather than his, it was still murder.

After the jury left to begin its deliberations at about 5:15 p.m., Bryant crossed the aisle and shook hands with both George and Julian, telling each he was a helluva good lawyer. It was the first civil word he had spoken to either of them, and it would be the last.

In the movies, the defendant and his lawyers usually sweat out the jury's deliberations in a comfortable attorney's room around a sumptuous, highly polished conference table with a big clock ticking off the tense minutes until a verdict is in.

In my case, defense team members took turns rotating into the small cinder-block holding cell in the basement of the courthouse where I was put to wait. Two wooden benches affixed to the walls and standing room accommodated only three people besides Linda and me. Two deputies sat watch in the corridor outside. We laughed some. Various of us offered a measured dose of optimism about the trial's outcome—at least a hung jury. We all felt relieved that it was over and that, come what may, we had given it our best shot.

One of the young lawyers had brought in food for our dinner, and I had just taken my first bite when a deputy came to tell us to get back into the courtroom. My chest tightened. *Something's wrong. They haven't been out long enough.* They had been deliberating only about an hour and a half, not enough time to be deadlocked in a hung jury.

We stood behind the defense table as the jurors filed in past us. None of them looked at me. *That's a bad sign. They never look at the defendant when they vote to convict.* As we sat down, I asked God to give me the strength to handle what I thought surely must be the end of all hope.

Judge Ritchie announced that the jury had him sent a note. They wanted to see the old "interview" in which Sheriff Reid asked me leading questions for the TV cameras the day after the crime. They asked for the magnifying glasses. (We had bought twelve magnifying glasses for them to examine photos with.) And they wanted a copy of the murder and manslaughter statutes to take into the jury room. The judge said they couldn't have in the deliberation room any of the things they asked for, but he read the statutes to them again. They filed out, stony-faced, looking neither at me nor at Bryant.

Back in the holding cell we speculated as to what their requests might mean. The magnifying glasses were definitely a good sign for us because the jurors wanted to see for themselves that Bryant had lied. The 1961 "interview" wasn't bad because it showed that I told the same story forty-four years before as I did on the stand. Inquiring about the statutes indicated that the jurors were at least considering manslaughter. Still, we were all less jovial now. As the hours passed, speech gave way to silence. At about 9:45, we were again called to the courtroom. The jury filed in once more, still stony-faced, looking straight ahead. Judge Ritchie announced that the jury wanted to have the murder and manslaughter statutes read to them again. Afterward, only Linda came back into the holding cell with me.

I asked her what she thought.

She leaned forward, reaching across the small space that separated us, and placed her hand over mine. "The way I see it," she said, "if they believed Rick Bryant's version of the crime, manslaughter wouldn't even be a possibility. Think about it. This is the second time they've asked for clarification between murder and manslaughter. To me, that means they've rejected the DA and his witnesses." She leaned back against the wall. "The good thing is, they believe you. The question now is whether they decide the crime was manslaughter or murder."

I leaned toward her and took hold of her hand, even though I knew it would look wrong if a deputy entered the cell. "There's just one thing I want to say, and I hope they don't have this fucking place bugged. But whatever happens, Junior, I just want you to know that I'll be okay. I mean, I have survived the worst they could throw at me for four decades, and I will survive whatever else they have in store for me." I looked her straight in the eye. "I need you to promise me right now that you will put your own best interest first if things don't go our way."

She gently extracted her hand from mine and smiled. "There'll be plenty of time to make these decisions if they are necessary. For now, let's keep a good thought."

It seemed as though only moments had passed, but it had been more than twenty minutes when George stepped into the cell and said, "The jury has reached a verdict."

Linda took my upper arm and guided me out the door. Smiling, she whispered, "It's gonna be okay. Let's go."

We took our places in the courtroom. Despite the late hour—10:10—it was packed with spectators, blacks on one side, whites on the other. We waited for the jury to make its entrance. When we had waited ten minutes, I turned to Julian for an explanation. He had none. It seemed to be getting very warm in the normally cold courtroom. I began sweating. My palms were wet. I reached for the bottle of water in front of me. Now it was 10:30, and the jury still had not returned. The tension in the room was electric, and the wait, for me, nearly unbearable.

The judge entered the courtroom and told everyone that, whatever the verdict was, no outbursts of any kind would be tolerated and that deputies would remove anyone who violated his order of silence. At 10:37 we rose as the jurors filed past us, looking neither to the right nor to the left. They all took their seats and stared straight at the judge—except for one woman who glanced at me fleetingly, with just the hint of a smile playing at the corner of her mouth.

My heart was pounding in my ears as George, Julian, and Ron rose with me to hear the jury's verdict. The bailiff took the written ballot from the foreman and gave it to the judge, who looked at it and handed it to the chief deputy clerk, who, with her voice breaking, announced that the jury had reached a unanimous decision. They had found me guilty. Of manslaughter.

My knees went weak and I was afraid I would fall. I turned to the jury and bowed my head in thanks and gratitude, but it was as if I were in a dream. The whole scene seemed unreal, as if it were happening to someone else. Julian, smiling, took my arm and gave it a victory squeeze. George was smiling. The jury filed out, and we took our seats—just in time, as I was light-headed, blood pounding in my ears.

The judge gave me the maximum sentence for manslaughter: twenty-one years. Because I had served more than double that, I was freed on the spot. Court was dismissed. Two deputies escorted me out the back door of the courtroom and put handcuffs on me for the ride back to the jail, where I'd be processed out.

"Hey," I said, balking at the cuffs. "Didn't you hear the verdict?"

"Just go with it, Wilbert," said Ron Ware. "I'm right behind you."

As Martin Luther King, Jr., day came to a close, I walked out of the Calcasieu Parish Correctional Center at midnight a free man. A crowd of mostly black citizens had gathered to celebrate my release and cheered wildly when they saw me. Surrounded by my legal team, I stopped briefly for the television cameras and print reporters.

"First of all I'd like to thank the jury from Monroe who gave me my freedom," I said, "and I'd also like to express my heartfelt apologies to the victims in this affair—their families, their relatives, and all of the lives in this community that my actions caused some suffering or misery or adversity. I know words are inadequate, but . . ." I choked up. Escorted through the crowd by deputies, my whole legal team moved in unison around me as we walked to two cars waiting in the parking lot, to the hooting and hollering of well-wishers. Moments later we were in a room at the Holiday Inn with my family. Someone brought in a couple of bottles of champagne so we could toast our victory. The unfamiliar brew was tart and sour on my tongue, not at all like the sweet taste of freedom.

After a couple of hours, I was alone with Linda. This too seemed unreal. Too drained even to shower, I lay down on the bed and pulled the covers over me.

"You're going to sleep fully dressed?"

I nodded. How could I explain that I was afraid to take off my lucky trial clothes, afraid that if I did I might wake up to find the verdict was just a dream? As it was, the cloud-soft mattress and cozy, warm comforter transported me far away from the steel bunk and thin waffle blanket that had been cold reality for most of my life. With Linda holding my hand, I exhaled and just let go.

14

Heaven

2005

I wake up in heaven every day.

I watch the sun rise on the face of the woman I have loved for twenty years, as she lies sleeping at my side. Curled into the hollow of Linda's bosom is one of our cats, Rodeo Joe, and on the pillow at my head is his brother Willie B, formerly the patriarch around here, who has yielded to me his job of watching over the household. When I rise, Willie B follows me to the back door to be let out and waits patiently with Ladybug, our third cat, for food to be put in their bowl. They now rely on me for their morning kibble, and I take it as a sign that I have become part of the clan. For reasons I can't quite articulate, their acceptance thrills me. It amazes me that cats can give me such pleasure and teach me so much about unconditional love and connections.

I rise early because I don't want to miss a thing. I know that in my mid-sixties, I'm on a short calendar.

Having so long dwelled in a hellish place, I recognize paradise when I see it. No, the streets are not paved with gold. They're common asphalt over which very little traffic flows. It's peaceful here. Chirping birds of all varieties nest in the old live oaks and make this place feel more like a park than a subdivision. I come from a world denuded of trees because they can be used to hide behind and obstruct the view of guards in the watchtowers on the lookout for signs of trouble. I love this green world—the fragrant, freshly mown grass, the flowering bushes that frame the property, the leafy boughs that canopy the house, the yard, the streets that carry normal people to and fro.

I brew coffee and listen to the cardinals sing and the woodpeckers tap as they rout out insects in the folds of the bark. I'm mesmerized by the aerial artistry of the hummingbirds as they hover at the feeder outside the picture window overlooking the backyard, then zoom off like cartoon UFOs. *Who would believe this?* I ask myself, for the umpteenth time. I stare in disbelief at my legs, bare from the knees down, leading to my sandaled feet, and feel the excitement of liberty. In prison I had to remain fully covered at all times, except when wearing flip-flops in the shower and shorts in the gym. I wiggle my unshod toes just for the fun of it, like a child playing with a new toy, and smile. *Who would believe that I am really here?*

I've been transported from a drab and colorless realm: a world almost totally devoid of love or beauty; a world in which our basic impulse to trust—that virtue by which we know ourselves and connect to others—makes treachery nearly inevitable; a world where decades-long friendships are betrayed overnight for an imagined chance at freedom or for the faintest hope of bettering one's conditions of confinement; a world where chaos and depravity are the norm and normalcy is the rarest feature of daily life; a world where softness has all but vanished in the hardscrabble struggle to survive; a world where brightness atrophies year by year as friends and family either die or just get on with their own lives, leaving you increasingly alone. To suffer deprivation on such a scale is a terrible punishment; to see its effects reflected in the lifeless or ferocious eyes of so many around you is worse, terrifyingly worse. I understand that prison is where society sends offenders to be punished for their crimes, but does any civilization really intend to create infernos that stamp out the humanity of those it sends there? I will never believe that about the ordinary men and women in whose name this is done.

Some people never recover from the deadening or coarsening effect of long-term deprivation. I was one of the lucky ones who had support and lifelines to the outside and an abiding belief that some unforeseen event or circumstance would eventually free me, and for me deprivation had an upside. Now that I'm free, I take extraordinary pleasure in life in all its diversity of forms, colors, and textures in a way I suspect few ordinary Americans can. Of course, I don't have the basic problems of sheer survival that confront many other long-termers upon their release: I have a roof over my head in a safe neighborhood, food to eat, and a partner with whom to build a new life. This is what I have longed for as long as I can remember. To me, this is heaven.

Life is so good I even love the Department of Motor Vehicles. One day I went there because I needed a photo ID. Even though I don't know how to drive, I still have to go to the DMV to get an official, state-issued identification card. As I enter the building, a white officer walks by, shakes my hand, and pats me on the back in congratulation. The place is packed and I take a number, like in the bakery I recall from childhood, and wait to be served. Several more people recognize me and wish me well. When my number is called, a pleasant, white, middle-aged woman instructs me to follow her to her workstation, where she asks what she can do for me.

"I need a photo ID," I tell her.

"Birth certificate?" she requests, all business.

I explain that I don't have one, that I've just gotten out of prison.

"Discharge papers?"

"No. I wasn't released through the normal process."

"How do you plan to get an ID without identification?" she asks.

I nervously offer her the only evidence of my identity I have, placing on her desk the New Orleans *Times-Picayune* front-page story on my release and pointing to the photo: "See? That's me. I'm even wearing the same clothes as in the picture." I hand over the front page of the Lake Charles *American Press*, which also has a photo of me, along with the Baton Rouge *Advocate*, and make my plea: "I was hoping you'd accept these as identification."

Suddenly her eyes light up and she smiles mischievously. "Oh, we know who you are. We heard you were in Baton Rouge and wondered when you were gonna show up." Stepping around her station to face the other women workers, she holds the newspapers up: "Get a load of this! These are his identification documents! Would you believe it?"

She has to get approval from her supervisor to accept them and is soon walking me through the other departments. Another white woman tells me to stand against a wall so she can take my picture. Neither of the women is happy with the result.

"You have to smile," says the photographer. "You have a beautiful smile." I flash my teeth at the camera. Both women approve the result. I ask the cost and reach for my wallet.

"Don't worry about this," one of the women says. Her eyes take in the roomful of women workers. She adds, "We'll take care of it. Keep your money. You'll need it. And good luck!"

Back home, Linda returns to find me in my study.

"I need to get a padlock to use at the Y," she informs me, dropping onto the sofa under the window.

"Look, I have the lock I used on my footlocker at the Calcasieu jail. You can have that if you want," I say, pleased to be able to offer something material to the household. I fish it out of the net sack holding the meager belongings I brought from the jail and explain to her how to use it. I tell her the combination.

She stares at me intently. "Do you realize that the numbers that open that lock—1, 15, 5—are the same as the date the jury freed you, January 15, 2005?"

I stare back at her. The one thing someone in jail always wonders is when he or she will get out. For nearly four years, while I was awaiting trial in Calcasieu Parish, I had the answer in the palm of my hand.

In John Blume's class at Cornell Law School, I look out into a sea of bright, young faces. I've come to the university to give the keynote address at a habeas corpus symposium, and the trip to his classroom is a bonus. I speak to the students about change of venue, and afterward, during the question-and-answer session, one of the students asks me what it's like to be free after so many years in prison. It's a question I get a lot.

"I understand why some immigrants fall to their knees and kiss the ground when they arrive in America," I begin. "I understand that gesture in a way you never will, never can." I pause, hoping that silence can add weight to my words. "You've lived your entire life in freedom. Like the air you breathe, it's always been there."

I can't find the words to adequately convey what I feel. How can I relate the simple joy of watching squirrels play a game of chase up and down the oak trees, the grandeur of a rose-colored camellia tree in full bloom, or the pleasure of looking in my closet and seeing a rainbow of shirts, jackets, trousers, jeans, and sweaters?

"Like refugees from other totalitarian societies," I tell the law students, "I understand that liberty means being able to speak freely, associate with whom you want, worship how and if you want, gather together without permission, live where you want, and move freely in the world without carrying identification on pain of being punished."

What I don't tell them is that, like other refugees, I bring with me to this free society the vestiges of life under the old regime: constant watchfulness, studying the faces around me, routine examination of the motives of newcomers in my life, and a lingering sense that I should have a witness with me at all times. I can't step out of my ingrained wariness as easily as I shed my prison denims. So despite my newfound liberty, I socialize very little and keep my business to myself. These mind-sets will fade, I hope, but it may take more time than I have.

Besides being a refugee, I am also a tourist here in this English-speaking country that is so different from the America I left behind in 1961. I'm not talking about just e-mail, iPods, cell phones, and the rest of the technology that has made people at once both more accessible and more isolated. Not even two decades of speaking trips outside the prison has prepared me for what I run into every day.

A visit to Walmart—there was nothing like this in 1961 Lake Charles—tells me a lot about my new world and how I might cope with it. I'm in search of a razor. When I finally find the right area, I am confronted with a mind-wrenching display that runs the entire length of one side aisle devoted to every kind of shaving apparatus imaginable. When I entered prison, there was just the metal razor that you screwed open and shut to change the blade. Bic then pioneered the plastic disposable. Here, I count at least twenty-five kinds of disposable razors cross-pollinating in bins below the racks of more upscale and durable devices, some with double, triple, or even quadruple blades or rotating heads to ensure a close, really close, shave. I have no way of knowing which of these instruments will do the job for me. And some of them cost as much as $100. *In Walmart!* The plethora of choices, the decisions that constantly must be made, are at first difficult for me. In the end, I leave with a pack of the same cheap Bics they sold in prison.

In the checkout lane I'm amazed to notice that at least three-quarters of the cashiers are black. I'm still very conscious of race because the outside world I left in 1961 was sharply divided and defined by race, as was the justice system during my long sojourn. In 1961 Lake Charles, I never saw a Negro cashier in any store outside the black neighborhood. Now I see African Americans working with money in stores, restaurants, banks, many of them in managerial positions supervising white employees. I'd heard and read about such things, but to actually see it amazes me.

This is definitely a more advanced society than the openly racist one I left behind, but it's a mystery to me. On a trip to the mall, I again see excess everywhere. I step into a store devoted entirely to gym shoes—excuse me, "sports shoes"—calibrated to accommodate the foot's every nuanced need while running, walking, strolling, jumping, biking, and cross-training. I gaze upon the floor-to-ceiling displays as if I'm taking in a cultural artifact like the Eiffel Tower. The old black-and-white high-tops I grew up with are here, too—I think as a fashion statement. They remind me that I'm a dinosaur who's been dropped into twenty-first-century America and, right now, the idyllic environs of Cornell Law School.

Ithaca, New York, a small but sophisticated city built around Cornell University, is breathtaking compared with Angola's eighteen thousand acres of flatlands. I join other faculty and some of the law students for dinner at a fancy French restaurant where I'm treated like a visiting dignitary. The place is fairly dark, which makes me uncomfortable for a number of reasons, not the least of which is that after four decades of eating prison food, I tend toward bright light so I can scrutinize my meal for foreign matter, like hairs or insect parts. This is a habit I can't shake even at home, where I know the kitchen is clean and the food properly prepared. I sit with my back to the wall—another holdover from prison. The menu comes with subtitles, but even when someone reads it to me in English, it's like hearing Greek. A lifetime of culinary deprivation has left me unprepared to cope with a place that doesn't have simple green salads, ordinary vegetables, common dishes. I'm too embarrassed to ask what a pomegranate reduction is. I try to play it safe by ordering a well-done steak with French fries. The waiter's smile is a little too broad when I request ketchup—and he regrets the restaurant has no hot sauce. I'm definitely outside my comfort zone, but the faculty and students, warm and genuine, make me feel as much at home as I can be in this strange land.

Deprivation on all fronts for so long now makes me want to acquire things. Linda helps me to shop wisely. Interwoven with our trips to large retail stores are visits to the St. Vincent de Paul Thrift Store. Today's resale stores—filled with Christian Dior, Perry Ellis, and Godchaux castoffs—bear no resemblance to the secondhand stores I recall from my childhood, where the merchandise was worn, in need of mending, or stained. One day shortly after my release, I bought several sport coats and two shirts for $11. The cashier recognized me, pulled $11 out of her own purse, and told me to have a great day.

This kind of compassionate generosity takes me by surprise every time. Conditioned by the stories I'd heard from ex-cons who returned to Angola, either as part of a ministry or as recidivists, about the difficulties they faced returning to society and how they had to try to hide their prison past or face scorn and abuse, I expected the same. In fact, because of my high profile, I expected worse. But I am greeted cordially by both blacks and whites. In one store, a white saleslady has finished her shift and is leaving for the day when she comes over to shake my hand. "There are some good buys on sweaters on the table around the corner," she says, palming me a $10 bill. Linda points out that $10 is a lot of money for a clerk who probably makes little more than minimum wage. When I'm waiting to pay for my sweater, a black man in line gives me $20 and says, "Man, have lunch on me."

I relied on the compassion of strangers for decades as I sought my freedom, but on a day-to-day basis, I've been self-sufficient for a long time. Moreover, in Angola, I had real power. Whatever was available, if it wasn't illegal, was mine if I wanted it. Out here, I have no power at all. I don't control anything, and I have no resources. I lack basic and essential skills such as math and driving. Finding myself dependent on others in so many ways is a huge psychological shift for me. It makes me even more grateful for the smallest kindnesses that come my way.

But life is more than compassionate encounters. Having been out about a month and a half, I've called deputy warden Darrel Vannoy to see about picking up my possessions from Angola. He phones back, informing me that Burl Cain wants to use the occasion to gather inmate leaders from around the prison for me to talk to, to give them hope. He wants me to come on a Monday or Tuesday, when the visiting room is closed. I ask Vannoy if it would be okay to separate the two events so I can pick up my stuff now and return another time to talk to the fellows. He says that's fine, and I ask if I can visit the *Angolite* offices and see my friends Lafayette Ballard, Calvin Duncan, and Sydney Deloch. He agrees.

We arrive at the prison by noon. My escort seems uncomfortable, though trying to hide it. It's probably because a white woman is with me, and he assumes she's either my wife or girlfriend. I introduce her as Dr. LaBranche, part of my defense team, and he seems a little more at ease.

Linda has never been into the bowels of Angola, so I'm describing what she's seeing. As we enter the A-Building, I see the gates, the security cage, the visitors in the visiting room to the left, the inmates on the other side of the gate, and all of the prison atmosphere I had suppressed comes rushing back. I force myself to ignore it because inmates are waving at me, thrusting their hands out to me. I represent their dream, their most passionate ambition in life—to be free. *I can't fold here.* We pass the cellblocks where men are being searched as they line up to go to the fields; they wave and yell hello. At the Main Prison Office complex, black inmates and officers alike come to shake my hand and congratulate me.

We visit with friends at the *Angolite* offices. I go into Douglas "Swede" Dennis's office for an interview. Swede, who never committed a crime against free society, was thrown into a violent jail in 1957 on a charge of vagrancy and killed another inmate in a fight. For that, he was sent to Angola during its bloodiest days and killed a tough-ass who was gunning for him, an act one warden called a "public service." I promise him that as soon as I get my life together, I will try to help him get out.

I've reached an agreement with the authorities that a classification officer will have permission to bring my forty banker's boxes of files out of the prison for me. Guards bring my two metal footlockers from storage and snap them open with a bolt cutter. I take one pair of shoes and leave the remaining food and clothing for whoever wants them. We leave for the visiting room, where we meet Sydney, whose legal advice led to my habeas petition for a new trial. We tell him we will do whatever we can to help him win his own release. Lafayette comes into the visiting room next, and I tell him also that I will do what I can to help him win release; he has always claimed innocence, and the police or prosecutors years ago destroyed the DNA evidence that he says will prove it. (I would eventually find out that DNA evidence often goes missing.) We're off then to Camp F to see Calvin. As we drive into the heart of the prison's eighteen thousand acres, I am again amazed at the beauty of the countryside, which belies the misery contained here. I thank Calvin for his legal aid, which helped free me, and promise him help in return, too.

It's 3:30 when we get back to the car. As we speed down the highway, leaving the prison increasingly behind, I feel relief, the tension falling away. Linda asks what it was like, going back.

"I am so glad to be out of that place—through with its madness," I say.

The biggest pain in prison, I explain, is the way you are assaulted psychologically and emotionally, the way in which you are robbed of any dignity as a human being and told in countless ways that you don't matter. Then there is the endless aggravation—the craziness, the madhouse atmosphere—that stems from stupidity ruling your world. People in supervisory positions in prison are often not selected on the basis of skill, experience, or ability, but because of politics or cronyism, which means that fools are often placed in positions of power. Stupid people tend to make stupid decisions and do stupid things, and it is this aspect of prison, compounded by the ignorance, childishness, self-destructiveness, irresponsibility, self-centeredness, and criminality of many prisoners, that makes daily prison life maddening. And stupidity takes no holiday; it is woven into the fabric of daily life. There is also the monotony, and the unparalleled boredom it breeds. Finally, there's the emotional deprivation—never being genuinely bonded with anyone or anything.

When we return to Baton Rouge, I am relieved to be home. I finally understand the concept of home. I have a family of one human mate and three felines to whom I belong and who belong to me. I have no words to describe how wonderful this is. I eat and stare out at a couple of cardinals strutting their stuff while Willie B dozes at the bottom of the tree. I delight in this—trees, pets, the simplest of things—and wonder idly how possessing wealth could make this any better. Not that I expect wealth.

John Whitley and Dwayne McFatter arrive to pick me up for a lunch date. I haven't seen the former warden and assistant warden since they testified at my trial. We go to a nice seafood restaurant beside a lake, where I am the only black. I realize that this is most often the case when I go out with friends. I find it ironic that I socialize almost entirely in a white world. But that's because almost all the people who tried to get me out of prison were white. Many of them stuck by me for decades, rallying support for my clemency appeals, talking to governors, visiting me, doing whatever they could. Other than black officials within the penal system who supported my work and my clemency efforts—and Loyola University's Ted Quant—I had almost no support from African Americans, outside the black Lake Charles community toward the end of my long struggle. I wasn't alone in that. Most of the people involved in prison reform or battling against the death penalty, most of the lawyers and activists fighting either for individual prisoners or for fairness and equity in the pardon and parole processes in

Louisiana, were white. With some exceptions, the blacks who came to the prison were ministers or gospel singers who played to a captive audience willing to have their souls saved if it meant a few hours' relief from the tedium of prison life, followed by a good meal.

Whitley and McFatter and I reminisce. They ask me how my new life is going. I tell them that, through my lawyers, I've heard from people from all over the world who wish me well, but that despite all my journalism awards and honors, I have yet to be offered a job. They express surprise at this. Like many others, my own family included, they think that my "celebrity" can automatically be translated into big bucks.

Personally, I'm not surprised at the lack of job offers. It would be a rare employer, TV station, or newspaper publisher who would be willing to hire a high-profile ex-con who has vocal detractors, some of whom may be their advertisers. I always knew I'd have to be self-employed. Most ex-cons try to hide their past for this very reason. But that's not an option for me.

I wonder how Michael Anthony Williams will fare. He's the lead story on the news tonight, exonerated by Barry Scheck's Innocence Project after spending twenty-four years in Angola for a rape that DNA has conclusively determined he did not commit. He's the ninth Louisiana prisoner freed from a wrongful conviction in the past two years. His parents died while he was in prison, and none of his six siblings has visited him in fifteen years. He went in at sixteen and, he is saying at his press conference, was sexually abused while guards turned their backs. He is justifiably proud of having survived his long struggle for vindication and freedom. He expresses the hope that he might be able to become an interior decorator. He smiles and shows the check for $10 that he received from the state upon his release to restart his life. Looking straight into the camera, determination filling his voice, Williams says, "But I'm gonna get a job."

Williams is optimistic about his future, like most men getting out of prison. They get out intending to stay out. Society, however, does not necessarily see Williams's imprisonment and ultimate vindication the same way he does. His triumph over tremendous odds is admirable, heroic even, but to many he will always be an ex-con above all else. His innocence doesn't necessarily remove the stigma of having been in prison, of being "different" because of that cultural experience, in a way that diminishes his attractiveness to potential employers.

I've been ironing and now hand Linda her jeans, freshly pressed and creased. She rolls her eyes and smiles, as if I've done something magnificent and foolish. I do all the ironing around here, along with the laundry, the dishes, the sweeping, and fixing the bed in the morning. I've taken to domesticity. I love taking care of our things, our house, our yard. I can't describe how happy I am just raking leaves or hauling garden soil.

It's been two months since my release, and I've been floating along carefree on the goodwill and generosity of my friends and loved ones. I've spent my days blithely fascinated by Google and our goose-down comforter, bowl-you-over fuchsia azaleas, and quick-as-a-wink e-mails.

And now Judge Ritchie reenters my life. He charges me with court costs of nearly $127,000. He decrees that despite his having declared me indigent, I am to pay for the cost of my fourth trial, because it was I who requested it. The fact that I did so because I was serving an unconstitutional sentence flowing from an unconstitutional trial is apparently immaterial, as is the fact that I served forty-four years in prison on a sentence that was dischargeable in ten and a half. Nobody is talking about reimbursing *me*. In fact, in the wake of the judge's order, someone writes to the Lake Charles newspaper and suggests that I should reimburse the state for the cost of my room and board all those extra years that they housed and fed me. The fact that no other criminal defendant in Louisiana history has ever been assessed the cost of his trial is not lost on Judge Ritchie. He simply asserts that he is not bound by what other judges have or have not done. He claims to have the power to make me pay for the salaries of the sheriff's deputies who stood guard in the courtroom; the cost of transporting, housing, and feeding the jury that freed me; and the cost of putting him and his staff up at a nice Monroe hotel during jury selection and feeding them at the city's best restaurants.

We note in our appeal of Judge Ritchie's order that the only thing we've been able to turn up comparable in all of American jurisprudence was what happened in the immediate aftermath of Emancipation, when conscripted prisoners filled the need for lost slave labor in the South. A freed slave would be arrested for some minor offense like lingering and fined, say, $2; but then he would also be slapped with "court costs" beyond the ability of any freedman to pay, making him slave labor under another name.

Judge Ritchie is incensed at the implied comparison. He also expresses concern that I'm going to write a book, for big money. I have submitted a proposal to write my autobiography, hoping that the lessons I've learned over forty years in prison can be helpful in making people understand what it is really like. Maybe the judge doesn't want me writing about Calcasieu Parish, about him, about Angola. A number of corrections officials, I was told, expressed surprise that I didn't bash Louisiana or Angola during my appearance on *Nightline* after my release. Frankly, it amazed me that people thought I would be mean or spiteful, considering that I built my journalistic reputation on telling the truth, good or bad.

If Ritchie's order is upheld, I wonder how I am going to contribute anything to the maintenance of our household. Linda has funded my freedom effort with her retirement savings and with the sacrificed years of employment that would have given her a pension. Now we are both without safety nets, and I realize that I don't even have Social Security and Medicare to fall back on since all my working years were spent in Angola, and that doesn't qualify you for those benefits.

I'm severely depressed for the first time as a free man.

"What are we going to do?" I ask Linda.

"What we've always done, Wilbert. Fight them. And in the meantime, take as much joy from life as we can, every day."

I try to do this, but in the wee hours and at other moments I am overtaken by anxiety over our future. This goes on for months until one day an old friend, Meredith Eicher, invites me to a street concert downtown. Meredith's mother, Elayn Hunt, was the first female director of corrections in Louisiana, in the 1970s. At the concert, she introduces me to Gary McKenzie, an attorney who specializes in bankruptcy law. Gary offers to file for bankruptcy for me to discharge Judge Ritchie's $127,000 in court costs. We agree to it. Six months later I'm declared bankrupt and free of debt. I'm now apparently worth about $4,500, which I received as a settlement from *Time* magazine for the years they gave reprint permission for an essay I wrote for them. I contribute the money to household expenses and sleep better at night.

I've been invited to New York to address the board of directors of the NAACP Legal Defense Fund, without whose help and resources I'd still be languishing in Angola. It is an important night, and Linda and I both work diligently on the speech I will give not only to thank them for what LDF did for me but also to try also to impress upon them that there is a great need for more legal assistance for people in prison, some innocent and others worthy of release. Thirty-six hours before we head to the airport, George Kendall calls with the news that Johnnie Cochran has just died of a brain tumor in Los Angeles. When I speak of Johnnie to his fellow board members and show them the EXPECT A MIRACLE pin he gave me, I am surprised that my voice disappears into a croak, and I cannot swallow back the tears that have come out of nowhere. I am embarrassed because I have trained myself for decades not to show emotion. A display like this would be regarded as weakness in prison, an invitation to trouble. Here, however, it seems cathartic for everyone, and no one appears to hold it against me. I hear myself say, "I can't do this," and a soft voice from the audience says, "Yes, you can—you can do it." I stop for a moment to collect myself, then finish the speech.

Afterward, we meet up with my former partner in documentary filmmaking, Liz Garbus, who introduces me to her husband, Dan. It's wonderful to see an old friend in a new setting, and like so many other longtime friends, Liz marvels that I am actually out of prison as I promised long ago I would be one day. It's a thrill to be with friends who'd given up hope that I'd ever obtain my freedom. It restores their faith in miracles.

After dinner, out on the street, Dan shows me how to tie the tie I've been carrying around in my pocket all evening. At the hotel, I practice knotting and unknotting it for half an hour so I'll remember how to do it.

The next morning when the wake-up call comes, I thank the operator. In turn, she says she hopes I'll have a great day. "Well, thank you very much," I say, impressed with the friendliness of these Big Apple folks.

"Who was that?" Linda asks. When I tell her, she breaks out in laughter.

"Mind telling me what's so funny?"

"*Sweetie!*" she says. "That's an automated system. You were conversing with a recorded message!"

"Well, hell, I didn't know," I say, laughing along with her.

I'm having the time of my life. I love New York—the grit and dazzle of Times Square, the grandeur of Grand Central Station, the solace of St. Paul's Chapel across from Ground Zero, where the Twin Towers fell as I sat in jail watching, a world away. It's a city to which Linda and I will return half a dozen times in my first year out, for various functions. At one, Barry Scheck presents me with the National Association of Criminal Defense Lawyers' Champion of Justice Award for my quarter century of journalism about prison, and George Kendall is given a similar award in recognition of his heroic work. Julian has received comparable honors in Louisiana.

I notice idly that I am spending more time in churches, temples, and synagogues than I ever would have dreamed. Prison soured me on organized religion. As I've said, I saw too many fake conversions by prisoners looking to claim rehabilitation without doing the hard work of changing their behavior. I saw too many priests, chaplains, and ministers who came to prison to save souls but didn't care about the rest of the person. I could see in too many of their faces that they came to Angola primarily because coming there made them feel good about themselves, and a little self-righteous.

Ironically, some of my closest and longest-standing friends have been nuns, priests, and ministers who live what they preach. I find myself at Wesley Methodist Church in Baton Rouge, where I've been invited to say a few words to an inner-city Boy Scout troop sponsored by the church. This is the ten-year anniversary of my first talk to them, when I learned that they were planning a summer outing to the famous scout camp at Philmont, New Mexico. Not all the boys had enough money to attend. I had $213 in my prison account, so I sent it to their scoutmaster. As a thank-you, they bought me a souvenir T-shirt from Philmont. Warden Cain said it was not allowed.

I talk to the scouts and their parents about freedom, and about the value of staying in school and making good life choices. Afterward, the scoutmaster, Elbert Hill, steps to the podium next to me, holding a small package wrapped in brown kraft paper and bearing the Angola mailroom's stamped notice to return to sender. It is an emotional moment for me when I open the package to find the souvenir T-shirt. Hill had saved the unopened package all these years, having faith that I'd get out of prison and he'd be able to give it to me.

Just as I'm ready to leave the podium, a young scout of about ten approaches. He steps to the microphone and tells me that the troop is very thankful that I helped them ten years ago in their time of need and announces that since I've just come out of prison, they decided to help me in my time of need and took up a collection. He hands me an envelope that contains a check for $213. I'm choked up but manage to say thanks and return to my seat.

My first summer as a free man has been great, but now there's a tropical storm brewing in the Gulf. As it takes shape, Hurricane Katrina is headed directly toward New Orleans. It makes landfall on the evening of August 29, and although we are nearly a hundred miles upriver, it causes massive damage here in Baton Rouge from downed trees. We lose electrical power, which means no air-conditioning in the sweltering heat, no fan, and no television. The next morning there's still no power, and the streets in this neighborhood of stately old trees are impassable because of fallen limbs, debris, and downed power lines.

I rig up a way to boil water so we can drip coffee. We more or less move out of the stifling house onto the back patio, where we're glued to the transistor radio for news. We learn to cook everything—even entire meals with rice and vegetables—on a small hibachi that has resided unused in the garage all summer. We begin cleaning up our yard and the street.

When our next-door neighbor manages to get a generator five days later, we go watch television at his house and get our first look at the devastation in New Orleans—dead bodies floating in the water, people on the roofs waiting for boats or helicopters to come, the hordes stranded outside the Superdome and marooned on the sizzling interstate for buses that, it turns out, have been waiting just outside the city for the okay to go in and rescue people. Animal rescue organizations are not being allowed to rescue animals, and some people are refusing to leave their home, rooftop, or asphalt patch without them. The tragedy worsens by the day. The incompetence of government and official leaders is nothing short of criminal.

After a week, we get our power back and are able to resume a fairly normal life. However, Baton Rouge's population has doubled overnight. Shopping even at the Walmart Superstore continues to feel like a war-torn Third World experience. There's no fresh meat, no bread, no milk or eggs, few staples. Many of the evacuees from New Orleans are now housed in Baton Rouge's convention center; others are spread out among the city's shelters, churches, synagogues, and temples. The streets are clogged with New Orleans cars and drivers who bring their

Big Easy U-turning ways to Baton Rouge's streets. At age sixty-three, I'd been making slow and uneven progress in learning to drive before the storm, but it's rush hour all the time now. There is no way I can process the information overload out on the streets, and I give up driving altogether.

With all the misery and chaos, we want to volunteer our services. I call the city of Baker, a town just north of Baton Rouge, and talk to the mayor, who claims to be a cousin of mine. He tells us to come help sort food at a distribution center. When we get there, there's nothing to do. The volunteers there direct us to a local church, which has more volunteers than evacuees, and nothing for us to do but re-sort and refold donated clothing in a back room. After an afternoon of that, we don't go back.

Linda hears on the news that there is a desperate need for volunteers to care for stranded dogs and cats at LSU's makeshift shelter. We go there. I stay at the desk outside, logging in visitors and workers who have to show ID because animals have been stolen. I cannot handle the inside, seeing the animals in cages; it's an emotional reflex left over from death row. I cannot stand seeing caging of any kind, to the point that I have to leave pet supply stores when I see fish in tanks and birds in cages. Linda emerges after four hours reeking of sweat, kitty litter, and hand sanitizer. She's in her element, radiant.

Early in September I receive a call from Catholic Charities asking if I'd be interested in helping at a turnaround oasis they've set up at the Bellemont Hotel in Baton Rouge for New Orleans police, firefighters, and other first responders to come for medical exams, immunizations, debriefing, counseling, and other assistance and services. I'm a little surprised at the request.

"Do you know who I am?"

"I do," the caller says. "I think you'll be a great asset."

"Hey," I say, "these are the people who have been putting their lives on the line to save folks for the last two weeks. If there's anything I can do to help them, count me in."

Linda and I report for duty at the Bellemont Hotel in the morning and LSU's animal shelter in the afternoon.

The situation at the Bellemont is heartbreaking. Men, mostly, spill from buses that ferry them here after they've spent days or weeks fishing people from attics and roofs in New Orleans, after sailing by those, dead or alive, whom they could not help. I've seen faces like this in

Ernie Pyle's photos of shell-shocked soldiers in World War II, faces
unable to fully engage the horror with which they had to deal. Many of
the cops and firefighters, upon recognizing me, express surprise that
I'm there to help them and shake my hand in thanks.

"I've lost everything," one dazed man says to me, as I help him fill
out the paperwork he needs to get in to see the doctors and counselors.
"My house—it's gone. Everything I've worked for my entire life, gone.
I'm fifty-nine years old, and I have to start over from scratch," he says.
"My pension—it's gone. My house . . ." He trails off. "I have nothing."
Then he recognizes me. His facial muscles relax just a bit. "But you
know what I'm talking about, don't you, Rideau?"

On our fifth day at the Bellemont, Linda and I are finishing our
shift as the reception committee for those needing services, guiding
them through the necessary paperwork, when Bruce Nolan, a *Times-
Picayune* reporter, arrives to do a story on the turnaround oasis. He's
surprised to see me there and asks me to hang around until he finishes
his interview with the man in charge. I say I will. After he leaves my station, a woman in blue scrubs whom I haven't seen before—a nurse, I
guess—strides from across the room to our table.

"Wilbert, you should have registered as a journalist," she says edg-
ily. I tell her I'm not here as a journalist but as a volunteer. She immediately walks away. It's quiet, no buses arriving, so I head to the
restroom. When I return, Linda tells me the woman in scrubs returned
and expressed hostility about my being there. "You think that of all the
places he could have volunteered to help, he just *happened* to end up
here?" she demanded. "And you don't think he's going to write about
this place?"

"Don't let it get to you," I say to Linda. "These kinds of things are
going to happen, that's all."

Soon after we arrive at home, the phone rings. We look at one
another and instinctively know it has something to do with the nurse.
On the line is the woman from Catholic Charities, who expresses thanks
for the wonderful job I've been doing. She says how much everyone has
appreciated my help—everyone except for one person who, familiar
with my background, was complaining about me.

"It's unfortunate," she says, "but I know you wouldn't want one bad
apple to spoil all the good work that you and Catholic Charities have
done and are still doing at the turnaround oasis." She suggests that for
the greater good, maybe I would consider not returning to the Bellemont. I say I don't want to be a distraction and will comply.

Five days later Hurricane Rita is in the Gulf. In Lake Charles, my sister Pearlene and her husband pick up my mother and make their way to our home. Some days later, they return to find my mother's house destroyed, like so many others. Mom moves in with my sister Mary in Houston. After six months, Mother moves into a refurbished house that, because it is in Lake Charles, I will never see. Everyone in my family realizes that owing to the hostility expressed toward me by some of the white townsfolk there, I will never return to Lake Charles. So I seldom get to see my elderly mother, who finds it increasingly difficult to travel. This hurts her heart, as it does mine.

We've returned to Baton Rouge after a trip of three days. Our cats act as though they'd been abandoned, and they stick to us like wallpaper. Rodeo refuses to leave the house at all. After going out for his constitutional, Willie B parks himself in my desk chair. Sangha, a young orphan who came to us after the hurricanes, follows Linda from room to room, crying to be held. Even Ladybug, whose lingering wildness stops her from entering the house, won't budge her nose from the back storm door until we take turns going out to pet her. God, it's good to be home. It's so much more than good. It's paradise to have a home, a place to be, a place where I am wanted and welcomed. I love my new life, which is more precious to me than all the kingdoms of the earth.

"Come feel this lump on Willie B's jaw," Linda says a few days later. We notice that he has lost a lot of weight. I feel the lump, which is hard and solid, not soft like the swelling that comes with infection. The next day we take him to the vet and learn that he has an oral cancer. The doctor prescribes medications, and Willie B's improvement is so dramatic that we take him to another vet for a second opinion. The diagnosis is confirmed. It is a question of days, not weeks, he tells us, until we will have to euthanize our friend, when his pain outweighs his quality of life. "It's the last thing you can do to show him that you love him," says the vet.

Willie B begins a clear and rapid decline. The bulge on his jaw grows daily. I'm convinced Willie B knows he is dying. I'm astounded by his equanimity, his stoicism, his strength. I can only pray that I will meet my end with the dignity he refuses to shed. The other cats also sense his illness, his vulnerability, his mortality, and keep their distance.

Last night Linda lay with Willie B on the sofa in my office, where he has taken up residence. They spent more than two hours in there,

Willie B uncharacteristically rolling around on her chest, forcing his forehead under her neck, trying to get as close to her as he could, insistently. This morning, he makes the rounds of all his favorite haunts in the neighborhood, literally stopping to smell the flowers in a deliberate way. I've gone with him, to photograph what is surely one of his final journeys. Too late, we realized that we have almost no photographs of him as an adult, and I'm trying to make up for it in one morning. When we return home, Willie B refuses to eat, refuses the medication that makes his physical condition tolerable. Linda is distraught, but even now Willie B, who has been her rock for the last twelve difficult years, has a strangely calming effect on her. I think he knows his role. We are all in my office, and Willie B moves from the sofa to the hallway, looks at me, and enters the coat closet, where it is dark and he is alone. A more feral cat would have simply walked off, like an elephant, to die. But Willie B long ago surrendered any wildness he had to his love for Linda. He stays in the closet for about ten minutes, then comes back, jumps in my lap for affection, leaves me, and jumps in Linda's lap. After a few minutes, he retires to the arm of the sofa and looks at us. It is a pleading kind of look. Like he's waiting for us to do something.

"I think he's telling us it's time," Linda says, swallowing hard but determined to remain calm for his sake. I agree. Willie B uncharacteristically steps willingly into the carrier, which I cradle on my lap during the thirty-minute trip to the vet, who knows we are coming and lets us wait in his private office until he is free. When he joins us, he takes Willie B from us and hooks up the sleeve for the needle that will administer the lethal cocktail. When we rejoin Willie B, Linda kisses him on his forehead and kneels so she is at eye level with him on his death table. She caresses him one last time, then holds his right front paw, where he will be killed, in her hand. His eyes lock on hers in what I can only describe as a knowing way, and they stay locked there until what is behind those eyes—life, consciousness, intelligence—vanishes.

Willie B is gone, just that fast. We return to the doctor's private office, where we take turns holding our departed cat for half an hour. If I had any doubts about the rightness of our decision, they evaporate when I feel my little friend finally at rest and realize how rigid with pain and stress he had become in his final days. Willie B was my first pet, and I loved him.

None of the death I witnessed at Angola affected me quite like this. Love had never been a factor, though losing Ora Lee Rogers and

C. Paul Phelps came close. At home, Linda's tears fall all over our forever-changed household. She's beyond the consolation of human words or kindness. Grief and loss define her. I think back forty-five years to the suffering, the sorrow I inflicted on Julia Ferguson's loved ones and ask God, again, to forgive me.

Linda retreats to prayers for the dead. She believes deeply that Willie B is on a path and that, maybe, she can help him on his way. This is one of the things I adore in her—her unconditional belief in the power of love. I envy her this devout belief.

Rodeo Joe, meanwhile, is deeply depressed and losing weight fast. He scours the neighborhood looking for Willie B. He stands sentry by the gate, staying out all night waiting for the return of his brother. Several weeks later, Rodeo is killed by a pack of stray dogs at dawn, in our front yard, his cries for help masked by the whir of the air conditioner as we sleep in the bedroom. I discover Rodeo's corpse and break the news to Linda. She is numb with grief. We make another sad trip to the crematorium. Rodeo's death casts a pall over our household, and, untutored in such piled-on domestic grief, I wonder if anything can redeem our joy. Ladybug cries day and night for her brothers, in vain.

Summer turns to fall, then winter. Miss Elsie, the best first neighbor anyone could have, decides her house is too difficult to keep up and moves to Mississippi to live with her son and daughter-in-law. A young couple, James and Jennifer, take her place, bringing their newborn and the hope and vigor of youth to our neighborhood.

One day a starving orange tabby shows up in our other neighbor's backyard, taking refuge from the cold in a spot of sun against the brick wall. Linda talks to him, feeds him.

"He's just like Willie B," she says. "Look at his markings."

It's true.

"Look," says Linda. "He's so sweet and gentle, so Zen, just like Willie B."

She believes Willie B has sent this castaway to us, and who am I to say he did not? We bring him into our home. Because of his color, we christen him Goldie. He bonds with Sangha and Ladybug. We go forward, with animals we love and care for. I tell Linda we are a family of discarded strays she has rescued. She smiles and says that we have all rescued her. As time passes, the days we grieve are outweighed by the days we live in wholeness.

It's spring again. I rise with the sun, brew coffee, set out food for the cats. The birds are starting to sing and a pair of squirrels play chase on the trunk of the old live oak out back. The spirits of my old friends still linger here, reminding me of the blessings of unconditional love. Yes, this is paradise. I go wake up Linda because I don't want her to miss a thing.

Acknowledgments

I am indebted to more people than I could include in this book, and more than I can possibly mention by name here, for their support, encouragement, and kindness over the course of my incarceration and since my release.

Without the help of the many guards and prison officials who saw something of value in me and opened doors of opportunity that allowed the best in me to emerge, neither this book nor my life as a journalist would have been possible. Also, to the many Angola prisoners who shared my experience of trying to improve themselves and the world we lived in, I want to say thank-you for your companionship and for helping me to keep faith and achieve some of my dreams.

To the journalists and editors who took notice of my efforts and treated me as a colleague during my quarter century as a prison journalist, I owe a special debt.

So many people befriended me along the way and eased the harshness of my prison life with letters, visits, friendship, love; although I cannot mention them all by name, I will never forget their contributions to my life.

My mother deserves far more thanks than I can give her for a lifetime of standing by me and never complaining about the hardship I brought upon her and my siblings.

My thanks go to East Baton Rouge Parish librarian Elva Jewel "Peggy" Carter, who contributed research to many *Angolite* articles and became a treasured personal friend, and to Louisiana State Library librarian Marc Wellman, another friend to whose research assistance this book owes much.

To Dr. Marianne Fisher-Giorlando, who brought her students to tour Angola every year and steadfastly supported both *The Angolite* and me, I owe great thanks.

For her unwavering support and readiness to help me anytime, any-where, I would like to thank my birthday buddy and longtime friend Leslie Turk.

I owe a great debt to the remarkable talent and generosity of the late Peter Golden, a Lafayette, Louisiana, dentist who traveled to Angola many times to save my teeth, pro bono, after they had all been declared beyond repair by the prison.

To Dr. Susan Jones of Lake Charles, I am grateful for the many times she came to the Calcasieu Parish jail during the last four years of my imprisonment to give me flu shots and other medical attention, pro bono.

My debt to lawyers is truly incalculable, beginning with Julian Mur-ray, Louisiana's "Atticus Finch" and best criminal trial lawyer, who fought for my freedom for two decades, pro bono.

I'm thankful that George Kendall brought not only his own pro bono legal brilliance to the fight to free me, but the resources of the NAACP Legal Defense Fund and the law firm of Holland and Knight. Those resources included talented young attorneys Laura Fernandez, Vanita Gupta, Chris Hsu, Parisa Tafti; and bright, energetic young law students Michael Block (Harvard), Katherine Bolton (NYU), Michael Bullerman (NYU), Deborah Cornwall (Harvard), Jerome Del Pino (NYU), Charles Hart (NYU), Annie Jacobs (NYU), Sarah Johnson (NYU), Dan Korobkin (Yale), Vivian Labaton (NYU), Susan Lee (NYU), Matt Mazur (Harvard), Michael Oppenheimer (CUNY), Susan Plotkin (NYU), Gretchen Rohr (Georgetown), Priy Sinha (NYU), Jonathan Smith (NYU), Aimee Sol-way (NYU), Maria Fernanda Torres (NYU), and Ben Wizner (NYU).

Ron Ware, the public defender in Calcasieu Parish who put his career on the line when he refused to go along with the attempt to judicially lynch me, has both my thanks and my great admiration.

To the late, consummate trial lawyer Johnnie Cochran, I am indebted not only for his pro bono legal help but for his steadfast faith in miracles, which reinforced my own.

My thanks go also to James Wood, the attorney just two years out of law school who defended me at my 1970 trial, but more important, whose testimony decades later helped me win the new trial that freed me in 2005.

To Ginger Berrigan, my first pro bono attorney and now a federal judge in the Eastern District of New Orleans, I offer my deepest gratitude for her faith in me and her unflinching support over the past thirty-five years.

I am grateful to Elaine Jones and her successor as president of the Legal Defense Fund, Ted Shaw, for undertaking the fight for judicial fairness for a guilty prisoner when there were, and are, so many incarcerated innocents begging for help, and not enough resources to meet the need.

To the jury of twelve ordinary citizens from one of Louisiana's most conservative parishes, I can only express gratitude that knows no bounds for the verdict that freed me.

I also owe thanks for the generosity of friends and strangers alike who have helped me since my release from prison.

To Catholic Charities' Prison Ministry Coordinator Linda Fjeldsjo and the St. Vincent de Paul Thrift Stores operated by the Catholic Diocese of Baton Rouge, I owe thanks for assisting me when I had nothing.

Dr. Frank J. Alvarez, III, and nurses Tina Davis and Leslie Murphy of the Baton Rouge Clinic have my great thanks for supplying me with free blood-pressure medication during my first year of freedom, when I could ill afford to buy it.

I would also like to thank Baton Rouge attorney Gary McKenzie and his assistant Audra Bodin, who worked pro bono to have me declared bankrupt to rescue me from unprecedented court costs meant to cripple my ability to rebuild my life.

I owe particular thanks to the Open Society Institute of the Soros Foundation for their financial support while I wrote this book and am honored to be among the many Fellows they support who are dedicated to relieving misery and doing good in this sometimes cynical world.

To Robert Barnett and Deneen Howell of Williams and Connolly, I owe thanks for jump-starting my life with their work to find a publisher for this book.

This book owes much to David Friend of *Vanity Fair* for his enthusiastic support and for his suggestion that I keep a journal as I awaited retrial in Lake Charles. Similarly, my thanks go to Ted Koppel for his good advice that I keep a journal of my first days and months of freedom. Both journals have proved immensely helpful in the writing of this book.

I am especially indebted to Jonathan Segal, my editor at Knopf, for taking a chance on me. His insightful suggestions and guidance have been invaluable to me in the writing of this book.

Finally, I am deeply grateful for Linda LaBranche, the petite Shakespeare scholar who became my knight in shining armor. Her friendship and love, first as my supporter and now as my wife, made everything else possible.

Index

293; habeas corpus petition filed
by, 236–7; at pardon board
hearing, 198, 208; at Polozola's
review of magistrate's
recommendation, 255; *20/20*
interview with, 197–8; at 2005
trial, 302, 303, 306, 308–12, 315,
320–2, 324–6, 328
Muslims, 97–8, 228, 292

Narcotics Anonymous, 99, 139
National Association for the
Advancement of Colored People
(NAACP), 50, 107, 135, 158,
341–2; Legal Defense Fund, 256,
274, 288, 302
National Association of Criminal
Defense Lawyers, 343
National Baptist Convention, 158
National Magazine Award, 152, 159,
206
National Public Radio, 205, 239,
303
National Weather Service, 320, 325
Native Americans, 313
NBC-TV, 159, 179
Neville, Aaron, 248
Neville Brothers, 196
New Orleans *States-Item*, 134, 141
New Orleans *Sunday Item-Tribune*, 35
New Orleans *Times-Picayune*, 78, 94,
153, 176, 177, 179, 184, 195, 250,
303, 346
New York Times, The, 159, 176, 179,
184, 304; *Magazine*, 161, 176
New York University, 302
Night Riders, 313
Nightline (television news program),
172, 184, 248, 341
Nolan, Bruce, 346
Noland, Christine, 237, 254–6
Northwestern University, 184
Norwood, W. J., 165

Ortega, Louis, 165
Ottinger, Sarah, 212, 216–17, 231
Owens, Donald Wayne, 197

Pardon Finance Board, 246
Parker, John, 237
Parker, Mack Charles, 33
Pastorek, Ken, 261
Peabody, Richard, 178, 240
Pence, Walter, 160, 164–5, 197
Penthouse magazine, 94, 134, 141,
155
Perlstein, Mike, 303
Person, Naomi, 239
Phelps, C. Paul, 133, 136–7, 140,
153, 154, 156, 160, 196, 242, 259;
as acting warden of Angola,
108–19, 123–5, 127, 138, 140–1,
204; and *Angolite*, 112–15, 130,
142, 144, 147, 152, 155, 168, 178,
214, 257; appointed head of
Department of Corrections,
130–1; death of, 235–6, 238, 349;
and executions, 188–9; firing of,
165–6; Linda and, 185; during
Maggio's tenure as warden, 142,
144–5, 147–8, 150, 167; profit-
and politics-driven corrections
system opposed by, 173; rehired
by Edwards, 172; retirement of,
194, 198; Rideau's release
supported by, 157, 177, 192–3,
195, 197; and Sinclair's informant
activities, 180–3
Phillips, Stone, 197–8
Pilgrimage for Life, 230
Pitcher, Sargent, 49, 51
Plaisance, Kenneth, 100–1, 103
Playboy magazine, 52
Polk, George, Award, 159
Polozola, Frank, 200–2, 241–2, 255,
256, 259, 277
Ponder, Elven, 50, 51, 58–60
Poret, Alton, 37, 39, 43, 57–8
Porter, William E., 106
preachers, inmate, 138
Prejean, Dalton, 214, 221, 222
Prejean, Helen, 174, 230–1
Prime Time Live (television
newsmagazine), 249
Prince, The (Machiavelli), 57

Printed in the United States
by Baker & Taylor Publisher Services